Books by Jeffrey St. John:

Countdown to Chaos
Noble Metals
Day of the Cobra
Constitutional Journal
Landmarks 1765–1990

A CHILD OF FORTUNE

A CHILD OF FORTUNE

*A Correspondent's
Report on the
Ratification of the U.S.
Constitution and Battle
for a Bill of Rights*

Jeffrey St. John

Foreword by
Warren E. Burger

Jameson Books, Inc.
Ottawa, Illinois

Jameson Books are available at special discounts for bulk
purchases for sales promotions, premiums, fundraising, or
educational use. Special condensed or excerpted editions can
also be created to customer specification.

For information and catalog requests write:

Jameson Books, Inc.
P.O. Box 738
Ottawa, IL 61350

815-434-7905

8 7 6 5 4 3 2 1   93 92 91

Printed in the United States of America

Distributed to the book trade by National Book Network.

ISBN: 0-915463-56-3

Library of Congress Cataloging-in-Publication Data

St. John, Jeffrey.
    A child of fortune: a correspondent's report on the ratification
of the U.S. Constitution and the battle for a Bill of Rights /
Jeffrey St. John.
        p.   cm.
    Includes bibliographical references and index.
    ISBN 0-915463-56-3
    1. United States—Constitutional History—Popular works.
    2. United States. Constitutional Convention (1787) I. Title.
KF4541.Z9S7 1990
342.73'029—dc20
[347.30229]   90-21386
                                                                    CIP

To the Printers and Editors in America
of the 1780s who made possible through
their newspapers the first truly national
political debate after the War of
Independence

... it is now a Child of fortune, to be fostered by some and buffeted by others. What will be the General opinion on, or the reception of it, is not for me to decide, nor shall I say any thing for or against it: if it be good, I suppose it will work its way good; if bad, it will recoil on the Framers.

General George Washington
  to Marquis de Lafayette, September 18, 1787, on the just-signed U.S. Constitution

CONTENTS

FOREWORD

★

Combining his skills as a journalist with a knowledge of history, Jeffrey St. John has produced another book that will enhance the knowledge of its readers—students and adults alike—about what every American should know—that it was a monumental task to secure the Constitution under which we have lived for more than 200 years. Here, Mr. St. John employs the same approach he used in *Constitutional Journal*, with its simulated day-by-day coverage of the Constitutional Convention. He gives to the ratification process in the thirteen States what modern journalism tries to do for presidential primary campaigns. It differs in that this book is written with restraint, born of a sense of history, that is the luxury of a writer free of the pressure of newspaper deadlines.

Few Americans, even those who are otherwise well read and well informed, understand that we almost did not get the Constitution that was drafted in 1787 and ratified in 1788—and that we were at first a nation of eleven, not thirteen, States. Perhaps no part of our history is so little understood. Almost everyone studies something about this in school. But how many appreciate the difficulty of ratifying the Constitution even in the state of Virginia where it survived by a mere ten-vote margin, 89 to 79? How many remember that even the leadership of George Washington, James Madison, and the young John Marshall had great difficulty overcoming the opposition of Patrick Henry, George Mason, and James Monroe?

The debate over ratification of the Constitution was the second, and most important, debate over the basic principles that brought new concepts of government into operation. The Federalist, nationalist concepts evolved by Washington, Hamilton, and others contended against the Anti-Federalist philosophy later adopted by the Jeffersonians. The debate was fierce but we must remember that revolutions are launched by men ready to risk all; unsuccessful revolutionists in that day would end up under a guillotine, on a scaffold, or in front of a firing squad. What would the new government be? And what kind of government should Americans have? Was there any need for a national government, and would a national government make the states superfluous? The Patrick Henrys wanted no part of a strong national government.

Mr. St. John's account illuminates this seminal debate, and offers a vivid portrait of the social and political complexion of America at the end of the eighteenth century. He reminds us that in those days, as in these, local politics and political personalities often figured as large as the great national issues. It is often helpful to be reminded that the Founding Fathers themselves were human beings, and subject to the same human frailties as others. Mr. St. John also makes clear that those who drafted and ratified the Constitution were not insensitive to the evil institution of slavery, but believed that their first and highest task was to create a government that would avoid a "balkanization" of the states into two or three "new republics." Even while the delegates in Philadelphia were struggling to make one nation out of thirteen, the Continental Congress, sitting in New York in July 1787, repudiated slavery for new states in the Northwest Territory by enacting the Northwest Ordinance.

Given the sad state of knowledge of our students—including many college graduates—about our history, this book and its companion, *Constitutional Journal*, should be required reading to graduate from high school.

> Warren E. Burger
> *Chairman, Commission on the*
> *Bicentennial of the U.S. Constitution*
> *Chief Justice of the United States, 1969–1986*

PREFACE

★

A Fist Fight over Freedom

Americans have always relished a good fight, particularly a political fist fight.

This is the story of the bare-knuckled, public combat over the ratification of the U.S. Constitution, September 18, 1787, through August 7, 1788. It is written as if the author were a correspondent filing weekly dispatches from the ratification battlefield.

Ratification was as much a struggle over political power to shape the future for the young country as a fight over two views of freedom.

One was rooted in the political order created after the War of Independence, which gave most of the political power to the States under America's first constitution, the Articles of Confederation.

The other was constructed during one sweltering summer of political statecraft at the Philadelphia Convention of 1787, which created the current U.S. Constitution. The document sought to reconcile personal liberty with the perceived need for a strong central government with powers to forge a political and economic common market among the thirteen separate, sovereign States. Europe plans to achieve in 1992 what America successfully accomplished over two centuries ago.

The Philadelphia Convention was held in secret, behind guarded closed doors, during four months. Although 55 delegates were elected and generally united for radical if not revolutionary political change, only 39 affixed their signature to the Constitution; three refused to sign and the others left for a variety of reasons before it was approved.

On the other hand, the ratification debate was conducted in public, lasted eleven months, was extensively reported by the press, and involved 1,648 quarrelsome, quixotic ratification Convention delegates in twelve States. (Rhode Island, dubbed Rogue Island by critics, did not hold a ratifying Convention until May 1790.) The vigorous Philadelphia Convention debates were a polite tea compared to the passionate, profound, and often profane ratification fights in each State.

During this public debate it was impossible for Americans from New Hampshire to Georgia, as well as on the Western and Southern frontiers, to think, talk, or argue about anything else but the new Constitution.

The normal life of the young semiwilderness nation slowed to a crawl as frontiersmen, farmers, mechanics, lawyers, doctors, politicians—current and aspiring—and printers confronted one another over the latest news and opinion contained in newspapers published in the cities and States of America in the 1780s.

The single burning issue during the ratification debates was over amendments to the Constitution, or as some at the time referred to them, a bill of rights. When the new Constitution emerged from Philadelphia in 1787 it did not contain guarantees of freedom of religion, press, speech, assembly, and trial by jury. . .and numerous other "rights" sought by many.

This volume, therefore, is as much the story of how the current U.S. Constitution was narrowly approved by the States, as the little-known saga of how and why the Bill of Rights was born in the incubator of the ratification debates.

Supporters of the Constitution resisted for nearly six months demands of its leading critics for amendments. In fact, most of the 95 newspapers in the nation not only supported ratification, but also remained silent on, or dismissed, the issue of amendments, or a bill of rights, including, ironically, press freedom. Some even charged that amendments were being used as a political weapon to effect its defeat.

Only after the Federalists and their supporters in the press came to realize that the new Constitution might be rejected outright, did they agree to recommend a series of amendments. These ultimately became the basis for the Bill of Rights, or the first ten amendments to the Constitution.

America's newspapers were indispensable to involving the people in the ratification struggle. They published the full text of the new Constitution for public study and debate. And during the weeks and months after it emerged from the secrecy of Philadelphia, newspapers became, next to personal letters, the primary source of information among the cities and the States, as well as a forum for a variety of essays for and against approval of the document.

In this age of global satellite communications, we can easily overlook just how primitive and slow was the pace of communications in the 1780s. In good weather, for instance, it took a letter or a newspaper mailed in Boston five to ten days to reach New York by horseback or coach.

We also forget, in this age of live television nightly newscasts and daily newspapers with full-color photographs and eye-catching graphics, just how crude were the newspapers at the time the U.S. Constitution was created, published, and publicly debated. Type was set by hand, there were no pictures, the presses were operated by hand. Most newspapers were published once a week, a few semi-weekly or daily.

Most consisted of a single folio, or crown sheet, folded once to make four pages. One page usually featured business and social advertisements, a half page was devoted to foreign news, and the remaining space included domestic items and essays on a wide variety of topics.

An exchange of newspapers through the mails allowed editors or "printers" in other cities to reprint one another's material. Thus, by this crude first "national news service" a single item or an essay would be reprinted in as many as fifty newspapers.

The Federalist Papers, for example, written by Alexander Hamilton, James Madison, and John Jay, were first published in New York City newspapers. Once they appeared in print, they were mailed to other papers—or passed along by individuals to friends in other States and cities for republication as part of what a foreign envoy in New York called "the paper war" of the ratification campaign.

During the last 200 years, the role of newspapers in the ratification debates of the American Constitution and in the making of the Bill of Rights has been largely unrecognized by both the public and the newspaper profession itself. The primary reason for this historical oversight is that only in the last half of this century have historians and scholars made a detailed study of the ratification period. And only in the last decade have they republished the massive amount of documentary material printed by the newspapers of the 1780s.

The dedication of this work to pioneer editors, or printers as they were called, of the 1780s is a long overdue public recognition of the crucial role they each played and of the unpaid debt this print and broadcast journalist believes all in the profession owe them. (A list of the newspapers of the period will be found in Appendix 1.)

Paradoxically, although the production of newspapers of the period was crude by today's terms, the papers contained some of the most profound political arguments in American history.

As political drama and theater, the ratification struggle has no peer. It is also a very human story, the most compelling in all of political history.

In filing these weekly "dispatches" from the 1780s, contemporary journalistic techniques—such as, "an observer notes," "James Madison is reported. . .," "a source says,"—are used to provide clarity and continuity for, and scholars' observations on, a complex set of ideas and events. The weekly dispatches are written in the present tense, and spellings and punctuation in direct quotes are carefully retained to preserve further the reader's sense of reading "this week's news." Nevertheless, this is a contemporary work of translation from scholarly works on the subject, supplemented by diaries, letters, published documentary evidence from the debates, and observations by contemporary historians.

The author has avoided personal opinions and conclusions out of the firm conviction that a fair and balanced report serves the goal of understanding far better than subjective opinions. Facts have a power of their own, and while complete objectivity is not possible, it is possible to present the factual essence of a historical subject so that the reader can make up his or her own mind.

In the final analysis, the ratification struggle was a public debate over the destiny of "We the People," and nothing like it had happened before, or has happened since, in our history nor in any other nation. Out of this ordeal for 3.9 million Americans (including 697,624 slaves and 59,557 free blacks) emerged not just the narrow approval of a new and novel national government, but also the creation of a raw political consensus for the creation of a bill of rights. The Philadelphia Convention and the ratification debates that followed changed forever the way the United States of America, and eventually the entire world, would view personal liberties and the exercise of political power.

ACKNOWLEDGMENTS

★

This report is first and foremost a translation based in part on the works of present and past historians. It has been supplemented by the published letters, diaries, and documentary records of the period between September 1787 and August 1788.

Four historians deserve special mention:

Dr. Forrest McDonald, University of Alabama, whose four decades of scholarship in American history of the 1780s and his over ten published works have been for this author an indispensable primary education of the period.

His 1985 work, *Novus Ordo Seclorum: The Intellectual Origins of the Constitution*, was of particular help for this book and the earlier one on the Philadelphia Convention. Dr. McDonald's blend of scholarship in and realistic perception of the politics of the eighteenth century is what makes all of his works unique.

His generous praise and support of *Constitutional Journal*, and his willingness to review this work and offer his comments and suggestions are more than appreciated.

Dr. Robert Allen Rutland, the University of Oklahoma at Norman, whose scholarship as editor of the *Papers of James Madison* has been invaluable, particularly his published works on the ratification period and the Bill of Rights.

The late (1905–1980) Dr. Merrill Jensen's pioneering works forced American historians to reexamine the first constitution, the Articles of Confederation, with more judicious judgment. He was also a force and an influence in the State Historical Society of Wisconsin, Madison, which published the multivolume *The Documentary History of the Ratification of the Constitution*. The editors and scholars who carried on what Dr. Jensen helped start deserve no end of praise and gratitude for their years of compiling and editing the documents relating to ratification. Without their efforts, headed by the series editor John Kaminski of the University of Wisconsin, Madison, this report would have suffered from serious historical anemia.

The late (1920–1977) Dr. Herbert J. Storing, of the University of Chicago, was editor of the seven-volume *The Complete Anti-Federalist*. Although he did not live to see all these valuable volumes published, they have proven to be an important supplement to our effort to provide the reader with a fair and balanced view of both sides of the ratification struggle.

During this author's own struggle to complete this, the second of three popular books on the making of the U.S. Constitution, several individuals and organizations offered support and encouragement.

The encouragement and support of retired Chief Justice of the United States Supreme Court Warren E. Burger are deeply appreciated. As chairman of the Commission on the Bicentennial of the United States Constitution and the Bill of Rights, he was generous in writing a foreword to our first book, and now to this volume.

One modern newspaper editor deserves special mention, Rich Martin, deputy managing editor of the *Roanoke Times & World News*, Roanoke, Virginia. He published in June 1988 four articles from this volume on the Virginia ratifying Convention. The series won the 1988 Benjamin Franklin Award, jointly awarded by the National Press Foundation, Washington, D.C., and the Bicentennial Commission.

Throughout the research and writing, Philip G. Benoit, communications director of Dickinson College, Carlisle, Pennsylvania, offered indispensable encouragement and support. So did Dr. Eugene W. Hickock, adjunct professor at Dickinson School of Law and founder of the 200-year-old college's Center for the Study of the Constitution.

Three college libraries and their staffs in south central Virginia were crucial in the research for this work: Joseph duPuy Eggleston Library, Hampden-Sydney College, Hampden-Sydney. Interestingly, two of the major opponents in the ratification drama were founders of this college, Patrick Henry and James Madison. The two other libraries were Dabney S. Lancaster Library, Longwood College, Farmville; and Sweet Briar College Library, Sweet Briar.

My sole assistant, who studiously verified quotes and sources, and patiently typed and prepared the manuscript, was Kathryn Boggs St. John, my wife, who receives the deep gratitude words cannot convey.

CHAPTER 1

★

September 20–27, 1787

General George Washington narrowly escaped death or serious injury this week when his carriage fell through rotting planks of a bridge spanning the Elk River in northeast Maryland. The terrified horses hung suspended fifteen feet over the rain-swollen waterway until local residents came to the rescue.[1]

The 55-year-old military hero of the American Revolution was on a four-and-a-half-day journey back to his Virginia plantation from the Philadelphia Constitutional Convention when the near-fatal accident occurred, on September 20. The President of the just-concluded four-month convention was reported to be unruffled by his narrow brush with death.

In the ten days since General Washington and thirty-eight of his fellow delegates signed the new proposed Constitution, on September 17, praise for the Convention's President and the document has filled the pages of key newspapers.

One observer reports that a wave of popular support for the Constitution has been heard in the cities and States of the country, in taverns, shops, markets, and on street corners. Support is due not so much to what the document contains as to the fact that General Washington and Dr. Benjamin Franklin signed it and both approve its ratification, which is required by nine of the thirteen States.[2]

A debilitating injury to or the death of General Washington at this time would be a crushing blow to those who expect him to be the unanimous choice as the first elected President under the new Constitution. Colonel Alexander Hamilton of New York and other supporters of the General believe that his enormous personal popularity

1

will be critical as they encounter personal prejudices and animosities toward parts of the Constitution during what he expects to be particularly heated debates in the individual States.[3]

Patrick Henry of Virginia, who refused to serve as an elected delegate at the Philadelphia Convention, because he "smelt a rat," is expected to be a formidable foe. Fellow Virginian James Madison, Continental Congressman, one of the major architects of the proposed national government, and General Washington's political confidant, believes that Mr. Henry is the single greatest enemy of ratification in Virginia.[4]

After the General arrived back at Mount Vernon on September 27, one of the first letters he wrote was to Mr. Henry. With it he enclosed a copy of the Constitution. In what appears to be an effort to soften Mr. Henry's anticipated opposition, the General took pains in his letter (a copy obtained by this correspondent) to point out that "the Constitutional door is open for amendments hereafter.

"From a variety of concurring accounts it appears to me," the General added, "that the political concerns of this Country are, in a manner, suspended by a thread."[5]

Following General Washington's example, delegates to the Convention have enclosed copies of the Constitution with letters dispatched to their friends. Also, publication of the document in newspapers and pamphlets has been like dropping a pebble in a pond, producing a widening ripple of public and private discussions.

The first newspaper to publish the new Constitution, on September 19, was the *Pennsylvania Packet*, owned by Philadelphia printers Dunlap and Claypoole. The firm may have been given the honor because it printed drafts of the document for delegates' use during the secret debates without leaking the contents. Since the document's initial publication, it has been reprinted as fast as printers can get their hands on it after delivery by express riders along post roads and by packet boats to other cities and States.[6]

Dr. Benjamin Franklin, who has spent most of his public life abroad, is reported to have sent copies to friends in England, France, and Italy.[7] Foreign affairs may play a role in the coming ratification fight, since America is saddled with a swollen foreign debt and it needs increased loans and trade from Europe.

The day after the document's publication in the *Pennsylvania Packet*, Dr. Franklin sent a copy to his sister, Mrs. Jane Mecom, remarking that his health at 81 is still good despite regular attendance, five hours a day, six days a week, at the four-month Convention. Some of his friends, Dr. Franklin added, "tell me I look better, and they suppose the daily Exercise of going & returning from the Statehouse has done me good."[8]

He concluded his letter with a hint of resignation and relief that the summer ordeal was finally finished, and the Constitution signed: "We have however done our best and it must take its chance."[9]

Chances for the Constitution in the Carolinas and Georgia are still unknown, because of the great distance from Philadelphia and delay of the mails. Its prospects in Pennsylvania, New Jersey, and Connecticut are favorable, according to reports reaching Congressman James Madison of Virginia, who has remained in Philadelphia.

In New York, the document has been received generally with favor, although the party in power, headed by the Governor, George Clinton, is determined to see it defeated. In Boston, the Constitution's reception has been extremely favorable, although its fate may be decided in Massachusetts' rebellious rural areas instead of in its cities. Ironically, Congressman Madison's own State of Virginia gives him the greatest worry.[10]

Edward Carrington of Virginia, a member of the Continental Congress in New York, fanned Mr. Madison's fears when he advised him in a September 23 letter that the same division that existed at the Philadelphia Convention has surfaced among Virginia's congressional members.[11]

Colonel George Mason and Governor Edmund Randolph refused to sign the document in Philadelphia, fearing its sweeping powers and the absence of a bill of rights. Colonel Mason, next to Patrick Henry and George Washington, is the most highly respected public figure in Virginia; he authored in 1776 that State's Declaration of Rights, the first in the Colonies.

The Continental Congress in New York received the new Constitution on September 20 with a letter of transmittal signed by

Convention President Washington requesting unanimous approval prior to submission to the States for ratification. Rather than act immediately, Congress voted to delay debate until September 26. This allowed time for ten Convention delegates, including Mr. Madison, to travel from Philadelphia to resume their congressional seats.[12]

Apparently the delay is a parliamentary ploy to ensure that the document will have sufficient defenders for the anticipated political ambush by those in Congress who want to amend it or block altogether its transmission to the States.

General Washington, in his transmittal letter to Congress, pointed out that "Individuals entering into society must give up a share of liberty, to preserve the rest."[13] Nevertheless, the Convention had difficulty deciding what liberties should be reserved to the States because of their diversity of geography, culture, commerce, population, and religion.

As General Washington said in his letter: "In all our deliberations on this subject, we kept steadily in our view that which appeared to us the greatest interest of every true American,—the consolidation of the Union,—in which is involved our prosperity, felicity, safety, perhaps our national existence."[14]

The word "consolidation" was like a thunderclap to Richard Henry Lee of Virginia, an influential member of Congress and an ally of Colonel Mason's. To the author of the resolves that led to the Declaration of Independence of 1776, consolidation sounds like a death warrant for the States as well as for individual rights. Mr. Lee told the nine States assembled in Congress this week that he favored sending the new Constitution to the States, but only if it were "bottomed upon a declaration or Bill of Rights, clearly and precisely stating the principles upon which this Social Contract is founded. . . ."[15]

The separate States, Mr. Lee said, had such precautions as "necessary to restrain and regulate the exercise of the great powers given to rulers."[16] He then outlined some of those rights:

> Freedom of religion; freedom of the press; trial by jury in civil and criminal cases; standing armies shall not be permitted in time of peace without two-thirds consent of the Congress under the new Constitution; free and frequent elections; independence of judges;

excessive bail and fines "or cruel and unusual punishments should not be demanded or inflicted." The people shall have the right to assemble peaceably to petition the legislature; and "Citizens shall not be exposed to unreasonable searches, seizure of their persons, houses, papers, or property."[17]

Mr. Lee knew he did not have the votes to carry his proposals. However, he did not suspect that the majority in Congress would *erase* from the official record the two days' debates on the new Constitution (September 26–27), including his bill of rights speech.[18]

As he bitterly commented later to Colonel Mason, ". . . the plan is to push the business on with great dispatch, and with as little opposition as possible, that it may be adopted before it has stood the test of reflection and due examination."[19]

Critics of the Constitution are already seething with anger that the Philadelphia Convention voted to keep secret its own official records of the four-month proceedings. On September 17, delegate Rufus King of Massachusetts proposed that the Journals of the Convention be destroyed, or deposited in the custody of Convention President Washington.

". . . a bad use would be made of them by those who would wish to prevent the adoption of the Constitution—" Mr. King said.[20] This correspondent has learned that neither General Washington, who now has possession of the official Journals, nor James Madison of Virginia, one of several delegates who took extensive notes, plans to make public any notes during the ratification debates.

Although the public is to be denied access to the debates of the Philadelphia Convention and of the Continental Congress in New York, newspapers are beginning to function as the forum for both sides in the ratification fight. Two essays, one for and one against the new Constitution, have already been published this week.

On September 26, a writer calling himself "An American Citizen" had published in the *Independent Gazetteer*, Philadelphia, the first public defense of the document, assuring readers that it is not true that the American President will be as powerful as the King of England. We have not been able to identify the author of this defense.

". . . there can be no danger, especially when we consider the solid foundations on which our national liberties are immoveably fixed, by the other provisions of this excellent constitution," the unidentified writer asserts.[21]

Meanwhile, in the *New York Journal*, an essay appeared on September 27 under the signature of "Cato" imploring readers to think for themselves when judging the Constitution, and not to put their trust in famous men but to question the measures proposed in the document.

"... the ambitious and despotic will entrap you in their toils, and bind you with the cord of power from which you, and your posterity, may never be freed ...;" warned "Cato."[22]

Colonel Alexander Hamilton is reported to believe that "Cato" is really his political enemy Governor George Clinton of New York. They exchanged bitter published charges in New York newspapers while the Philadelphia Convention was in session.

The ratification contest is likely to last eight or nine months, Colonel Hamilton forecasts in a memorandum written this week, a copy of which this correspondent obtained. He believes, moreover, that although powerful forces will stop at nothing to defeat the Constitution, "the probability seems to be on the side of its adoption. ...

"But it is almost arrogance," he admits, "in so complicated a subject, depending so intirely on the incalculable fluctuations of the human passions, to attempt even a conjecture about the event."[23]

As Indian summer creeps across the country and the harvest is about to reward a spring and summer of sweat, the news this week of General Washington's narrow brush with death is beginning to appear in newspapers from New Hampshire to Georgia.

The *Pennsylvania Gazette*, for example, reported the incident, insisting that the sparing of the General's life was as providential as his survival of the July 1755 ambush of General Braddock's army in the French and Indian Wars. After having two horses shot out from under him and his tunic pierced with four musket balls, it was predicted that God had preserved the life of then Colonel Washington as a future blessing for the country.

". . . This prophecy has been literally fulfilled," the *Pennsylvania Gazette* observed. "May not the providential preservation of the valuable life of this great and good man, on his way home from the Convention, be for the great and important purpose of establishing, by his name and future influence, a government, that will render safe and permanent the liberties of America, which he has acquired with his sword?"[24]

CHAPTER 2

September 28–October 4, 1787

Two dissenting members of the Pennsylvania Legislature were seized at their lodgings by an angry pro-Constitution mob this week, dragged through the streets of Philadelphia, and forced to complete a quorum, sitting through a session at the State House while a majority voted to make Pennsylvania the first State to call for a convention to ratify the new Constitution.[1]

One observer reported that the mauled pair sat grimly in the assembly chamber on September 29 with "clothes torn and faces white with rage." At one point a dissenter rushed for the door only to be seized and returned to his seat by physical force.[2]

Ironically, the incendiary incident took place in the same State House where the new Constitution was written and signed (on September 17) and where the Declaration of Independence was approved in 1776. The near-riotous event has shattered Philadelphia's positive air of approval since the document was first published ten days ago.

The wild affair started when nineteen minority members of the State Legislature, opposed to the new Constitution, went into hiding in an effort to deny the assembly a quorum. The majority maintains this device was to postpone, until the next general election, consideration of a motion to approve a constitutional ratifying Convention. The Pennsylvania assembly was facing mandatory adjournment at noon, September 29, and a general election is coming in November, when an Anti-Federalist Assembly might be elected. Also, delay would have denied Pennsylvania the honor of being the first State to call a convention and frustrate the majority's strategy of action rather than argument.[3]

"... What are held out as inducements to act with such precipitation," dissenter William Findley asked in a long speech, "as some Members say the *honor* of being foremost; but I would rather say the *dishonor* of acting unfederally. ... This is one reason of waiting the recommendation of Congress. ..."[4]

Congress in New York had, in fact, unanimously approved transmitting the new Constitution to the States as Mr. Findley spoke in Philadelphia. A Pennsylvania Congressman immediately dispatched the news to Philadelphia with an express rider who changed horses on the way and was in the saddle all night. Reining in his lathered mount at the State House the early morning of September 29, the rider rushed in with a copy of the Congressional resolution. It was then that seizure of the dissenters was ordered for the involuntary quorum. Passage was then ensured of the measure calling for an election of delegates to be held on the first Tuesday in November for a State ratifying Convention.[5]

Five days later, the Anti-Federalist minority counterattacked in the pages of the October 4 *Pennsylvania Packet*, citing the facts of the mob action, and adding, "On this outrageous proceeding we make no comment."[6]

In an essay addressed to their constituents, the minority maintained that they absented themselves from the assembly as a protest against the majority that were acting with haste, surprise, and without notice as required by the rules. Besides, the sixteen added, the Convention that created the new Constitution during the summer consisted of State delegates who were from the same party and elected from Philadelphia to the exclusion of rural areas.

"You will therefore perceive," the essay continued, "that they had no authority whatever from the legislature, to annihilate the present confederation and form a constitution entirely new, and in doing which they have acted as mere individuals, not as the official deputies of this commonwealth."[7]

To bolster their arguments, the dissenters cited the refusal of three delegates to sign the new Constitution: Colonel George Mason and Governor Edmund Randolph, both of Virginia, and Elbridge Gerry of Massachusetts.

The mob action, as well as its alleged sanction by the political leaders in Pennsylvania who favor the new Constitution, has unleashed a sulfuric firestorm of public statements. In New York, a similar debate is smoldering this week over the tactics of the majority in the Continental Congress.

"It is certainly the most rash and violent proceeding in the world to cram thus suddenly into men a business of such infinite moment to the happiness of millions," Congressman Richard Henry Lee of Virginia bitterly observed of the September 28 vote by Congress, sending the new Constitution to the States.[8]

Mr. Lee and his allies were defeated by a majority in Congress in their efforts to censure the Philadelphia Convention for exceeding its power. They also failed in an effort to convene a second convention for writing amendments to the new Constitution—including a bill of rights.

In an October 1 letter to Colonel George Mason, Mr. Lee alleges that the majority is misrepresenting the term "unanimously" in the Congressional resolution transmitting the document to the States. Congress "unanimously" *agreed to the action,* not to its contents, Mr. Lee maintains.[9]

With obvious bitter reference to the haste in Congress, he says, "The greatness of the powers given, and the multitude of places to be created produce a coalition of monarchy men, military men, aristocrats and drones, whose noise, imprudence and zeal exceeds all belief."[10]

Mr. Lee's letter to Colonel Mason is certain to be used by Virginia's opponents to the new Constitution, including Patrick Henry. General George Washington and James Madison have already conceded that the opposition of Mr. Henry, along with that of Colonel Mason and Mr. Lee, represents a dangerous threat to ratification in their State and elsewhere.

Mr. Madison admitted as much this week in a September 30 letter to General Washington. Writing from New York, he provides a detailed account of the debates in Congress, in which he has played a prominent part. Mr. Madison acknowledges the dissent of Mr. Lee and others in the Congress and reports to General Washington that the "serious division" was terminated by the "unanimous" compromise to send the document to the States without endorsement.

"The general voice of this City seems to espouse the new Constitution," Mr. Madison adds. "It is supposed nevertheless that the party in power is strongly opposed to it. The Country must finally decide, the sense of which is as yet wholly unknown."[11]

Since returning to Mount Vernon from the Philadelphia Convention, General Washington has turned his attention to the five farms that make up his plantation. One observer reports that he has turned a deaf ear to the suggestion he will be unanimously chosen first President under the new Constitution, if it is ratified by the necessary nine States. He is reported to find the idea an enemy to his hopes for peaceful retirement and is determined to remain aloof from the growing angry debate over ratification.[12]

A source close to the General reports that the letters he has written contain no mention of the new Constitution, although most of the letters he receives contain news and opinion on nothing else. Instead, General Washington is focusing on family, finances, crops, and animals. For example, he is anxiously awaiting word from a friend with the names of the eight hunting hounds presented him as a gift.

He has a list of names but needs to have a description of each dog so "that I might know how to *apply* the names ... without it, I shall find myself at a loss," the General said in a brief letter he posted during his return journey to Mount Vernon after presiding as President of the four-month Convention.[13]

In sharp contrast, Colonel Alexander Hamilton, former military aide to General Washington, is throwing himself into the battle for ratification in New York State. He must have been pleased to read this week in the New York *Daily Advertiser* a sharp attack on his political foe Governor George Clinton of New York. Signed "Caesar," the essay was a reply to Governor Clinton's September 27 attack, signed "Cato," on the Constitution.

"Caesar" accuses "Cato" of being a demagogue, one who is forever crying how public liberties are being invaded. This, "Caesar" maintains, is only a means to personal power ends by flattering the multitude into believing that all power is seated in the people.

"For my part," "Caesar" adds, "I am not much attached to the *majesty of the multitude,* ... I consider them in general as very ill qualified to judge for themselves what form of government will best suit their particular situations; ..."[14]

One observer reports that Colonel Hamilton believes the "Caesar" essay ill advised in its approach, more a public display of personal dislike of Governor Clinton and the multitude than an intelligent and reasoned defense of the new Constitution.[15]

Sources also say that just this week he has proposed to John Jay of New York, the current Secretary of Foreign Affairs of the confederated government, a joint collaboration on a series of newspaper essays to counter the growing number of hostile articles appearing in print. The series will not have the names of its authors, but the planned "papers" will carry the *nom de plume* "Publius" and will explain the new Federal Constitution and defend it against every possible attack.[16]

One such attack has already appeared in print, signed by Colonel George Mason of Virginia. The essay echoes his arguments made at the Philadelphia Convention, which led to his refusal to sign the document.

"There is no declaration of rights," Colonel Mason argues at the very onset of his October 4 essay, "and, the laws of the general government being paramount to the laws and constitutions of the several states, the declarations of rights in the separate states are no security."[17]

The proposed House of Representatives, the 62-year-old respected Virginia statesman maintains, has the "shadow" rather than the "substance" of popular representation. The Senate's power to alter money bills, originating in the House, along with its shared appointment power with the President, Colonel Mason argues, "will destroy any balance in the government, and enable them [the Senate and President] to accomplish what usurpations they please upon the rights and liberties of the people.

"The judiciary of the United States," he adds, "is so constructed and extended as to absorb and destroy the judiciaries of the several states, thereby rendering laws as tedious, intricate, and expensive, and justice as unattainable, by a great part of the community, as in England; and enabling the rich to oppress and ruin the poor."[18]

The office of Vice President is unnecessary, Colonel Mason further asserts. It was created by the Philadelphia Convention and for "want of other employment, [he] is made president of the Senate, thereby dangerously blending the executive and legislative powers. . . ."[19]

The five Southern States, Colonel Mason also warns in his October 4 essay, will have their commerce ruined by the requirement that only a simple Congressional majority is needed to enact all commercial and navigation acts. This gives the Northern and Eastern States a monopoly, he says, and a license for economic extortion against the South.

"This government will commence in a moderate aristocracy," the tall, white-haired Virginia statesman predicts. "It is at present impossible to foresee whether it will, in its operation, produce a monarchy or a corrupt oppressive aristocracy. It will most probably vibrate some years between the two, and then terminate in the one or the other."[20]

This week demonstrates the depth and degree of political passion on both sides of the ratification ramparts. Words, in this passionate war for power to decide the future, appear aimed at mortally wounding the opposition rather than converting to either cause.

CHAPTER 3

October 5–11, 1787

General George Washington and Dr. Benjamin Franklin were attacked in print this week as pawns of the "wealthy and ambitious" for their support of the new Constitution. The document was also denounced for erecting an unaccountable powerful national government that "would be in practice a permanent ARISTOCRACY."[1]

The rapierlike assault was published in the October 5 edition of Philadelphia's *Independent Gazetteer* under the *nom de plume* "Centinel," who is believed to be, according to one source, the prominent Pennsylvanian legislator and jurist George Byran.[2] He and other Pennsylvania lawmakers angrily allege that supporters of the new Constitution are stampeding the State toward approval of the document without the benefit of discussion or debate.

Since September 17, when General Washington and Dr. Franklin signed the Constitution in Philadelphia, their role in the four-month secret Convention has been widely praised in the press. Their support is seen as critical to ratification by a necessary nine States.

But the blunt broadside of "Centinel" this week may signal a deliberate effort of opponents of the Constitution to dilute their influence. He is charging that they have been duped by a conspiracy of a powerful few who believe they have the right "to lord it over" their fellow creatures.

The "Centinel" essay states, for example, that although General Washington and Dr. Franklin have "the welfare of their country at heart," they are, because of political inexperience and old age, being used by sinister and secret forces that have contrived a crisis to justify adoption of the new Constitution.

". . . These characters," the essayist adds, "flatter themselves that

15

they have lulled all distrust and jealousy of their new plan, by gaining the concurrence of the two men in whom America has the highest confidence, and now triumphantly exult in the completion of their long meditated schemes of power and aggrandisement."[3]

The powers granted to the proposed national government to tax and regulate commerce, according to the author, amount to a death sentence upon the States, which will be "melted down into one empire." So vast a nation as America can be governed and remain free only if composed of confederated small republics or States, autonomous in the administration of local affairs and liberties while "united in the management of their foreign and general concerns.

"It would not be difficult to prove," "Centinel" adds, "that any thing short of despotism, could not bind so great a country under one government; and that whatever plan you might, at the first setting out, establish, it would issue in a despotism."[4]

The secrecy of the recent Philadelphia Convention was assailed, moreover, as a suppression of free inquiry and discussion. The absence in the new Constitution of safeguards for liberty of the press, "that grand *palladium of freedom* and *scourge of tyrants*," argues "Centinel,"[5] is compounded by the absence of a bill or declaration of personal rights.

A bill of rights in the new Constitution was first proposed at the Philadelphia Convention by Colonel George Mason of Virginia and was rejected. It was again rejected when proposed by Richard Henry Lee of Virginia during the debates over the Constitution in the Continental Congress in New York, in late September, before it was sent to the States.

Nevertheless, a bill of rights has become a burning political issue in the already inflamed ratification debates. In response to the first "Centinel" essay, James Wilson of Pennsylvania is the only one of Pennsylvania's Constitutional Convention delegates willing publicly to defend the Constitution. He spoke out at length before an outdoor gathering this week in the yard of the Philadelphia State House where the document was framed and signed.[6]

"... the insidious attempts, which are clandestinely and industriously made to pervert and destroy the new plan, induce me the more readily to engage in its defence," the stout Scottish-born lawyer said, squinting through his thick, rounded spectacles at the hushed outdoor crowd.[7]

Those who charge that the Convention deliberately omitted a bill of rights to protect the liberty of press and trial by jury, Mr. Wilson says, do so out of motives that have little to do with those important rights. If, in giving the new Congress the power to regulate commerce, the Convention had also granted the power to "regulate literary publications," there could be genuine cause for concern.

"In truth, then," Mr. Wilson said as his Scottish burr became more pronounced, "the proposed system possesses no influence whatever upon the press; and it would have been merely nugatory, to have introduced a formal declaration upon the subject; nay, that very declaration might have been construed to imply that some degree of power was given. . . ."[8]

It is a fabrication, he went on, that trial by jury in civil cases is abolished in the new Constitution. "The cases open to a jury, differed in the different states; it was therefore impracticable, on that ground, to have made a general rule," he added.[9]

Another false charge is that the separate States will be destroyed by the new Constitution. Indeed, the 45-year-old Pennsylvania lawyer added, the document depends for its very existence on the continued operation of the States. Those who assert the States will be destroyed do so because their power, political position, and even wealth under the current confederated system of separated States will be affected, he declared.

"If there are errors," Mr. Wilson concluded, "it should be remembered, that the seeds of reformation are sown in the work itself, and the concurrence of two thirds of the congress may at any time introduce alterations and amendments."[10]

Critics in the audience later described Mr. Wilson as "the principal fabricator" of the Constitution in a "Dark Conclave" and vowed to continue their attacks on him and others seeking election to the Pennsylvania ratifying Convention, slated for late November.[11] The opposition charges, with some substance, that the Convention is being dictated by the majority, which is eager to have Pennsylvania the first State to ratify the document.

James Wilson's October 6 speech is an answer as much to the

October 4 published objections of Colonel George Mason of Virginia as to the October 5 "Centinel" attack on General Washington, Dr. Franklin, and the new Constitution.

Meanwhile, at Mount Vernon, General Washington received a letter from Colonel Mason enclosing his objections to the Constitution, which had been published in Philadelphia. In his October 7 letter, a copy having been obtained by this correspondent, he suggests that a second national convention be called to consider amendments.[12]

Although the General's response to his old friend and fellow Virginian was polite, but cool, he revealed in a separate letter (October 10) to James Madison his real attitude toward Colonel Mason's publishing his criticism of the new Constitution.

"He has I am informed rendered himself obnoxious in Philadelphia by the pains he took to disseminate his objections amongst some of the seceding members of the Legislature of that State," the General implying that Colonel Mason has allied himself with extreme critics of the new Constitution in Pennsylvania.[13]

One observer reports, moreover, that the disagreement between the two, which first surfaced during the Philadelphia Convention, has become so strong that it has permanently shattered their longtime personal friendship. General Washington believes that Colonel Mason's objections are the products of "pride" and "want of manly conduct" that prevent him from abandoning his opposition.[14]

General Washington is becoming alarmed at the growing volume of critical articles on the new Constitution appearing in city and State newspapers. In an October 10 letter to his friend the poet David Humphreys, he expresses fear that the ratification debate will be influenced by the "sinister views of too many characters" appearing in print. What are needed, he says, are "good pens" writing openly in newspapers in favor of ratification.[15]

General Washington's fear that friends of the new Constitution are losing the war of words is likely to increase when he receives copies of three separate essays published this week in the Poughkeepsie (New York) *Country Journal*. The essays are signed "The Federal Farmer" and are believed to be authored by Colonel George Mason's close ally Richard Henry Lee of Virginia, although this cannot be confirmed.[16]

The Virginia Governor believes that after an extensive examination of the alleged defects of the Articles, the Convention gave too much power, or "energy," to the proposed national government. To remedy this, he explains in his letter, he proposed in Philadelphia that State ratifying Conventions and a second "General Convention" be convened to consider amendments. When the Convention rejected his proposal, he decided to withhold his signature with the view that in Virginia his proposals might find support among the people.

". . . no man can assure himself," Governor Randolph adds, "how a constitution will work for a course of years, until at least he shall have the observations of the people at large. I also fear more from inaccuracies in a constitution than from gross errors in any other composition; because our dearest interests are to be regulated by it, and power, if loosely given, especially where it will be interpreted with great latitude, may bring sorrow in its execution."[26]

He believes that if the Constitution were submitted to the people, Virginians would reject it entirely, with the prospect of withdrawing from the Union. "This formidable event I wished to avert, by keeping myself free to propose amendments, and thus, if possible, to remove the obstacles to an effectual government," Governor Randolph concludes.[27]

One observer believes that by taking this "middle course," the Virginia Governor has placed himself in a pivotal position of influence. He believes that his State will ultimately decide the fate of the document and be in the position to insist on amendments as a bill of rights.[28]

CHAPTER 4

★

October 12–18, 1787

A savage Indian-settler war in southern Georgia is reported to have erupted, with many dead and wounded on both sides, according to a member of the Virginia House of Delegates who revealed this week details of the September 21 bloody battle involving one hundred fifty Creek Indians and an equal number of white settlers. In the immediate aftermath of the hand-to-hand fighting, Georgia officials were reported to be "preparing for a vigorous Indian expedition."[1]

Also this week, on October 15, the Governor of Georgia presented to his Executive Council a copy of the new Constitution. One observer believes that the explosion of fresh fighting between the Creeks and the settlers is almost certain to guarantee the document's ratification in thinly populated Georgia. The State is expected to look to any new national government for military assistance to cope with any future Indian-settler conflicts.[2]

In New York, Congressman James Madison of Virginia, still attending sessions of the Continental Congress, reports this week that Georgia has declared martial law and is fortifying its capital in Savannah. Mr. Madison blames Imperial Spain for the "dangerous war with the Creek Indians" and alleges that "the Indians derive their motives as well as their means from their Spanish neighbours."[3]

Since June 1784 Spain has kept the Mississippi River closed to American commerce and navigation. That act set off a political earthquake among the thirteen Confederated States. Its aftershocks plunged the Continental Congress into a bitter sectional dispute that came close to splitting the Confederacy into three parts and provoking a war with Imperial Spain.[4]

During the recent Philadelphia Convention, the delegates wrote

23

into the new Constitution a provision requiring a two-thirds Senate approval of all treaties. This provision was approved, in part, to prevent any future national government from surrendering American navigation rights to the Mississippi,[5] a river vital to the Southern States.

Congressman Madison wrote to General Washington expressing concern that the Mississippi issue might be injected into the already incendiary ratification debates. In his October 14 letter, a copy having been obtained by this correspondent, Mr. Madison reveals that a South Carolina Congressman has been circulating to friends the printed text of a speech he gave in secret Continental Congress debates a year ago on the politically explosive Mississippi question. Charles Pinckney III supported the position that the U.S. give up navigation rights on the Mississippi for twenty-five years in exchange for American access to the markets of the Spanish Empire.[6]

Mr. Madison writes that the subject is still "too delicate in my opinion to have been properly confided to the press."[7]

What apparently worries Congressman Madison and General Washington is the use Patrick Henry of Virginia may make of the Mississippi issue in opposing the new Constitution. In the past, Mr. Henry has been a vocal and influential critic against giving up U.S. rights on the river, charging that the proposal was part of a conspiracy of Northern merchants to sell out the commerce of Virginia and the South. The issue was one of the reasons given by the famous orator of the American Revolution for refusing to serve as a delegate to the recent Philadelphia Convention.[8]

General Washington, since the Constitution was published, has sought to win over Mr. Henry to the cause of ratification. The public circulation of Mr. Pinckney's speech might revive the issue and provide Mr. Henry with a plausible pretext for leading a powerful coalition to defeat ratification of the document in Virginia.

"His printing the secret paper at this time could have no motive but the appetite for expected praise," observes Mr. Madison.[9] General Washington concurred in his reply, sarcastically observing that Congressman Pinckney is unwilling "to loose any fame that can be acquired by the publication of his sentiments."[10]

The youthful, wealthy South Carolinian, who was a delegate to the Federal Convention, has also been circulating in New York a copy of a plan for a national government that he had submitted at the Convention. It was never formally acted upon or debated. He is now reported to be claiming a share of credit for framing the new Constitution. Mr. Madison, who regards himself as one of the principal architects of the document, is clearly annoyed at Mr. Pinckney's claim.[11]

General Washington's efforts to persuade Patrick Henry to support ratification may be in vain. James Monroe, in a letter to James Madison, flatly states that the retired five-term Governor of Virginia will oppose ratification. He further states in his October 12 letter that Mr. Henry's influence and the refusal of Colonel George Mason and Governor Edmund Randolph of Virginia to sign the Constitution represent "powerful opposition" to ratification.

"It will perhaps agitate the minds of the people of this State, more than any subject they have had in contemplation since commenc't of the late revolution," predicts James Monroe, the 29-year-old former Congressman from Virginia.[12]

The widening divisions in the State over the Constitution have produced bitter feelings. Mr. Madison, for example, wrote General Washington on October 18 from New York insisting that Colonel Mason's reasons for refusing to sign the new Constitution were superficial if not insincere. Mr. Madison asserts that the recently published reasons given by the 62-year-old Virginia statesman for not signing were not raised in Philadelphia, they either were ". . . not previously thought of, or must have been wilfully concealed."[13]

General Washington admits in a letter to his former chief of artillery, Henry Knox, that Governor Randolph's and Colonel Mason's refusal "to subscribe to the proceedings of the Convention will have a bad effect in this State. . . ." He accuses them of alarming the people and appealing "to the fears of the people. . . ."[14]

The hero of the American Revolution suggested in other correspondence that Colonel Mason's published objections to the Constitution were effectively answered by the October 6 Philadelphia speech of James Wilson of Pennsylvania. General Washington wrote to his friend David Stuart praising Mr. Wilson as "able, candid, and honest a Member as any in Convention." He enclosed a copy of Mr. Wilson's speech in his letter, dated October 17, and asked Mr. Stuart to have it republished if possible, as it would be "of service" in the ever-widening war of words in city and State newspapers.[15]

The *Pennsylvania Herald*, meanwhile, published an essay signed "A Democratic Federalist," attacking Mr. Wilson's speech. The essay, believed to have been authored by Richard Henry Lee of Virginia, an ally of Colonel Mason's, disputes Mr. Wilson's contention that a bill of rights guaranteeing freedom of the press is unnecessary.

"Under the enormous power of the new confederation, which extends to the *individuals* as well as to the *States* of America," the "Democratic Federalist" argues, "a thousand means may be devised to destroy effectually the liberty of the press—There is no knowing what corrupt and wicked judges may do in process of time, when they are not restrained by express laws."[16]

This is why, according to the "Democratic Federalist," a bill of rights must also contain a guarantee of jury trials in civil cases as well as a freedom of the press provision. He accuses Mr. Wilson of being "ingenious" and asserts that *"trial by jury in civil cases, is by the proposed constitution entirely done away with, and effectually abolished."*[17]

This may be an effort to prejudice the press against the new Constitution. However, the gentleman presented a technical but well-informed argument for jury trials in civil cases.[18]

Meanwhile in Virginia, General Washington believes that if Governor Edmund Randolph were converted to the ratification cause, he would swing other votes in the State and checkmate the efforts of Patrick Henry, George Mason, and Richard Henry Lee. An observer reports that one inducement for the politically ambitious Virginia Governor may be a high appointive post in a new national government.[19]

Richard Henry Lee is apparently well aware of the importance of Governor Randolph. Just this week Congressman Lee in New York penned a long letter, a copy of which this correspondent obtained, to the 34-year-old Governor urging amendments to the

Constitution by "calling a new convention for the purpose of considering them."[20] However, efforts last month in Philadelphia and New York to convene a second convention were defeated.

It is clear that both sides in the ratification battle are waging a war of words in the newspapers to influence the various State ratifying Conventions.

On October 16, the Connecticut General Assembly unanimously adopted a resolution providing for the election of delegates to a State ratifying Convention to be held in Hartford the first week of January 1788.[21] One observer reports that even while the Philadelphia Convention was in session this past summer the newspapers of the State published a multitude of articles favorable to the new Constitution. As a result, the State's clergymen, lawyers, physicians, merchants, and veterans of the Revolutionary armies are reported to be solidly in favor of ratification.[22]

The day after Connecticut acted, the Massachusetts General Court* issued a call for a State ratifying Convention. However, the Constitution may face militant opposition similar to what it has encountered in Virginia. Principally, but not exclusively, the reason is that Convention delegate Elbridge Gerry of Massachusetts joined Colonel Mason and Governor Randolph of Virginia in refusing to sign the document in Philadelphia.

Newspapers in Philadelphia, New York, and Boston favoring ratification have launched a barrage of criticism against the three dissenters.[23]

In a letter to the President of the Senate and Speaker of the House in Massachusetts, Mr. Gerry defended his refusal to sign. The 43-year-old Massachusetts merchant and Signer of the Declaration of Independence and Articles of Confederation maintains he was sent to Philadelphia only to amend the Articles and not to approve an entirely new Constitution.

"It was painful for me," Mr. Gerry adds, "on a subject of such national importance, to differ from the respectable members who signed the constitution: But conceiving as I did, that the liberties of America were not secured by the system, it was my duty to oppose it."[24]

*Legislature.

Nevertheless, in a private letter written from New York on the same day, he predicted that if the Constitution is adopted "it will lay the foundation of a Government of *force & fraud*, that the people will bleed with taxes (at every) pore, & that the existence of their liberties will soon be terminated."[25]

Boston newspapers are predicting that farmers, mechanics, sailors, laborers, merchants, and men of independent fortune will benefit materially if the document is ratified.

"... for nothing short of a firm and efficient government can dissipate the gloom that involves every present prospect," states the *Boston Gazette* on October 15. "... All these evils will gradually subside, till they finally disappear, if we but have the wisdom and firmness speedily to adopt the New Federal Constitution."[26]

Speed is the last thing that dissenters Elbridge Gerry and Richard Henry Lee want. As Congressmen attending sessions of the Continental Congress in New York, they are reported to be plotting a strategy of delay. Congressman Lee in particular has been turning out a steady stream of articles critical of the Constitution and conferring with New York Governor George Clinton, who also opposes ratification.[27] One observer says that Colonel Lee has been working with allies in Pennsylvania and Delaware hoping to delay the decisions in those States.[28] His correspondence with Colonel Mason in Virginia reveals, this correspondent has learned, that Colonel Lee has become the principal intellectual leader of the opponents to ratification.

Colonel Alexander Hamilton of New York has assumed a similar role for the Federalists. He is reliably reported to be planning a series of newspaper articles to counter the growing number of hostile pieces appearing in print. He is seeking the assistance of James Madison, who is remaining in New York and who has been urged by General Washington to give explanations of the Constitution since "none could give them with more accuracy."[29]

Joining Colonel Hamilton in the authorship of the forthcoming series of newspaper articles is John Jay, currently Foreign Secretary of the Confederation. It was Mr. Jay who first proposed that the U.S. give up navigation rights on the Mississippi River for twenty-five years, igniting the firestorm that plunged the thirteen States into an acute political crisis. During the last three years, Secretary Jay, with the aid of General Washington, has sought to resolve the explosive question with quiet diplomatic efforts with the Spanish.

Reports this week that the Spanish may have encouraged the Creek Indians to make war on white settlers in southern Georgia may serve to strengthen the arguments for adoption of the Constitution. Mr. Jay is known to believe that Spain's closing the Mississippi to the Confederation and Great Britain's barring American use of the St. Lawrence River are powerful justifications for forming a new union "to put and keep them in *such a situation* as, instead of *inviting* war, will tend to repress and discourage it."[30]

In the meantime, the Spanish envoy to the Continental Congress wrote to Madrid in a secret diplomatic dispatch, a copy having been obtained by this correspondent, "that the paper war in the Newspapers over the new System of Government" clearly indicates "its establishment will be delayed a long time."[31] He also wrote that he wouldn't be surprised if a new convention were called next year.

The "paper war in the newspapers" has been generally void of humor, although an exception was provided this week in the October 17 issue of the Philadelphia *Freeman's Journal*.

"Oratory can do wonderful things—" observed an anonymous author opposed to the Constitution, "one of the Athenian sages is reported to have made so moving a speech upon the miseries of human life, that more than half his audience rose from their benches, and went home with a determined resolution to hang themselves before night."[32]

CHAPTER 5

October 19–25, 1787

Two heroes of the American Revolution found themselves on opposite sides of the ratification battlelines this week when Patrick Henry rejected George Washington's efforts to secure his public support for the new Constitution. The former five-term Governor of Virginia made known his opposition in a brief letter to General Washington, a copy having been obtained by this correspondent.

"I have to lament," Mr. Henry wrote on October 19 to General Washington, "that I cannot bring my mind to accord with the proposed Constitution. The Concern I feel on this account is really greater than I am able to express. Perhaps mature Reflections may furnish me Reasons to change my present Sentiments...."[1]

However, on October 22 Mr. Henry is reported to have expressed a more candid view to Colonel Thomas Madison, cousin of Congressman James Madison of Virginia.

"I can never agree to the proposed plan without Amendments, tho' many are willing to swallow it in its present form...," Governor Henry wrote.[2]

Richmond has been a riot of rumors in the last week as members of the Virginia House of Delegates arrive from as far away as the Kentucky counties to consider the new Constitution. The buckskin-clad Kentuckians, carrying long rifles and short scalping knives used in Indian fighting, are a rude contrast to Tidewater delegates dressed in fine imported linen cloth suits. As the Indian summer heat swept across the city, they met in taverns, inns, private homes, and public buildings, reportedly counting heads and collecting rumors about the possible fate of the document.[3]

When the legislators were called to order this week and Mr.

Henry had arrived to take his seat, most of the delegates were prepared to approve a State ratifying Convention. It was still uncertain whether critics of the Federal Convention would try to use this session to promote amendments to the Constitution and a second federal convention.[4]

Governor Henry, looking older than his 51 years, made his opposition clear during the October 25 session. He was first to his feet to oppose a resolution calling for a State Convention for the narrow purpose of ratifying or rejecting the Constitution. He wanted the right of the Convention to propose amendments as a condition to ratification.

Francis Corbin, a young former Tory who had sought an education in England during the War and whose father had been a royal official, was a poor choice, one observer notes, to offer the resolution on behalf of the Federalists.[5]

John Marshall, a handsome 32-year-old Henrico County lawyer, veteran of the War of Independence and a staunch supporter of the proposed Constitution, adroitly sought to disarm Governor Henry and defuse his politically explosive amendment proposal. Agreeing that the ratifying Convention should have the power to propose amendments, he said he did not want the resolution allowing for amendments to imply that Virginia disapproved of the document.[6]

The compromise resolution offered by Mr. Marshall was unanimously adopted, stipulating that proceedings of other State ratifying Conventions should be submitted to the Virginia Convention for "full and free investigation and discussion." In a counterattack, Governor Henry later proposed a resolution, which was adopted, that approved paying expenses of any Virginia Convention delegate who might consult with other States for the purpose of considering appropriate amendments and paying expenses of delegates to another federal convention should one be agreed upon.[7]

Colonel George Mason, an ally of Governor Henry's, watched this week's inconclusive scrimmage in the Virginia House of Delegates with a degree of anxiety. Rising to support Mr. Henry's proposal,

Colonel Mason also justified his refusal to sign the Constitution in Philadelphia.

"I thought it wrong, Mr. Chairman—" the 62-year-old statesman stated. "I thought it repugnant to our highest interests—and if with these sentiments I had subscribed to it, I might have been justly regarded as a traitor to my country. I would have lost this hand," gesturing with his right hand, "before it should have marked my name to the new government."[8]

Since his return to Virginia from the Federal Convention in Philadelphia, Colonel Mason has been recovering from serious neck and head injuries received in a coach accident near Baltimore.[9] The accident may not have been as painful to him as the reception he is reported to have received from his constituents, rumored to be enraged at his refusal to sign the Constitution.

Besides attacks in the newspapers, it had been reported that bodily harm to Colonel Mason might result if he made an appearance among outraged Alexandria citizens, when returning in late September from Philadelphia to his home in nearby Gunston Hall.[10]

The Mayor of Alexandria, a port town at the mouth of the Potomac River, is said to have warned Colonel Mason that public opinion is so inflamed against him that he could not guarantee his personal safety. Nevertheless, according to a reliable source, Colonel Mason demanded that the town crier call an assembly so that he could address the people.

When the citizens of Alexandria had gathered, he calmly and succinctly outlined his objections to the Constitution. When he had finished, according to this source, the awestruck assembly silently parted and made a path for him as he walked to his horse. However, a heckler reportedly called after him, perhaps aware of his recent head and neck injuries: "Mr. Mason, you are an old man, and the public notices that you are losing your faculties."

"Sir," retorted Colonel Mason as he swung into the saddle, "the public will never notice when you lose yours."[11]

The inflamed opinion against Colonel Mason in northern Virginia may be traced in some measure to the fact that General Washington at nearby Mount Vernon strongly favors the Constitution. One observer believes this may well neutralize the opposition in Virginia

of Colonel Mason, Patrick Henry, and two former Governors of the
State who were also Signers of the Declaration of Independence:
Thomas Nelson, Jr., and Benjamin Harrison. General Washington
had sent copies of the proposed Constitution to both gentlemen, as
he had to Governor Henry.

Former Governor Harrison replied, "My objections chiefly lie
against the unlimited powers of taxation, the regulation of trade,
and the jurisdictions that are to be established in every state altogether independent of their laws. The sword and such powers will,
nay, must, sooner or later establish a tyranny."[12]

The presently elected Governor, and former Governors, may
oppose the Constitution, but Congressman James Madison has told
General Washington that the chief threat to Virginia's ratification
is Patrick Henry's proven oratorical sway over the people.[13]

At the same time, one observer believes that the cause of
ratification from the onset was dealt a needless injury because the
document was created in secrecy.

Just this week the secrecy issue surfaced in the Philadelphia
Freeman's Journal. In the October 24 issue, "Centinel" skillfully
tied Convention secrecy to the absence of a bill of rights protecting
press liberty and other "invaluable" personal rights. Insisting that
secrecy was dictated "by the genius of Aristocracy" at the
Philadelphia Convention, "Centinel" maintains that despite the support of General Washington and a "splendor of names," a sinister
plot is maturing to rob the people of their liberties.

"The authors of the new plan," the essayist adds, "conscious that
it would not stand the test of enlightened patriotism, tyrannically
endeavoured to preclude all investigation.—If their views were
laudable; if they were honest,—the contrary would have been their
conduct, they would have invited the freest discussion. Whatever
specious reasons may be assigned for secrecy during the framing
of the plan, no good one can exist, for leading the people blindfolded
into the implicit adoption of it. Such an attempt does not augur the
public good—It carries on the face of it an intention to juggle the
people out of their liberties."[14]

Refusal to make public the records of the Constitutional

Convention debates has apparently handed critics of the Constitution a powerful weapon to fan public fears. One observer has pointed out that the secrecy of the Philadelphia conclave produced an aura of mystery and suspicion and that keeping secret the minutes of the debates reinforces charges that sinister motives underlay the document's creation.[15]

Even the U.S. Minister to France, Thomas Jefferson, has been critical that the Convention kept its debates secret. "I am sorry," Mr. Jefferson wrote from Paris to John Adams in London where he is serving as U.S. Minister to Great Britain, "they [Convention delegates] began their deliberations by so abominable a precedent as that of tying up the tongues of their members. nothing can justify this example but the innocence of their intentions, & ignorance of the value of public discussions."[16]

Because Mr. Jefferson was the author of the Declaration of Independence, his view of the new Constitution will carry considerable influence, despite the fact he was in Paris during the Convention.

James Madison this week, in a lengthy, seventeen-page letter to the American envoy, for the first time conceded that he was profoundly disappointed with the results of the Philadelphia Convention. He had repeatedly sought and failed to have the proposed national government armed with the power to veto all State laws. Mr. Madison knows that Mr. Jefferson opposes such power but in his October 24 letter he attempted to persuade his fellow Virginian that the power was necessary. Otherwise, he doubted the new Constitution would reform what Mr. Madison perceives as the existing paramount political evil: the power of the States to pass unjust laws.[17]

It is unlikely, however, that the 36-year-old Virginia Congressman will openly renew his campaign for national veto power over State laws during the current ratification debates. If he does, critics of the Constitution could point to the proposal as proof that the secret aim of its advocates is the consolidation of the thirteen States into a single republican empire.

★

Just this week, "Cato," alleged to be New York Governor George Clinton, assailed in the October 25 issue of the *New York Journal* the new Constitution as a plan for consolidation of the States into one government. "Cato" states that such a government cannot *"form a perfect union, establish justice, insure domestic tranquility, promote the general welfare, and secure the blessings of liberty to you and your posterity"* because, as he states, the proposed government is founded on principles contradicted by ancient and contemporary experience.[18]

"Cato" quotes French philosopher Montesquieu that liberty can flourish only in small republics with limited geography, whereas in large republics covering an extensive land mass the public good is sacrificed to a thousand views. The immense territory of America, its diverse climates, commerce, and customs would create a consolidated republic and become "like a house divided against itself.

"...you must risque much, by indispensably placing trusts of the greatest magnitude, into the hands of individuals, whose ambition for power, and aggrandizement, will oppress and grind you—where, from the vast extent of your territory, and the complication of interests, the science of government will become intricate and perplexed, and too misterious for you to understand," developing into a despotic monarch, which, Mr. Locke remarks, *"is a government derived from neither nature, nor compact."*[19]

Despite such attacks, James Madison expresses confidence that the small States will approve the Constitution because of commercial and political self-interests, ignoring alarmist abstract arguments of future consequences to freedom.

"New Jersey appears to be zealous," Mr. Madison writes from New York to Virginia Governor Edmund Randolph on October 23. "Meetings of the people in different counties are declaring their approbation, and instructing their representatives."[20]

The New Jersey Legislature is expected next week to approve resolves for electing delegates to a State ratifying Convention. One observer reports that near-unanimous praise for the Constitution is due directly to freeing New Jersey from the pressure of paying impost duties to New York and Pennsylvania.[21] The small State has been described by its neighboring States as a cask being tapped at both ends.

The large States, such as Massachusetts, New York, Pennsylvania, and Virginia, still give Mr. Madison worry. Virginia's Governor Edmund Randolph reports in a letter to Mr. Madison that, in his opinion, the "tide is turning" in the State in favor of the Anti-Federalists: "New objections are daily started, and the opinions of Mr. Henry gain ground. He and I have had several animated discourses, but he recedes so far from me that we must diverge after a progress of half a degree further."[22] Nevertheless, he's not yet publicly declared himself, not even to Mr. Madison: "I have thought proper to postpone any explanation of myself, except in private, until every thing is determined which may relate to the Constitution."[23]

Mr. Madison is reported to believe that the only effective strategy is to prevent Governor Randolph from falling under the influence of Patrick Henry. One observer reports that Mr. Madison regards the current Virginia Governor as a "weighty and wobbly stone" to be wedged out of the Henry line and converted by a mixture of argument and flattery. One form of flattery is to convince Governor Randolph that his political stature in the State can approach that of former Governor Henry if he becomes a warm friend rather than a cold foe of the Constitution.[24]

Although Congressman Madison is in New York and is seeking to shape events in his own State through correspondence, at the same time he is reported to be making his influence felt nationwide. By remaining in New York and attending sessions of the Continental Congress, he is able secretly to manage the forces favoring ratification.

CHAPTER 6

October 26–November 1, 1787

If General George Washington allows the idea to prevail that he will not accept election as President of a new national government, "it would prove fatal" to ratification of the Constitution in some States, according to the stylistic penman of the document, Gouverneur Morris.

The colorful 35-year-old lawyer, financier, and Pennsylvania delegate to the recent Philadelphia Constitutional Convention made the blunt prediction this week in a letter to General Washington, a copy of which was obtained by this correspondent.

In his October 30 letter, Mr. Morris wrote the 55-year-old military hero of the American War of Independence that had he not attended the Convention and signed the document it would have "met with a colder Reception, with fewer and weaker Advocates" and with more vigorous opponents than it now has.

"No Constitution is the same on Paper and in Life," Mr. Morris adds. "The Exercise of Authority depends on personal Character; and the Whip and Reins by which an able Charioteer governs unruly Steeds will only hurl the unskilfull Presumer with more speedy & headlong Violence to the Earth. The Horses once trained may be managed by a Woman or a Child; not so when they first feel the Bit. And indeed among these thirteen Horses now about to be coupled together there are some of every Race and Character. They will listen to your Voice, and submit to your Control; you therefore must I say *must* mount the Seat."[1]

It is widely assumed by friend and foe alike that if ratification of the proposed Constitution is secured, General Washington will be unanimously elected President. He is reported by one observer to have turned a deaf ear to the idea. Allegedly he prefers Mount

Vernon as a retirement refuge, as if it could fend off a world that looks to him for leadership.[2]

Mr. Morris's letter is not without irony. Immediately after the Philadelphia Convention the peg-legged Pennsylvanian (he lost his limb in a carriage accident) vowed *not* to support the Constitution, concluding that it lacked sufficient central powers. But it is reliably reported that Colonel Alexander Hamilton of New York convinced Mr. Morris that the document, with all its alleged weaknesses, remains America's only hope.[3] Nonetheless, the New York lawyer could not convince the Pennsylvania lawyer to collaborate on a series of newspaper articles explaining and defending the document.

The first of the projected series, signed "Publius," appeared this week in the New York *Independent Journal*. Colonel Hamilton, widely believed to be the author, insists that the fate of the "American Empire" and the preservation of liberty and property hinge on ratification of the Constitution. If the document is defeated, he warns in the October 27 essay, it will be the "general misfortune of mankind. . . .

"Among the most formidable of the obstacles which the new Constitution will have to encounter," he adds, "may readily be distinguished the obvious interest of a certain class of men in every State to resist all changes which may hazard a diminution of the power, emolument, and consequence of the offices they hold under the State establishments. . . ."[4]

A reliable source says that the immediate aim of the series of articles is to influence the election of pro-Constitutional delegates to New York's ratifying Convention.[5] Already six State Legislatures—Pennsylvania, New Jersey, Connecticut, Massachusetts, Virginia, and Georgia—have called for State ratifying Conventions.

However, New York's 48-year-old Governor, George Clinton, is an opponent of the Constitution and a bitter political enemy of Colonel Hamilton's. He is reported to be delaying a decision in anticipation that five other State Conventions might reject the document, making it unnecessary for New York to act.[6]

Furthermore, this observer says the Governor is not certain a New York Convention can be trusted to follow his wishes.[7] It is believed that Governor Clinton ordered two New York delegates to the Philadelphia Convention, John Lansing and Robert Yates, to return home in mid-July in the hope of breaking up the Convention. Colonel Hamilton was then the sole New York representative.

The former military aide to General Washington attended only six weeks of the four-month secret conclave. In the end, he expressed dislike of the compromise document, but nevertheless signed it. He now appears determined to defeat Governor Clinton's efforts to scuttle the Constitution.[8]

The handsome 32-year-old lawyer and legislator may have had Governor Clinton in mind when, in the first "Publius" essay, he warns against political demagogues pandering after support of the people in the name of safeguarding their liberties.

"History will teach us . . .," "Publius" wrote, "that of those men who have overturned the liberties of republics, the greatest number have begun their career by paying an obsequious court to the people, commencing demagogues, and ending tyrants."[9]

"Publius" goes on to charge that opponents of the Constitution have the secret aim of forming separate confederacies and predicts this would lead to dismemberment of the Union if the proposed Constitution is rejected.

"It will therefore be of use to begin by examining the advantages of that Union, the certain evils, and the probable dangers, to which every State will be exposed from its dissolution," Colonel Hamilton adds, promising to take up the subject in the next essay.[10]

Several observers report that Colonel Hamilton's long-range political goal is to gain adoption of the Constitution, however weak he may perceive its powers. Once in place he would work to enlarge the national government's powers to make it "workable."[11]

However, these observers point out that Colonel Hamilton and his allies have failed to appreciate the powerful appeal, and the depth of feeling over the absence, of a bill of rights in the Constitution to protect the people against oppressive acts of future rulers.[12]

In the six weeks since the document was signed in Philadelphia and published in city and State newspapers, the absence of a bill of rights has become an issue similar in its political impact to a fire bell rung in the middle of the night, alarming even those favoring reform.

James Wilson of Pennsylvania, a 45-year-old Constitutional Convention delegate, sought to explain the absence of a bill of rights in an October 6 Philadelphia speech. The scholarly Scottish-born lawyer insisted a bill of rights is not needed in the Constitution since most of the States already have such protections. His speech was widely published and subjected to an avalanche of printed attacks.

Just this week the *New York Journal* published four separate, lengthy essays assailing Mr. Wilson. One was signed "Brutus," who, a source maintains, is Robert Yates, a New York Convention delegate.[13] Mr. Yates is a 49-year-old lawyer, New York judge, and ally of Governor Clinton. "Brutus" points out that the new Constitution specifically states the document shall be the supreme law of the land.

"It is therefore not only necessarily implied thereby, but positively expressed," the November 1 essay states, "that the different state constitutions are repealed and entirely done away, so far as they are inconsistent with this, with the laws which shall be made . . . under the authority of the United States; of what avail will the constitutions of the respective states be to preserve the rights of its citizens?"[14]

The day before this "Brutus" broadside, the New York *Independent Journal* published the second essay of the "Publius" series. A source reports that its author is the Foreign Secretary of the current Confederation, John Jay of New York. The 42-year-old lawyer and diplomat is said to be secretly collaborating with Colonel Hamilton on a series of newspaper articles defending the proposed Constitution.[15]

Ignoring the burning issue of a bill of rights and the charge that the separate States will be swallowed up under the proposed national government, "Publius" maintains the separate States should be one nation, under one Federal government, rather than three or four confederacies.

"Providence," he argues in the October 31 essay, has ordained the nation as one united people, ". . . descended from the same ancestors, speaking the same language, professing the same religion, attached to the same principles of government, very similar in their manners and customs, and who, by their joint counsels, arms, and efforts, fighting side by side throughout a long and bloody war, have nobly established general liberty and independence.

"This country and this people seem to have been made for each other and it appears as if it was the design of Providence, that an inheritance proper and convenient for a band of brethren, united to each other by their strongest ties, should never be split into a number of unsocial, jealous, and alien sovereignties."[16]

This is the first time since the ratification debate erupted that a principal advocate of the Constitution has sought to justify on religious grounds a document that, unlike the Declaration of Independence, does not mention religion or ask for "Protection of Divine Providence." However, since the end of the War of Independence, public sentiment has been growing that the postwar period has witnessed a decline in moral and religious values.

For example, the *Virginia Independent Chronicle* of Richmond published "A Proposal for Reviving Christian Conviction," written by an anonymous Episcopal minister. He maintains that a "cold indifference towards religion" has crept over all segments of the population. Civil institutions, the author argues, require religious sanction.

"Those who doubt of the good effects arising from the operation of religious principles," he adds, "need only turn their thoughts to the state of Pennsylvania, and contemplate the happy and flourishing condition of that province from its first settlement."[17]

Nonetheless, the religious piety of nonviolent Quaker Pennsylvania appears to have had little influence on the verbally vehement ratification debate in that State. Writing from New York about his observations in the Continental Congress, Nicholas Gilman, 32-year-old New Hampshire Congressman and delegate to the Philadelphia Convention, says, "The intemperance of a number of the members of the Pennsylvania Legislature has made enemys to the new plan—but not such as to render the adoption of it very doubtful."[18]

Foes of the proposed Federal government have been using with great effect descriptions of how the Pennsylvania Legislature, in late September, allegedly incited a Philadelphia mob to drag two dissenting members to the State House in order to secure a quorum for approval of a State ratifying Convention. One observer reports that tactics of the pro-Constitution forces in Pennsylvania have aroused indignation in other States and caused some who favored the plan to change their views.[19]

In recent weeks, the Philadelphia newspapers have been filled with articles both praising and denouncing the Constitution, almost to the exclusion of other news. One penman, describing himself as "An Old Whig," writes in the Philadelphia *Independent Gazetteer* of his fears about the power of the new and novel office of President. After George Washington's term, the anonymous essayist argues, the country is likely to have a King or a Caesar and, therefore, a bill of rights is imperative to preserve personal liberties.

"If we are not prepared to *receive a king*," the "Old Whig" adds, "let us call another convention to revise the proposed constitution, and form it anew on the principles of a confederacy of free republics; but by no means, under pretence of a republic, to lay the foundation for a military government, which is the worst of all tyrannies."[20]

The day before, on October 31, the *Pennsylvania Gazette* took sharp issue with a recent "Centinel" essay that attacked General George Washington and Dr. Benjamin Franklin as ignorant or foolish pawns of the powerful and well born.

"What a variety of methods do the opposers of our new constitution pursue, to prevent the adoption of it," the newspaper replied.

It went on to observe, "A New York writer, under the signature of BRUTUS, wishes to have three confederacies—that is, three times the officers, and three times the expence of the proposed plan. *If the union is preserved*, it can have nothing to fear from the British Colonies on the North, or the Spanish on the South; *but if it should be divided into three parts*, European politics would soon play off *one* against *another*."[21]

Thus, for the first time since the ratification debate began, advocates have publicly used the argument that a strong central government must be adopted to keep at bay Great Britain and Imperial Spain. Last week Congressman James Madison asserted that the bloody battles in late September between Georgian settlers and Creek Indians were supported by motives and materials from Imperial Spain.

"Individuals complain also," Congressman Madison revealed, "that their fugitive slaves are encouraged by East Florida. The policy of this is explained by supposing that it is considered as a discouragement to the Georgians to form settlements near the Spanish boundaries."[22]

The Continental Congress's response has been to send a resolution to the Governors of Georgia, South Carolina, and North Carolina authorizing the appointment of one commissioner in each State to conclude a peace treaty with the Creeks in Georgia and the Cherokee Nation in North Carolina. The October 27 secret communication from the Secretary of the Continental Congress, a copy of which this correspondent obtained, states that peace should be established by diplomacy, with money being appropriated for "this business." The Confederation does not maintain a military force equal to or exceeding the Spanish, who would aid the Indians if war develops.[23]

Colonel Hamilton and Foreign Secretary Jay can be expected to argue in their "Publius" essays that the dangers posed by Great Britain and Imperial Spain can be met only by a strong central government headed by a strong leader behind whom a single nation of States can unite.

Colonel Hamilton, Secretary Jay, Gouverneur Morris, and other supporters of the proposed Constitution look to General Washington as that leader. Colonel Hamilton sent to the General this week a copy of his first "Publius" essay, indicating how closely he and other advocates are working with the 55-year-old master of Mount Vernon to secure ratification.[24]

General Washington is reported by one observer to be pleased with the "Publius" essay, predicting that the essays "will merit the notice of posterity" because they ably discuss "the principles of freedom and the topics of government...."[25]

In recent days Secretary Jay is said to have become seriously ill and may be unable to continue his collaboration with Colonel

Hamilton. As a result, other pro-Constitutionalists, among them James Madison, are being approached by Colonel Hamilton to aid in writing the newspaper series.[26]

As Mr. Morris wrote to General Washington this week: "... public Opinion ... must not be neglected in a Country where Opinion is every Thing."[27]

CHAPTER 7

★

November 2–8, 1787

Pennsylvania's pro-Constitutionists were swept to a decisive victory this week in an election of delegates to a State ratifying Convention, ensuring that Federalist forces would dominate the conclave when it formally meets later this month.

James Wilson, a leader in the Federal Convention, was the only candidate in the November 6 balloting who was also a delegate to the Philadelphia Convention.[1] One observer reports that opposition attacks on all the Pennsylvania delegates who signed the new Constitution have been so verbally violent that of those delegates only Mr. Wilson's name was put on the ballot, as a political precaution.[2]

Anti-Federalist foes of the document placed Dr. Benjamin Franklin's name on the ballot in a futile effort to draw votes for their party. The 81-year-old President of the Executive Council of Pennsylvania received more votes than any of the opposition candidates because of his personal popularity, not because of party position. Although Philadelphia voted overwhelmingly for pro-Constitution delegates, the victory did not restrain a mob of rioters from stoning a boarding house where several Pennsylvania Assembly opposition members were lodged.[3]

One observer insists that the special Pennsylvania delegate election was timed to prevent effective organization by the Anti-Federalists. Caught off guard, they have denounced the speed with which the election was called.[4] The opposition is also charging that the election was unfair because most of the 70,000 eligible voters in the State were not informed an election was to be held. As a consequence, they argue, only 13,000 voted for the 46 members of the forthcoming ratifying Convention.[5]

James Wilson answered the opposition by charging that the Anti-

Federalists are out to defeat the document more from a concern for the loss of power and profitable State posts, than from a concern that the Constitution will destroy personal liberties. The opposition's objection to granting the proposed national government powers of direct taxation ignores the positive benefits for dealing collectively with the States and with the Confederation's swollen debts, Mr. Wilson says.

"The State of Pennsylvania particularly," the 45-year-old lawyer predicts, "which has encumbered itself with the assumption of a great portion of the public debt, will derive considerable relief and advantage. . . ."[6]

This week's special election virtually ensures that Pennsylvania will approve ratification. However, in Massachusetts, a critical State as to size along with Pennsylvania, Virginia, and New York, the outlook for the new Constitution is overcast with dark clouds of doubt.

Just this week Constitutional Convention delegate Elbridge Gerry of Massachusetts, one of the three who refused to sign the document on September 17, stirred up a storm. In a letter published in the November 3 edition of the *Massachusetts Centinel*, the 43-year-old Signer of the Declaration of Independence and of the Articles of Confederation charged that the Philadelphia Convention acted illegally; it was empowered only to amend the current Articles, not to write a new Constitution. For this reason and others, he says, he refused to sign it.

"Others may suppose," he adds, "that the Constitution may be safely adopted, because therein provision is made to *amend* it. But cannot *this object* be better attained before a ratification, than after it? And should a *free* people adopt a form of Government, under conviction that it wants amendment?"[7]

Mr. Gerry's published criticism of the Constitution has infuriated pro-Constitution forces in the State. His two fellow delegates who did sign the document, Rufus King and Nathaniel Gorham, are reported to be angry and worried over the impact of Mr. Gerry's opposition. Henry Jackson, a Boston merchant and political ally of the two, is quoted as saying that Mr. Gerry's "infamous" letter "has done more injury to this Country . . . than he will be able to make atonement in his whole life. . . ."[8]

During the last two weeks, Massachusetts has approved the election of delegates and the calling of a ratifying Convention. The latter's makeup is likely to be split between merchants from the cities favoring ratification and farmers from the rural areas opposing.[9] A similar division has developed in Pennsylvania, New York, and Connecticut.

An effort was launched just this week to convince "tillers of the land" that the new Constitution will revive prosperity in American agriculture by the regulation of foreign trade. Oliver Ellsworth, a Federal Convention delegate from Connecticut, made this argument in the November 5 edition of the Hartford *Connecticut Courant*, under the *nom de plume* "A Landholder."[10]

"Every foreign prohibition on American trade," observes the 42-year-old jurist, "is aimed in the most deadly manner against the holders and tillers of the land, and they are the men made poor. Your only remedy is such a national government as will make the country respectable; such a supreme government as can boldly meet the supremacy of proud and self-interested nations. . . ."[11]

This argument is likely to have a powerful appeal since agriculture is the main pursuit of 90 percent of the population of the thirteen States. A recent depression in foreign trade, falling prices for exported agricultural products, and new restrictions on U.S. goods in Europe are problems that defy solutions under the current Confederated government.[12]

The "Landholder" and other Federalists promise a return to prosperity by a regulation of trade and guaranteed higher prices for commodities, if the Constitution is adopted.

"Artful men," Mr. Ellsworth says in his published letter, "may insinuate the contrary—tell you let trade take care of itself, and excite your jealousy against the merchant because his business leads him to wear a gayer coat, than your œconomy directs. But let your own experience refuse such insinuations. . . . You cannot expect many purchasers when trade is restricted, and your merchants are shut out from nine tenths of the ports in the world."[13]

Foreign trade and foreign threats appear to be the two most potent arguments in the Federalists' political arsenal. Both issues were linked in the latest "Publius" essay, published in the November 7 issue of the New York *Independent Journal.*

The author of the essay is rumored to be John Jay, Foreign Secretary of the Confederated government, who allegedly is collaborating with Colonel Alexander Hamilton of New York on the newspaper series.

In this latest essay, "Publius" promises that under the new government citizens will be safer from "foreign arms and influence" than they have been under the current system of confederated States. Foreign commerce will also be more secure, "Publius" says, because a national government will honor its treaties and act to protect overall interest, rather than thirteen separate States motivated by sectional and local considerations.

Savage Indian conflicts are less likely, "Publius" predicts, under a new national government. In several instances, he charges that Indian hostilities have been "provoked by the improper conduct of individual States, who, either unable or unwilling to restrain or punish offences, have given occasion to the slaughter of many innocent inhabitants.

"The neighborhood of Spanish and British territories," the essayist adds, "bordering on some States and not on others, naturally confines the causes of quarrel more immediately to the borderers. The bordering States, if any, will be those who, under the impulse of sudden irritation, and a quick sense of apparent interest or injury, will be most likely, by direct violence, to excite war with these nations; and nothing can so effectually obviate that danger as a national government, whose wisdom and prudence will not be diminished by the passions which actuate the parties immediately interested."[14]

In a followup November 7 essay in the New York *Independent Journal,* "Publius" (allegedly John Jay) reminds his readers that as American trade grows, so will the dangers of confrontation with rival countries. He points, as examples, to Spain's closing the Mississippi River to American navigation and to Great Britain's excluding the thirteen States from using the St. Lawrence River. If war erupted between a State and one of these foreign powers, "Publius" asks, would the others "spend their blood and money" in another State's defense? Or, would they play off one State against another?

"The history of the states of Greece," the essayist continues, "and of other countries, abounds with such instances, and it is not improbable that what has so often happened would, under similar circumstances, happen again."[15]

European envoys accredited to the Confederated government in New York have not reacted privately or publicly to the two "Publius" essays published this week. It would doubtlessly come as a shock if they suspected they were written by the Confederation's Foreign Secretary! But in England, reaction to the Constitution is beginning to emerge. Copies of the document arrived in England in late October, after nearly six weeks' voyage, and last week it was published in six London newspapers.[16]

Mrs. Abigail Adams, wife of the American Minister to Great Britain, John Adams, writes from London that the "Form of Government" is received by officials as a "Sublime work" and that "... it is so good that they are persuaded the Americans will not accept it."[17]

Thomas Lee Shippen, a law student in London and the son of a prominent and pioneering Philadelphia physician, also writes to his father this week of the document's reception: "... The people here extol as the master piece of policy, and the Convention as a Roman Senate—We stand six inches higher at least than we did. In Westmr Hall this morning I felt the barristers press my hand harder than usual, and I found it was because my Country had improved so much ... in ye science of Govt. ..."[18]

Another American is equally excited. John Brown Cutting, a 32-year-old former secretary to American envoy John Adams, is completing his legal studies in London and writes that the document is "the most stupendous Fabric" of republican government "that ever was invented...to perpetuate political freedom, civil happiness and national reknown...."

"I extol every member of that Convention," he adds, "whose name is annexed to the work, and fancy and foresee marble monuments and bronze busto's to his honor, starting into form from the future gratitude of posterity—. . . one may venture to predict that the suffrages and approving sanction of nine states must make the architects of such an eminent Edifice at least memorable if not immortal."[19]

Nevertheless, in at least two States the powers of the new and novel office of President were denounced as dangerously comparable to the King of England. "Cato," suspected to be New York Governor George Clinton, predicts in the November 8 issue of the *New York Journal* that the ten-mile square of land set aside for the seat of the new national government will become similar to the European courts, a place for the minions and favorites of a monarch-President to gain fortune and hold power isolated from the community at large.

". . . he is the generalissimo of the nation," warns "Cato," "and, of course, has the command and controul of the army, navy and militia; he is the general conservator of the peace of the union—he may pardon all offences, except in cases of impeachment, and the principal fountain of all offices and employments. Will not the exercise of these powers therefore tend either to the establishment of a vile and arbitrary aristocracy, or monarchy?"[20]

In antislavery Quaker Pennsylvania, opponents to the Constitution seek to use the clause that extends slavery until 1808 as an argument why the document is dangerously deceitful. "Centinel," in the November 5 edition of the Philadelphia *Independent Gazetteer*, lashes out at the language in the document that describes slaves only as "persons." The essayist maintains that it is against the declared sense of other States' efforts not to "put an end to an odious traffic in the human species"; that such traffic "is especially scandalous and inconsistent in a people, who have asserted their own liberty by the sword" in the recent War of Independence.

"The words are dark and ambiguous;" "Centinel" adds, "such as no plain man of common sense would have used, [and] are evidently chosen to conceal from Europe, that in this enlightened country, the practice of slavery has its advocates among men in the highest stations."[21]

Ever since the Constitution was published six weeks ago, Quakers in Pennsylvania and other States are reported deeply disturbed by the Constitution's extension of the slave trade for twenty years. During the last two decades Quakers have been successful at prohibiting the slave trade on the State level. Six States either now prohibit slave trade or have tightened earlier laws, and one State imposes a heavy duty on imported slaves. Quakers are petitioning other States, particularly Rhode Island, the center for the overseas slave trade. (Rhode Island did not attend the Philadelphia Convention.)

One source reports that while Quakers generally favor the proposed Constitution, they are not expected to be active in the fight over ratification. This is said to be partly because of the slavery-extension provision, but more importantly because of their general policy not to engage in politics.[22]

If opponents to the Constitution hope to use the slavery issue as a political weapon in the forthcoming Pennsylvania ratifying Convention, the nonpolitical, antislavery Quakers in the State are not likely to give their assistance. The Convention debate will probably be bitter, if not abusive, with the Anti-Federalist minority waging a war of words against the Federalist majority while privately conceding they do not have the votes to prevail.

James Wilson, instrumental in drafting the Constitution, is likely to assume leadership of the majority in the ratifying conclave. He is also likely to bear the burden of answering the militant opposition. The Scottish-born lawyer has already stung the opposition with the charge that they fear the loss of power and profit, not liberty, if the new Constitution is approved.

"Cincinnatus" did not hesitate to turn those same charges against the pro-Constitutionalists.

"Perhaps these very violent gentlemen for the new establishment," he replied in a newspaper essay, "may be actuated by the same undue motives. Perhaps some of its framers, might have had its honours and emoluments in view. When you have let loose suspicion, Mr. Wilson, there is no knowing where it will end. Perhaps some may be audacious enough to suspect even—YOU."[23]

With such denunciations, the ratification Convention in Quaker Pennsylvania promises to be anything but peaceful and friendly.

CHAPTER 8

November 9–15, 1787

Diminutive Delaware placed itself in the position this week of becoming the first of the necessary nine States to ratify the new Constitution, perhaps denying the honor to its giant sister State and neighbor, Pennsylvania, which is in a rush also to ratify first.

On November 10, the Delaware Assembly, without debate or dissent, adopted a resolution calling for a State ratifying Convention to meet on December 3. Thomas Collins, Delaware President, on presenting the document to the lawmakers, recommended it "as a subject of the most important consideration, involving in its adoption not only our prosperity and felicity, but perhaps our national existence."[1]

Delaware's two political factions are reported to favor ratification, principally because the small State views the new Constitution as an instrument for improving its commercial future. Long-standing economic and cultural connections, fostered by the Delaware River, have prepared the tiny State for union with Pennsylvania and New Jersey.[2]

Because of Pennsylvania's fierce factionalism, Delaware is likely to have the honor as the first State formally to ratify the Constitution, shaped in some measure at the recent Federal Convention in Philadelphia by Delaware's most famous statesman, John Dickinson.

The 55-year-old former President of both Pennsylvania and Delaware was one of the few delegates at the recent constitutional conclave who personally participated in every phase of the American Revolution, beginning with the Stamp Act in 1765. Mr. Dickinson has been called the "Penman of the Revolution" because of his writings that paved the way for the Declaration of Independence. The highly respected Delaware statesman wrote the first draft of the current Articles of Confederation. As a delegate to the recent Federal Convention, Mr. Dickinson influenced the creation of the power-sharing formula between the proposed national government and the existing thirteen States contained in the Constitution.

Therefore, Mr. Dickinson is reported alarmed at the growing volume of criticism published against the new Constitution in the newspapers. He is said to be preparing to take up his pen again for a series of newspaper essays defending the document, to abate anxieties that the States will be destroyed if the Constitution is ratified.[3]

Just this week one of the most persistent critics of the Constitution, Richard Henry Lee of Virginia, was in Mr. Dickinson's State arguing for a delay in ratification. When in Wilmington, according to one source, the Continental Congressman passed out published essays hostile to the document, maintaining that powerful opposition was forming against the document.[4]

One such essay is signed "Cincinnatus," believed to have been authored by Congressman Lee's younger brother, Arthur, who served in Europe as a diplomat during the recent War of Independence. Attacking the idea of a standing army in time of peace, "Cincinnatus" argues in the November 15 issue of the *New York Journal* that ancient Rome and Greece lost their liberties only after they had established a peacetime standing army and embarked on the road to conquest, for a standing army and tyranny were concomitant.

"Let then the people rightly understand," the essayist sarcastically states, "that one blessing of the constitution will be, the taxing them to support fleets and armies to conquer other nations, against whom the ambition of their new rulers may declare war."[5]

Readers of the New York *Independent Journal* were treated this week to a pair of "Publius" essays that also used history, but to support the Constitution, emphasizing the dangers of foreign aggression and underscoring the causes of war between confederated states.

In the November 10 essay, believed to have been written by Foreign Secretary John Jay, "Publius" argues that not until union was achieved in Great Britain, particularly between England and Scotland, was there permanent peace.

"We may profit by their experience," the essay continues, "without paying the price which it cost them. Although it seems obvious to common sense that the people of such an island should be but one nation, yet we find that they were for ages divided into three, and that those three were almost constantly embroiled in quarrels and war with one another."[6]

In what appears to be an appeal to the fears of Southern States, the essay also argues that any future confederacy in America is likely to be dominated by Northern States, furthering the potential for sectional war and opening the way for foreign aggression. This would come about, "Publius" argues, as North and South each seek foreign alliances, as has happened in Europe.

"And here let us not forget," Mr. Jay counsels, "how much more easy it is to receive foreign fleets into our ports, and foreign armies into our country, than it is to persuade or compel them to depart. How many conquests did the Romans and others make in the character of allies, and what innovations did they under the same character introduce into the governments of those whom they pretended to protect."[7]

History was used again in the second "Publius" essay published this week, believed to be authored by Colonel Alexander Hamilton of New York, to underscore the perceived causes for past wars between confederated states and foreign nations. In the November 14 essay, "Publius" points out that in both the ancient and the contemporary past, favorites of rulers have been willing to wage wars for personal power. And, he adds, because of bigotry, petulance, or intrigue, even women have on occasions been the cause of wars.[8]

Continuing his case, he states that the defensive and offensive wars of ancient Sparta, Athens, Rome, and Carthage, all republics, arose from commercial conflicts, as did the wars in Europe involving England, Holland, France, and Spain. In the face of such evidence and experience, Colonel Hamilton asks, can the current Confederation of American States expect "peace and cordiality," given the human imperfections, weaknesses, and evils inherent in a society of every shape.

"To look for a continuation of harmony," the essay states, "between a number of independent, unconnected sovereignties in the same neighborhood, would be to disregard the uniform course of human events, and to set at defiance the accumulated experience of ages."[9]

To bolster his argument, Colonel Hamilton cites the current chaotic credit of the country, the allegedly lax and ill administration of the current Confederated government, and the recent violent disturbances in Pennsylvania, Massachusetts, and the "State of Franklin." The last, beset by internal discord and external Indian attacks, was formed out of western lands of North Carolina in December 1784, even though North Carolina has rescinded its initial agreement and the "State" has not been recognized by the Confederation.[10]

Just two weeks ago, the Continental Congress in New York sent to the Governors of North Carolina, South Carolina, and Georgia instructions to begin peace talks with the Cherokee and Creek Indians to prevent the spread of a generalized war between white settlers and Indian tribes in the tri-State region.[11]

In late September, fresh fighting broke out between settlers and the Creeks in southern Georgia. Congressman James Madison of Virginia alleges that Imperial Spain supplied the "motives as well as their means" to the Creeks.[12] One observer charges that Imperial Spain, to defend its Florida and Louisiana possessions, has secretly been promoting the secession of the frontier territories of Kentucky and Tennessee through bribery, by shutting the Mississippi River to American commerce, and by exploiting sectional antagonism between East and West.[13]

Georgia, as a consequence, is expected to ratify the new Constitution, hoping to guarantee its protection from future Indian attacks and the alleged intrigues of Imperial Spain.

However, the *Gazette of the State of Georgia,* published in Savannah, has printed criticism of the Constitution. An "Essay by a Georgian" appeared in the November 15 issue, and although the writer likes "the plan," he is troubled by its proposed powers of taxation, powers for providing a standing army in time of peace, the regulation of elections by a national Congress, and failure of the document to provide for the right to trial by jury in civil and criminal cases and failure to provide for freedom of the press.

"I beg you to call to mind," the essayist continues, "our glorious declaration of independence, read it, and compare it with the federal constitution; what a degree of apostasy will you not then discover: Therefore, guard against all encroachments upon your liberties so dearly purchased with the costly expence of blood and treasure."[14]

In North Carolina and South Carolina, the reception of the Constitution is reported to be favorable, but with the same reservations that have been voiced in private and published in public from New Hampshire to Georgia: the need for a Federal bill of rights. Federalist leaders, such as James Wilson of Pennsylvania, maintain that such a provision is not needed since a majority of the States already have these safeguards in their State constitutions or laws.

But South Carolina physician and historian David Ramsay pleaded with a close associate of Mr. Wilson's to include in Pennsylvania's ratification document a bill of rights, to set a pattern for other States. The 38-year-old member of the South Carolina House in a November 10 letter to Philadelphia physician Benjamin Rush, a copy having been obtained by this correspondent, argues that such a provision would undercut critics of the Constitution in his State and other States.

"I assent to Mr. Wilsons reasoning," Dr. Ramsay writes, "that all is retained which is not ceded; but think that an explicit declaration on this subject might do good at least so far as to obviate objections. . . . I would not make these alterations conditions of acceptance; I would rather trust to the mode of alteration proposed in it [the amending process] than hazard or even delay the acceptance of the proposed plan."[15]

The absence of a bill of rights has become the most persuasive argument of the Anti-Federalists in the nearly two months since the Constitution was signed in Philadelphia. Dr. Ramsay appears to be the first of the Federalist supporters, however, to recognize the political danger posed by the issue and the need to deny its continued effective use by critics of the document.

The de facto leader of the Federalists, General George Washington, appears to share with Mr. Wilson the belief that the Anti-Federalists are using the issue of a bill of rights solely to defeat the document's ratification. One observer reports that General Washington believes some opponents hold "sinister views," meaning dishonest debtors who fear the new Constitution will force them to honor contracts, local politicians who will lose power under the proposed national government, and demagogues who wish only to fish in turbulent political waters.[16]

General Washington revealed his own views toward the opposition in a letter to his nephew, Bushrod Washington, a copy having been obtained by this correspondent. In the November 10 missive written from Mount Vernon, the 55-year-old former President of the Philadelphia Convention indicates he is irritated that the foes of the document appear more active in the newspapers than do its friends.

"They build their objections," General Washington charges, barely suppressing his anger, "upon principles that do not exist, which the Constitution does not support them in, and the existence of which has been, by an appeal to the Constitution itself flatly denied; and then, as if they were unanswerable, draw all the dreadful consequences that are necessary to alarm the apprehensions of the ignorant or unthinking."[17]

General Washington advises his nephew as an elected member of the Virginia House of Delegates how to conduct himself. It cannot be confirmed, but it is likely that the letter is intended to be read by a wider audience and is the General's way of indirectly making his own views known, using his prestige to counteract criticism of the Constitution.

One observer reports, for example, that his letters are meant to have influence in directing the Federalist forces and expects they will be quoted and published in order to exert powerful influence on public opinion.[18] Last week, newspapers in New Jersey, Pennsylvania, and Massachusetts published brief items describing General Washington's part in the Constitutional Convention as a way to use his name and prestige to bolster support for ratification.[19]

The *Boston Gazette* provides an additional justification for ratification, arguing in a November 12 essay that Providence has given America the opportunity to become a haven for the oppressed people of the world.

"It was reserved for us," the *Boston Gazette* notes, "in the annals of fate, to open an ASYLUM for the oppressed in every quarter of the Globe, but it remains to complete the noble work, by establishing a government which shall *secure* the blessings of liberty to ourselves, our posterity, and the emigrant, from tyranny who may fly to these hospitable shores.–Heaven, to all its other favours, now presents the golden opportunity. . . ."[20]

The ratification struggle has also given the 95 newspapers in the cities of the thirteen States an opportunity and importance they have not heretofore had. This prestige was put to rhyme this week by the *Albany Gazette*, with publication of "The News-Mongers' Song for the Winter of 1788":

Come on brother scribblers, 'tis idle to lag.
The CONVENTION has let the cat out of the bag,
Write something at random, you need not be nice,
Public spirit, Montesquieu, and *great Dr. Price,*
>> *Down, down, down derry down.*

Talk of *Holland & Greece,* and of *purses & swords,*
Democratical mobs and congressional Lords:
Tell what is surrendered and what is enjoy'd,
All things weigh alike, boys, we know, in a void.
>> *Down, down, &tc.*

Much joy, brother printers! the day is our own,
A time like the present sure never was known:
Predictions are making—predictions fulfil,
All nature seems proud to bring grist to our mill.
>> *Down, down, &tc.*[21]

CHAPTER 9

November 16–22, 1787

Quaker-settled Pennsylvania this week became the first State to convene a ratifying Convention, only to have its first formal session beset by bickering over whether its daily proceedings should open with prayer.

On November 21, sixty-nine elected delegates assembled at the Philadelphia State House, attended by what one observer reports is a large impatient majority favoring ratification and unwilling to tolerate delay from a militant minority.[1]

The proposal that each session of the Convention open with prayer was offered by Dr. Benjamin Rush, a prominent Philadelphia physician and Signer of the Declaration of Independence. The 42-year-old former military surgeon pointed out that from the first Continental Congress to the current one, elected lawmakers always asked for divine blessing before beginning deliberations.

Several delegates objected, arguing that a nondenominational clergyman could not be found to cover the diverse religious affiliations of the delegates. Besides, it was also argued, the Convention that framed the government of Pennsylvania and its General Assembly never began its business sessions with prayer.

"That the convention who framed the government of Pennsylvania," replied Dr. Rush, "did not preface their business with prayer, is probably the reason that the state has ever since been distracted by their proceedings."[2]

Although the prayer proposal was postponed, disagreement at the onset is a forecast of opposition efforts to contest every issue. The Anti-Federalist delegates, who number around twenty, are reported by one observer to concede they cannot defeat ratification. Their strategy is to argue for amendments in the form of a bill of rights and to call for a second Federal convention.[3]

In the last two weeks, Pennsylvania newspapers have aimed their argumentative arrows at the delegates to the State's ratifying Convention.

This week, for example, Federalist leader James Wilson, writing as "A Plain Citizen" in the November 22 issue of the Philadelphia *Independent Gazetteer*, appealed to the Convention to reject the ideas of a second Federal convention and of amendments.

If one State, argued the former Pennsylvania delegate to the Federal Convention who helped draft the new Constitution, can offer amendments, all States can. As a consequence, "the petty interests of a single state" will make of the Federal plan "a parcel of narrow, partial and illiberal proposals, jumbled together in one confused chaos, which would require no less than the omnipotent *fiat* of Jehovah to reduce them to order or consistency with each other."[4]

A bill of rights, or amendments, has become the principal battle flag carried by Anti-Federalists from New Hampshire to Georgia. Just this week, the architect of the proposal, Colonel George Mason of Virginia, had his objections to the new Constitution published in the *Massachusetts Centinel*.

"There is no Declaration of Rights," insists Colonel Mason, "and the laws of the general government being paramount to the laws and constitution of the several States, the Declarations of Rights in the separate States are no security."[5]

Colonel Mason's published views are likely to reinforce those of Elbridge Gerry of Massachusetts, who caused a storm in the State in recent weeks not only by refusing to sign the new Constitution in Philadelphia, but also by publishing his reasons in State and city newspapers. Both Colonel Mason and Mr. Gerry have been targets of attacks by pro-Constitution newspapers for their refusal to sign the document.

Mr. Gerry wrote in a letter, a copy having been obtained by this correspondent, that if the document is adopted he will support it. But, he adds, "as it now stands I think it neither consistent with the principles of the Revolution, or of the Constitutions of the several States. . . ."[6]

Mr. Gerry suffered a serious political setback this week when he failed to secure election as a delegate to the Massachusetts State ratifying Convention. The State's three other delegates to the Federal Convention, however, in the November 19 balloting, were elected to the ratifying Convention, as well as the State's popular Governor, John Hancock. The delegate elections divided the State; the country people split over ratification, and the city residents solidly support it.[7]

The Federalist majority in Massachusetts intends to trade on Governor Hancock's popularity. And, according to one observer, is prepared to hold out to him, in return for his support, the prospect of election as first President of any new national government, if General Washington declines to run. The 50-year-old politically ambitious Governor and Signer of the Declaration of Independence has remained noncommittal about the Constitution, but Federalist leaders in the State are reported to believe that he can be brought around to support ratification by a combination of flattery and bargaining.[8]

Reports are that Federalist leaders in Massachusetts have settled on a political strategy radically different from that of the majority in Pennsylvania. Impressed and alarmed about how the tactics of hurry and force in that State are having a negative impact, political craft is to replace the arrogance and verbal abuse of the Anti-Federalists. The Federalists in Massachusetts apparently have taken to heart biblical advice to be as "wise as serpents" but to appear as "harmless as doves," intending to deal skillfully with the opposition in the State with patience, conciliation, and moderation.[9]

Meanwhile, in New York, critics of the Constitution exhibited in their published essays traits of the screaming hawk rather than of the peaceful dove. In the November 21 issue of the *New York Journal*, for example, an essay titled "A Countryman from Dutchess County" stopped short of calling Dr. Benjamin Franklin a hypocrite.

"The Doctor is at the Head of a humane Institution for promoting the Emancipation of Slaves, or abolishing Slavery; yet lends his Assistance to frame a Constitution which evidently has a Tendency not only to enslave all those whom it ought to protect; but avowedly encourages the enslaving of those over whom it can have no Manner of Right, to exercise the last shadow of Authority."[10]

According to one source, the author of the essay is believed to be De Witt Clinton, the 18-year-old nephew of the New York Governor,

George Clinton, a bitter critic of both the Constitution and Colonel Alexander Hamilton, one of its major defenders. It is widely rumored in New York that the 32-year-old Colonel Hamilton is the author of a series of newspaper articles signed "Publius," which defend the Constitution.

The "Publius" series is intended to influence the selection of delegates to New York State's ratifying Convention, but the lengthy essays have thus far failed in their objective. The articles, according to one observer, have not responded to the concerns of the opposition in the mistaken belief that the State's Anti-Federalists can be persuaded that a strong Federal union is needed; whereas their concerns are that such a union endangers personal liberty.[11]

No fewer than four separate "Publius" essays were published this week, the first in the New York *Independent Journal* on November 17. Colonel Hamilton in this essay warns that without a new Union, internal war could erupt among the current Confederated States over Western land claims and commercial rivalries. Sharp differences over how to pay the existing swollen debt and what share should be assumed by each State are also likely to be additional sources of conflict without a new strong national government, according to Colonel Hamilton.

"For it is an observation, as true as it is trite," the essay adds, "that there is nothing men differ so readily about as the payment of money."[12]

The following day, in the November 18 issue of the *New York Packet*, "Publius" may have given additional ammunition to the critics of the Constitution and their fear of a standing peacetime army. Colonel Hamilton argued that the "ardent love of liberty" may have to give way to the need of the nation as a whole for safety from external danger and the preservation of the nation's independence from Europe.

Besides, the former military aide to General Washington adds, an increase in wealth, and the arts of industry and finance have "produced an entire revolution in the system of war, and have rendered disciplined armies, distinct from the body of the citizens, the inseparable companions of frequent hostility."[13]

A firm Union, "Publius" notes in the third essay published this week, in the New York *Independent Journal,* will be of crucial importance to the peace and liberty of the States and will become a fortress against domestic faction, insurrection, and revolution.

"It is impossible," the essay notes, "to read the history of the petty republics of Greece and Italy without feeling sensations of horror and disgust at the distractions with which they were continually agitated, and at the rapid succession of revolutions by which they were kept in a state of perpetual vibration between the extremes of tyranny and anarchy."[14]

Foes of the Constitution have drawn from such ancient disorders the false conclusion, according to "Publius," that the same fate awaits America if the document is ratified. Critics have argued that so vast a nation as America can preserve liberty and order only by a confederation of small republics, and not by a consolidated or Continental Republic over the vast geography of America.

"Publius," in reply, argues that advocates of such a view ignore progress in political science, unknown by the ancient republics that perished in the flames of war, anarchy, and tyranny. These "discoveries" include: separation of powers, legislative checks and balances, court systems with judges holding their office during good behavior, and election of representatives by the people.

". . . these are wholly new discoveries," Colonel Hamilton adds, "or have made their principal progress towards perfection in modern times. They are means, and powerful means, by which the excellences of republican government may be retained and its imperfections lessened or avoided."[15]

The fourth "Publius" essay published this week was authored, according to one source, by Congressman James Madison of Virginia. Until now the essays have been written by Colonel Hamilton and John Jay. However, because of illness, the Foreign Secretary of the Confederation has been forced to discontinue his contributions.[16]

Mr. Madison confirmed his secret participation in the "Publius" newspaper project in a letter he wrote to General Washington (a copy of which this correspondent obtained). His November 18 letter reveals that he returned to New York from Philadelphia after canceling plans to return to Virginia, apparently to accept Colonel Hamilton's offer to coauthor the series after Secretary Jay's illness.

In his letter, he enclosed the first seven "Publius" essays and requested that the General arrange for their republication in Virginia through a third party to counter the spirit of criticism against the Constitution after the initial flush of favorable comment in the State.

"I will not conceal *from you*," Congressman Madison wrote to General Washington, "that I am likely to have such a *degree* of connection with the publication here as to afford a restraint of delicacy from interesting myself directly in the republication elsewhere. You will recognize one of the pens concerned in the task."[17]

Although both Colonel Hamilton and Congressman Madison were privately disappointed with the outcome of the Philadelphia Convention, they have thrown themselves into the ratification fight. One observer reports that Mr. Madison did not expect to take part in the current campaign. He changed his mind after witnessing in recent weeks a flood of Anti-Federalist newspaper essays savaging the Constitution he had a crucial role in creating.

According to this same observer, he is likely to bring to the "Publius" enterprise a prodigious, analytical power, and a greater working knowledge of the Constitution than Colonel Hamilton has. He has, for example, many of the memorandums he had prepared prior to the Philadelphia Convention, and has the only complete set of notes of the secret four-month conclave. This gives him an enormous advantage in defending the document.[18]

Mr. Madison's first essay was published this week in the November 22 issue of the New York *Daily Advertiser*. He argues that society is divided into "clashing interests," or factions, and although the causes cannot be removed, the effects can be controlled. An extended republic, with elected representatives, can better accommodate and control the fires of faction than a pure democracy in which the people directly participate. Pure democracies, he argues, have, in the past, been spectacles "of turbulence and contention; have ever been found incompatible with personal security or the rights of property, and have in general been as short in their lives as they have been violent in their deaths.

"Theoretic politicians," the "Publius" essay adds, "who have patronized this species of government, have erroneously supposed that by reducing mankind to a perfect equality in political rights, they would, at the same time, be perfectly equalized and assimilated in their possessions, their opinions, and their passions."[19]

An extended republic as proposed in the Constitution, according to Mr. Madison, provides a check against violent faction, fed principally by an unequal distribution of property which a majority in a pure democracy might demand by force from a minority. The first object of government is the protection of property rights as well as of "unequal faculties of acquiring property."

"A rage for paper money," "Publius" concludes, "for an abolition of debts, for an equal division of property, or for any other improper or wicked project, will be less apt to pervade the whole body of the Union than a particular member of it. . . .

"In the extent and proper structure of the Union, therefore, we behold a republican remedy for the diseases most incident to republican government."[20]

CHAPTER 10

November 23–29, 1787

The preambles in the new Constitution and the Declaration of Independence became weapons this week in the Pennsylvania ratifying Convention battle over whether a bill of rights was needed or was unnecessary in the Constitution.[1] The debate was given additional drama by the sharp clash of positions punctuated by foreign accents of the delegates.

Scottish-born lawyer and recent delegate to the Federal Convention, James Wilson, 45, spoke in a thick burr as he peered through his rounded spectacles when answering the arguments of Irish-born Anti-Federalist leader John Smilie, also 45. The War of Independence veteran and professional politician was one of those dissenters besieged at their boarding house by a Philadelphia mob on November 6.[2] His recent personal experience may have provided additional reasons for demanding a bill of rights.

In rebuttal, Mr. Wilson told the delegates, "Here, Sir, it is expressly announced: 'We, the people of the United States, do ordain, constitute, and establish.' . . . This single sentence in the preamble is tantamount to a volume, and contains the essence of all the bill of rights that have been or can be devised; for it establishes at once, that in the great article of government, the people have a right to do what they please."[3]

It is mistaken, Mr. Wilson went on, to assert that because Great Britain has a declaration of rights, rooted in the Magna Carta, that America should emulate England. Those rights are granted by a king, he added, whereas "here, Sir, the fee simple of freedom and government is declared to be in the people, and it is an inheritance with which they will not part."[4]

In reply, Mr. Smilie directed the attention of delegates to the language of the State constitutions and the preamble to the Declaration of Independence. In each, it specifically states, he said, that men by nature are endowed "with certain natural, inherent and inalienable rights," whereas in the new Constitution such wording is wanting. Although authority "naturally rests in the people," Mr. Smilie continued, specific steps are necessary for the people to exercise their right to alter and abolish government.

"The truth is," Mr. Smilie added in his lilting Irish brogue, "that unless some criterion is established by which it could be easily and constitutionally ascertained how far our governors may proceed, and by which it might appear when they transgress their jurisdiction, this idea of altering and abolishing government is a mere sound without substance. Let us recur to the memorable declaration of the 4th of July, 1776."[5]

Since the Pennsylvania Convention first met, the Federalist majority, led by Mr. Wilson, has beaten back all efforts of the Anti-Federalists, led by Mr. Smilie, to delay adoption with lengthy debate. Demands for a bill of rights by the minority would create delay, requiring amendments the majority maintains were not authorized by the Federal Convention. The document must be taken as a single proposition without alterations, Mr. Wilson warned the delegates.

When an effort was made by the Anti-Federalists to enter into the ratifying Convention journals reasons of delegates for ratifying or rejecting the Constitution, the proposal was overwhelmingly rejected.[6]

The rush to ratify may be tied to the desire of Pennsylvania's Federalists to be first among the States to approve the Constitution. Delay, because of a drawn-out bill of rights debate, might give that honor to Delaware, which this week elected delegates to its own ratifying Convention, to convene on December 6.

Delaware's two political parties are reported to support ratification, increasing prospects that the smallest State will be the first. Delegate elections on November 26 were reported to have turned on local issues, not on the new Constitution.

However, one observer reports that efforts at intimidation of the

Whigs (or the Anti-Federalists) with armed militia, and the Tory party (the pro-Constitutionalists) moving polling stations, and instilling a fear of bloodshed, cut balloting from the normal 1,100 that usually vote (from a total population of 59,000) to less than 700. Nearly 400 have reportedly signed a petition to the State Legislature demanding a new election for delegates.[7]

In contrast, New Jersey's election of delegates to its State ratifying Convention this week was without a ripple. Like Delaware, the State is expected to ratify the Constitution because it believes it will derive commercial advantages by a Federal regulation of trade, an advantage it does not now have under the Articles of Confederation. Perhaps for this reason, few in New Jersey have openly expressed opposition to ratification.[8]

In Boston, a pair of essays published this week in the *Massachusetts Gazette*, signed "Agrippa," attacked the powers in the new Constitution to regulate trade and to tax as a potential tyranny. The essays, believed to have been authored by former Harvard University Librarian James Winthrop, insist the chief dangers of the Constitution are destruction of the separate States and a stifling of commerce by excessive regulation.

"It is a fact justified by the experience of all mankind," the essayist asserts, "from the earliest antiquity down to the present time, that freedom is necessary to industry. We accordingly find that in absolute governments, the people, be the climate what it may, are [in] general lazy, cowardly, turbulent, and vicious to an extreme. On the other hand, in free countries are found in general, activity, industry, arts, courage, generosity, and all the manly virtues."[9]

Ancient Greece and Rome, according to "Agrippa," perished because "war was the employment" for freemen, whereas domestic work was consigned to slaves. By contrast, the essayist goes on, the great commercial republic of Carthage retained its freedom longer than Rome because the spirit of free commerce became the bond of union among its citizens.

"Our great object therefore," Mr. Winthrop ("Agrippa") concluded, "ought to be to encourage this spirit. If we examine the present state of the world we shall find that most of the business is done in the freest states, and that industry decreases in proportion to the rigour of government."[10]

The contrary was also advocated this week, in two published "Publius" essays. The rigorous use of power by the proposed new national government in foreign trade and the use of indirect taxation are necessary, "Publius" suggests.

In the November 24 edition of the New York *Independent Journal*, "Publius" warns that European maritime states already view America as a potential rival in trade. The power of a new national government to exclude nations like Great Britain from American ports and the creation of a Federal navy should be future policies of a United States of America, according to the essay, believed to have been written by Colonel Alexander Hamilton of New York.[11]

Such power would also safeguard America's neutrality among European rivalries. With a Union of the States, thriving commerce, and a Federal navy, America in the future could become "the arbiter of Europe in America"[12] as national interests dictate. A weak commerce and disunion, the essay warns, would make the nation vulnerable to the predatory powers of Europe that respect neutrality only when defended by adequate power.

"Let Americans," Colonel Hamilton asserts, "disdain to be the instruments of European greatness! Let the thirteen States, bound together in a strict and indissoluble Union, concur in erecting one great American system, superior to the control of all transatlantic force or influence, and able to dictate the terms of connection between the old and the new world!"[13]

In a followup essay, in the November 27 issue of the New York *Independent Journal*, "Publius" also argues that government should promote private commerce as the best basis for creating national wealth. Taxation of that wealth, to support the government, should be in proportion to the quantity of money in use and the speed by which it circulates.

However, the essay warns that the experience in Europe, particularly in France, and in the separate American States, dictates that such taxes be indirect.

"It is evident from the state of the country," the essayist adds, "from the habits of the people, from the experience we have had on the point itself, that it is impractical to raise any very considerable sums by direct taxation. Tax laws have in vain been multiplied; new methods to enforce the collection have in vain been tried; the public expectation has been uniformly disappointed, and the treasuries of the States have remained empty."[14]

One national government would be more able to impose duties than is practicable to the individual States, "Publius" says. He proposes that the larger portion of revenue should come from indirect taxes on consumption and duties on imports. If the revenue is not derived from commerce it will fall with an oppressive hand on private property, he predicts. Besides, the taxing of imported "spirits" would be favorable "to the morals, and to the health of the society" and help curtail consumption of this "national extravagance."[15]

How the Spanish and French envoys based in New York will react to the proposal of "Publius" for taxing imported spirits is not known. However, this week, in a secret diplomatic dispatch, the French envoy, Louis Guillaume Otto, forwarded to Paris an assessment of the ratification debate.

"... the two parties abuse each other in the public papers," the envoy's dispatch observed, a copy having been obtained by this correspondent, "with a rancor which sometimes does not even spare insults and personal invectives.... This spirit of argument is even pushed to intolerance in regard to foreigners and they absolutely want us to take a side for or against the new Constitution. Some politicians trying to be shrewder than others have even suggested that this Constitution was bad since it was approved by foreign Ministers."[16]

In this regard, rumors have been circulating in recent weeks that the French envoy had a hand in the secret Philadelphia Convention. One source says the rumor orginated with dissident Maryland delegate John Francis Mercer.[17] The 28-year-old lawyer left the Federal Convention early, and rushed home to organize opposition to ratification.

★

The Maryland House of Representatives voted this week to have the delegates to the Federal Convention personally give testimony about the secret conclave. One source reports the resolution was the work of Anti-Federalists in Maryland seeking an official forum to denounce the Constitution.[18]

One delegate, Daniel Carroll, 57, in a letter to Dr. Benjamin Franklin, a copy having been obtained by this correspondent, revealed that in the November 29 Maryland House session, he used excerpts from the 81-year-old philosopher's speeches at the Philadelphia Convention. This is a clear violation of the vow of secrecy taken by every delegate.

The wealthy Maryland planter indicated that he was compelled to use the material in violation of the secrecy rule to counter the penetrating Anti-Federalist arguments of a fellow delegate, State Attorney General Luther Martin.[19] Mr. Martin, like Mr. Mercer, left the Philadelphia Convention early and has been active in efforts to block ratification.

In his November 29 appearance before the Maryland House, Mr. Martin, 43, provided the first detailed "insider's" view of the four-month secret Convention that drafted the Constitution. He revealed, for example, that the closed-door debate was far more acrimonious than has been admitted or openly acknowledged up to now.

Mixed with these revelations—a violation of Mr. Martin's own oath of secrecy—was a slashing attack on the work of the Convention in general, and on General Washington and Dr. Franklin in particular. The two were accused of neglecting the rights of the States and the liberties of the people.

"The ratification of this Constitution," Mr. Martin insisted, "is so repugnant . . . to the Terms on which we are all bound to amend and alter [the Articles of Confederation], that it became a matter of surprise to many that the proposition could meet with any countance or support."[20]

CHAPTER 11

November 30–December 6, 1787

The power of the "People" and the power of the "States" became rhetorical ramparts of the Pennsylvania ratifying Convention this week, one side using the terms as verbal volleys to defend, the other side to discredit, the new Constitution.

William Findley, 46, an opposition delegate born in Londonderry, Ireland, formulated the terms of the debate when he charged that the document is an instrument for "consolidation," not "confederation" of the separate States.

". . . the proposed Constitution," the writer-orator observed in his lilting Ulster accent, "establish[es] a general government and destroy[s] the individual governments, from the following evidence taken from the system itself. In the Preamble, it is said, '*We the People*,' and not '*We the States*,' which therefore is a compact between individuals entering into society, and not between separate states enjoying independent power and delegating a portion of that power for their common benefit."[1]

In his lengthy rebuttal, James Wilson insisted that the States were made for the people as well as by them and the people have the undeniable power to form either a general or a State government in whatever form or manner they choose. The preamble to the Declaration of Independence gives the people this power, the former delegate to the Philadelphia Convention added, whereas the new Constitution preserves the States.

". . . from the very nature of things," the Pennsylvania lawyer added, "and from the organization of the system itself, the state governments must exist, or the general government must fall amidst their ruins; indeed so far as to the forms, it is admitted they may remain; but the gentlemen seem to think their power will be gone."[2]

It is the very "system" and "powers" proposed, replied the 49-year-old delegate Robert Whitehill, that do little to "illuminate the darkness of our doubts."[3] This document, the veteran Pennsylvania lawmaker insisted, emanated in the darkness of the Philadelphia Convention and must terminate in the destruction of the States. A despotism of a deliberate design is what awaits America, he charged.

The system contains the seeds of its own self-preservation to perpetuate itself, Mr. Whitehill warned, "seeds which will vegetate and strengthen in proportion to the decay of state authority, and which will ultimately spring up and overshadow the thirteen commonwealths of America with a deadly shade. . . .

"For, Sir," he added, "the first article comprises the grants of powers [to Congress to make all laws] so superlative in their nature, and so unlimited in their extent, that without the aid of any other branch of the system, a foundation rests upon this article alone, for the extension of the federal jurisdiction to the most extravagant degree of arbitrary sway."[4]

The high tenor and tone of the Convention debate quickly waned when Dr. Benjamin Rush, 42, suggested that supporting separate thirteen States by the opposition amounted to the sin of idolatry.

". . . this passion for separate sovereignty," observed the Philadelphia physician and Signer of the Declaration of Independence, "had destroyed the Grecian Union. This plurality of sovereignty is in politics what plurality of gods is in religion—it is the idolatry, the heathenism of government."[5]

Opposition leader William Findley insisted that Dr. Rush welcomed, and even "rejoiced" in, the eventual consolidation and annihilation of the States. This would come about, he predicted, in part by the taxing power granted to the new Congress.

"The powers given to the Federal body for imposing internal taxation," the Irish-born Pennsylvania lawmaker observed, "will necessarily destroy the state sovereignties, for there cannot exist two independent sovereign taxing powers in the same community, and the strongest will of course annihilate the weaker."[6]

Fear that the States will be swallowed up by the national government is not confined to a minority of dissenters in Pennsylvania.

Samuel Adams of Massachusetts expressed the same concerns to Richard Henry Lee of Virginia in a December 3 letter, a copy of which this correspondent obtained.

"I confess," wrote the famous New England leader of the American Revolution, "as I enter the Building I stumble at the Threshold. I meet with a National Government, instead of a fœderal Union of Sovereign States."[7]

In the last six weeks, Continental Congressman Lee has sought to persuade Samuel Adams to support his proposals for amendments, or a bill of rights. Apparently the 55-year-old Virginian has succeeded in convincing the influential 65-year-old Massachusetts leader of the dangers of a document without amendments.

Writing as "Candidus" in the December 6 issue of the *Independent Chronicle* of Boston, Mr. Adams called on State ratifying Conventions to retain the "original plan" of the Federal Convention while also proposing amendments or a bill of rights. If this cannot be accomplished, he added, a second Continental Convention of the States should be called to achieve that end.

"Candidus" disputed arguments of the advocates of the Constitution that the problems of the country trace to a lack of energy in government. The new Constitution will not restore peace and happiness to the country, the Puritan-bred Revolutionary leader warned, because the principal "evils we now experience" have arisen from a desire for "luxurious living of all ranks and degrees. . . .

"No government under heaven," the essayist stressed, "could have preserved a people from ruin, or kept their commerce from declining, when they were exhausting their valuable resources in paying for superfluities, and running themselves in debt to *foreigners,* and to *each other* for articles of folly and dissipation:—While this is the case, we may contend about forms of government, but no establishment will enrich a people, who wantonly spend beyond their income."[8]

With Samuel Adams of Massachusetts making common cause with Virginian dissenters Richard Henry Lee, Colonel George Mason, and Patrick Henry, it clearly indicates that the Anti-Federalist forces in these two large States have gained political ground since the Constitution was signed and published eleven weeks ago.

Rufus King of Massachusetts, 32, a lawyer and delegate to the Philadelphia Convention, is reported by one observer to have written to General George Washington that the absence of a bill of rights has created "an apprehension that the liberties of the people are in danger and a distrust of men of property or education have a more powerful effect on the minds of our opponents than any specific objections against the Constitution."[9]

In turn, General Washington has conceded that Virginia's decision to hold its ratifying Convention seven months from now, on the first Monday in June 1788, is a double-edged sword.

". . . if those States whose conventions are to meet sooner," he acknowledges in a December 3 letter, a copy having been obtained by this correspondent, "should adopt the plan I think there is no doubt that they [Virginia's delegates] will be followed by this, and if some of them should reject it, it is very probable that the opposers of it here will exert themselves to add this State to the number."[10]

The 55-year-old retired military hero of the American Revolution concedes that opposition in Virginia is gaining strength. He attributes this to the "opposers" appealing to "the passions of the people," with the purpose of rousing "their fears." It is "idly vain," he maintained in another letter written this week, for the foes of the document to work for amendments at this time. General Washington is convinced, moreover, that behind this effort is a desire for "disunion," or "separate Confederacies."[11]

In an effort to influence public opinion, the General enclosed in his letter to his friend, David Stuart, copies of the "Publius" essays believed to have been authored by Alexander Hamilton of New York and James Madison of Virginia.

"If there is a Printer in Richmond," the General suggests, "who is really well disposed to support the New Constitution he would do well to give them a place in his Paper. . . . Altho' I am acquainted with some of the writers who are concerned in this work, I am not at liberty to disclose their names, nor would I have it known that they are sent by *me* to *you* for promulgation."[12]

Four more "Publius" essays were published in New York this week for a total thus far of seventeen. A November 30 essay, appearing in the *New York Packet,* said to have been authored by James Madison, seeks to refute the assertion of the Anti-Federalists that so vast a territory as America cannot be governed by a national government. This is an error, "Publius" maintains, by confusing a democracy with a republic.

". . . in a democracy," he explains, "the people meet and exercise the government in person; in a republic, they assemble and administer it by their representatives and agents. A democracy, consequently, will be confined to a small spot. A republic may be extended over a large region."[13]

If Europe can claim credit for the discovery of representative government, "Publius" adds, America can claim credit for discovering the concept of an extended representative republic that safeguards private rights and public happiness. Had the leaders of the American Revolution not sought new political forms, the nation might now be the melancholy victim of misguided counsels of the past that have "crushed the liberties of the rest of mankind.

"Happily for America," the essayist adds, referring to the leaders of the Revolution, "happily, we trust for the whole human race, they pursued a new and more noble course. They accomplished a revolution which has no parallel in the annals of human society. They reared the fabrics of governments which have no model on the face of the globe. They formed the design of a great Confederacy, which it is incumbent on their successors to improve and perpetuate."[14]

The defects of the current Articles of Confederation were described in the December 1 issue of the *New York Packet* by "Publius," believed to be Colonel Hamilton. At present, the essay states, the government cannot repel foreign aggression because it has neither troops nor treasury and therefore cannot compel Imperial Spain to reopen the Mississippi River to American commerce.

". . . the evils we experience," the essay adds, "do not proceed from minute or partial imperfections, but from fundamental errors in the structure of the building, which cannot be amended otherwise than by an alteration in the first principles and main pillars of the fabric."[15]

A followup essay in the *New York Packet* of December 4, alleged also to have been written by Colonel Hamilton, predicts that the only alternative to the new Constitution may be a major civil war between the States, with foreign powers encouraging any dissensions.

"This may be considered as the violent death of the Confederacy," the essayist asserts. "Its more natural death is what we now seem to be on the point of experiencing, if the federal system be not speedily renovated in a more substantial form."[16]

"Publius," in the New York *Independent Journal* of December 5, also maintains that fears the States will be swallowed up by a national government are unfounded. The people of each State are "apt to feel a stronger bias towards their local governments" than toward the proposed government Union.[17]

"It will always be far more easy," the essay predicts, "for the State governments to encroach upon the national authorities, than for the national government to encroach upon the State authorities."[18]

CHAPTER 12

★

December 7–13, 1787

Delaware wounded the pride of Pennsylvanians this week by securing for itself a special niche in the nation's history. On December 7 it became the first State to ratify, unanimously, the new Constitution.[1]

Pennsylvania was forced to settle for second place. On December 12, by a divided vote of 46 to 23, delegates approved the document after weeks of bitter debate. At times Convention delegates came perilously close to physical fights.[2]

According to one source, when the news of Delaware's unanimous ratification was announced at the State House in Philadelphia, opposition delegate John Smilie acidly observed: ". . . the State of Delaware had indeed reaped the honor of having first surrendered the liberties of the people to the new system of government."[3]

News of the thirty delegates' vote in Dover, Delaware, is expected to spread rapidly south to Georgia and north to New Hampshire. Nevertheless, it will be some weeks before the entire country hears the news or reads it in the newspapers.[4] The news reached Philadelphia first, but the nearby Baltimore *Maryland Journal*, the second out-of-State newspaper to report on Delaware's vote, observed that "Pennsylvania is debating the ground by inches. . . ."[5]

The Delaware proclamation, drained of any prideful language, said in part that the Deputies of the People of the Delaware State, "in behalf of ourselves and our Constituents, fully, freely, and entirely approve of, assent to, ratify and confirm the said Constitution."[6]

The Delaware President, Thomas Collins, sent to the Secretary of the Continental Congress in New York the formal ratification documents with a proclamation granting ten square miles "for the

Seat of the Government of The United States, wherever they may make Choice of the same within this State."[7]

During the Federal Convention last summer, considerable debate was devoted to a permanent national capital. The ten-square-mile Federal territory concept was created to avoid the possibility of jurisdictional disputes between the States and the new national government.[8]

In sharp contrast to the sulfuric ratification debates in the Pennsylvania State House during the last several weeks, the Dover, Delaware, Convention was a placid session, held four days with only one ripple of dissent disturbing the calm surface.

On December 3, nine protest petitions signed by 369 voters were presented to the Convention from one of the three counties in the State demanding a new election of delegates. The protests charged that armed, unlawful force had been used to rig the election of delegates in the County of Sussex. The Convention refused to order a new election and seated the ten delegates who were alleged to have been elected by the threat of musket balls rather than by paper ballots.[9]

John Dickinson, Delaware's most prominent political leader and delegate to last summer's Federal Convention, took no part in his State's ratifying Convention. He is, however, preparing to publish a series of essays urging ratification of the Constitution by other States.

Past experience, Mr. Dickinson observed, should provide a warning to critics of the Constitution; by refusing to relinquish their own interests, ". . .their measures may. . .tend to draw down the same distractions upon us, that desolated Greece."[10]

Dr. Benjamin Rush, a close friend of Mr. Dickinson and a delegate to the Pennsylvania ratifying Convention, made a similar appeal this week to dissident delegates. He pleaded with them to sign Pennsylvania's instrument of ratification in a righteous decision of unanimous approval.

A millennium of "virtue and happiness" will be the consequence of the document's acceptance, the prominent Philadelphia physician predicted. The hand of God was employed in its creation, he said, as certain as the hand of Providence had parted "the Red Sea to give a passage to the children of Israel or had [fulminated] the Ten Commandments from Mount Sinai!"[11]

The same voice that thundered on Mount Sinai "thou shalt not steal," he asserted, now proclaims in the ears of every dissenting delegate, "thou shalt not reject the new federal government. . . ."

"Think, sir, of its effects upon our State of Pennsylvania," Dr. Rush added in his ardent address. "Let this Constitution be the umpire of all our past disputes. Here let us this night bury the hatchet of civil discord and smoke the calumet of peace together!"[12]

One dissident delegate, Robert Whitehill, rebuffed the offered olive branch, saying he regretted that "so imperfect a work should have been ascribed to God."[13] The Cumberland County delegate read petitions from 750 of his constituents, and he was "praying" that the new Constitution not be approved unless amendments, particularly a bill of rights, were adopted.

James Wilson, leader of the Federalist majority, has maintained during the weeks of Convention debate that a bill of rights is unnecessary and beyond the body's "narrow compass" to accept or to reject the new Constitution.

Mr. Wilson and Thomas McKean, 53, a fellow delegate and the Chief Justice of Pennsylvania, are angered at the news that Delaware has been the first State to ratify. They blame opposition tactics for their State's failure to be the first. Every article of the document has been contested by the militant minority, only to be answered in lengthy detail by leaders of the Federalist majority.

". . . it is high time our proceedings should draw towards a conclusion," Mr. Wilson said, controlling his Scottish temper but not his burr. "Perhaps our debates have already continued as long, nay, longer than is sufficient for every good purpose."[14]

Looking directly at the opposition delegates, the lawyer went on to charge that the day-to-day objections have been repeated over and over, with the real intent of influencing other States, infecting them with discontent, and a fever of fear that the new Constitution is the enemy of liberty.

"By adopting this system," he said, concluding a lengthy speech delivered in two parts over a day and a half, "we shall probably lay a foundation for erecting temples of liberty in every part of the earth. . . . It will be subservient to the great designs of Providence with regard to this globe; the multiplication of mankind, their improvement in knowledge, and their advancement in happiness."[15]

A humorous moment in the otherwise grim, grueling Convention came when Chief Justice McKean, a Signer of the Declaration of Independence, delivered a lengthy rebuttal to the objections of the opposition. As he concluded, a thunderclap of applause broke from the otherwise quiet audience in the packed gallery.

"No, Sir, this is not the voice of the people of Pennsylvania," angrily replied opposition delegate John Smilie, "and were this Convention assembled at another place, the sound would be of a different nature, for the sentiments of the citizens are different indeed. . . . I will add, that such conduct, nay were the gallery filled with bayonets, such appearance of violence would not intimidate me, or those who act with me, in the conscientious discharge of a public duty."[16]

Chief Justice McKean coolly replied that "The gentleman, sir, is *angry*—because other folks are *pleased*."[17] He went on to insist, half humorously, that the opposition's fears of the Constitution amounted to: "*if the sky falls, we shall catch larks; if the rivers run dry, we shall catch eels*," which, he added, amounted "to a sound, but then it was a mere sound, like *the working of small beer*."[18]

Just before the final 46-to-23 vote for ratification, a list of fifteen amendments prepared by the opposition were read to the Convention. They were offered on the understanding they would be made part of the official record and presented to the people of Pennsylvania to consider after the Convention voted for ratification and adjourned.

James Wilson, apparently seeing an opportunity to bring the contentious Convention to a favorable, swift conclusion, agreed. He would be happy, he told the Convention, that the amendments "would appear upon the Journals [of the Convention], as an evidence of the motives which had prevailed with those who framed and supported it, and that its merited rejection would permanently announce the sentiments of the majority respecting so odious an attempt."[19]

The following day, opposition delegate Robert Whitehill bitterly complained that the fifteen resolutions had not been inserted in the record and demanded it be done. The motion was opposed by the majority, with Mr. Wilson calling on Mr. Smilie to reduce the motion to writing.

"Indeed, sir," responded the Irish-born delegate indignantly, "I know so well that if the honorable member from the city says the articles shall not, they will not be admitted, that I am not disposed to take the useless trouble of reducing my motion to writing, and therefore I withdraw it."[20]

The fifteen amendments guarantee freedom of religion, of speech, and of the press; jury trials in both state and national courts; and freedom from unwarranted search and seizure. They also propose various structural changes in the Constitution and conclude with a final amendment guaranteeing State sovereignty, and restricting the power of the new national government to specific delegated functions.[21]

Besides refusing to allow the drafted bill of rights to be made part of the Pennsylvania ratifying Convention record, one source has told this correspondent that the Federalist majority bribed the Convention shorthand reporter, Thomas Lloyd, not to publish the entire proceedings as he had originally planned. This source says Mr. Lloyd will publish only the speeches of the Federalist majority.[22]

The minority is expected to publish in friendly newspapers its bill of rights proposals, and its allegations that the Federalists achieved ratification through haste and the use of violence. The minority also intends to include an attack on the Federal Convention's secrecy.[23]

One observer believes that the ruthless tactics of the majority to make Pennsylvania first to ratify amounted to a "majority *coup d'etat*," motivated primarily by the desire to have Philadelphia selected as the permanent seat of the new national government.[24]

There may be a price to be paid by the Pennsylvania Federalists for their hurried victory. They have given ammunition and encouragement to Anti-Federalist forces in other State ratifying Conventions. One observer believes that the minority in Pennsylvania has unwittingly provided a formula for Federalists in other States, who may use the bill of rights issue as a way to win over the wavering votes of those who favor the Constitution but, fearful of its great powers, also want a bill of rights.[25]

In the immediate aftermath of Pennsylvania's ratification vote this week, 81-year-old Dr. Benjaman Franklin, carried in his sedan chair, led a jubilant procession of officials from the State House through the streets of Philadelphia to the Court House, where the ratification proclamation was publicly read.[26]

The bells of Christ Church proclaimed the news to the city as a militia artillery team fired a Federal salute thirteen times on the Market Street docks. At the Sign of the Rainbow tavern, thirteen toasts were offered to the health and prosperity of the new national Ship of State. Later that evening, a boat symbolizing the U.S.S. *Constitution*, mounted on a wagon drawn by five horses, paraded through city streets, offering "fixed expectation of the revival of commerce and navigation under this happy government."[27]

CHAPTER 13

★

December 14–20, 1787

After three days of consideration at the Blazing Star tavern in Trenton, thirty-one sober delegates of the New Jersey ratifying Convention unanimously approved this week the new Constitution.[1]

New Jersey's December 18 decision follows ratification last week by Delaware and Pennsylvania, bringing the total number of States to three, with six still needed for the document to have legal force as the law of the land. The Delaware Valley trio has long had cultural and commercial connections, facilitated by the Delaware River, and those connections have prepared them for closer union.[2]

The formal public reading of New Jersey's proclamation of ratification received a thunderous welcome by cheering crowds in the Trenton courthouse square. A light infantry company's cannon fired no fewer than fifteen separate salutes, thirteen for the United States and one each for Delaware and Pennsylvania.[3]

Later in the taverns, thirteen toasts were offered. One was for the fallen dead in the late War of Independence. Another to the United States: "May the American drums soon beat reveille to the dawn of the new government, and tattoo to anarchy and confusion."[4]

The *Pennsylvania Packet* used New Jersey's ratification to lecture militant dissenters at the recent State ratifying Convention in Philadelphia. The paper argued that New Jersey's adoption of the document challenges Pennsylvania's minority argument that the new national government will destroy freedom.

Nearly every field in New Jersey, the paper noted, "has been dyed with the blood of its militia" in the name of freedom. Nearly every farm in the State was plundered by the British army during the late war.

"No commercial influence, no *terror* of an applauding gallery," the *Pennsylvania Packet* angrily added, "no legal sophistry had any weight in the Convention of that *patriotic* state in producing the ratification. The men who pretend to love liberty more than the citizens of *New Jersey* must show that they have done half as much in its defense before they can be believed."[5]

Despite this biting criticism, the *Pennsylvania Packet* published this week a lengthy dissent by the minority, signed by twenty-one of the twenty-three members at the Pennsylvania Convention who voted against ratification.

Decrying the secrecy of the Constitutional Convention, the Anti-Federalist minority report of December 18 charged the Federalists with using force and fraud in the Pennsylvania ratifying Convention to secure approval.

"As this government will not enjoy the confidence of the people," the report predicts,"but be executed by force, it will be a very expensive and burthensome government. The standing army must be numerous, and as a further support, it will be the policy of this government to multiply officers in every department: judges, collectors, tax-gatherers, excisemen and the whole host of revenue officers will swarm over the land, devouring the hard earnings of the industrious. Like the locusts of old, impoverishing and desolating all before them."[6]

Included in the dissenters' document are the fifteen amendments submitted to the Pennsylvania Convention as a bill of rights. Since the issue was first raised by the Anti-Federalists, it has gained growing popular political appeal. Just this week, the advocates of a bill of rights received unexpected support from overseas.

Thomas Jefferson, U.S. Minister to France, in a December 20 letter to Congressman James Madison, a copy of which this correspondent obtained, says he approves of many features of the new Constitution. But, he does not like the omission of a bill of rights. The author of the Declaration of Independence does not agree with the argument that it is unnecessary.

Minister Jefferson contends that "a bill of rights is what the people are entitled to against every government on earth, general or particular, and what no just government should refuse, or rest on inference."[7]

One knowledgeable observer has concluded that if Mr. Jefferson persists with this position, it may powerfully aid the advocates of a bill of rights in other State ratifying Conventions. He has already written to others making his views known. These letters may be used in the growing campaign for amendments.[8]

Since the Constitutional Convention concluded three months ago, Mr. Madison and other Virginia Federalists in a steady stream of letters have sought to influence Mr. Jefferson. Despite the fact that he took no part in framing the Constitution, his fame and influence as the author of the Declaration are believed to be considerable—even removed from the current ratification battle scene by a two-month Atlantic voyage and an overland coach trip to Paris.

Mr. Jefferson's letter was posted in France the same day that Mr. Madison responded to an earlier letter in which he had expressed the belief that the current Confederated government could be reformed rather than replaced entirely.

"The Treasury Board," writes Mr. Madison in his December 20 letter, in trying to persuade the diplomat that he is mistaken about reform, "seem to be in despair of maintaining the shadow of Government much longer. Without money, the Offices must be shut up, and the handful of troops on the frontier disbanded, which will probably bring on an Indian war, and make an impression to our disadvantage on the British Garrisons within our limits."[9]

The failures of the Confederated government to reform its finances and to provide for defense against foreign dangers are two issues that foes of the Constitution have chosen to ignore. At the same time, friends of the document have hammered away at the failure of the Confederated government to deal with the swollen domestic and foreign debt and the dangers posed by Imperial Spain in Florida and Great Britain in Canada.

Colonel Alexander Hamilton, writing this week in three separate "Publius" essays, deals with the alleged defects of the current Articles of Confederation; the need for a strong national government; and why, despite widespread popular opposition, America needs a peacetime standing national army and navy.

In the December 14 issue of the *New York Packet*, "Publius" maintains that under the Articles of Confederation a system of requisitioning men for a national army, from the States during the War of Independence, proved as expensive as it was injurious to the conduct of the conflict.

"It gave birth," writes the former military aide to General Washington, "to a competition between the States which created a kind of auction for men. In order to furnish the quotas required of them, they outbid each other till bounties grew to an enormous and insupportable size."[10]

"Publius" further argues, in the *New York Packet* on December 18, that so vast a republic as America cannot be a real Union unless a strong national government possess the power to enforce national policy, freely arrived at by the people's representatives.

"The circumstances that endanger the safety of nations," the essay adds, "are infinite, and for this reason no constitutional shackles can wisely be imposed on the power to which the care of it is committed. This power ought to be coextensive with all the possible combinations of such circumstances; and ought to be under the direction of the same councils which are appointed to preside over the common defence."[11]

The next day in the New York *Independent Journal*, "Publius" maintains that power to raise armies should remain with the new Congress, not with the President. The Constitution's mandate concerning appropriations for a standing army for only two years at a time provides "great and real security" to those worried about a standing army in time of peace, according to Mr. Hamilton, alleged author of this essay.

Real and present dangers are colonies in the South that are subject to Spain's dominance, and Great Britain's settlements in the north. Each nation has Indian allies, who are America's natural enemies, "Publius" warns. These two nations are principal maritime powers as well, and if America means to be a commercial nation and be secure on this side of the Atlantic, Colonel Hamilton argues, the government will need not only a national army, but also a navy.

"Though a wide ocean separates the United States from Europe," the essay adds, "yet there are various considerations that warn us against an excess of confidence or security. . . . The improvements in the art of navigation have, as to the facility of communications, rendered distant nations, in a great measure, neighbors."[12]

Colonel Hamilton and other supporters of the Constitution have charged that critics of the document have no alternative to offer. Until now, many Anti-Federalists have insisted that the crisis confronting the country is being blown out of proportion to justify a seizure of power. All the reform that is required, they argue, is amendments to the Articles of Confederation.

Samuel Adams of Massachusetts, writing as "Candidus" in the December 20 issue of Boston's *Independent Chronicle*, broke with this belief. He offers, instead, a seven-point alternative plan to the Articles and to the new Constitution.

It is true, the influential New England leader of the American Revolution writes, that the governments of the States have for many years been in decline. But in order to "remedy these evils," he asks, shall we now pass to the other extreme in the mistaken idea that the country has no alternatives?

The resolves of the Continental Congress of April 1783 offered a reform program, "Candidus" argues, that gave Congress new exclusive powers to deal with problems of debt, commerce, and defense. This plan for a commercial Confederation of States should be considered as a prudent alternative to the new Constitution that lacks a bill of rights.

"The Constitution proposed," continues Mr. Adams, "may aggrandize a few individuals: *The offices of honor and profit, may please the AMBITION of some, and relieve the EMBARRASSMENTS of others*. It may serve to multiply Judicial controversies, and embarrass the citizens of the several States, by appeals to a Federal Court. It may give an undue influence to Congress, by the appointment of a numerous Body of officers. It may discourage *Industry*, by promoting an infinite train of dependents and seekers.—But the great object of commerce,—our national respectability,—together with industry and frugality, would probably be the happy consequences of a Commercial Confederation."[13]

It is doubtful that Mr. Adams' alternative plan will gain much support. Three States have already agreed to ratify the Constitution. Neighboring New Hampshire just this week has called for a ratifying Convention. Earlier this month North Carolina did the same, and Georgia has elected delegates to a ratifying Convention which is expected to begin next week with the clear prospect it will become the fourth State to approve.

Congressman James Madison of Virginia may regard Samuel Adams as a threat to ratification in the large, important State of Massachusetts. In a letter to General George Washington, a copy having been obtained by this correspondent, Congressman Madison urges the General to try to influence the "precarious index of public sentiment" in Massachusetts by communicating to any gentlemen he may know "[his] good wishes for the plan."[14]

The Christmas season is here, but it has not brought much cheer to Mount Vernon, as General Washington confides to a friend the gloomy view that ratification for a "General Government is now suspended by a thread...."[15]

CHAPTER 14

December 21–27, 1787

The Christmas spirit of "Peace on Earth, Good Will Toward Men" was shattered this week when Federalists and Anti-Federalists came perilously close to armed confrontation in the western Pennsylvania town of Carlisle.[1]

Although no one was killed or gravely injured, the near "riot" of December 26 was the latest in a series of explosive incidents in the State over ratification of the Constitution. In late September and early November, mobs in Philadelphia besieged critics of the Constitution in their boarding house, throwing stones at the windows. In another incident, two Anti-Federalist Assemblymen were forcefully dragged by Federalists to the State House to complete a quorum to call for a ratifying Convention.[2] During the ratifying Convention the debates grew so angry that delegates were reported to have come close to physical blows.[3]

The "Carlisle Riot" erupted in the late afternoon of December 26 when armed Anti-Federalists drove from the town square a Federalist group preparing a victory bonfire and the firing of a cannon. Burning the gun carriage and a copy of the Constitution, the Anti-Federalists shouted: "Damnation to the forty-six; long live the virtuous twenty-three," referring to those delegates who voted for and against the document.[4]

The following day, the Federalists returned to the town square armed with muskets and fixed bayonets, determined to celebrate ratification at the risk of their lives. However, after firing a few musket volleys into the air, the group retired from the town square vowing to seek legal rather than lethal redress. In turn, the Anti-Federalists were satisfied to burn in effigy Federalist leaders James Wilson and Thomas McKean, Chief Justice of Pennsylvania.[5]

The comic "Riot at Carlisle" contained the potential for turning bloody and tragic. According to the Scottish-born President of Carlisle's Dickinson College, Charles Nisbet, meetings held in town by Anti-Federalists on December 24 urged the "People to take up Arms in Defence of their Rights."[6]

Failing to secure a bill of rights in the Pennsylvania ratifying Convention, critics of the Constitution have turned their attention to other States, such as Massachusetts. This week, for example, a writer terming himself "Poplicola" warned readers of the December 24 *Boston Gazette* of the tyrannical designs of Pennsylvania Federalist leader Thomas McKean.

The Chief Justice of Pennsylvania was quoted from a speech he had recently given in the State ratifying Convention that "DESPOTISM, if wisely administered, *is the best form of government ever invented by the ingenuity of man!*" The essayist asserted that the "pride and madness, not *ingenuity* of man, *invented* DESPOTISM."[7]

During this Christmas week the ratification debate took a new and ugly turn.

A slashing personal attack on Elbridge Gerry of Massachusetts and Colonel George Mason of Virginia was published in the December 24 issue of the *Connecticut Courant*. Both refused to sign the Constitution at the Federal Convention in Philadelphia. Since September 17, their objections have been widely published and subjected to public discussion and newspaper denunciations.

Oliver Ellsworth of Connecticut, a Philadelphia delegate who also did not sign but now supports the Constitution, assailed Mr. Gerry and Colonel Mason in an essay signed "The Landholder." He charges Mr. Gerry with "barefaced selfishness" by favoring redemption of "old Continental Money," implying that he did so to profit personally. Mr. Ellsworth also charged that the reasons they gave at the secret Philadelphia Convention for not signing are different from those published in the newspapers.

"Instead of waiting till the Convention rose," the essayist caustically observes of Mr. Gerry, "before you consulted your friends at New-York, you ought to have applied to them at an earlier period, to know what objections you should make. They could have instructed you as well in August as October. With these advantages you might have past for a complete politician, and your duplicity might never have been detected."[8]

Growing opposition to the Constitution, Mr. Ellsworth insists, is due to Colonel Mason and Mr. Gerry manipulating the fears and ignorance of the masses. In Virginia, the opposition stems, he asserts, from "the madness of Mason, and the enmity of the Lee faction to General Washington. Had the General not attended the convention nor given his sentiments respecting the constitution, the Lee party would undoubtedly have supported it, and Col. Mason would have vented his rage to his own negroes and to the wind."[9]

Mr. Ellsworth is aware, nevertheless, that Colonel Mason during the secret Philadelphia Convention offered the most eloquent and impassioned denunciation of slavery of any delegate. A source has provided this correspondent with a copy of a few transcripts of the debates and they show Colonel Mason stating:

"This infernal trafic originated in the avarice of British Merchants. The British Govt. constantly checked the attempts of Virginia to put a stop to it. . . . Every master of slaves is born a petty tyrant. They bring the judgment of heaven on a Country. As nations can not be rewarded or punished in the next world they must be in this. By an inevitable chain of causes & effects providence punishes national sins, by national calamities."[10]

Furthermore, the secret transcripts reveal Mr. Ellsworth taking exception to Colonel Mason's charge that Eastern, or New England, shipping interests had a "lust of gain" by profiting from slavery as carriers of such human cargo.[11] Mr. Ellsworth must also know, according to one reliable source, that his Connecticut colleague Roger Sherman had concluded a deal privately last June 30 with John Rutledge of South Carolina whereby New England delegates would go along with the extension of slavery until 1808 if the South supported political protection of its shipping interests.[12]

Colonel Mason is aware of the deal. However, because each delegate swore an oath of secrecy at the Constitutional Convention, he has apparently refused to break his oath and divulge what he knows as a form of self-defense. Congressman Richard Henry Lee has probably been told by Colonel Mason what actually transpired in Philadelphia, but he has not revealed it in the Anti-Federal cause.

Congressman Lee of Virginia is the de facto leader of the Anti-

Federalists, as Congressman James Madison of Virginia is one of the Federalist leaders. In the weeks after the Philadelphia Convention, both remained at the Continental Congress in New York authoring essays and organizing support in various States for their respective causes.

Congressman Lee decried in a December 25 essay the personal attacks on Mr. Gerry, Colonel Mason, and himself. Such personal attacks are not from true Federalist patriots, he says in signing himself "The Federal Farmer." They are from anti-Republicans who secretly wish a new national government as a way to abolish the States. The true Republicans are, he avers, those who wish amendments and are willing to debate the facts and not indulge in "personal attacks" to divert public attention from the dangers of the document.

"These ardent advocates," Congressman Lee adds, "seem now to be peevish and angry, because, by their own folly, they have led to an investigation of facts and of political characters, unfavourable to them, which they had not the discernment to foresee."[13]

Mr. Lee has effectively formed an opposition alliance with George Clinton, New York Governor, and Samuel Adams in Massachusetts, two large States that remain doubtful for ratification. A Virginia Signer of the Declaration of Independence, Mr. Lee, 55, has become the most influential Anti-Federalist leader and champion of amendments or a bill of rights.

Perhaps for this reason he has been identified as the author of the "Federal Farmer" essays, by an anonymous writer signing himself "New England" in the December 24 issue of the *Connecticut Courant*.

"New England" attacked Mr. Lee as a slave-owning Virginian meddling in the politics of the region. Terming the "Federal Farmer" essays a form of "poison," the essayist questions "what honest motives" could induce a slave-owning Virginia planter to become a guardian of New England's freedoms when such concerns would be better directed toward the people of New Zealand!

"If we are not mistaken," the anonymous author charges, addressing Mr. Lee personally, "all your cant about liberty, democracy and aristocracy, is hypocritical, or else arises from a real ignorance of the nature of political liberty—in your practical sense, liberty can only mean a privilege for gentlemen planters to do what they please—in no conversation, in no intercourse with mankind, have you been known as the guardian or protector of that depressed race of men whose toils have enabled you to live in affluence, and at leisure plot dissentions and mischief to your country."[14]

It is doubtful that such savage personal attacks on Mr. Lee are likely to have an effect on New England political leaders like Samuel Adams of Massachusetts. Their friendship dates back to 1775 when they assumed leadership roles in the struggle for independence against Great Britain.

Both are reported to agree that the Constitution must contain a bill of rights. The Virginia Congressman was one of the first to raise the issue, in late September, before the Continental Congress sent the document to the States for ratification.[15] Since then he has apparently persuaded Mr. Adams that amendments will preserve the freedom they fought for and won in the American Revolution.

Just this week, General Charles Warren, 61, urged Old Patriots, among them Samuel Adams, and the authors of the Constitution to examine the principles of the American Revolution and the document and judge whether they are consistent or contrary. Writing in the December 27 issue of the *Independent Chronicle* of Boston as "Helvidius Priscus," General Warren praised Colonel Mason's and Elbridge Gerry's refusal to sign the document as well as their courage to submit their dissent to the world.

In turn, the descendant of one of the *Mayflower* passengers attacked James Wilson of Pennsylvania and the delegates to Philadelphia who framed the Constitution. Many of them, he says, "were infants" when the struggle with Great Britain was waged and know nothing of the costs by the blood of heroes and friends to emancipate America from tyranny.

". . .let them examine," Mr. Warren asserts of Federalist supporters, "the principles of the late glorious revolution, and see how far they comport with the opinions in vogue. And before they embrace the chains of survitude, let them scrutinize their own hearts, and inquire, if their pride and their independency of spirit, will suffer them to lick the hand of a despotic master."[16]

Meanwhile, in New York, Colonel Alexander Hamilton is arguing that the freedoms gained in the late war would not have been won without military force. And those freedoms will not remain secure from foreign dangers in the future, he says as "Publius" in the December 21 *New York Packet*, unless a national standing army is allowed to the national government.

The bravest of the State militia during the War of Independence "know the liberty of their country could not have been established by their efforts alone"[17] and required the assistance of the professional army and navy of France. The traditional domestic fear of a standing national army in time of peace is offset by the reality of the foreign dangers now facing the nation.

"The territories of Britain, Spain, and of the Indian nations in our neighborhood," he observes, "do not border on particular States, but encircle the Union from Maine to Georgia. The danger, though different in degrees, is therefore common. And the means of guarding against it ought, in like manner, to be the objects of common councils and of a common treasury."[18]

The State of Georgia is reported to have convened its ratifying Convention in Savannah this week. If the vast, yet thinly populated State ratifies, it will be the first Southern State to do so. The continuing war with the Creek Indians, allegedly sponsored by Imperial Spain, is likely to force Georgia to choose between what Savannah merchant Joseph Clay has termed two evils.

"The new plan of government for the Union," writes the delegate to the Georgia ratifying Convention, "I think will be adopted with us readily; the powers are great, but of two evils we must choose the least. Under such a government we should have avoided this great evil, an Indian war."[19]

In New York, the Secretary of the Continental Congress reveals that Georgia is raising an army of 3,000 men "to enter into a serious War with the Creek Indians."[20]

"I am also informed," he writes to the Governor of Connecticut on December 27, "that the States of Massachusetts and Virginia have diverted to their own state purposes the supplies which were to have come from them into the public treasury, so that Congress is like to be left without the means of keeping up the few troops on the frontiers, or even to support the forms of Government and defray the current expences."[21]

CHAPTER 15

December 28, 1787–January 3, 1788

Besieged to the South and West by Imperial Spain and her Creek Indian allies, frontier Georgia nodded toward the North and a national union this week, becoming the fourth State to ratify the new Constitution.[1] Georgia's action was independent of the extensive, often-heated debate in the Northern States, and slow midwinter travel has delayed word reaching this Southern-most State that three other States have preceded it.

Meeting in the State capital, Augusta, the ratifying Convention formally declared the document approved by Georgia on January 2 by a unanimous vote, 30 to 0. A state of martial law and a vow by Georgia's Governor, George Handley, to give no quarter in any war against the Creeks was an ominous overture to ratification by the first Southern State.

"The regular troops will be marched into the Indian country, putting to death all who make opposition," Governor Handley vowed. "Mercy will not be granted on any other terms than a total surrender of their country and themselves. . . .should they obstinately persevere in their fruitless endeavors to continue the war against us, we shall make their towns smoke with fire and their streets run with blood. . . ."[2]

The Governor has agreed to delay such Draconian measures to give peace commissioners time to negotiate a treaty with the Creeks in Georgia and the Cherokees in South Carolina and North Carolina. Shortly after the outbreak of fresh fighting between the Creeks and Georgian settlers in late September, the Continental Congress in New York appointed peace commissioners to try and effect a settlement with the tribes of the tri-State region to defuse the potential for a generalized Indian war.[3]

Georgia's swift approval of the Constitution this week was, according to one observer, not due entirely to the Creek threat and Imperial Spain's intrigues.

Unlike other States embroiled in debates over a bill of rights and the powers of the proposed national government before agreeing to the Constitution, Georgia's concerns may begin to surface after ratification. It is hopeful about the probable impact the document will have on Western territorial expansion, with a united nation offering more protection on its Western flank, and the impact on private debts.[4]

According to Henry Osborne, Georgia's Chief Justice, the State suffers from "wounded credit" caused by a flood of inflated paper currency amid a drought of gold and silver coin. Even the meager amount of silver coin circulating in the State, according to the jurist, has been "mutilated" by "dishonest men" who have "cut" it for dishonest purposes.

"I cannot help regretting that our paper currency should still continue depreciated to one-third its nominal value . . . ," the delegate to the Georgia ratifying Convention said. "The Federal Constitution has wisely taken away from each of the states the power of emitting a paper money; therefore no further emission (happily for us) can ever be made by the state. The fear of that power being again exercised was, I firmly believe, the primary cause of the depreciation."[5]

No other issue at the Federal Convention in Philadelphia last summer received more support from a majority of delegates than the clause in the new Constitution forbidding the States from issuing their own paper money. Delegates from nearly every State were reported unanimous in agreeing that of all the economic evils of the post-War period, inflated paper money has been one of the principle engines in the destruction of the country's prosperity and morals.

". . . this is a favorable moment to shut and bar the door against paper money," Connecticut delegate Oliver Ellsworth reportedly told the Constitutional Convention on August 16. "The mischiefs of the various experiments which [have] been made, [are] now fresh in the public mind and [have] excited the disgust of all the respectable part of America."[6]

★

Oliver Ellsworth, 42-year-old Connecticut jurist, is one of the 174 elected delegates who took their seats this week when the first formal session of the Connecticut ratifying Convention met in Hartford on January 3.[7] Connecticut is the first New England State to convene and is being watched closely by Massachusetts, expected to convene its own Convention next week.

Connecticut's Convention delegates who support the Constitution see it primarily as an instrument for revivial of the State's economy. For instance, in a series of essays, "A Landholder" (allegedly written by Mr. Ellsworth) maintains that farmers of the State and elsewhere will enjoy increased income from the domestic and foreign sale of their commodities if the document is ratified. In the past, Connecticut politics have been polarized between the merchants of the cities and the farmers in the countryside.

"The produce of the country," Judge Ellsworth writes, "is in general down to the old price, and bids fair to fall much lower. It is time for those who till the earth in the sweat of their brow to inquire the cause, and we shall find it neither in the merchant or farmer, but in a bad system of policy and government, or rather in having no system at all."[8]

The State's political leaders see the current system of taxation also as an economic evil. Each State currently has the power to tax imports from abroad and from other States by a system of "imposts." Critics charge this has created an uncommon market of economic chaos among the States and has allowed cheap foreign imports to flood the country at the expense of domestic commerce.

"We are all groaning under an intolerable burden of public taxes," complains an essay signed "A Farmer" and published in the *New Haven Gazette*, "and at the same time lamenting the scarcity of cash and the difficulty of vending the produce of our farms. . . ." With the proposed regulations and restrictions, "Our neighbors, New York, Rhode Island, and Massachusetts, would not be sucking the blood of our circulating medium by their state impositions."[9]

The Constitution proposes, in effect, a common market of the States, giving the national government power to regulate domestic and foreign commerce. The document would also give the new Congress power to levy imposts, or duties, on imports and domestic consumer goods in the form of excise taxes. The States would be denied their existing power of internal tariffs on goods produced in one State and exported to another.

Colonel Alexander Hamilton of New York, believed to be one of the original authors of the proposed policy of taxation, offers in three "Publius" essays this week a defense and an explanation of the taxing powers contained in the Constitution.

In the December 28 issue of the *New York Packet*, he says that the new national government cannot rely for its revenue on the existing system of contributions from the thirteen States. Such a system is the cause of the current economic chaos and would do little to deal with the existing swollen foreign and domestic debt.

An independent power of taxation, "Publius" states, "would enable the national government to borrow as far as its necessities might require. Foreigners, as well as the citizens of America, could then reasonably repose confidence" in trade.[10]

Critics of this independent taxing power, Colonel Hamilton writes in a followup essay in the *New York Packet* of January 1, are wrong when they charge that this power will pave the way for a tyranny by taxation and end in the destruction of the individual States.[11]

". . . the individual States should possess," "Publius" asserts, "an independent and uncontrollable authority to raise their own revenues for the supply of their own wants . . . an attempt on the part of the national government to abridge them in the exercise of it, would be a violent assumption of power, unwarranted by any article or clause of its Constitution."[12]

Despite such sweeping assurances, "Brutus," in an essay published in the *New York Journal* on December 27, remains unconvinced. The author is believed to be Robert Yates, an ally of New York Governor George Clinton. Both are bitterly contesting at every step the efforts of Colonel Hamilton. Governor Clinton has delayed the call for a State ratifying Convention, which Colonel Hamilton is seeking to influence with his published essays.

"Brutus" predicts that in time the States will not have the power to raise revenues except by permission from the national Congress. The gradual accumulation of powers by the national legislative, executive, and judicial branches will override those parallel branches in the individual States, he predicts, with their being "subordinate to the general government, and engaged by oath to support it, and will be constitutionally bound to submit to their decisions."[13]

As a concrete illustration, "Brutus" cites the power to impose excise taxes. What this really means, he points out, is a tax on every article used or consumed by every class in society. Such a tax, he predicts, will fall on consumers in the city as well as on those in the countryside and will become an unlimited form of taxation, not limited as its advocates maintain.

"A power that has such a latitude," the essay asserts, "which reaches every person in the community in every conceivable circumstance, and lays hold of every species of property they possess, and which has no bounds set to it but the discretion of those who exercised it[,] I say such a power must necessarily, from its very nature, swallow up all the power of the state governments."[14]

General George Washington and other advocates of the Constitution view the States' abuse of their power, ironically in the imposition of unprecedented rates of taxation, as one of several reasons why the document must be ratified. General Washington may take some consolation in the fact that the Confederated government is not the only country struggling with chronic financial problems.

In a letter to Thomas Jefferson, U.S. Minister to France, a copy having been obtained by this correspondent, General Washington says he is relieved to learn that the finances of France and England are in such a woeful state that a war between the two powers will be delayed.

It will give America time, he says, to form a national government with the separate States and thereby prevent them from forming alliances "with the European powers which can involve them in their political disputes," which will be ruinous to the future of the American Republic, so pregnant with potential greatness.

"... whenever a contest happens among them," General Washington adds, "if we wisely and properly improve the advantages which nature has given us, we may be benefitted by their folly.... I conceive under an energetic general Government such regulations might be made, and such measures taken, as would render this Country the asylum of pacific and industrious characters from all parts of

Europe, would encourage the cultivation of the Earth by the high price which its products would command, and would draw the wealth, and wealthy men of other Nations, into our bosom, by giving security to property, and liberty to its holders."[15]

The author of the Declaration of Independence shares with the military hero of the American Revolution this vision of the future. However, Mr. Jefferson writes from Paris this week that his high opinion of the abilities and honesty of the framers of the Constitution does not prevent thinking for himself when judging the document.

"I suppose I see much precious improvement in it," he observes in his December 31 letter, but adds that he sees "some seeds of danger which might have been kept out of sight of the framers by a consciousness of their own honesty & a presumption that all succeeding rulers will be as honest as themselves."[16]

The Marquis de Lafayette, after reading the Constitution sent to him in Paris by General Washington, has endorsed its boldness but has two fears: first, the lack of a bill of rights; second, the General may refuse election as America's first President.

". . . But in the Name of America," the Marquis urges the General, "of Mankind at large, and Your Own fame, I Beseech You, my dear General, Not to deny Your Acceptance of the office of President for the first Years—. . . ."[17]

CHAPTER 16

★

January 4–10, 1788

The sword, the purse, and the cross sowed dragon's teeth at the Connecticut ratifying Convention this week, forcing Federalist leaders to settle for a 128-to-40 margin rather than unanimous approval of the new Constitution on January 9.[1]

The dissent of nearly one-third of the delegates came as a surprise, since it was widely assumed that Connecticut would, in becoming the fifth State to ratify, do so unanimously.

Federalist leaders in the State are reported so infuriated, even with those who voted for ratification but raised doubts during Convention debates, they are vowing to destroy the political careers of those delegates who did not give unquestioning support.[2]

The six-day Convention was held in a Hartford church heated with wood-burning stoves to ward off the cold New England winter for the 168 delegates and an overflow spectator crowd.

A confrontation developed between Federalists elected as State officials and Anti-Federalist farmers and former officers of the Continental Army. General Jeremiah Wadsworth spoke for the veterans when he objected to the provision in the Constitution giving the Congress power over "both the sword and purse."[3]

At least eighty of the Convention delegates have first names taken from the Old Testament—Aaron to Zebulun—evidence of the strong religious strain in Congregational Connecticut. The clergy is believed to have a large influence in State politics.[4]

Omission in the preamble of the Constitution of "a firm belief of the being and perfections of the one living and true god" may have caused some delegates to vote against the document. Delegate William Williams raised the issue, only to have it and other objections buried in rebuttal speeches rich in religious and biblical rhetoric.[5]

"Though no enthusiast," Dr. William Samuel Johnson told the Hartford Convention, "I cannot but impute it to a signal intervention of Divine Providence that a Convention from states differing in circumstances, interests and manners should be so harmonious in adopting one grand system. If we reject [this] plan of government ... I fear our national existence must come to a final end."[6] Dr. Johnson was a delegate in Philadelphia and signed the document.

From the time the Philadelphia Convention concluded and the Connecticut ratifying conclave convened, the State has been an island of outward calm encircled by an angry sea of public debate in neighboring Massachusetts and New York. An absence of dissent in Connecticut may have misled many to believe that unanimous approval was certain.

However, observers have told this correspondent that Connecticut's Federalist leaders, in concert with almost all the State's newspapers, conspired to suppress all public objections to the Constitution.

According to one source, not only did the State's newspapers refuse to publish almost all Anti-Federalist essays, but officials allegedly sought to stop circulation of Anti-Federalist pamphlets shipped in from other States. Whereas Connecticut Federalists found unlimited space in the State's newspapers and took advantage of their complete freedom from opposition to attack Anti-Federalists in Massachusetts, New York, Pennsylvania, and Virginia.[7]

The most eloquent and explosive dissent in Connecticut took place outside the Convention meeting hall. It was delivered by Dr. Benjamin Gale, a prominent physician and businessman, at a Killingworth, Connecticut, town meeting. His speech was circulated as a printed pamphlet throughout the State.

In particular, Dr. Gale attacked the Constitution for extending slavery for twenty years. Connecticut ships carry such cargo, Dr. Gale observed, tearing families apart while single slaves are sold like cattle and "lashed like horses." Rather than designate in the document that "*Negroes* was intended by the word *persons*," Dr. Gale continued, it would have been better to have said nothing in a new Constitution that is being hurried by its supporters as if "the salvation of our souls depended upon our adopting it *immediately*."[8]

Permitting trade in *"bodies and souls of men"* for another twenty-one years, the 72-year-old physician and author of several published books on religion added, means that such a system of government is itself a form of slavery.

"For what have we been contending and shedding our blood and wasting our substance," he asked, "but to support the rights of men. I am told our reverend clergy in general are much engaged to support this new plan of government, but if this is really the case, they may in future preach and pray to the Africans that may be imported by virtue of this new Constitution."[9]

Since the ratification struggle began last September, the slavery issue has played almost no part in the newspaper or Convention debates of the five States that have approved the document. When it has surfaced, it has done so not as a moral issue but as a weapon to discredit individuals.

Oliver Ellsworth of Connecticut, for example, in a "Landholder" essay last month, impugned the motives of Colonel George Mason of Virginia, an opponent of the Constitution. At the Philadelphia Convention, Colonel Mason objected to the provision permitting slaves to be imported until 1808 and he refused to sign the document.

But Judge Ellsworth states, "Mr. Mason has himself about three hundred slaves and lives in Virginia, where it is found by prudent management they can breed and raise slaves faster than they want them for their own use, and could supply the deficiency in Georgia and South-Carolina; and perhaps Col. Mason may suppose it more humane to breed than import slaves...."[10]

Colonel Mason gave one of the most passionate speeches in the Philadelphia Convention denouncing the slave trade. He had also proposed a bill of rights, an issue that has since become a major battle cry for Anti-Federalists. Judge Ellsworth may have sought to discredit the issue by attacking the author of the proposal as a slave owner who allegedly profits from the odious practice. The bill of rights issue surfaced briefly at the Connecticut Convention this week, but it was dismissed by Samuel Huntington, the State's Governor, as unnecessary.

"This is a new event in the history of mankind," Governor Huntington told the delegates. "Heretofore, most governments have been formed by tyrants and imposed on mankind by force. . . . This noble attempt does honor to our country. While I express my sentiments in favor of this Constitution, I candidly believe that the gentlemen who oppose it are activated by principles of regard to the public welfare. If we will exercise mutual candor for each other . . . we may long continue to be a free and happy people."[11]

However, in the immediate aftermath of the Convention, critics have expressed in private their anger and bitterness, fearing to express their views openly. Many have charged in private correspondence that the Federalist majority ruthlessly directed high-handed tactics and "malevolent, vindictive tempers" toward any "that dare either write, speak, or act or even think against their own Dagon Constitution."[12]

The State's major newspapers and Federalist leaders deny allegations that the press was closed to dissent and that delegates were subjected to relentless abuse and threats of ruin to their public careers.

Jonathan Trumbull, Jr., former secretary to General George Washington, wrote to the hero of the American Revolution this week that as an eyewitness to the debates in Connecticut, he can report they were conducted with great liberality, candor, and fairness, which "I hope will have a happy influence on the Minds of our Brethren in the Massachusetts. . . ."[13]

The key New England State's ratifying Convention opened on January 9, the day Connecticut concluded its deliberations. The Boston State House was rejected as too small to accommodate the 355 elected delegates, the largest number of any State Convention thus far. Several days were spent searching for a site large enough to conduct business. Finally, Mr. Moorheads Meeting House, on Milk Street, was selected. Carpenters were brought in to build a public gallery to seat up to 800 and the press.[14]

Foul weather during the opening session this week matched the grim attitude of a solid Anti-Federalist bloc of delegates. Most are from the rural and western part of the State where echoes of the recent Shays's Rebellion are still influencing public opinion.

The abortive armed revolt, led by Captain Daniel Shays in late 1786 and early 1787 to prevent court foreclosures on debt- and tax-ridden Massachusetts farmers, was ruthlessly suppressed by State officials. According to one observer, Shays's Rebellion was instrumental in convening last summer the Federal Convention in Philadelphia. The Shays's "mobs" and disorders in five other States sent shockwaves of alarm throughout the country, creating a stampede of support for a new and strong national government to deal with what was perceived as spreading "anarchy."

But the vindictive and insensitive manner in which the rebellion was put down polarized Massachusetts politics, according to this same observer, by reviving fears and suspicions about the dangers of a powerful government, whether in Boston at the State level or under the new Constitution at the national level. Ironically, the document is currently in danger of being defeated in Boston because of a rural backlash against all but local government. If defeated in Massachusetts, the document could be doomed in New York and Virginia, the two other large States.[15]

Federalist leaders, aware of the odds and of the uphill fight they face, have decided on a strategy of smiling and polite stealth, rather than follow the Federalist rough-and-rude rush to ratification in Pennsylvania and Connecticut.

This week, for example, Federalists raised no objections when it was proposed that dissenter Elbridge Gerry, one of three who refused to sign the Constitution in Philadelphia, be seated at the ratifying Convention to answer delegate questions. Mr. Gerry had declined last fall to seek a seat in the Convention, certain he would be defeated by a Federalist.[16]

Delegate Caleb Strong, who secured election to the State Convention and was at Philadelphia with Mr. Gerry, plans to offer a motion that no ratification vote should be taken until a free and full debate on the document has been conducted.

A vote now, before Federalists have had time to woo and win undecided votes, might end in defeat. It was the Federalists who were also reported to have suggested the Convention move to a larger location to accommodate spectators, permitting them to pack the galleries with pro-Constitution supporters.[17]

Federalists also moved with great political skill and stealth when they secured the election of the State's popular Governor, John

Hancock, as President of the Convention. The vain, yet popular, hero of the American Revolution was elected Governor, in part, because of a promise of amnesty for Shays's rebels. Twenty-nine delegates at the Boston Convention had followed Captain Shays, some of them officers.[18]

Governor Hancock has remained neutral on the new Constitution, but is believed to be receptive to Federalist flattery and even an opportunity to serve in national office. The *Worcester Magazine* reported that Governor Hancock is being talked about as the first Vice President under the new Constitution.[19]

Samuel Adams, a Signer of the Declaration of Independence, along with Mr. Hancock, has also been under Federalist pressure to support ratification. However, the influential New England leader of the American Revolution is reported to have announced at a private dinner this week his opposition to ratification. The news swept swiftly throughout Boston.

In response, Federalists convinced the Boston Association of Tradesmen and Mechanics, constituents of Mr. Adams and an influential group in the city's politics, to issue on January 7 a resolve widely published in pro-Federalist newspapers. The statement supports ratification without amendments. It also argues that adoption would mean a revival of trade, navigation, and work for tradesmen and mechanics who, otherwise, might be "compelled to seek employ and subsistence in strange lands."[20]

Thus, during the first week of the Massachusetts ratifying Convention, the blunt and outspoken Samuel Adams was subdued and silent, offering no objections to a document he regards as dangerous if it remains unamended.[21]

CHAPTER 17

★

January 11–17, 1788

Rural delegates to the Massachusetts ratifying Convention served blunt notice this week that the new Constitution was not the Ten Commandments and that its "aristocratic" supporters in the cities were not prophets divinely ordained to lead them into a new promised land.

"We ought to be jealous of rulers. All the godly men we read of failed—nay, [I] would not trust a flock of Moseses," Abraham White told the 355 delegates in opposing the powers granted to Congress to regulate elections.[1]

In reply, Rev. Samuel West asked, "Is it probable that we shall choose men to ruin us? Are we to object to all governments? and because power *may* be abused, shall we be reduced to anarchy and a state of nature?"[2]

General Samuel Thompson expressed surprise that a clergyman, so learned and revered, would counsel the people to have little fear of powerful Federalist rulers.

"This, sir, is quite contrary to the common language of the clergy," General Thompson said, "who are continually representing mankind as reprobate and deceitful, and that we really grow worse and worse day after day.... I extremely doubt the infallibility of human nature. Sir, I suspect my own heart, and I shall suspect our rulers."[3]

According to one observer, this distrust of all government by a large number of rural delegates is rooted in the democratic New England town meeting where all delegated power is held suspect. A tradition of annual elections has been regarded as a check on the abuse of power.

The new Constitution calls for election to the House of Representatives for two years and to the Senate for six, raising fears that these longer terms will allow elected officials to become an entrenched and self-perpetuating political aristocracy. Feeding this fear is the rivalry between the agricultural and the commercial sections of Massachusetts, cast as a conflict between back-country democracy and city aristocracy.[4]

"We need not talk of the power of an aristocracy," Fisher Ames assured his fellow delegates, fearful of the power of Congress to regulate national elections. "The people, when they lose their liberties, are cheated out of them. . . . A democracy is a volcano, which conceals the fiery materials of its own destruction."[5]

Democracy has been cited as the principal cause for the recent Shays's Rebellion in the State. Armed debt-ridden western Massachusetts farmers laid siege to the State courts to prevent collections of debts and taxes. The abortive, largely bloodless rebellion polarized politics in Massachusetts and sent shockwaves throughout the other States. A sizable segment of the Anti-Federalist delegates at the ratifying Convention either participated in the armed rebellion or sympathize with the insurgents.

Massachusetts is the first true test for the Federalists in a large State. Delaware, Pennsylvania, New Jersey, Georgia, and Connecticut ratified the document easily. During the last three months, however, the State has been exposed to a rising volume of published Anti-Federalist essays with considerable effect on the thinking of rural delegates.

The conclave is reported to be evenly divided and has the largest number of elected delegates of any ratifying Convention thus far convened. Rural delegates in homespun and with the leathery look of plowmen have no more idea of the outcome than the more worldly and wealthy merchant and lawyer delegates in tailored broadcloth.

In the New England port city of Boston, increasingly turning toward the sea and away from the land for its prosperity, speculation on the final outcome is heard everywhere in the taverns and on downtown wharves. In other States, all eyes and ears are turned toward Boston, awaiting news by express rider or packet boat. Dutch bankers, French ministers, London merchants, and Americans abroad anxiously await news whether the new Constitution will survive its first serious test.[6]

In New York, Congressman James Madison of Virginia has written to General George Washington, a copy of the letter having been obtained by this correspondent, providing intelligence from this first week of debates in Massachusetts. It is "very ominous," he reports, that Shays's delegates have made common cause with those from the province of Maine seeking separate status as a State. The Maine delegates fear the Constitution will prevent peaceful, legal separation.

"The decision of Massachusetts either way will involve the result in this State [New York]," Mr. Madison writes General Washington. "The minority in Penna. is very restless under their defeat. If they can get an Assembly to their wish they will endeavor to undermine what has been done there. If backed by Massts. they will probably be emboldened to make some more rash experiment."[7]

Mr. Madison has remained in New York as a member of the Continental Congress while authoring with Colonel Alexander Hamilton a series of newspaper essays under the signature "Publius." The literary-political partnership is reportedly designed to influence selection of delegates to the New York State ratifying Convention.[8]

Not until this week did the New York Governor, George Clinton, place before the State Legislature, meeting in Poughkeepsie, the proceedings of the Philadelphia Convention that concluded last year on September 17. One observer believes this delay was deliberate, allowing time for other States to reject the document and thus negate New York's having to call a ratifying Convention.[9]

However, the threat that New York City, a commercial center for the State, might secede if the new Constitution were not debated in a formal convention may have moved Anti-Federalist Governor Clinton to act. John Jay, Secretary of Foreign Affairs of the Continental Congress, is reported to have written to General Washington: "An idea has taken Air, that the Southern part of the State will at all Events adhere to the Union, and if necessary to that End, seek a Separation from the northern."[10]

In his speech to the New York Legislature on January 11, Governor Clinton neither praised nor condemned the Constitution. Instead, he noted with satisfaction the settlement of boundary disputes with Massachusetts and Pennsylvania. He expressed dissatisfaction that New York continues to import luxury items from abroad which, in his words, "drains us of our wealth, and is the source from which most of our present difficulties proceed."[11]

Governor Clinton is reliably reported to have left public criticism of the Constitution to the two New York delegates he appointed, who permanently left the Philadelphia Convention halfway through its four-month ordeal. Robert Yates and John Lansing outlined in a letter to the Governor their reasons for leaving early and for opposing the document.

That the letter was published this week in the January 14 issue of the New York *Daily Advertiser*, along with Governor Clinton's speech to the Legislature, is regarded as no coincidence. The letter had been transmitted to the Legislature by the Governor without comment.

They asserted they had been sent to Philadelphia specifically instructed to amend the current Articles of Confederation, not to write a new Constitution creating a national government with powers certain to destroy the States and personal liberties.

"It is with the sincerest concern we observe," their letter states, "that in the prosecution of the important objects of our mission, we have been reduced to the disagreeable alternative of either exceeding the powers delegated to us, and giving our assent to measures which we conceived destructive of the political happiness of the citizens of the United States; or opposing our opinion to that of a body of respectable men. . . ."[12]

Colonel Alexander Hamilton was the third New York delegate in Philadelphia and he has charged that Governor Clinton recalled his two allies with the aim of trying to wreck the work of the Convention."[13]

Ever since he signed the document, a furious war of words has been waged between Colonel Hamilton and the Clinton forces in the New York newspapers under a series of *nom de plumes*.

Just this week, for example, Colonel Hamilton's partner in the "Publius" series, alleged to be Congressman James Madison, defends the work of the Convention as the product of Divine Providence. In the January 11 issue of the New York *Daily Advertiser,* "Publius" expresses amazement that the Philadelphia conclave overcame so many difficulties.

"It is impossible for any man of candor," he asserts, "to reflect on this circumstance without partaking of the astonishment. It is impossible for the man of pious reflection not to perceive in it a finger of that Almighty hand which has been so frequently and signally extended to our relief in the critical stages of the revolution."[14]

The following day, January 12, in the New York *Independent Journal,* "Publius" observes that in every case of ancient history the framing of a government has never, until now, fallen to an assembly of men, but fallen to some individual of preeminent wisdom and approved integrity.

Yet, he notes, the critics of the new Constitution differ among themselves as to a cure for a patient suffering from a potentially life-threatening disease.

"The prescription is no sooner made known, however," he adds, "than a number of persons interpose, and, without denying the reality or danger of the disorder, assure the patient that the prescription will be poison to his constitution, and forbid him, under pain of certain death, to make use of it."[15]

The most persistent and effective criticism of the document is the absence of a bill of rights. But "Publius" points out that the Articles of Confederation contain no bill of rights either.

Some of these same critics, he says, also complain that the Constitution permits the importation of slaves for twenty more years, while they support retaining the Articles, which have no restriction on the institution.

"It is a matter of wonder and regret," the essayist observes, "that those who raise so many objections against the new Constitution should never call to mind the defects of that which is to be exchanged for it. It is not necessary that the former should be perfect: it is sufficient that the latter is more imperfect."[16]

Nevertheless, the debates in the Massachusetts Convention demonstrate that these arguments do not address the central fear that animates opponents of the Constitution: unchecked power in the hands of the aristocracy—the "rich and ambitious," "lawyers, and men of learning—." According to one observer, this is the most pervasive dread of those hostile to ratification.[17]

Frustration of Federalist leaders to deal with this argument was expressed by Rufus King, a delegate to the Massachusetts ratifying Convention and a signer in Philadelphia of the Constitution.

". . . an apprehension that the liberties of the people are in danger," he writes from Boston to James Madison in New York, "and a distrust of men of property or Education have a more powerful Effect upon the minds of our Opponents than any specific Objections against the constitution—. . . . But every Attempt to remove their fixed and violent Jealousy seems hitherto to operate as a confirmation of that baneful passion—"[18]

CHAPTER 18

★

January 18–24, 1788

Facing the prospect that the new Constitution is heading for the reefs of shipwreck, Federalist captains at the Massachusetts ratifying Convention this week sought secretly to chart a new course. In a desperate effort to transform a looming narrow defeat into a narrow victory, they appealed to "honest doubters" among the delegates to vote for ratification, with bill of rights amendments held out as a possibility.[1]

The new course to rescue Federalist fortunes was revealed in a letter Rufus King wrote this week to Congressman James Madison in New York, a copy having been obtained by this correspondent.

"We are now thinking," the 32-year-old Massachusetts lawyer and convention delegate reveals, "of amendments to be submitted not as a condition of our assent & Ratification, but as the opinion of the Convention subjoined to their Ratification—This scheme may gain a few members, but the issue is doubtful—"[2]

Since publication of the new Constitution, in September 1787, Anti-Federalists like Richard Henry Lee of Virginia have urged that the two houses of Massachusetts insist on a bill of rights in the form of amendments as a condition for ratification.[3]

A minority at the Pennsylvania ratifying Convention failed late last year to secure amendments as a form of a bill of rights. In Virginia the fight for amendments has been led by former Governor Patrick Henry and Colonel George Mason. Colonel Mason refused to sign the new Constitution as a Virginia delegate to the Federal Convention. The most persistent and effective argument of the published Anti-Federalist essays has been demands for amendments, rather than outright rejection of the document.

★

At the Massachusetts ratifying Convention this week, dissident delegates took up the demand for amendments by attacking the powers of Congress over both the sword and the purse. Maine delegate General Samuel Thompson warned that Great Britain operated under the secrecy of taxation by picking "the subjects' pockets, without their knowing of it" and he charged that the new Constitution empowers Congress to do the same.

"But where is the bill of rights," General Thompson asked, "which shall check the power of this Congress; which shall say, *Thus far shall ye come, and no farther.* The safety of the people depends on a bill of rights. If we build on a sandy foundation, is it likely we shall stand?"[4]

In response, James Bowdoin, former Massachusetts Governor, insisted that the new Constitution is itself "a declaration of rights." The document contains numerous checks on the power of Congress, and the power of Congress is the power of the people, he argued. If imperfections are found in the operation of the new Constitution, they may be corrected by amendments as provided for in the document, he said.

"If the Constitution should be finally accepted and established," the former Governor concluded, "it will complete the temple of American liberty, and, like the keystone of a grand magnificent arch, be the bond of union to keep all the parts firm and compacted together."[5]

Some Anti-Federalist delegates may be wondering whether bribe money will be the mortar for Massachusetts' part of the arch. Earlier this week the Convention was stunned to read in the *Boston Gazette and Country Journal* of January 21 bold headlines proclaiming:

Bribery and Corruption!!!
The most diabolical plan is on foot to corrupt the members of the Convention, who oppose the adoption of the new Constitution. Large sums of money have been brought from a neighboring state for that purpose, contributed by the wealthy. If so, is it not probable there may be collections for the same accursed purpose nearer home?[6]

Faces flushed with anger, Federalist leaders waved the newspapers in the Convention hall and indignantly ordered a committee to investigate. According to one observer, some Anti-Federalist leaders may have hoped the charges were true. While the bribery bombshell sputtered and died for want of evidence, the allegation only deepened the brooding bad feelings on both sides.[7]

At one point, those feelings nearly exploded into a fist fight. Elbridge Gerry, invited by the Convention to answer questions from delegates because of his role as a delegate at the Federal Convention in Philadelphia, sought the floor to volunteer information. Federalist delegate Judge Francis Dana objected, unwilling to give the non-signer of the Constitution an opportunity to propagandize against the document as an unelected delegate to the ratifying Convention.

According to Rufus King, Mr. Gerry then attempted to answer Judge Dana. Both sides of the packed Convention hall apparently joined in a shouting debate about whether Massachusetts' most outspoken critic of the Constitution should be heard. The President of the Convention ordered adjournment rather than run the risk of rising tempers ending in violence.

"Mr. Gerry immediately charged Mr. Dana with a design of injuring his Reputation," added eyewitness Rufus King, "by partial information, & preventing his having an Opportunity to communicate important Truths to the Convention; this charge drew a warm reply from Mr. Dana, the Members collected about them, took sides as they were for or against the Constitution, and we were in Danger of the utmost Confusion. However, the Gentlemen separated—"[8]

One observer reported later that Mr. Gerry angrily vowed never to return to the Convention, despite anguished appeals from his supporters. While his vow delighted the Federalists, the incident made a hero of Mr. Gerry and damaged Federalist credibility.[9]

The near fist fight and bogus bribery charge may have emboldened the opposition into trying to force adjournment of the Convention. General Thompson first raised the issue, suggesting that Massachusetts wait five or six months and "see what our sister states" decide.

"There are some parts of this Constitution which I cannot digest;" General Thompson told the delegates, "and, sir, shall we swallow a large bone for the sake of a little meat? Some say, Swallow the whole now, and pick out the bone afterwards. But I say, Let us pick off the meat, and throw the bone away."[10]

Fellow Maine delegate Samuel Nason proposed repeal of a previous vote for a section-by-section debate of the Constitution. This would have opened up the Convention for a general discussion of the document and also have set the stage for a motion to adjourn. Delegates were running out of money and were in urgent need of an early decision, Mr. Nason insisted.

Federalist delegates sought to smother the incendiary proposal with speeches while their supporters in the packed galleries hissed at the proposal. However, it was influential Samuel Adams, who had been strangely silent since the delegates had convened, who succeeded in throwing cold water on the potential Anti-Federalist bonfire.

The 65-year-old New England leader of the American Revolution said that he was sorry to learn of the financial distress of some delegates, but that he favored "a full investigation" of the Constitution and was opposed to the motion to end the section-by-section debate. Loans might be extended to those delegates in financial distress, he added.

"We ought not," he told the hushed Convention hall, "to be stingy of our time, or the public money, when so important an object demanded them; and the public will expect that we will not . . . we should proceed as we began."[11]

Mr. Adams' remarks clearly signaled to the Anti-Federalists that he has jumped their ship. One observer reports that he may have been forced to by his constituency, who are Boston mechanics* and tradesmen. Paul Revere is the acknowledged leader of Boston artisans, who support ratification. The silversmith, just before the opening of the Convention, marched with a delegation to Mr. Adams' home and confronted him with their solid support for ratification.[12]

This correspondent has also learned that Mr. Revere's successful efforts at persuading Samuel Adams to "convert" to ratification may have been at the secret request of Federalist leaders. According to one source, Mr. Adams attended a secret meeting this week at the palatial Boston home of Governor John Hancock, along with Federalist leader Rufus King and three other gentlemen.[13] Their purpose was to convince the Governor that he too should support the Constitution, although we have no word about Mr. Adams' specific participation.

*Boston's skilled craftsmen called themselves artisans or mechanics.

Governor Hancock, although elected as President of the Massachusetts ratifying Convention at the insistence of Federalist leaders, has so far been absent from the Convention and has not yet signified his attitude about the Constitution. The popular but vain Governor offered as an excuse for his absence a painful attack of the gout. But Mr. King believes that the health of the politically astute Governor will recover "as soon as a majority is exhibited on either Side."[14]

According to several reliable sources, the Governor was told at the secret meeting that only his popularity could decide the ratification issue in the State and that only he could be the savior of the country. He could do this by agreeing to support a bill of rights in the form of nine amendments. In return, he would receive support for re-election and perhaps even be given serious consideration as a candidate for Vice President, or even for President if General Washington declined election, or if Virginia did not ratify the new Constitution.[15]

". . . if Mr. Hancock does not disappoint our present Expectations," Rufus King observes in a letter to Congressman James Madison, "our wishes will be gratified. But his character is not entirely free from a portion of caprice. . . ."[16]

The willingness of Massachusetts Federalists to support amendments to win over delegates who are "honest doubters" represents a radical departure from their previous position. Federalists throughout America have adamantly opposed any amendments during the ratification process.[17]

Nathaniel Gorham, a delegate to the Federal Convention as well as the Boston-based ratifying conclave, maintains that without the expediency of recommending amendments, the Constitution is likely to go down in a narrow defeat.

". . . I am pretty well satisfied," he wrote to Congressman James Madison, "we shall loose the question, unless we can take of[f] some of the opposition by amendments. I do not mean those to be made the condition of the ratification—but recommendatory only. Upon this plan I flatter myself we may possibly get a majority of 12 or 15—& not more."[18]

★

Nevertheless, there is a silent undercurrent working to the benefit of the Anti-Federalists in this State in the form of a deeply rooted sectional distrust of the South. According to one observer, this prejudice arises not only from opposition to the system of slavery but also from North-South differences in climate, geography, dialect, and attitudes about religion.[19]

Anti-Federalist delegates also object to thinly populated and slave-owning Georgia being allowed three representatives in a national legislature, with slaves being counted as three-fifths of a person for purposes of computing the number of representatives for each State. Whereas densely populated Massachusetts, with no slaves, will be allowed only eight representatives. Rather than concede that the three-fifths formula was an appeasement of the South to secure adoption of the Constitution in the Federal Convention, Federalists this week justified the compromise as a step toward future abolition of the evil institution.

In 1808 the Federal government will be empowered by the Constitution (once it is ratified) to prohibit the importation of slaves into the country.

James Madison of Virginia, writing as "Publius" in the January 22 issue of the *New York Packet*, agrees that postponement of that prohibition is unfortunate, but offers a positive view.

"It ought to be considered," he notes, "as a great point gained in favor of humanity, that a period of twenty years may terminate forever, within these States, a traffic which has so long and so loudly upbraided the barbarism of modern policy; that within that period, it will receive considerable discouragement from the federal government, and may be totally abolished. . . ."[20]

CHAPTER 19

January 25–31, 1788

Governor John Hancock left his "sick bed" this week to make an entrance at the Massachusetts ratifying Convention, wrapping himself in the mantle of political physician prepared to bind up the wounds of Convention division with the prescriptive balm of conciliation.

The popular 51-year-old handsome Governor was elected President of the Convention January 9 but made no appearance until January 30, pleading a painful attack of gout that confined him to his home. However, knowledgeable observers report the illness was a convenient excuse for the Governor to absent himself "because he wishes first to know, on which side the majority will be. . . ."[1]

In full view of the 355 delegates and the packed spectator galleries, Governor Hancock was carried to the President's chair in the hall, his feet still wrapped in bandages.[2] The Secretary of the Convention, George R. Minot, Esq., commented later that the ceremony surrounding his entrance seemed "to approach to servility, and looked like the blind adoration paid to Kings."[3]

Governor Hancock's sudden, dramatic appearance was apppparently timed by Federalist leaders to begin a drive to secure a ratification ballot after successfully delaying a vote. One source reports that Federalist leaders have been privy to the floor strategy of the opposition by placing informants in their private meetings.[4]

This week Federalists had a ready answer for every argument advanced by the opposition. Dissident delegate Amos Singletary sought to hold rural delegates to a hard line by suggesting that the Constitution was a power play by the wealthy and educated professionals of the cities.

"These lawyers, and men of learning, and moneyed men," he told the Convention, "that talk so finely, and gloss over matters so smoothly, to make us poor illiterate people swallow down the pill, expect to get into Congress themselves; they expect to be the managers of this Constitution, and get all the power and all the money into their own hands, and then they will swallow up all us little folks, like the great *Leviathan*, Mr. President; yes, just as the whale swallowed up *Jonah*."[5]

Jonathan Smith, a ploughman from the rugged western farming region of the Berkshire hills, rose in rebuttal with a "few words to my brother ploughjoggers" on the "black cloud that rose in the east last winter, and spread over the west."[6]

Immediately a delegate objected, insisting the remark was out of order. He demanded to know what Shays's Rebellion, an armed revolt of debt- and tax-ridden Massachusetts farmers in late 1786 and early 1787, had to do with the new Constitution? Samuel Adams' surprise comment cut the air like a whip: "The gentleman was in order—let him go on in his own way."[7]

The new Constitution, Mr. Smith went on, is a cure for the kind of violent disorders that endangered life, liberty, and property in the State. Specifically answering Mr. Singletary, Mr. Smith said he did not think the worse of the new Constitution because it was favored by lawyers, men of learning, and money men. All the delegates are embarked on the same course and all will sink or swim together.

Shall we, he asked, "throw the constitution overboard because it does not please us alike? Suppose two or three of you," he said, switching from a sea to a soil metaphor, "had been at the pains to break up a piece of rough land, and sow it with wheat; would you let it lie waste because you could not agree what sort of a fence to make? . . . . I say, Take things in time; gather fruit when it is ripe. There is a time to sow and a time to reap; we sowed our seed when we sent men to the federal Convention; now is the harvest, now is the time to reap the fruit of our labor; and if we won't do it now, I am afraid we never shall have another opportunity."[8]

One observer has informed this correspondent that while there is no denying the blunt eloquence of the Berkshire ploughman, he may have had some artful assistance from the Secretary of the Convention, Federalist George Minot, who has penned a history of Shays's Rebellion.[9]

Frustrated at their effort to divide the Convention along class lines, Anti-Federalists then sought to rally a majority against the Constitution with a slashing attack on the slavery clause.

"Mr. President, shall it be said," thundered General Samuel Thompson, "that, after we have established our own independence and freedom, we make *slaves* of others? O! Washington, what a name has he had! How he has immortalized himself! But he holds those in slavery who have as good a right to be free as he has. He is still for self; and, in my opinion, his character has sunk fifty per cent."[10]

Despite assurance from influential Samuel Adams that the Constitution opens the door to end the evil institution in twenty years, one observer reports that many delegates will probably follow the course announced this week by delegate James Neal and vote against ratification because of the slavery issue.[11]

"My profession," said the Quaker from Maine, "obliges me to bear witness against anything that favors making merchandise of the bodies of men, and unless this objection is removed I cannot put my hand to the constitution."[12]

Federalist leader General William Heath sought to dull the sharp cutting edge of the slavery issue by arguing it was not within the power of the conclave to do anything for or against slavery. The Federal Convention in Philadelphia went as far as it could politically, he explained, confining importation of slaves to existing States, whereas the Continental Congress in New York has outlawed its existence in new States.

"I ardently hope," General Heath continued, "that the time will soon come when our brethren in the Southern States will view it as we do, and put a stop to it; but to this we have no right to compel them. . . . Each state is sovereign and independent to a certain degree, and the states have a right, and they will regulate their own internal affairs as to themselves appears proper; and shall we refuse to eat, or to drink, or to be united, with those who do not think, or act, just as we do? Surely not. We are not, in this case, partakers of other men's sins. . . ."[13]

★

These words had hardly died away when Federalist leader Theophilus Parsons surprised and confused the opposition by moving that the Convention assent to and ratify the new Constitution. According to one observer, this was General Heath's signal to set the stage for Governor Hancock to assume his secretly designated role as conciliator of the Convention.[14]

General Heath, after an appeal to patriotism and posterity, suggested that since "many gentlemen appeared opposed to the system," is there not, he asked, a way for such minds to be relieved from such embarrassments? Answering his own question, he suggested that after ratification the first members of the new Congress be instructed to press for necessary additional paragraphs to the new Constitution.

". . . I cannot but flatter myself," General Heath told the still hall, "that in this way the gentlemen of the Convention will have the difficulties under which they now labor removed from their minds. We shall be united: the people of the commonwealth and our sister states may be united."[15]

The vagueness of the proposition was put into focus when Governor Hancock surprised the delegates by addressing the Convention. His "painful indisposition of body," he explained, had prevented his attendance but he had been kept informed on the proceedings; because of the objections of some gentlemen he felt an obligation to "hazard a proposition" for their consideration.

"My motive," Governor Hancock added, ". . . arises from my earnest desire to this Convention, my fellow-citizens, and the public at large, that this Convention may adopt such a form of government as may extend its good influence to every part of the United States, and advance the prosperity of the whole world."[16]

The Governor then read to the Convention nine proposed amendments. And although he did not expressly claim their authorship, he left the clear impression that they were of his own creation. But one observer has revealed that the amendments had been prepared by Federalist leaders and handed to the Governor to read.[17]

In turn, the Federalist leaders are reported to have compiled the nine amendments from the writings of moderate Anti-Federalist

Richard Henry Lee of Virginia, from the minority of the Pennsylvania ratifying Convention, and from objections to the new Constitution raised in the Massachusetts Convention.[18]

The amendments are alleged to have been drafted by Theophilus Parsons, one of the five gentlemen who had attended a secret meeting at the Governor's home. At that meeting, Governor Hancock agreed to act as conciliator of the Convention and to introduce the nine amendments. In return, he was assured of support for his re-election and a promise of consideration for President or Vice President under the new Constitution.

One observer reports that the Secretary of the Convention, George R. Minot, considers the whole process a mockery. Mr. Minot peeked over Governor Hancock's shoulder as he read his address and noticed the nine amendments were in the handwriting of a Federalist leader.[19]

Samuel Adams, who had also been a participant in the secret deal with the Governor and Federalist leaders, rose to address the Convention after Mr. Hancock had awed most of the delegates with his sincerity. There are reports that the delegates believed the proposition came from Governor Hancock's deepest convictions and praised his presentation as a masterful stroke of conciliation.[20]

Mr. Adams predicted that the proposition "must have weight in other states, where Conventions have not yet met" and create a sentiment of unity against external enemies. As far away as Virginia, objections have been raised, he said, and in Pennsylvania one-third of the Convention opposed the new Constitution without amendments or a bill of rights. Should there be large minorities in several other States, he added, "I should fear the consequences of such disunion.

"I apprehend, sir," Mr. Adams said, addressing Governor Hancock, "that these states will be influenced by the proposition which your excellency has submitted, as the resolutions of Massachusetts have ever had their influence. If this should be the case, the necessary amendments would be introduced more early and more safely."[21]

Mr. Adams then seconded Governor Hancock's propositions and a large committee was proposed to formalize the proposal. According to Federalist leader Rufus King: "We have a Majority of Federalists on this Committee and flatter ourselves the result will be favorable—"[22]

One observer reports that not only were the Anti-Federalist delegates surprised by Governor Hancock's appearance, but also his proposals left them without any counterstrategy. Bewildered and dismayed, the opposition is preparing to stall by requesting time to consider the very amendments many had militantly demanded previously.[23]

John Quincy Adams, the 20-year-old son of the U.S. Minister to Great Britain, John Adams, reports the Federalists will not now put up a candidate to oppose Governor Hancock's re-election.

"The very men," the youthful Adams wrote of Massachusetts Federalists, "who at the last election declared the Commonwealth would be ruined if Mr. Hancock was chosen, have now done every thing to get him in. . . ."[24]

CHAPTER 20

★

February 1–7, 1788

Boston went "wild with joy" this week after clamoring church bells and booming cannons in the seaport city announced the news that the Massachusetts ratifying Convention had, on February 6, become the sixth State to approve the new Constitution, doing so by a narrow 19 ballots out of 355 cast.[1]

An analysis by one observer of the 187-to-168 vote concludes that delegates living in counties close to or touched by the sea voted for ratification, whereas most delegates from the interior of Massachusetts and the province of Maine voted against approval.[2] However, interior Berkshire County voted Federalist.

Federalist leaders privately concede that Governor John Hancock's influence was crucial in persuading a handful of Anti-Federalist delegates to vote for ratification. One Federalist went so far as to assert that had Governor Hancock not "appeared in Convention, it was more than probable the *important* question would have been lost—"[3]

On January 31, Governor Hancock personally laid before the packed Boston Convention nine amendments secretly prepared by Federalist leaders. Although recommendations only, one observer believes the "conciliatory proposition" was the beginning of the end for the Anti-Federalists, tipping the scales toward the narrow Federalist victory.[4]

Playing a supporting role in the skillfully orchestrated Federalist political drama was Samuel Adams. Rising in support of Governor Hancock's nine propositions, the 65-year-old Signer of the Declaration of Independence emphasized that the first proposition, reserving all powers to the States not delegated to the new Congress, was of particular importance.

"This appears, to my mind," Mr. Adams told the Convention, "to be a summary of a bill of rights, which gentlemen are anxious to obtain. It removes a doubt which many have entertained respecting the matter. . . ."[5]

However, Anti-Federalist Samuel Nason did have doubts. The Confederated government, he replied, was a sacred instrument he had sworn an oath to uphold. Now, if the new Congress can be given the power to dissolve that compact, to what can we trust? The new Constitution begins by stating "We, the people of the United States," whereas the current Articles of Confederation declares "We the States."

"If this, sir, does not go to an annihilation of the state governments," he insisted, "and to a perfect consolidation of the whole Union, I do not know what does."[6]

Federalist delegate Rev. Thomas Thacher maintained that internal and external dangers require the Convention to think not of a single city or state, but of one continental nation.

". . . On the one hand," he went on, "the haughty Spaniard has deprived us of the navigation of the River Mississippi; on the other, the British nation are, by extravagant duties, ruining our fisheries. Our sailors are enslaved by the pirates of Algiers. Our credit is reduced to so low an ebb, that American faith is a proverbial expression for perfidy, as Punic faith was among the Romans. Thus we have suffered every species of infamy abroad, and poverty at home."[7]

Apparently sensing the tide was running against them, opposition delegate Major Thomas Lusk followed the Reverend Mr. Thacher with an attack on the slavery provision of the Constitution. He went on to link "poor natives of Africa" kidnaped and sold in slavery to the article in the document prohibiting religious tests for election to national office. Disregarding a religious qualification, Major Lusk said, made him shudder "at the idea that Roman Catholics, Papists, and Pagans might be introduced into office, and that Popery and the Inquisition may be established in America."[8]

"And let the history of all nations be searched," shot back Rev. Isaac Backus, a Baptist minister, ". . . and it will appear that the imposing of religious tests hath been the greatest engine of tyranny in the world. And I rejoice to see so many gentlemen, who are now giving in their rights of conscience in this great and important matter. . . ."[9]

Anti-Federalists were reported by one observer to have made a final, but futile, bid to block a showdown vote this week by proposing adjournment of the Convention so that nearby towns could discuss the propositions. The move lost 229 to 115, and was followed by former opponents rising to announce they would vote for ratification.[10]

On February 6, Samuel Adams puzzled and alarmed both sides by offering additional amendments to the nine already proposed. Specifically, "that the said Constitution be never construed to authorize Congress to infringe the just liberty of the press, or the rights of conscience; or to prevent the people of the United States, who are peaceable citizens, from keeping their own arms; or to raise standing armies, unless when necessary for the defense of the United States, or . . . to prevent the people from petitioning, in a peaceable and orderly manner . . . for a redress of grievances; or to subject the people to unreasonable searches and seizures of their persons, papers or possessions."[11]

It was received by both sides like a lighted fuse sputtering toward a powder magazine. The Anti-Federalists supposed the "Old Patriot" would never have offered additional amendments unless he believed the powers of the new Constitution posed a real danger. The Federalists feared that Mr. Adams would cost them their new converts.[12] And so his proposal was defeated.[13]

Observers are divided in their opinions why the proud and once bold New England leader of the American Revolution put himself in the position of suffering a self-inflicted humiliation.

One concludes that Mr. Adams sought to satisfy those delegates who felt the amendments introduced by Governor Hancock fell far short of the required bill of rights.[14] Another maintains that Mr. Adams saw his former ally Governor Hancock winning all the glory and could not resist a final effort to capture some for himself.[15]

★

Indeed, Governor Hancock did cover himself with glory as the great conciliator of the Convention. Most delegates remained ignorant of the secret political compact both leaders had concluded with the Federalists that made this week's narrow victory possible.

"The question now before you," Governor Hancock stated just before the critical vote, "is such as no nation on earth, without the limits of America, has ever had the privilege of deciding upon. As the Supreme Ruler of the Universe has seen fit to bestow upon us this glorious opportunity let us decide upon it; appealing to him for the rectitude of our intentions, and in humble confidence that he will continue to bless and save our country."[16]

In the wake of the narrow 19-vote victory, at least a half-dozen opposition delegates rose to express their support for the Constitution, vowing to return home and urge their constituents to submit cheerfully now that the question has been decided.

". . . the Constitution had had a fair trial," insisted Major Benjamin Swain, "and that there had not, to [my] knowledge, been any undue influence exercised to obtain the vote in its favor. . . ."[17]

Nevertheless, according to one observer, at least three rural delegates refused to vote for ratification out of a "disgust at the unfair methods which were taken in order to obtain a vote."[18]

It is not clear just what the trio meant. But another witness maintains that Federalist leaders spread the word among rural delegates, many of whom had exhausted their funds because of the unexpected length of the Convention, that if the Constitution were adopted, there would be no difficulty respecting pay for delegate service. If, on the other hand, the document were defeated, they would have to look to the State Treasurer, who had confessed his coffers were empty.[19]

George R. Minot, Secretary of the Convention, favors the Constitution but even he questions the public assertion that the contest was fairly won by his side. The Federalists, he admits, packed the Convention and "no stone was left unturned" to bring Anti-Federalists to renounce their principled opposition.

"*Bad* measures in a good cause," the Convention Secretary is quoted about Federalist tactics, "never was there a political system introduced by less worthy means, than the new constitution."[20]

Federalist leaders conceded at the onset of the Convention that the opposition was in the majority and accurately expressed the sentiment of the voters who had elected them. But according to James Madison of Virginia, the Anti-Federalists in Boston had no plan except to defeat ratification. Despite their vast numbers, Madison noted, "there was scarce a man of respectability, and not a single one capable of leading the formidable band."[21]

Just what impact this week's Federalist victory in Massachusetts will have on those remaining States that still must convene ratifying Conventions, will take some weeks to determine. Most Federalists throughout the country conceded before the February 6 vote in Boston that a defeat in Massachusetts would have meant a certain death warrant for the document.

"The decision of Massachusetts," insisted Virginia Congressman Edward Carrington, "is perhaps the most important event that ever took place in America, as upon her in all probability depended the fate of the Constitution."[22]

Perhaps for this reason alone, when the city's church bells and booming cannon announced the news of ratification, "The Boston people . . . lost their senses with joy," as Henry Knox, Massachusetts Revolutionary General, phrased it.[23]

Cartoons, pamphlets, and poems were distributed in the streets by enthusiastic supporters, apparently confident that Massachusetts' achievement would lead to ratification in the remaining States. According to one Boston newspaper, Convention delegates on both sides joined together: "All appeared to be willing to bury the hatchet of animosity, and smoke the calumet of union and love."[24]

Some 4,500 representatives of the trades and professions joined a "Grand Procession" through the streets of Boston and adjacent towns to mark the victory.[25] Federalist leaders, one observer notes, did everything possible to promote harmony, particularly among opposition rural delegates, as all dined on roast ox washed down with New England rum.[26]

Throughout Boston this improvised verse could be heard sung to the tune of "Yankee Doodle Dandy":

The 'Vention did in Boston meet,
But State-house could not hold 'em,
So then they went to Fed'ral-street,
And there the truth was told 'em—

> Yankee doodle, keep it up!
> Yankee doodle, dandy,
> Mind the music and the step,
> And with the girls be handy.

They ev'ry morning went to prayer,
And then began disputing,
'Till opposition silenc'd were,
By arguments refuting.

> Yankee doodle, keep it up! &c.

Then 'squire Hancock like a man,
Who dearly loves the nation,
By a concil'atry plan,
Prevented much vexation.

> Yankee doodle, &c.

He made a *woundy* fed'ral speech,
With sense and elocution;
And then the 'Vention did beseech
T' adopt the Constitution.

> Yankee doodle, &c.

. . . .

Now Politicians of all kinds,
Who are not yet decided;
May see how Yankees speak their minds;
And yet are not divided.

> Yankee doodle, &c.

So here I end my fed'ral song,
Compos'd of thirteen verses,
May agriculture flourish long,
And commerce fill our purses!

> Yankee doodle, keep it up!
> Yankee doodle, dandy,
> Mind the music and the step,
> And with the girls be handy.[27]

CHAPTER 21

★

February 8–14, 1788

With bone-chilling cold sweeping down from British-controlled Canada, New Hampshire on February 13 became the seventh State to convene a ratifying Convention and a majority of delegates are reported to have instructions from their constituents to turn a cold shoulder to ratification.[1]

One observer tells this correspondent that "for the first time" Federalist leaders may have misjudged the strength of Anti-Federalist forces. Overwhelming newspaper support for the new Constitution in New Hampshire may be blinding many Federalists to a growing revolt against ratification in the rural back country.[2]

This observer also points out that unlike the Conventions in Pennsylvania and Massachusetts, Anti-Federalists in New Hampshire have an articulate and persuasive leader in Joshua Atherton, a lawyer experienced in politics and a former jailed British loyalist.[3]

The 51-year-old passionate advocate of State sovereignty chose the slavery clause in the Constitution as his principal argument why New Hampshire should reject the document. In the just-concluded Massachusetts Convention, the slavery issue and the lack of religious qualifications for holding office in a national government influenced many rural delegates to vote against ratification. Both issues surfaced this week at the snowbound New Hampshire Convention.

". . . we will not lend the aid of our ratification to this cruel and inhuman merchandise, not even for a day," Mr. Atherton vowed. "There is a great distinction in not taking a part in the most barbarous violation of the sacred laws of God and humanity, and our becoming guaranties for its exercise for a term of years. Yes, sir, it is our full purpose to wash our hands clear of it. . . ."[4]

Another observer has informed this correspondent that opposition leaders are pressing for an early ballot in the belief a majority of delegates will vote down ratification. Anti-Federalist leaders are also prepared to follow the example of Massachusetts and demand a bill of rights in the form of twelve amendments.[5]

Before last week's narrow ratification vote in neighboring Massachusetts, nearly every Federalist leader in the State was confidently predicting that if the Boston Convention concurred, New Hampshire "would not be one week in session."[6] The first week's session in Exeter has apparently shocked Federalist leaders into the grim realization that their confident march into the future has come to a sudden halt.[7]

Federalists in other States have suffered from the same snare of overconfidence, perhaps brought on by their joy at the critical victory in Massachusetts. The narrow 19-vote margin out of 355 cast was possible only because Federalists in Boston accepted Anti-Federalist demands for amendments to be considered later.

James Madison of Virginia, writing from New York to General George Washington, observes that the amendments are a "blemish, but are in the least Offensive form." He confidently predicts that in New Hampshire there "seems to be no question that the issue there will add a *seventh* pillar, as the phrase now is, to the fœderal Temple."[8]

Express riders and packet boats, slowed by severe weather conditions, have yet to reach New York and Philadelphia with the news that the seventh pillar of the Federal Temple may be resting on a shaky foundation.

One observer reports that Federalists failed to realize that in New Hampshire, as in Massachusetts, delegates closer to seaports and rivers support ratification, anticipating that new Federal trade regulations will revive prosperity. Whereas, delegates in the isolated back country, independent and deeply religious, form a narrow majority and see their liberties endangered by a document which they also perceive sanctions slavery and godlessness.[9]

Last week, before the opening of the Convention in Exeter, Anti-Federalist writer Thomas Cogswell, in the February 8 issue of Exeter's *Freeman's Oracle*, directed a warning to the delegates that the new national government may rest on a sandy ground.

Writing as "A Friend to the Rights of the People," the essayist decries the absence of a religious test for holding office, the slavery clause, and the power of Congress to raise a standing army and navy. The powers of the new Congress to make all laws, to set the members' own salaries, to allow terms of office for more than a year, and to levy taxes will, he predicts, feed the craving appetites of men for gain. The "high taste of foreign courts will be relished by Congress"[10] and stretched as far as the patience and abilities of the people will bear.

". . . the truth is," he adds, "power long continued, makes men giddy, turns the head, and heart too, many times. The most promising characters, at first, have proved the worst in less than six years. Nero was one of the best among the Roman Emperors, at his first entering the Imperial throne, in a short time, he proved a monster of iniquity."[11]

In view of such potential for corruption under the new Constitution, Thomas Cogswell concludes the absence of a religious test is all the more alarming.

". . . when a man has no regard to God and his laws," he observes "nor any belief of a future state; he will have less regard to the laws of men, or to the most solemn oaths or affirmations; it is acknowledged by all that civil governments can't well be supported without the assistance of religion. . . ."[12]

With the exception of Rhode Island, most States, like Pennsylvania (even though it is more liberal in religious matters), have in their Constitutions requirements that anyone seeking public office swear a religious oath affirming a belief in God and in the divine inspiration of the holy Bible.[13]

When the Federal Convention in Philadelphia last summer adopted a prohibition against such oaths, most delegates were well aware that the provision would risk opposition during ratification debates. Delegates to the Connecticut and Massachusetts ratifying Conventions did raise the issue along with the absence of annual elections. Some delegates voted against ratification because of one or both issues.

Congressman James Madison of Virginia, one of the few Federalist leaders who have studied theology, sought this week to deal with the issues of a religious oath and annual elections. Writing as "Publius" in the February 8 issue of the *New York Packet*, Mr. Madison argues that the sole qualification for election to the House of Representatives, besides the age of 25, should be "merit of every description" and not "any particular profession of religious faith."[14]

In the following day's issue of New York's *Independent Journal*, "Publius" went on to assert that annual elections, while a safeguard against the abuse of power because of prolonged tenure in office, would be not as practical at the national level as at the State level.

"The distance which many of the representatives will be obliged to travel," the essay adds, "and the arrangements rendered necessary by that circumstance, might be much more serious objections with fit men to this service, if limited to a single year, than if extended to two years."[15]

Mr. Madison has experienced firsthand the difficulties of attending sessions of the Continental Congress in New York because of bad weather and impassable roads. In the last year alone, the Continental Congress often lacked a quorum to conduct business because of dangerous and difficult travel conditions.

One observer notes that even with the urgency of communicating information about ratification debates and Conventions, it has taken a full five days for the Congressman in New York to receive a letter from Rufus King of Boston confirming that Massachusetts has narrowly ratified the new Constitution.[16]

This same observer reports that the "snail-like slowness of the post" is compounded by postmasters routinely opening and reading letters. So notorious is the practice, that the principal author of the new Constitution, among others, has taken to writing in cipher particularly to Thomas Jefferson, the American Minister to France.[17]

A few days ago, in fact, General George Washington, in writing to the Marquis de Lafayette in Paris, stated he had no reserve about committing his views on the new Constitution in letters, "although by passing through the Post offices they should become known to all the world"; for, in truth, "I have nothing to conceal on that subject."[18]

Similar charges were made late last year when Anti-Federalist leaders Richard Henry Lee of Virginia and Elbridge Gerry of Massachusetts complained that their posted correspondence was being opened and read, and letters even disappeared. Since the first of the year, Anti-Federalist leaders have also charged the post office with waylaying newspapers containing their essays opposing the new Constitution.[19]

In Pennsylvania, for example, Anti-Federalists insist that Federalists used their influence with postal officials to prevent New York–printed essays from reaching Philadelphia in time for debates at the State ratifying Convention and even paid postmasters and postriders bribes to destroy Anti-Federalist material. Federalists have denied the charges, insisting the opposition is merely trying to stir up trouble.[20]

Anti-Federalists in Pennsylvania also insist that the printed dissent of the opposition at the State ratifying Convention in Philadelphia was delayed by postal officials so it would not reach Boston in time to be read by the delegates at the Massachusetts ratifying Convention.[21]

The charges of a Federalist conspiracy might have some substance if the only complaints came from Anti-Federalist printers. But an observer has told this correspondent that pro-Constitution printers along the Eastern seaboard have also expressed dismay at the failure of the postal system to deliver *their* newspapers. Nevertheless, Anti-Federalists are reported to be prepared to make an issue of the problem as a Federalist conspiracy for political advantage.[22]

"Those influential vehicles, the newspapers," angrily asserts "Centinel" in the Philadelphia *Independent Gazetteer,* "with few exceptions, have been devoted to the cause of despotism, and by the subserviency of the P——— O———, the usefulness of the patriotic newspapers has been confined to the places of their publication, whilst falsehood and deception have had universal circulation, without the opportunity of refutation."[23]

Behind such bitter words is a reality faced by Anti-Federalists: of the 95 newspapers published in the cities and States of the nation, a majority are overwhelmingly pro-Federalist. According to one observer, only a half-dozen newspapers support the Anti-Federalists. Understandably, printers are located primarily in the populated areas, where they receive their strongest financial support. And it is these areas that are strongly pro-Constitution. Despite this advantage in the ratification debate, Federalists have mounted a relentless campaign of pressure against Anti-Federalist newspapers.[24]

Last year Anti-Federalists launched a bitter attack on Federalists, alleging that their control of a majority of the newspapers has led to a pervasive refusal to publish their essays. The issue of being denied access to newspapers has been linked to the absence of a bill of rights in the Constitution, particularly a provision safeguarding press liberty.

". . . In America," writes Anti-Federalist "Philadelphiensis" in the January 23 issue of the Philadelphia *Freeman's Journal*, "the freedom of the press is peculiarly interesting: to a people scattered over such a vast continent, what means of information or redress have they, when a conspiracy has been formed against their sacred rights and privileges? None but the press. This is the herald that sounds the alarm, and rouses freemen to guard their liberty."[25]

CHAPTER 22

★

February 15–21, 1788

The newly appointed French envoy to the Continental Congress predicted this week that ratification of the new Constitution by six States means "that one of the most important revolutions on this Continent is on the eve of being consummated."[1]

Comte de Moustier, who arrived in New York just last month, also predicted in his February 16 secret diplomatic dispatch to the Minister of Foreign Affairs in Paris, that Massachusetts' ratification of the Constitution provides the necessary political momentum for the eventual establishment of a new national government.

". . . from now on we must think about the conduct we should observe toward the United States which will take on a completely different existence from that which they had until now," the 37-year-old French envoy observed in his dispatch,[2] a copy of which has been obtained by this correspondent.

Almost two-thirds of the swollen American foreign debt is owed to France for its loans and military assistance during the War of Independence. A source close to the French monarchy maintains that this financial support is the root of that country's current state of financial insolvency and political instability.[3] In February 1787 an Assembly of Notables was convened in Paris to effect financial and political reforms, but failed.[4]

Ironically, the conclave broke up on May 25, the day the Constitutional Convention in Philadelphia began its own effort at political and economic reform. Just this week Congressman James Madison of Virginia reported, in a letter written from New York, that various sources in Europe indicate that approaching events in France "may almost amount to a revolution in the form of its Government."[5]

One observer notes that not until this year has the French Crown pressed the U.S. Minister to France, Thomas Jefferson, for payment on the large sums owed. The author of the Declaration of Independence is reported to be acutely embarrassed by the large decade-old debt. He is also anguished about American failure to pay French officers who fought for American independence.[6]

The French, as well as other European nations, have followed the course of the American ratification debates closely with a view to how the outcome will affect their own positions in the New World.

The debate over the Constitution is now in its fifth month with nine States required to give legal force to the document. The new French envoy, who will present his credentials to the Continental Congress next week, concludes that European powers are no longer in a position "either to foster, or to hinder adoption of the new Constitution. . . .

"It can be presumed that England awaits the moment of decision on this present crisis in order to take a definitive stand with regard to the united States," observes Comte de Moustier of France's principal European rival. "Without having a representative here, she has maintained so many partisans and she takes care to maintain so many Emissaries, that she can give all the attention to the movements of these States that her interests require without giving that appearance. . . ."[7]

John Adams, U.S. Minister to Great Britain, reported this week that the London government looks with favor on the Constitution and is willing to conclude a new commercial treaty with America once the document is ratified. In his February 14 letter to John Jay, Foreign Secretary of the current Confederated government, Minister Adams urges "prompt Acceptance" of the Constitution so America can begin to pay off its foreign debts to the French, the British, and the Dutch.[8]

Minister Adams, who is expected to return to the United States in the spring, published in London last month the third volume of his *Defence of the Constitutions*, a series of commentaries that have been both praised and denounced in his home country. The 53-year-old Signer of the Declaration, like Thomas Jefferson, played no part in drafting the new Constitution because of diplomatic service abroad. However, the opinions of both still carry influence in the current ratification struggles in the States.

In his third volume, Minister Adams concludes that the current Confederated government is inadequate for the future of a nation so vast in size, population, and potential wealth and commerce. The new Constitution is better suited "to unite their wills and forces, as a single nation. . . .

"But the conception of such an idea," he adds, "and the deliberate union of so great and various a people, in such a plan, is, without all partiality or prejudice, if not the greatest exertion of human understanding, the greatest single effort of national deliberation that the world has ever seen."[9]

Thomas Jefferson in Paris, however, in his correspondence during the past two months makes it clear that although he supports the new Constitution, the absence of a bill of rights in the document is its principal defect.

Last December, the 44-year-old envoy wrote James Madison and others in America expressing his support for the new Constitution but suggested amendments in the form of a bill of rights. Mr. Jefferson's correspondence is being circulated by Anti-Federalists to support their campaign for amendments. One observer reports that Congressman Madison believes Mr. Jefferson's letters have been damaging to the cause of ratification.[10]

". . . I think our governments will remain virtuous for many centuries," Minister Jefferson predicts to Congressman Madison, "as long as they are chiefly agricultural; and this will be as long as there shall be vacant lands in any part of America. When they get piled upon one another in large cities, as in Europe, they will become corrupt as in Europe."[11]

A division between the cities and the agricultural areas is already evident, playing a critical role in the ratification debates. In the Conventions of Pennsylvania, Connecticut, and Massachusetts, for example, delegates from along the great corridors of commerce—the seacoast, Connecticut and Ohio Rivers, and Shenandoah Valley—

and the cities, whose material interests will be advanced and strengthened, have generally favored ratification and the Federalists. Whereas rural delegates and those from the interior and agricultural areas, more conservative and suspicious of a distant national government, have generally opposed ratification and supported Anti-Federalist demands for a bill of rights.[12]

This same pattern emerged in the New Hampshire Convention sitting in Exeter. Rural delegates have a narrow majority to defeat approval, as partially confirmed by General Benjamin Lincoln of Massachusetts in a letter to General George Washington. Accounts from New Hampshire, wrote General Lincoln, "are vague and uncertain, things do not look as well as we wish they did."[13]

When Massachusetts narrowly approved the Constitution on February 6, Federalists confidently assumed that New Hampshire would shortly follow. However, Anti-Federalists in the State have shown surprising strength among delegates from the back country. Observing the New Hampshire proceedings, a Maine gentleman observed, "it is with them as it was with us, the Country Members Mostely against, the Traiding Towns for it."[14]

One source reports, moreover, that New Hampshire Federalists have been infuriated by Anti-Federalists from Massachusetts who have come into their state armed with pamphlets for use by Federalist opponents. Federalists are also alarmed and dismayed to learn that at least "40 towns in New Hampshire have instructed their delegates in Convention to vote against the Constitution."[15]

New Hampshire's Anti-Federalist Thomas Cogswell fanned the flames of opposition with a published essay addressed to members of the Convention under the title "A Friend of the Republic." Adopting the new Constitution without a bill of rights, he insists, means surrendering liberties, privileges, and immunities of New Hampshire into the hands of a new and powerful Congress.

"Every honest man," he says, "ought to be bold enough to declare his rights—at least, such great and essential ones, as never ought to be trusted to the caprice of any set of man—And you, gentlemen, I hope will be bold enough to spurn at a Constitution, offered you without a Bill of Rights; and receive none unless the most essential ones are enumerated."[16]

The bill of rights issue has bedeviled Federalists ever since it was first proposed last year by Colonel George Mason of Virginia at the Philadelphia Federal Convention. Ironically, summary rejection of the proposal has given critics of the Constitution their most persuasive argument against it.

One observer points out that despite all the solemn, shrill, sensible, absurd, clever, and vulgar arguments against the Constitution, the demand for a bill of rights flows from a legitimate fear of the corrupting effects of political power.[17]

The most vigorous advocates of a bill of rights, according to another observer, have been older men who less than fifteen years ago lived under the corrupt, unlimited power of the British Parliament and King. With few exceptions, vigorous advocates of the new Constitution are younger men who did not experience, or participate fully in, the main intellectual and physical struggle against Great Britain. Anti-Federalist leaders are in their 50s and 60s and are called "the old patriots of '75" by the press; a majority of the Federalists are in their 30s and 40s.[18]

Eighty-two-year-old Dr. Benjamin Franklin, who spent many of the last fifteen years abroad, this week in a letter to a friend in France summarized the fears of both the Federalists and the Anti-Federalists. Confident the Constitution will be ratified, he adds, ". . . though there is a general dread of giving too much *Power* to our *Governors*, I think we are more in danger from too little Obedience in the *governed*."[19]

Dr. Franklin also expresses concern about "the internal troubles" in France, where he had served as U.S. Minister for nine years before Thomas Jefferson replaced him.

Late last year, William Short, private secretary to Minister Jefferson, wrote to Mr. Madison and observed that war or peace in Europe this spring will depend on the finances of France.

"This will be a revolution completely operated in the government in this country," Mr. Short noted, referring to attempts by the Finance Minister to reform the country's taxes and finances. "Should it effect a permanent constitution this country will unquestionably be the richest & most powerful in the world in twenty years."[20]

France may be a wealthy country, but the government has been overwhelmed by the nearly five-billion-franc debt incurred because of aiding the American War of Independence. At the same time, King Louis XVI cannot raise taxes on the poor or on the many privileged groups who are exempt. The current fiscal crisis confronting France is fast turning into a political crisis.[21]

Compounding France's fiscal-political problems was a crop failure that exploded into hunger riots in Paris last August. Rioters shouted revolutionary slogans and burned some government ministers in effigy. One observer reports a struggle for power is currently under way in France between the King and his belief in the absolute power of the monarchy and those demanding he share power in the name of reform and liberty.[22]

Minister Jefferson is hopeful that out of the current financial-political ferment in France will come constitutional reform along the lines of that in America. However, Arthur Young, a British writer on agriculture, who has traveled extensively in France in the last year, is less optimistic after witnessing the Paris riots.

"One opinion," he observed, "pervaded the whole company, that they are on the eve of some great revolution in government; . . . a great ferment in all ranks of men, who are eager for some change. . . ."[23]

Thus, while the new French envoy to the Continental Congress in New York writes to Paris that the ratification debate is the consummation of "one of the most important revolutions on this Continent," an equally important revolution on the European continent may be just beginning.

CHAPTER 23

February 22–28, 1788

The forward momentum of Federalists was suddenly frozen in its tracks this week as news spread throughout snow-blanketed New England towns and cities that New Hampshire adjourned its ratifying Convention without voting to accept or reject the new Constitution.

Instead, the State set a June date to reconvene, buying time for thawing out opposition and saving the document from the frostbite of defeat.[1]

One Boston newspaper reported this week that on February 22, in the session before the Exeter Convention adjourned, delegates did vote narrowly to reject the document, 54 to 51. However, one observer has told this correspondent that Federalist leaders prevented the vote from being officially recorded. At the same time, they swiftly moved for adjournment over the strenuous objections of Anti-Federalist leaders. This recorded vote carried, 56 to 51.[2]

Federalist leaders have convinced fence-sitting delegates to go along with the adjournment ploy, suggesting they return home and persuade their constituents to issue new instructions. The delegates are returning to their homes armed with twelve proposed amendments believed to be recommendations, but not conditions, for ratification. Massachusetts Federalists won ratification by a narrow margin earlier this month with the same approach of offering recommendations.

During the ten days the New Hampshire Convention met at a Congregational church in Exeter, Federalists ran into a granite wall of opposition from back-country delegates who were instructed by their constituents to reject the Constitution. Finally, some were swung over, but Federalist leaders concluded that adjournment until June was the only arrow left in their quiver.[3]

New Hampshire's Governor and delegate to the Federal Convention in Philadelphia, John Langdon, admitted this week in a letter to General George Washington that "contrary to the expectation of almost ev'ry thinking man, a small majority of (say four persons) appeared against the system, this was the most astonishing to ev'ry man of any information. . . ."[4]

One observer reports that when New Hampshire convened its Convention on February 13 the Anti-Federalists had a forty-vote advantage, only to have it eroded by a series of Federalist efforts. One strategy, according to this observer, was a well-timed dinner party, apparently with more than strong tea served, to delay the selected Anti-Federalists from attending and voting.[5]

Federalists in New England and New York, while privately expressing deep disappointment, predicted in public this week that New Hampshire will eventually vote to ratify. According to one source, what gives them the greatest worry is the impact New Hampshire's adjournment will have on those States that have yet to ratify.[6]

General Washington, for example, is reliably reported to have counted on New Hampshire, Maryland, and South Carolina approving before Virginia. This would strengthen Federalist forces before his deeply divided State decides. Now, for the first time, he is very troubled that the climate for acceptance in Virginia will be considerably worsened.[7]

Meantime, the flagging spirits of Anti-Federalists everywhere are expected to fly higher as news of New Hampshire's action slowly makes its way south during one of the worst winters in a generation. The news is certain to be received in New York with gloom by the Federalists, who were barely able to muster sufficient support to call a Convention, and with glee in Philadelphia by Anti-Federalists, who had been, they charge, badly treated.[8]

Congressman James Madison of Virginia has admitted to close associates that adjournment in New Hampshire was an "expedient" to "prevent a rejection."[9] But the price has been "no small check to the progress of business" and an encouragement to Anti-Federalists in New York, Pennsylvania, and Virginia.[10]

★

Since the conclusion of the Federal Convention last September, Congressman Madison has remained in New York to attend sessions of the Continental Congress. However, much of his time and effort have reportedly been directed toward waging a war of words in the newspapers, authoring with Colonel Alexander Hamilton a series of essays published under the *nom de plume* "Publius."

It is being rumored that the 36-year-old Virginia lawmaker has authored at least half of the sixty essays published thus far. As many as four in one week have appeared in New York newspapers and been reprinted elsewhere. In addition, he is said to have written since last September no fewer than forty-five lengthy letters, mainly to Thomas Jefferson in Paris and to associates and friends in Virginia. At least twenty of these letters have been addressed to General Washington at Mount Vernon, providing him with a steady stream of information on the ebb and flow of the ratification fight.

Late last week Mr. Madison informed the General that he will be returning to Virginia to stand for election as a delegate to the Virginia ratifying Convention. Elections are expected to begin next week and the Convention is scheduled to convene in Richmond the first week in June.

General Washington and other Virginia Federalists have been pressing the Congressman to make the race. He indicates in his February 20 letter to the General, a copy having been obtained by this correspondent, that he does not look forward to verbal duels with Patrick Henry and other Virginia critics of the Constitution.

"I foresee that the undertaking," Mr. Madison writes, "will involve me in very laborious and irksome discussions: that public opposition to several very respectable characters whose esteem and friendship I greatly prize may unintentionally endanger the subsisting connection. . . ."[11] He is alluding to his close personal and political relationship with many in Virginia who now oppose the Constitution which he helped to create.

Mr. Madison is being kept informed by friendly correspondents in the Virginia Commonwealth of the activities of Patrick Henry, the former five-term Governor, and Colonel George Mason. Mr. Henry refused to serve as a delegate in Philadelphia and the latter refused to sign the document in Philadelphia, decrying the absence of a bill of rights.

While most Federalists in Virginia and elsewhere welcome Massachusetts' recent ratification, one observer reports that the recommendation for amendments has given an influential boost to the bill of rights cause.[12] If New Hampshire follows in its neighbor's footsteps and insists on amendments when the delegates reconvene in June, it may strengthen the hand of critics in Virginia.

First advocated by Colonel Mason and championed by Congressman Richard Henry Lee of Virginia, the bill of rights issue is the most persuasive argument the critics of the document have employed in the five-month ratification battle. In Virginia, the issue may play a critical role at the Richmond ratifying Convention.

However, equally influential is Patrick Henry, who is holding the document hostage to fear and uncertainty about centralized power. Second only to General Washington, the spellbinding orator is held in the highest regard in Virginia. Kentucky will be sending delegates to the Richmond Convention and in recent months Mr. Henry is reported to have written incendiary letters to leaders in that Virginia province, warning that the Mississippi River will be lost forever to Imperial Spain if the new Constitution is adopted.[13]

The Mississippi River is considered vital to interior Virginia and Kentucky trade as the main transportation route. Patrick Henry is expected to make good use of the Spanish claim to the Mississippi to induce frontier Kentucky to oppose ratification.[14]

The Attorney General for the Kentucky district, Harry Innes, just last week made it clear that adoption of the Constitution "would be the destruction of our young & flourishing country" because the document vests the power to regulate commerce in the new Congress.

"Our interests and the interests of the Eastern states," he warns, "are so diametrically opposite to each other that there cannot be a ray of hope left to the Western Country to suppose that when once that interest clashes we shall have justice done us. . . . So long therefore as Congress hath this sole power & a majority have the right of deciding on those grand questions we cannot expect to enjoy navigation of the Mississippi."[15]

Attorney General Innes reports that despite five inches of snow, the Indians continue to be hostile in Kentucky with horse stealing posing a survival problem to hunting frontiersmen. Kentuckians also fear that the Constitution's granting Congress power over the State militia "may leave us in a defenceless State and subject us to the ravages of the Merciless Savages. . . ."[16]

On the other hand, Georgia ratified the Constitution on January 2 partly from the belief that the new national government would strengthen its ability to deal with Indian attacks. Since last year Georgia has been fighting a savage Creek Indian–settler war on its southern border. There are also reports that the Cherokees in North Carolina and South Carolina are threatening to put on war paint and take up the tomahawk. Mr. Madison and others in the Continental Congress have been working with meager resources to prevent a generalized Indian war in Georgia and the Carolinas.

Mr. Madison has alleged that Imperial Spain is behind the Indian war in Georgia and may seek to exploit discontent in Kentucky over the Constitution in an effort to make the region a Spanish province.[17] Privately, Mr. Madison has expressed his belief that behind Patrick Henry's opposition to the Constitution is his alleged goal of forming a separate Southern Confederacy.[18] Such a development would serve the ambitions of Spain and shatter any possibility of an American union.

The Federalists' fear of Governor Henry's opposition is, therefore, not confined to his prestige and oratorical powers to sway public opinion in Virginia. There are geopolitical advantages that Imperial Spain might net by fishing in the troubled waters of Kentucky and by keeping the Mississippi River closed to American navigation.

These fears are well founded. When Spain first closed the vital waterway in 1784, the issue produced one of the worst sectional disputes in the history of the Continental Congress, for there were the dual threats of a war with Spain and the splintering of the thirteen States into two or three separate sectional confederacies.[19]

Frontier settlers have in recent years demanded statehood. Like those in the province of Maine seeking separation from Massachusetts, Kentuckians may fear that the Constitution threatens their chances for independence.

Spain and Great Britain can profit from political unrest in the independent-minded frontier settlements, particularly if any single state or province breaks away. For instance, Great Britain has closed the St. Lawrence to American navigation and is seeking to detach the Vermont territory from the Confederation. The territory has been denied admission as the fourteenth State because of the conflicting land claims of New York and New Hampshire.[20]

Vermont is still seeking admission, as are Maine and Kentucky. If frustrated because of sectional disputes, they might be willing to accept protection and trade concessions from either Great Britain or Spain.

Nevertheless, as one observer points out, Kentucky's application for status as a State has been received with indifference, if not coolness, by New England. This only confirms for Patrick Henry that New England is prepared to see the Mississippi remain closed, leaving Virginia and Kentucky impoverished while the New England States grow prosperous and wealthy.[21]

Little wonder that James Madison dreads returning to Virginia to stand for election for the ratifying Convention and face the oratorical colossus Patrick Henry.

"He will be the main pillar of the constitution," Thomas Jefferson in far-off Paris had predicted of Congressman Madison, "but though an immensely powerful one, it is questionable whether he can bear the weight of such a host."[22]

CHAPTER 24

★

February 29–March 6, 1788

Rhode Island took the phrase "We the People" literally this week and ordered a public referendum on the new Constitution rather than follow other States and elect delegates to a ratifying Convention.

The action of the proud, tiny New England State of 38,000 is viewed by one observer as consistent with its refusal to send delegates to the Philadephia Federal Convention last summer. Calling a ratifying Convention now would be a confession of error for not participating in the summer-long conclave that created the Constitution.[1]

Rhode Island has been a thorn in the side of other States ever since the independent State was founded by the religious nonconformist Roger Williams in 1636. Besides occasionally defying the Continental Congress, its policy in recent years of issuing inflated paper money has enraged its sister States.[2] However, in varying degrees seven other States have indulged in the inflationary practice, one of the principal reasons the Federal Convention was convened.

"Rogue Island" is the persistent term of derision used by critics, particularly after the State government contrived to pass a law punishing with fines any creditor who refused to accept inflated State currency. A new national government would force Rhode Island to pay its debts in gold and silver, ending the feathered nest of the controlling agrarian party.[3]

The Constitution, ratified by six States at this writing, specifically denies States the power to print paper money, and requires them to coin only gold and silver as tender of payment on debts. During the Federal Convention last summer, Rhode Island was held up by some delegates as an illustration of the dishonorable measures and "length to which a public body may carry wickedness & cabal."[4]

One source in Boston tells this correspondent that the State government met last week to prepare a public statement denouncing sister States for deserting the Articles of Confederation.[5] The *Salem Mercury* (Massachusetts) reported on February 26 that political leaders in Rhode Island are planning to charge "the several states who have adopted the new constitution, with treason."[6]

Ever since Rhode Island refused to send delegates to Philadelphia, it has been subjected to an unprecedented wave of public and private attacks. A minority within the State, made up primarily of merchants, has sought to break the political stranglehold the agrarian party has on the State by favoring adoption of the Constitution.

The *Newport Herald*, the lone Federalist voice in the State, argued in its February 14 issue that a State ratifying Convention would be a "step of repentance" and remove the "foul stains" inflicted on the State by its political leaders.

". . . a perseverance of unfederalism," warns the *Newport Herald*, "will bring on this State the merited punishment for our national degeneracy, and establish us as a monumental example of the truth of that adage, '*Those whom GOD wills for destruction he first makes mad.*'"[7]

While the current Rhode Island government has been attacked for its debasement of the currency as a form of fraud against its sister States, the volume of virulence of attacks on it may also be because of its view of property. Shortly after coming to power, the radical paper-money party was rumored to be considering a bill that would equalize the distribution of property every thirteen years.[8]

Rhode Island's announcement this week of a public referendum rather than a State ratifying Convention has delighted Anti-Federalists. Nevertheless, because of its reputation as a "rogue," its example is not likely to have any real influence on other States. According to one observer, the popularity of Anti-Federalism in the State has contributed to its unpopularity elsewhere; the State's brand of Anti-Federalism has even proven elsewhere to be an embarrassment to Anti-Federalist leaders.[9]

Few Anti-Federalist publications have rushed to the tiny State's defense. The one exception was the Philadelphia *Freeman's Journal*.

Significantly, in its defense the newspaper pointed out that the State has outdone Pennsylvania "in the glorious work of freeing the negroes in this country" and of outlawing slave importation since 1784.[10]

Extension of the slave trade in the Constitution until 1808 has contributed to Rhode Island's opposition to the document, particularly among Quakers. A sizable number of delegates to recent ratifying Conventions in Connecticut, Massachusetts, and New Hampshire opposed the document solely because of the slavery issue.

New England Federalists are reported to be more annoyed at Rhode Island's calling a public referendum than concerned that it may influence other States. Rufus King of Massachusetts predicts that balloting in town meetings around the State on the first Monday in March will end in defeat for the document "by a majority of two to one; probably by a still larger majority."[11]

New Hampshire's adjournment of its Convention on February 22 without ratifying is more troubling to Federalists than Rhode Island's expected rejection of the Constitution. Already Federalists have launched a campaign in the press to influence New Hampshire delegates to vote for ratification when they reconvene in June.

Oliver Ellsworth addressed "the CITIZENS of New-Hampshire" in the March 3 issue of the *Connecticut Courant*. The Federalist leader, writing as "The Landholder," warned that only ratification can save the State from becoming an appendage of British Canada or Nova Scotia.

"Though separated from the government of Britain," the 43-year-old Connecticut jurist observes, "at no less price than the blood of your bravest sons, you border on her dominions—She is our enemy. . . . Her force may easily be pointed through your whole territory, and a few regiments will effectually banish resistance."[12]

Fear of foreign invasion and weakness of the current Confederated government to check any aggression are a Federalist argument that is being used with considerable effectiveness. Georgia ratified the Constitution in large measure because of fear that the current Indian war with the Creeks has been inspired by Imperial Spain as part of her secret campaign to annex American frontier territory in the South and the West.

The opposite is true in Virginia. Fear of Imperial Spain is working against Federalists. Opposition leader Patrick Henry is prepared to use Spain's closing of the Mississippi River in the forthcoming Virginia Convention. According to one observer, the five-time Virginia Governor has written letters to potential Kentucky delegates to the ratifying Convention alleging that the Constitution will mean permanent loss to Southern trade on the river, suggesting that their interests are being sacrified by Northern States.[13]

This week Virginia began a month-long process of electing delegates to its ratifying Convention, to be held in Richmond during the first week in June. Former Governor Henry is expected to win a Convention seat handily, an appalling prospect for Virginia Federalists, who fear him for his powers of oratorical persuasion more than any other person in America.

Congressman Edward Carrington of Virginia is reported to have told Congressman James Madison in mid-February that Virginia Federalists face real trouble. Not only does Governor Henry have "blind followers" on his home ground, but friends of the Constitution are timid and too cautious.

"Of this however I am pretty certain," states the 40-year-old Mr. Carrington, "that the doctrine of amendments has taken such strong ground, that the direct adoption of the Constitution cannot be well expected should less than Nine States have adopted when our Convention comes to set."[14]

Shortly after Mr. Madison received this disturbing intelligence, he wrote General George Washington that he had reluctantly decided to return to Virginia from New York and seek election as a delegate. His friends have warned him that he faces defeat unless he wages a vigorous campaign.[15]

According to an observer, Federalist candidates in Virginia lack the advantage they have held in Northern States of placing prominent figures against relatively unknown and inexperienced candidates. In Virginia, Federalists will be coming up against Anti-Federalists drawn from a long list of imposing professional and political men.[16]

Virginia Federalists, as a consequence, are reported to be taking great care in selecting their candidates. Personal popularity, family influence, public reputation, business, and financial power are some of the considerations. One observer says it will be hard for the people of the State to reject such prominent Virginians.[17]

They are also counting on electing candidates who served General Washington as officers in the Continental Army. According to one source, a large number of them favor the Constitution and as a group have worked in the last six months in the various States to secure ratification.[18]

The overwhelming support of former military officers is believed to be due in large measure to the influence of General Washington. This week he wrote Congressman Madison, praising him for his decision to seek election as a delegate to the Virginia Convention.

"The determination you have come to," warmingly writes the General, "will give pleasure to your friends ... the consciousness of having discharged that duty which we owe to our Country, is superior to all other considerations. ..."[19]

Since his return to Mount Vernon last September, after serving as President of the Federal Convention in Philadelphia, General Washington has remained, publicly, removed from the ratification struggle. However, a steady stream of correspondence and visitors keeps him well informed. In return, he writes to friends at home and abroad offering his unequivocal support for the Constitution.

One observer informs this correspondent not only that these letters have had great weight in directing the movement of Federalists, but also that published excerpts have had a direct, powerful influence on public opinion. Without General Washington, according to this source, the battle of Virginia for ratification might be lost.[20]

Nevertheless, the 56-year-old hero of the American Revolution is disturbed at persistent efforts to have him declare his candidacy as the first President under the Constitution. Part of his concern may stem from a genuine desire for retirement from public life and part from embarrassing financial problems.

Upon returning to Mount Vernon, he discovered, one source reports, his entire crop had been "destroyed by one of the severest droughts." With many mouths to feed, he is said to be short of cash to make up for the natural disaster and to pay his back taxes on his five farms that make up his beloved estate.[21]

Another reliable source reports, moreover, that he has had to put off the Sheriff of Fairfax County on three occasions when an attempt was made to collect back taxes. Reportedly, he has received a warning that his unproductive land holdings in the western portion of Virginia will be sold if the taxes on Mount Vernon are not paid.[22]

"I never felt," General Washington confided to a friend, "the want of money so sensibly since I was a boy of 15 years old as I have done for the last twelve months and probably shall do for twelve months more to come."[23]

CHAPTER 25

★

March 7–13, 1788

The Attorney General of Maryland, Luther Martin, this week called on former delegates to the Philadelphia Constitutional Convention to disavow "anonymous slanders" published against Elbridge Gerry of Massachusetts for opposing the Constitution and for allegedly seeking to use his position in the secret conclave last summer for personal financial gain.

Mr. Martin, in the March 7 issue of the *Maryland Journal*, challenges the author of a series of "Landholder" essays to make known his identity or be branded "the wretched dupe and tool"[1] of fabricators of false "assertions meant to injure the reputation of individuals" in Philadelphia who opposed the creation of the new Constitution.[2]

"... Sir, I am really at a loss," the 44-year-old militant Anti-Federalist earlier stated, "which most to admire—the depravity of this writer's heart, or the weakness of his head."[3]

Several sources have confirmed for this correspondent that the series of "Landholder" essays are being written by Oliver Ellsworth of Connecticut, who also served with Mr. Martin as a delegate in Philadelphia. Since late last year, the "Landholder" essays have been attacking Mr. Gerry and Mr. Martin in particular and Anti-Federalists in general.

One source says that the slashing sallies are short on facts and long on exaggeration. They delight Federalists but infuriate prominent Anti-Federalists who are the victims of Judge Ellsworth's vigorous, vituperative essays.[4]

Last week, for example, in the *Maryland Journal*, "Landholder" repeated his charge that Mr. Gerry introduced a resolution in

Philadelphia calling for redemption of old Continental currency because he held so much of the nearly worthless paper money.

Only when the proposal was defeated, according to "Landholder," did the 43-year-old Massachusetts merchant oppose the document out of "barefaced selfishness" and with "the utmost rage and intemperate oppositon to the whole system he had formerly praised."[5]

Luther Martin, a delegate from Maryland, insists that he never heard Mr. Gerry make such a proposal in Philadelphia and that both consistently opposed the new Constitution and refused to sign it because it did not contain a bill of rights and safeguards for the rights of the States.

Lashing out last week, "Landholder" charges that Attorney General Martin is hardly a credible source since by his "ignorance in politics and contradictory opinions," he "exhausted the politeness of the Convention, which at length prepared to slumber when you rose to speak. . . .

"You, sir," the essay continues, "had more candour in the Convention than we can allow to those declaimers out of it; there you never signified by any motion or expression whatever, that it stood in need of a bill of rights, or in any wise endangered the trial by jury. In these respects the Constitution met your entire approbation; for had you believed it was defective . . . it was your indispensable duty to have proposed them."[6]

Attorney General Martin replies that he sought to have a bill of rights considered in Convention, but was rebuffed. ". . . ambition and interest had so far blinded the understanding of some of the principal framers of the Constitution," that had they accepted his proposal it would have frustrated their secret, sinister ambitions.

"I most sacredly believe," he adds, "their object is the total abolition and destruction of all state governments, and the erection on their ruins of one great and extensive empire, calculated to aggrandize and elevate its rulers and chief officers far above the common herd of mankind, to enrich them with wealth, and to encircle them with honors and glory. . ."[7]

One observer questions whether Mr. Martin's motives for militant opposition to the Constitution do not contain some element of self-interest. Under Maryland's current laws, he, as well as others, has sought to use inflated paper money to make extensive purchases of land confiscated from British owners. The new Constitution denies States the power to traffic in inflated paper money and contains the potential for former British loyalists to sue for return of their confiscated property.[8]

Nevertheless, Oliver Ellsworth may have his own motivation for repeatedly lashing in print Elbridge Gerry of Massachusetts with unsubstantiated allegations. He may have been attempting to reduce Mr. Gerry's influence in the ratification debate in that State before last month's narrow 19-vote victory. And, in recent weeks, "Landholder's" attacks on Maryland Attorney General Martin may be because Maryland is the next State to hold a ratifying Convention, to begin April 21.

Over the winter, critics of the Constitution in Maryland and Virginia have sought to form a coalition, one observer notes, to frame a series of amendments, or a bill of rights as they are referred to, for the Southern States. Luther Martin and other Maryland Anti-Federalists are planning to use dilatory tactics to delay any ratification vote in the Maryland Convention, and may even try to follow New Hampshire's recent example and adjourn without voting. This will put additional pressure on Federalists in Virginia to agree to concessions, and, in turn, if successful, the Anti-Federalists will have greater leverage in Maryland when its ratification Convention reconvenes.[9]

Another source reports that for the first time General George Washington is worried about the prospects for ratification in Virginia, particularly if the Anti-Federalists in Maryland move to delay a vote before Virginia meets. He has confided to his former military aide James McHenry, who was a Maryland delegate in Philadelphia along with Luther Martin, that Maryland's postponement would adversely affect decisions in both South Carolina and North Carolina and provide New York with a pretext for rejection.[10]

"Decisions, or indecisions then with you," General Washington gravely adds, "will in my opinion, determine the fate of the Constitution, and with it, whether peace and happiness, or discord and confusion is to be our lot."[11]

This correspondent has learned that General Washington regards the move in Maryland to adjourn without a decision as good as a rejection. So seriously does he regard the threat, that he is delicately urging his Federalist friends in the State to make every effort to frustrate the plans of the Anti-Federalists.[12]

Luther Martin is one of the few Anti-Federalists willing to challenge openly General Washington's and Dr. Benjamin Franklin's support of the Constitution.

". . . If it was the idea of my state," he replied to the "Landholder," "that whatever a Washington or Franklin approved, was to be blindly adopted, she ought to have spared herself the expence of sending any members to the Convention, or to have instructed them implicitly to follow where they had led the way."[13]

Since the Constitutional Convention adjourned last September, Maryland Attorney General Martin has hammered away at the theme that the Constitution is really the product of a conspiracy by the wealthy and well born. In replying to the "Landholder," for example, Mr. Martin accuses Oliver Ellsworth of trying to prevent the veil of secrecy of the Convention from being drawn aside.

". . . a veil which was interposed," he says, "between our proceedings and the Public, in my opinion, for the most dangerous of purposes, and which was never designed by the advocates of the system to be drawn aside . . . , is only for the purpose of deception and misrepresentation."[14]

Next to the absence of a bill of rights, the secrecy of the Philadelphia Convention is the most effective political issue employed by the Anti-Federalists. The Convention at the start of its proceedings secured from each delegate an oath of secrecy for their lifetime. At the conclave's conclusion, it was voted to give General Washington custody of the minutes of the Convention debates.

One reliable source says that Rufus King of Massachusetts proposed the records be entrusted to General Washington or destroyed as "a bad use would be made of them by those who would wish to prevent adoption of the Constitution—"[15]

Whether Mr. King had Luther Martin and other dissenters in Philadelphia in mind, it is not clear. However, during the last six months the Maryland Attorney General has been the only delegate openly to disavow his oath of secrecy. He has provided considerable details about the secret debates, and charged that the secrecy rule was intended to conceal a conspiracy.

As a result, the secrecy rule, while crucial during creation of the Constitution, has cast a cloud of doubt over the document during ratification. The published attacks on Mr. Martin by "Landholder" have given Anti-Federalists cause to charge they are also designed to discredit him because he is providing details of the conspiracy.

Last month, for instance, an essay appeared in the February 5 issue of the *Independent Gazetteer*, Philadelphia, signed "Centinel." The writer maintained that published attacks on the former Maryland delegate to the Federal Convention confirm the existence of a conspiracy.

". . . He has laid open the conclave," the essayist asserts, "exposed the dark scene within, developed the mystery of the proceedings, and illustrated the machinations of ambition. His public spirit has drawn upon him the rage of the conspirators, for daring to remove the veil of secrecy . . . : all their powers are exerting for his destruction; the mint of calumny is assiduously engaged in coining scandal to blacken his character, and thereby to invalidate his testimony. . . ."[16]

Considerable doubt is being expressed by observers that Luther Martin will have any effective influence on the ratification contest in his State. One believes that although he is brilliant, his reputation as a heavy drinker and his use of inflammatory rhetoric prevent many from taking him seriously. Furthermore, he is widely regarded in Maryland as a faithful servant of Samuel Chase and owes his Attorney General post to that Signer of the Declaration of Independence.[17]

Another source reports that Samuel Chase is widely regarded in the State as an opportunist who made money from the War of Independence. Feared by many, respected by some, and loved by very few, the 46-year-old lawyer has long favored paper money—earning the enmity of the more established aristocratic conservatives in the States.[18]

The bombast of Luther Martin and the energy of Samuel Chase, together with the opposition of other Anti-Federalists, have managed to convince Federalists that the course of ratification in Maryland will be difficult, despite the influence and support of General Washington. By a steady stream of newspaper essays and public speeches, the Anti-Federalists are giving the appearance of vigorous opposition, apparently eroding the quiet strength of the Federalists.[19]

The April 7 election for delegates to the Maryland ratifying Convention, to be held in Annapolis, will test whether the Chase–Martin Anti-Federalists can overcome their ragged reputations and the fact that General Washington is widely known in Maryland to favor ratification.

Although he maintains a public posture of neutrality, privately the General expresses anger at calls by the Constitution's critics for a second Federal convention to consider amendments.

"... I have wondered," General Washington has confided to a close friend, "that sensible men should not see the impracticality of the scheme. The members would go fortified with such Instructions that nothing but discordant ideas could prevail ... there is no alternative, no hope of alteration, no intermediate resting place, between the adoption of this [the Constitution], and a recurrence to an unqualified state of Anarchy, with all its deplorable consequences."[20]

CHAPTER 26

★

March 14–20, 1788

The Anti-Federalist charge that the President under the new Constitution will become as powerful and tyrannical as the King of England was subjected this week to one of the most systematic Federalist refutations since the ratification debate erupted six months ago.

Ever since the Constitution was published last September, some Anti-Federalists have assailed the document as squinting toward monarchy, insisting the powers of the novel new office are comparable to those of a King.

Just last week, for example, the essayist "Philadelphiensis" in the Philadelphia *Independent Gazetteer* predicted that ratification will, in a short time, produce anarchy and civil war.

"How can we suppose," he asks, "that the president general, being once in full possession of his unlimited powers, would deliver them back again to the people; the supposition is preposterous; he must be more than *man* if he would; a more dangerous king is not in the world than he will be; liberty will be lost in America the day on which he is proclaimed...."[1]

In response to, or anticipation of, such arguments, "Publius" in the *New York Packet* this week seeks to demonstrate that the powers of the new President are similar rather to those of the governors of the separate States than to those of the King of England. In a point-by-point comparison, he argues, for example, that:

• The President is elected by the people for *four* years; the King of Great Britain is a "perpetual and *hereditary*" prince.

167

- The President is subject to impeachment; the King "is sacred and inviolable."
- The President's power of veto over the Congress is qualified; the King's power over acts of the British Parliament is "absolute."
- The President commands military and naval forces; the King also has this right, and in addition to "*declaring* war" he can *raise* and *regulate* armies and fleets on his own.
- The President has the power to make treaties with the Senate's concurrence; the King "is the *sole possessor* of the power of making treaties."
- The President has no power of spiritual jurisdiction; the King is "the supreme head" of the national church.

"What answer shall we give," the essayist asks, "to those who would persuade us that things so unlike resemble each other? The same that ought to be given to those who tell us that a government, the whole power of which is in the hands of the elective and periodical servants of the people, is an aristocracy, a monarchy, and despotism."[2]

The author, believed to be Colonel Alexander Hamilton of New York, further argues that some of the power of the new President is less than that of the current Governor of New York (an Anti-Federalist). Moreover, many of the powers set down in the Constitution, according to "Publius," are currently being exercised by the Governors of New York, Maryland, and Delaware.[3]

One observer with access to the still secret debates of the Federal Convention confirms for this correspondent that the delegates in Philadelphia borrowed extensively from several State Constitutions and from the Articles of Confederation in framing the Constitution.[4]

During the Convention last summer, rumors were rampant that the delegates were considering a monarchial form of government and were even contemplating inviting the son of George III to become King of the United States. Leaders of the Convention admitted that they had received so many letters asking if the rumors were true, they were forced to issue a rare public statement.

"... tho' we cannot, affirmatively," the August 22, 1787, statement read in the *Pennsylvania Journal*, "tell you what we are doing, we can, negatively, tell you what we are not doing—we never once thought of a king."[5]

Members of the Maryland delegation in Philadelphia may have been partially responsible for giving credence to the persistent charge that the Convention contemplated a monarchy. Luther Martin, Maryland's Attorney General, has insisted that fellow delegate John Mercer recorded over twenty delegates who favored a royal government after weeks of deadlock over what form the Executive should take.[6]

The office of President is a novel proposal, and apparently delegates were concerned about demagogues or middling politicians, with a republican form of government perhaps unable to remove perceived difficulties. Thus, Colonel Hamilton, as a New York delegate, is believed to have told the Convention on June 18 that though he did not favor a monarchy, "I believe the British government forms the best model the world ever produced. . . ."[7]

From these circumstances, Anti-Federalists have woven a web of arguments that the Constitution is a secret monarchist snare fabricated by the wealthy and the well born. However, one observer points out that fears of a single, powerful President eligible for reelection were expressed by many of the ardent supporters of the Constitution during the debates in Philadelphia.[8]

Governor Edmund Randolph of Virginia, when a single Executive was first proposed, denounced the proposal as the "foetus of monarchy" and warned, according to a source, that America should not adopt a new national government on the British model.[9]

Just this week, Georgia delegate William Pierce, influential in securing ratification in his State, was quoted in the March 20 issue of the *Gazette of the State of Georgia* (Savannah) that despite his support of the Constitution, his single most solid objection to the new government is the power given to the Executive.

"The authority which the President holds," he says, "is as great as that possessed by the King of England. Fleets and armies must support him in it. I confess however that I am at a loss to know whether any government can have sufficient energy to effect its own ends without the aid of a military power."[10]

Colonel Hamilton disputes that the powers of the President are inconsistent with the genius of republican government. As "Publius" in the March 15 issue of New York's *Independent Journal*, he gives his reasons.

"Energy in the Executive," he argues, "is a leading character in the definition of good government. It is essential to the protection of the community against foreign attacks; it is not less essential to the steady administration of the laws; to the protection of property against those irregular and high-handed combinations which sometimes interrupt the ordinary course of justice; to the security of liberty against the enterprises and assaults of ambition, of faction, and of anarchy."[11]

Since last October, Alexander Hamilton and Congressman James Madison have sought to keep secret, even from fellow Federalists, their authorship of some 70 "Publius" essays. However, it is now an open secret that since the essays have appeared principally in the New York newspapers their purpose is to influence election of Federalist delegates to the New York ratifying Convention. A reliable source informs this correspondent that plans are under way to publish the lengthy essays in a single volume in time to influence the ratifying Conventions of both New York and Virginia.[12]

Mr. Madison has returned to Virginia from New York to stand for election as a delegate to the State ratifying Convention. One source reports that he stopped at Mount Vernon to confer with General Washington and to discuss political strategy. At this meeting, Mr. Madison is believed to have renewed his suggestion that the General publicly endorse the Constitution.[13]

General Washington has made it clear in his private correspondence that he strongly favors ratification of the Constitution, but he has refrained from openly endorsing it. Nevertheless, at least one of his recent letters, strongly supporting the document, has found its way into print, causing him worry and anxiety. The French envoy in New York has grasped the reasons for the General's concern.

"In the uncertainty existing at this time over the success of the new plan of Constitution," observes Comte de Moustier, "the General will be pained to see that his opinion has been published, which after all that has been said on the election of a President, he will not appear to be impartial."[14]

General Washington has been subjected to persistent pleas, from home and abroad, that he agree to serve as the United States' first President. For instance, fellow delegate Gouverneur Morris of Pennsylvania, in a letter to the General last October, predicted that "... should the idea prevail that you would not accept the Presidency it would prove fatal in many Parts."[15]

The General's youthful wartime aide, Marquis de Lafayette, is reliably reported to have written from Paris since the first of the year at least two impassioned pleas. In his February 4 letter, the Marquis says that he agrees with U.S. Minister Thomas Jefferson that the new Constitution's want of a bill of rights and the powers of the Executive are grounds for worry. But with the General serving as the first President, "Every dangerous Seed Will Be a Glorious Sheet in the History of my Beloved General. . . ."[16]

Federalists apparently not only view General Washington's hero status as crucial in carrying ratification, but also see his acceptance of the Presidency as one way to refute the argument of Anti-Federalists that the powers of the new, novel office are comparable to those of the King of England

Nine days after adjournment of the Philadelphia Convention, the first public statement predicting that the General would be selected as the first President was made in the *Pennsylvania Gazette*.

"While the deliverers of a nation in other countries," the newspaper wrote on September 26, "have hewn out a way to power with the sword, or seized upon it for stratagems and fraud, our illustrious Hero peaceably retired to his farm after the war. . . .—Can Europe boast of such a man?—or can the history of the world shew an instance of such a voluntary compact between the *Deliverer* and the *delivered* of any country, as will probably soon take place in the United States."[17]

Besides possessing world renown as the military leader who defeated the armies of King George III, General Washington has an unequivocal record as a vocal opponent of monarchy.[18] Anti-Federalist predictions that the powers of the President will become as extensive as those of the monarchy of England are not likely to prove persuasive. During the last decade, moreover, whenever the Continental Congress or the States appeared unable to resolve a crisis, some advocated monarchy as a solution. Federalist writers also used the threat of a monarchy to obtain a hearing for a stronger central government.[19]

During the Philadelphia Convention, delegates were reportedly sensitive to the charge that the secret conclave was intent on creating an American King. Nevertheless, one observer has concluded that during the deadlocked debate over the shape of the Executive, when Maryland delegate John Mercer recorded 20 delegates favoring a monarchy, rumors may have been deliberately circulated to test public opinion.[20]

Also, South Carolina delegate Pierce Butler has revealed that the powers of the President would not have been so great "had not many of the members cast their eyes towards General Washington as President; and shaped their Ideas of the Powers to be given to a President, by their opinions of his Virtue."[21]

CHAPTER 27

★

March 21–27, 1788

Seafaring Rhode Island sent a defiant shot across the bow of its sister States' ship this week when, in overwhelming numbers, voters scuttled ratification of the new Constitution.

Returns from a popular State-wide referendum held March 24 reveals that of the 6,000 eligible Rhode Island voters, 2,945 rejected ratification, and only 237 voted for adoption.[1]

Because an overwhelming defeat in Rhode Island was widely anticipated, according to one observer, Federalist leaders in the State instructed their supporters to stay away from the polls. So effective was the boycott that the balloting in the Newport and Providence town meetings recorded only 12 votes for ratification in both cities.[2]

John Collins, the Rhode Island Governor, a supporter of ratification, wrote to the President of the Continental Congress in New York that the calamitous rejection was designed not "to give any Offence to the respectable Body who composed the Convention," but to express the view of the "people in general," who prefer the known Articles of Confederation to the unknown new Constitution.[3]

Few New England Federalists, before this week's vote of rejection, went out of their way to try and influence Rhode Island to reverse its militant opposition to ratification. Last week, however, Connecticut's Oliver Ellsworth, writing as "The Landholder" in the March 17 issue of the Hartford *Connecticut Courant*, lashed out against the Anti-Federalist majority over its persistent support of paper money.

"The distress," Judge Ellsworth wrote, "to which many of your best citizens are reduced—the groans of ruined creditors, of widows and orphans demonstrates that unhappiness follows vice, by the unalterable laws of nature and society. I did not mention the stings of conscience, but the authors of public distress ought to remember that there is a world where conscience will not sleep."[4]

In the last two weeks, Rhode Island has been the target of unrelenting criticism by its sister States for issuing large amounts of unsecured paper. According to one observer, "the paper money scheme" has driven its currency down in value to seven or eight cents on the Spanish dollar. He suggests, however, that the critics of the State have overstated, for political reasons, the amount of fraud and corruption involved in these policies.[5]

Rhode Island's paper-money policy and its political system of direct democracy have been held up by critics as evil examples to show why the new national government of representation, or republicanism, is preferable. One observer maintains that the State does not deserve more than one-tenth of the mud thrown in its direction recently.[6]

Since founded by religious nonconformist Roger Williams, the State has been a practitioner of direct democracy and a haven for persecuted Puritans, Jews, and Quakers. One source reports that the State's Quakers, despite their specific prohibition against involvement in secular political activities, have waded into the paper-money war.

Last month Rhode Island Quakers submitted a petition to the State Legislature denouncing the depreciation of paper money and calling for repeal of the laws that make the near-worthless currency legal tender. Federalists have since charged that Anti-Federalists concluded a political deal whereby the Quakers would maintain silence on their paper-money repeal proposal in exchange for Anti-Federalist support for outlawing the slave trade in Rhode Island.[7]

The Constitution was published last year and since then Quakers throughout the States have criticized the document because it extends slavery until 1808. Rhode Island Quakers see abolition in their State as essential because it is from the seaports of Providence and Newport that ships set out to ply the African slave trade. Quakers, along with other antislavery groups, since October of last year, have been working to prohibit the trade in five States with the clear prospect of success by the fall of 1788.[8]

For the clergy of other faiths, working for an end to the slave trade, the Constitution presents a conflict between principle and practical politics. For example, Congregational clergyman Samuel Hopkins, in Newport, Rhode Island, believes that the 20-year extension of the slave trade by the Philadelphia Convention will curse the country in the future if efforts are not now made to end it.

"At the same time it appears to me," he says, "that if this constitution be not adopted by the States, as it now stands, we shall have none, and nothing but anarchy and confusion can be expected. —I must leave it with the Supreme Ruler of the universe, who will do right, and knows what to do with these States. . . ."[9]

Dr. Benjamin Rush, Signer of the Declaration of Independence, reported late last month that efforts by the Anti-Federalists to gain support from Quakers for defeat of the Constitution by using the slavery clause have been met with silence and contempt.

He maintains the Quakers are solidly in favor of ratification because they "consider very wisely that the Abolition of slavery in our country must be gradual in order to be effectual, and that Section of the Constitution which will put it in the power of Congress twenty years hence to restrain it altogether, was a great point obtained from the Southern States. . . .

". . . If it [the Constitution] held forth no other advantages," adds the prominent Philadelphia physician, "that a future exemption from paper money & tender laws, it would be eno to recommend it to honest men."[10]

In the absence of a detailed voter analysis of the returns from Rhode Island this week, it is difficult to determine what specific role the slavery and paper-money issues played in the overwhelming rejection of ratification. Federalist leader James Madison of Virginia is reported to believe that the paper-money issue played a principal role in the outcome.[11]

Cyrus Griffin of Virginia, the Contintental Congress President, told Congressman Madison in a letter this week, a copy having been obtained by this correspondent, that Rhode Island's rejection is symptomatic of trouble for the Constitution in other States. New Hampshire has adjourned until June without a decision. Massachusetts ratified by only 19 votes, "formidable opposition" exists in New York and Virginia, and in Pennsylvania a vocal minority is working to reverse that State's affirmative ratification vote—all of which "operating together," an apprehensive President Griffin grimly concludes, "will prevent the noble fabrick from being enacted."[12]

Mr. Madison has recently returned to Virginia from New York to stand for election as a delegate to the Virginia ratifying Convention, slated to convene in Richmond the first week in June. He reports this week that he is chagrined to find his home county "filled with the most absurd and groundless prejudices against the fœderal Constitution. I was therefore obliged . . . to mount for the first time in my life, the rostrum before a large body of the people, and to launch into a harangue of some length in the open air and on a windy day."[13]

Although Mr. Madison was absent for most of the campaign, he is reported this week to have won over three opponents, to the surprise and delight of Virginia Federalists. However, one observer reports that since his return, local residents have told him that last summer's severe drought in the State and the savage winter have produced hard economic conditions that may have a direct bearing on ratification.[14]

A promise that the new Constitution will cure the real, and imagined, economic problems facing the country is being pressed by advocates of ratification in Virginia, as well as in neighboring North Carolina, slated to begin electing delegates to a State ratifying Convention next week.

Hugh Williamson, North Carolina delegate to the Philadelphia Convention, etched, for example, a bleak economic portrait under the current Articles of Confederation: a shortage of hard money, proliferation of paper money, loss of trade, a swollen domestic and foreign debt, and lack of money to pay troops to guard the American frontiers from foreign troublemaking.

"The proposed system," the 53-year-old North Carolina lawmaker observed to residents of his State, "is now in your hands, and with it the fate of your country. We have a common interest, for we are embarked in the same vessel. At present she is in a sea of troubles, without sails, oars or pilot; ready to be dashed into pieces by every flaw of wind. You may secure a port, unless you think it better to remain at sea."[15]

Although the Constitution was advanced as an instrument for economic reform, Anti-Federalists assert that its advocates have misrepresented, if not distorted, the actual state of the nation's economy under the Articles. Writing as the "Federal Farmer," Richard Henry Lee, former Congressman of Virginia, maintains that many of the economic problems facing the country are consequences of the War of Independence and require time to remedy.

"We are hardly," insists the 56-year-old Signer of the Declaration of Independence, "recovered from a long and distressing war: The farmers, fishmen, &c. have not yet fully repaired the waste made by it. Industry and frugality are again assuming their proper station. Private debts are lessened, and public debts incurred by the war have been, by various means, diminished; and the public lands have now become a productive source for diminishing them much more. I know uneasy men, who wish very much to precipitate, do not admit all these facts: but they are facts well known to all men who are thoroughly informed in the affairs of this country."[16]

Just as the War of Independence with Great Britain split families into loyalist and patriot camps, the Constitution has created political cleavages between father and son. For example, John Adams, until recently the U.S. Minister to Great Britain, is a strong public advocate of the new Constitution. Whereas his 20-year-old son, John Quincy, opposes it, disputing Federalist arguments that only the Constitution can cure the country's economic ills.

". . . our situation it is true," he writes, "is disagreeable; but it is confessedly growing better every day, and might very probably be prosperous in a few years without any alteration at all, but even if some alteration be *necessary*, where is the necessity of introducing a *despotism*, yes, a *despotism:* for if there shall be any limits to the power of the federal Congress, they will only be such as they themselves shall be pleased to establish."[17]

John Adams, after nearly ten years of diplomatic service in Europe, is reported this week to be on his way back to America. Although the Signer of the Declaration of Independence from Massachusetts has been removed from domestic politics during this past decade, his published writings have kept his name before the American public.

Earlier this year the second volume of his *A Defence of the Constitutions of the Governments of the United States* went on sale in America and the third volume is due out this spring. While widely praised, the work has also been attacked by critics on this side of the Atlantic for its admiration of the British constitution. James Madison's father, a Virginia planter, believes that Minister Adams' writings indicate that he has spent too much time among the monarchies of Europe and that he maintains a bias for a monarchy for his own country.[18]

James Madison, the son, is equally critical of *A Defence*. In a letter last year to Thomas Jefferson in Paris, Mr. Madison acknowledged that the work excited a good deal of attention during the Philadelphia Convention and revived admiration in America for the British political system.

"Men of learning," observed Mr. Madison, who himself reads Greek, Latin, and Hebrew, "find nothing new in it. Men of taste, many things to criticize. And men without either, not a few things, which they will not understand. It will nevertheless be read, and praised, and become a powerful engine in forming the public opinion."[19]

Since it has become known that Minister Adams is returning home from London, his family, friends, and supporters are beginning to promote his political future as Vice President if the new national government is approved by the required nine States. His daughter, Abigail Adams Smith, wrote from London last month scolding her brother John Quincy for wishing that their father come home to retirement and his books.

"... the Americans in Europe say he will be Elected Vice President—besides my Brother independant of other important Considerations—he would not I am well Convinced be Happy in Private Life....—he is of opinion that some *new* form of Government for our Country is necessary—he does not wholy approve of the one which has been offered—but he thinks that the People had better adopt it as it is—and then appoint a new Convention to make such alterations as may prove necessary."[20]

One observer has told this correspondent that Minister Adams has been less than candid with the American public as to his actual views of the Constitution. While praising it in public and to Federalist leaders like James Madison, in private he has sided with Anti-Federalists in supporting a bill of rights and a second Convention.[21]

Next to outright defeat of the Constitution, Federalists fear that a second Convention will wreck the work of the first. Should Minister Adams' inconsistent views become known to the de facto intellectual leaders of the Federalists, Congressman Madison might use his influence with General Washington to frustrate Mr. Adams' political ambitions for high office in the new national government. Mr. Madison already has a decidedly negative opinion, alleging that Mr. Adams wants the Presidency for himself while "he has made *himself obnoxious to many*, particularly in the *Southern states by the political principles avowed in his book.*"[22]

CHAPTER 28

★

March 28–April 3, 1788

Federalist storm-warning flags went up this week in the Chesapeake Bay States of Maryland, Virginia, and North Carolina as election returns in two of the States forecast hazardous conditions for the Constitution.

Returns this week from North Carolina's election of delegates to its ratifying Convention reveal that opponents of the document scored a two-to-one "landslide," virtually ensuring Anti-Federalist domination when the conclave meets in late July. According to one observer, Federalists are dismayed but not surprised by the outcome of the balloting, blaming defeat on "3 or 4 designing Men, of influence in the back Counties."[1]

North Carolina's election returns follow the pattern in other States that have thus far considered the new Constitution. Federalist support and strength generally have come from the cities and seacoast commercial interests, whereas Anti-Federalist opposition to the Constitution, without amendments, has come mostly from rural, interior agricultural areas.[2]

The State extends five hundred miles from the Atlantic coast to the Blue Ridge Mountains, and beyond them almost four hundred miles to the Mississippi River. Imperial Spain's closing of the waterway to American commerce and navigation has led to the charge by Patrick Henry of Virginia, widely believed in North Carolina, that adoption of the Constitution will mean a renunciation of American access to the river. Equally important is the fear of settlers in the interior of the State that they will lose their lands if the Constitution is ratified, particularly if the Western areas became separated from the States.[3]

General George Washington this week denounced as "unfair and unjust" the Anti-Federalist charge that settler lands and access to the Mississippi will be lost if the Constitution is adopted. He insists the argument was used in the just-concluded month-long delegate elections in Virginia to "inflame the passions" of the "ignorant" as a way to prejudice voters in the frontier interior of the State against the document.[4]

The General conceded in an April 2 letter from Mount Vernon, a copy having been obtained by this correspondent, that New Hampshire's late February postponement of a decision until June ". . . has entirely baffled all calculation upon the subject, and will strengthen the opposition in this State."[5]

At this writing, it is a matter of speculation how much actual influence the surprise New Hampshire postponement has had on Virginia's just-concluded election of Convention delegates. However, one observer reports that Virginia Federalists are particularly alarmed at the setback, fearing it has boosted Anti-Federalist morale as well as, perhaps, indicated that their ideas are beginning to take hold.[6]

One Virginia Federalist, elected as a delegate to the Richmond ratifying Convention, slated to meet in June, has written Congressman James Madison asking him to urge his friends in Maryland and South Carolina to resist Anti-Federalists' efforts to have both States follow New Hampshire's example. Maryland will hold its Convention later this month and South Carolina in May.

". . . The adjournment of the New-Hampshire convention," observes George Nicholas, "puts an end to the hope that nine will adopt before the meeting of our convention, but it will be a great matter to have the sanction of eight states. Maryland and South-Carolina are the only ones which are now to meet. . . ."[7]

One observer reports that the election returns from Virginia reveal that neither friends nor foes have captured a large delegate majority like that piled up in neighboring North Carolina. The questionable strength of the document's critics and of its advocates in Virginia clearly offers a confused, uncertain outlook.[8]

However, the Virginia elections were polite drawing-room contests compared to the bare-knuckles conduct of both sides in neighboring North Carolina.

One source reports, for example, that at a Dobbs County polling station, fists and curses were exchanged. In the riotous darkness, with candles knocked over, the sheriff was "knocked almost senseless," and the ballot box he was guarding carried away, whereupon a Federalist was heard to cry: "Well done, Boys, now we'll have a new Election."[9]

Federalists then appealed to Governor Samuel Johnston to order a special election, and he promptly complied. Later, when the broken ballot box was found, and the spilled ballots retrieved and counted, both sides asserted that their candidates would have been elected.[10]

During the heated campaign, unsubstantiated stories were circulated that Anti-Federalist leader Willie Jones had denounced General Washington as a *"damned rascal, and traitor to his country, for putting his hand to such an infamous paper as the new Constitution."*[11]

The influential Anti-Federalist leader denied in the North Carolina press that he ever made such a statement. Mindful of the General's prestige and the potentially damaging effect of the charge by Federalists, Willie Jones went out of his way to praise Washington in print as "the first and best character in the world."[12]

Just as Federalists are using Washington's name and fame in their war of words, Anti-Federalists in North Carolina are countering with Patrick Henry. He is reported to have been in touch with foes of the Constitution in the State. Each side is counting on outside influences.

According to another observer, this is why the two sides in North Carolina agreed to delay their State's ratifying Convention until late July. Each side believes that by summer, decisions by every other State are likely to aid its cause.[13]

If North Carolina is divided between seacoast commercial interests and interior settlers-farmers, divisions also exist along debtor and creditor lines. Debtors, and those denounced as dishonest and cunning, favor paper money, while creditors support the hard-money position of the Constitution.[14]

Most North Carolina farmers are convinced, moreover, that the Constitution was created to benefit the Eastern commercial interests at the expense of the Westerners, who believe they will be forced to pay higher taxes to support a fleet and a standing army to protect American commerce.[15]

Similar sectional differences surfaced in the just-concluded Virginia delegate elections. Federalists nearer the seacoast easily won seats to the June ratifying Convention in Richmond. Elections farther inland proved to be hotly contested, and in the far west Kentucky territory, Anti-Federalists took nearly all the contests.

One observer concludes that Virginia Anti-Federalists have fought the Federalists to a standstill in the older parts of the State and have won over settlers in Kentucky. The credit for this is being given to Patrick Henry's persistent campaign of criticism of the document.[16]

Congressman Madison readily concedes in a letter to General Washington that Patrick Henry's "torch of discord" turned Kentucky into a flashpoint and should Maryland and South Carolina reject ratification or postpone, the impact in Virginia might prove fatal.

". . . The difference between even a postponement and adoption in Maryland," he adds, "may in the nice balance of parties here [in Virginia], possibly give a fatal advantage to that which opposes the Constitution."[17]

Mr. Madison himself narrowly won election in his home district of Orange. Friends had warned him that unless he exerted himself by personally campaigning and by lobbying a key Baptist leader, he faced defeat. The Baptists in the State had almost embraced the Anti-Federalists' belief that the Constitution posed a peril to religious liberty because it lacked a bill of rights.[18]

Opponents of Mr. Madison derived most of their support from Baptists. However, his supporters reminded them that in 1786 he had led the successful fight in the State for passage of the Virginia Statute for Religious Freedom. One observer believes that this argument, and his hour-and-three-quarter speech on the Orange Court House steps in the bitter cold and snow before the county's only poll opened, won him his narrow victory.[19]

Federalists were both surprised and relieved, agreeing that Mr. Madison is the only person in Virginia, if not in the country, who can challenge Patrick Henry in the forthcoming ratification Convention in Richmond. Cyrus Griffin, President of the Continental Congress in New York, confirmed this widely held opinion when he wrote Mr. Madison, "We all much rejoiced to hear of your election" for you are "absolutely necessary to counter-act" the Anti-Federalists, headed by Patrick Henry.[20]

The former five-term Virginia Governor easily won election in his district, Prince Edward County. George Mason and James Monroe also secured seats. Each represents a faction in the Anti-Federalist opposition. Governor Henry and Colonel Mason represent the militants, and Colonel Monroe the moderates.

Anti-Federalists are counting on the election of Virginia's current Governor, Edmund Randolph, as an endorsement of their principles.[21] Governor Randolph, along with Colonel Mason, refused to sign the new Constitution in Philadelphia.

However, one source maintains that Mr. Madison, by a series of secret letters over the last few months, may have converted Governor Randolph to the Federalist cause. In these letters Mr. Madison has allegedly questioned the motives of the opponents of the Constitution, arguing that the real aim of Patrick Henry is disunion.

Mr. Madison is confident that Governor Randolph will stand with the Federalists when the Convention meets in Richmond during the first week in June, but the question remains what role he might play at the crucial political conclave.[22]

"The Governor is so temperate in his opposition and goes so far with the friends of the Constitution that he cannot properly be classed with its enemies," Congressman Madison confidently wrote to Thomas Jefferson in Paris shortly after Governor Randolph's election as a delegate.[23]

A reliable source reports that Mr. Madison has not been alone in his efforts to convert Governor Randolph from his position of calling for a second Convention to secure amendments before ratification, as demanded by Patrick Henry, George Mason, and other Anti-Federalists.

On January 8, General Washington, either on his own or at the urging of Mr. Madison, wrote to the Governor an adroit, persuasive letter designed to win him entirely over as an advocate of the document he had refused to sign.[24]

"To my Judgement," General Washington wrote his former military aide-de-camp, "it is more clear than ever, that an attempt to amend the Constitution which is submitted, would be productive of more heat and greater confusion than can well be conceived. . . . it is the best Constitution that can be obtained at this Epocha, and that this, or a dissolution of the Union awaits our choice, and are the only alternatives before us."[25]

The weight of General Washington's warning of "disunion" and of Governor Randolph's memory of military service at the side of his hero may carry more influence than all the finely woven arguments of James Madison.

CHAPTER 29

★

April 4–10, 1788

Maryland Federalists swept to an overwhelming victory this week in delegate elections to the April 21 ratifying Convention in Annapolis, amid Anti-Federalist charges of "fraud" and "ballot box stuffing."[1]

One observer reports that both sides in Baltimore "manipulated the polls shamelessly." When the voting was over, the Federalists led shipbuilders and merchants in a victory parade of several thousand.[2]

Anti-Federalists are charging that in the port city of Baltimore foreign seamen, armed with clubs, intimidated citizens, "chiefly Germans," keeping them from voting while nonresidents were allowed to vote. The charge of fraud, one observer tells this correspondent, is one way to bolster Anti-Federalist morale after their staggering defeat.[3]

After a three-month campaign in Baltimore, Annapolis, and the Maryland countryside, Federalists swept fifteen counties, whereas only two went solely with the Anti-Federalists.[4]

Late last year the Maryland Legislature set the first week in April for delegate elections, and Federalists have since been fearful that vocal Anti-Federalists in the State would wage a close contest. But the unconfirmed vote results show that when the Annapolis Convention meets, Federalists are expected to have 64 delegates to the Anti-Federalists' 12.[5]

If such a commanding majority holds up in official returns, it is almost a certainty that Maryland will ratify the new Constitution and become the seventh State to approve.

Even last-minute thundering in the press by Maryland's Anti-Federalist Attorney General, Luther Martin, failed to hold back the Federalist tide.

In the *Maryland Journal* of March 28, for example, Mr. Martin warned that "the whole history of mankind proves" that government, once granted power, works to expand it at the expense of rights reserved to people, until they end in slavery. A sane person would indignantly reject poison offered by a physician to cure a physical disorder, he said.

"... With the same indignation ought you, my fellow-citizens," Attorney General Martin counseled, "to reject the advice of those *political quacks*, who, under pretence of healing the disorders of our present government, would urge you *rashly to gulp down* a constitution, which, in its present form, unaltered and unamended, would be as certain death to your liberty, as *arsenick* would be to your bodies."[6]

One observer tells this correspondent that despite a steady stream of newspaper essays, plus some entertaining tavern speeches on court days, the Anti-Federalists' failure in Maryland can be traced to their "ineptness" in failing to master the election process, relying almost entirely on public speeches and published articles.[7]

Nevertheless, Federalists in both Maryland and Virginia are still worried that their opponents might play one remaining card. The Maryland Convention has been empowered by the State Assembly to adjourn from day to day until the results of the Virginia Convention, set for June, are known.

General George Washington and Congressman James Madison have repeatedly warned about the employment of this tactic, lest it should boost the morale of Virginia Anti-Federalists and give them "a fatal advantage."[8]

Federalists know they cannot risk another adjournment, as they had in New Hampshire during late February. The political momentum for ratification would be lost if a second State voted for adjournment.

Luther Martin and a few other Maryland Anti-Federalists may have personal reasons for not wanting the Constitution adopted; their own financial positions might be threatened. After defeat of the British, Mr. Martin and other well-known families purchased at bargain prices extensive land that had been confiscated from British owners and they paid for it with depreciated State currency.

Adoption of the document would pose a direct threat to those in

Maryland who engaged in such dealings, according to one observer, since the new Constitution might allow British property owners to sue for return of their confiscated lands.[9]

Maryland Federalists effectively used these issues during the recent delegate elections to discredit their militant opponents.

Meanwhile, in Pennsylvania charges of another form are being made, this time by Anti-Federalists. In recent weeks they have waged a savage campaign in the press alleging that prominent supporters of the Constitution have mounted a conspiracy "to defraud the public out of the millions lying in the hands of individuals by the construction of this system, which would, if established, cancel all debts now due to the United States."[10]

This explosive charge was first made last February and was repeated March 24 in the Philadelphia *Independent Gazetteer* by "Centinel." According to the essayist, Dr. Benjamin Franklin conspired with others at the Philadelphia Convention to include in the document an *ex post facto* clause to allow individuals and States to default on owed war debts.

"The discovery of the intended fraud," "Centinel" charged, "which for magnitude and audacity, is unparalleled, must open the eyes of the deluded to the true character and principles of the men who had assumed the garb of patriotism, with an insidious design of enslaving and robbing their fellow-citizens. . . ."[11]

The allegations appear as part of a determined Anti-Federalist effort to discredit signers and supporters of the document and at the same time to overturn the ratification vote of Pennsylvania. Only weeks after its approval last December, a petition drive was launched in six western counties demanding the Pennsylvania Assembly not confirm ratification. Last week, the legislative body adjourned without acting on the petition with 6,005 signatures.[12]

Of all the States, Pennsylvania has thus far become the most bitter battleground between friends and foes of the new Constitution. Newspapers favoring one side or the other have been the primary weapons in this war of words in which truth has been the first casualty. According to one source, for example, both Federalists and Anti-Federalists have had printers publish forged or faked letters.[13]

Dr. Benjamin Franklin, America's most famous printer, is alarmed at "the spirit of rancor, malice, and *hatred*" carried on by the State's newspapers during the last seven months of the ratification debate.

In an essay titled "On the Abuse of the Press," prepared for the Philadelphia *Pennsylvania Gazette*, which he founded in 1729, the 82-year-old philosopher called on printers to be more discreet about what they published. Ironically, the *Gazette* refused to publish his essay.[14]

Although Dr. Franklin continues to serve as President of Pennsylvania, he has not been active in the State in championing the document since publication of the Constitution last September, nor has he attempted overtly to use his enormous prestige to influence other States. Nevertheless, newspapers favoring ratification never miss an opportunity to link his name with General Washington's as favoring ratification.[15]

A reliable source also reports that since his daily participation last summer in the Constitutional Convention (he never missed a day's session), Dr. Franklin's health has steadily declined. Unable to attend meetings of the Pennsylvania Council since early January, Dr. Franklin admitted to a friend on February 11 that he had been "very ill with a severe fit of the [bladder] stone which followed a fall I had on the stone steps . . . whereby I was much bruised and my wrist sprained, so as not to be capable of writing for several weeks."[16]

The *Federal Gazette* just this week published an essay authored by Dr. Franklin, or one that had been written for him. In the April 8 issue of the Philadelphia newspaper, he draws parallels between the dissent Moses encountered after delivering the Ten Commandments from Mount Sinai and the current opposition to the new Constitution.

"On the whole it appears," he wrote in part, "that the Israelites were a People jealous of their newly-acquired Liberty . . .; they suffer'd to be work'd upon by artful Men, pretending Public Good; with nothing really in view but private Interest, they were led to oppose the Establishment of the *New Constitution*, whereby they brought upon themselves much Inconvenience and Misfortune."[17]

Dr. Franklin may have been moved to use the biblically based argument to counter efforts to overturn Pennsylvania's ratification vote and to cool the politically overheated climate in the State.

Last month, for instance, Militiamen from several counties in the Carlisle area, said to number 5,000, marched to the town and demanded the release from jail of seven Anti-Federalists who were arrested last December for allegedly inciting a riot in the wake of the State's ratification vote. They had refused parole and insisted on having their case heard. According to one source, an "accommodation" was reached and the imprisoned men were released and the charges later dropped.[18]

Since the Carlisle riot, both sides have talked of substituting weapons for words. One observer says that the Federalists actually fear an armed outbreak from their adversaries. An unnamed Federalist has been quoted as declaring that five thousand lives would be "a small sacrifice, a cheap purchase for the establishment of the new constitution."[19]

Anti-Federalists insist that unless a second Federal convention is called to enact amendments in the form of a bill of rights, the nation will soon witness "all the horrors of a civil war."[20]

These statements and allusions to a civil war have not persuaded the de facto intellectual leader of the Federalists, James Madison. He has made it clear that he believes a second convention "would be wholly abortive" of the first. He also believes that some Anti-Federalists who are promoting such a scheme "secretly aim at disunion."[21]

Despite this week's smashing Federalist election victory of delegates in Maryland, Congressman Madison in an April 10 letter to General Washington warns that the danger of postponement at the Annapolis Convention is still very real. He enclosed a letter he has written to a mutual friend in Maryland warning of the danger, and asked the General to put a postal wafer on it and forward his letter to the address of their friend.[22] With the letter going by way of Mount Vernon, General Washington will be endorsing the letter's contents, without signing his name to it.

Until now, General Washington has refrained from intervening directly in the ratification debates and process. Apparently he is taking Mr. Madison's concerns to heart and a source reports that he is prepared to urge his "Maryland friends" to prevent Anti-Federalists from postponing the Annapolis Convention, which he believes would be equivalent to a rejection.[23]

At this date, it is not clear how much weight General Washington contributed to the Federalist sweep this week in neighboring

Maryland. One observer says that personal influences played almost no role in the Anti-Federalist defeat, but that issues dominated and dictated the election outcome. Voters, he says, chose those delegates who reflected their own views.[24]

In Pennsylvania and Massachusetts, the foremost members of the bar were, it was alleged, ready to "browbeat" less learned voters to accept the document. In Maryland, by contrast, the Anti-Federalist ranks were made up almost exclusively of men from the legal profession. According to one observer, while some plain men of the soil sought election as delegates in Maryland, most of the candidates were lawyers with long experience in politics, with the single goal of defeating ratification.[25] Luther Martin and Samuel Chase were among them. Apparently political experience clashed with the election process; voters' minds were more on issues than on the men themselves.

Ironically, when the new Constitution was framed by the 55 delegates in Philadelphia last summer, 34 were lawyers.[26]

CHAPTER 30

★

April 11–17, 1788

South Carolina Federalists sank Anti-Federalists' hopes for watering down or scuttling the new Constitution by piling up this week a two-to-one majority in the election of delegates to the May 12 State ratification Convention.[1]

The defeat was compounded by a bizarre development in the wake of this week's balloting. The most articulate Anti-Federalist leader made it known, despite his election to the ratifying Convention, that he will refuse to take his seat.

Rawlins Lowndes, a prominent Charleston lawyer, judge, and former President of South Carolina, broke ranks with the ruling seacoast establishment and almost alone represented the Anti-Federalist opposition when the Constitution was first debated by the State Legislature earlier this year.[2]

The South Carolina House of Representatives took up the issue of the Constitution on January 16 and debated setting a date for delegate elections, and the time and place for a ratifying Convention. However, the session turned into a fierce three-day denunciation and defense of the document.

Judge Lowndes stunned the packed assembly when he denounced the powers granted to the Federal Senate and President in the Constitution as comparable to, and even exceeding, those of the monarchs of Europe.

"Now, in the history of the known world," he asked, "was there an instance of the rulers of a republic being allowed to go so far? Even the most arbitrary kings possessed nothing like it."[3]

General Charles Cotesworth Pinckney, a South Carolina delegate to the Philadelphia Convention, rose in rebuttal. He rejected Judge

Lowndes' assertion that the new Congress would be dominated by Northern numbers and imperil the South in general and South Carolina in particular by the regulation of trade and the making of treaties.

"The comparison made between kings and our President was not a proper one," added General Pinckney. "Kings are, in general, hereditary, in whose appointment the people have no voice; whereas in the election of our President, the people have a voice. . . ."4

Despite rebuttal by four other Federalists, Judge Lowndes stubbornly stood his ground. The new Constitution is an experiment, he said, and warned that when it is adopted "the sun of the Southern States would set, never to rise again." He then singled out the slavery clause in the document that permits continuance of the traffic until 1808.

"Why confine us to twenty years, or rather why limit us at all?" Judge Lowndes asked the stunned, hushed House. ". . . this trade could be justified on the principles of religion, humanity, and justice; for certainly to translate a set of human beings from a bad country to a better, was fulfilling every part of these principles. But they [Northerners] don't like our slaves, because they have none themselves, and therefore want to exclude us from this great advantage."5

This was the first time since the ratification struggle began that a defense of slavery has been openly offered in any of the States. It also was the first time that it has been linked with an Anti-Federalist.

In Pennsylvania and the New England States, Anti-Federalist opposition to the Constitution has been, in part, because the document sanctions the continuation of the institution for two more decades and allows States the right to recover fugitive slaves.

Since Judge Lowndes' proslavery speech on January 16 in Charleston, newspapers in Southern, Mid-Atlantic, and New England States have reprinted his remarks, some expressing vigorous disagreement.

Last month, for example, the March 19 edition of the *Pennsylvania Gazette* made it clear that the Anti-Federalist minority in Pennsylvania is always a friend "to the abolition of negro slavery, and the states of Rhode-Island and Massachusetts, who consider slaves as *freed* by coming into their jurisdiction, can never expect to agree with the gentlemen in Carolina. . . ."6

South Carolina's population is estimated to be 150,000 whites and 48,000 Negroes.[7] General Pinckney maintained last January that the Philadelphia Convention, by allowing South Carolina to count its slaves as three-fifths of a person, for purposes of determining representation in the new Congress, did not concede "too much to the Eastern States, when they allowed us representation for a species of property which they have not among them. . . .

". . . I am as thoroughly convinced as that gentleman is," the General said, gesturing toward Judge Lowndes, "that the nature of our climate, and the flat, swampy situation of our country, obliges us to cultivate our lands with negroes, and that without them South Carolina would soon be a desert waste."[8]

Representatives from the interior and frontier settlements of the State may have found reason to be unnerved by General Pinckney's words. Not over slavery, but with the idea that South Carolina's delegation to the Federal Convention, composed exclusively of men from the ruling Charleston establishment, succeeded in securing the counting of a slave as three-fifths of a white person, even though their own greater numbers do not command equal representation in the South Carolina Legislature.

One observer points out that a sizable number of Anti-Federalist delegates elected this week are chiefly farmers and frontiersmen from the upcountry and middle agricultural area of the State. Many feel they have never been given their fair share in governing the State or in its delegation to last year's Federal Convention, particularly since many are also veterans of the daring and highly effective guerrilla war, led by Francis "Swamp Fox" Marion against the British after defeat of Continental troops in South Carolina in 1780.[9]

The disparity between population and representation, one source says, has grown greater for most of this decade. For example, 80 percent of the State's population lives in the interior back country, and only 20 percent lives in the three districts in the low country around Charleston. Yet the planters, merchants, and lawyers around the port city command the lion's share of the seats in the State House and Senate.[10]

Bitter resentment at this state of affairs manifested itself last January when South Carolina's House was confronted with the vote for the city in which the ratification Convention should be held. The low-country representatives favored Charleston; the back country favored Columbia. By the narrowest of votes, 76 to 75, Charleston won.[11]

The election this week of Convention delegates reflected the continuing sectional differences. An unofficial canvas by this correspondent reveals that when the Convention meets in Charleston on May 12, the Federalists will have 149 seats to 73 for the Anti-Federalists, with 121 Federalists representing 20 percent of the white population.[12]

Since the stormy meeting of the South Carolina Legislature last January, both sides have sought to enlist outside help. The Anti-Federalists have made use of Virginians Patrick Henry, Richard Henry Lee, and Colonel George Mason. Pamphlets, speeches, and protests of Anti-Federalists in Pennsylvania have also been circulated within the State, particularly in the back country.[13]

The better educated and more powerful low-country Federalists have imported and reprinted the "Publius" essays, believed to be authored by Colonel Alexander Hamilton of New York and Congressman James Madison of Virginia. One observer reports that newspaper editors in South Carolina, afraid to offend their merchant supporters, have "clamped their columns shut to Anti-Federalist essays," thereby throwing the whole influence of the press on the Federalist side.[14]

Federalists elsewhere view adoption by South Carolina and Maryland as crucial to building momentum for adoption in Virginia. A setback in these two States might imperil ratification in Virginia, which is already facing formidable opposition.

Congressman Madison just last week revealed in an April 10 letter to General George Washington that he has been in communication with allies in South Carolina "on the critical importance of a right decision there" to effect a favorable one in Virginia.[15]

Opposition in Virginia, as in both North and South Carolina, emanates from farmers and frontiersmen in the interior, especially in the Kentucky territory of Virginia. Mr. Madison reveals in a letter last week, a copy having been obtained by this correspondent, that he has also written letters to allies in Kentucky to counteract the campaign being waged there by former Virginia Governor Henry.

Mr. Madison is pessimistic about his efforts, in part because the Continental Congress in New York has refused to act on Kentucky's application to become the fourteenth State.

"There are individuals," Congressman Madison added, "who will throw obstacles in the way, till Vermont can be let in at the same time. And others, I suspect, who will do the same, with the covert view of irritating Kentucky into an opposition to the new government."[16]

The failure of the Continental Congress to act on the statehood applications of Kentucky and Vermont is viewed by Federalists as one more reason why the Constitution should be adopted.

Just this week the April 17 issue of the Fredericksburg *Virginia Herald* republished an essay that originally appeared in a Charleston newspaper, authored by "Civis." A source has revealed that the author is David Ramsay, a Federalist member of the South Carolina House of Representatives. "Civis" attacked the current Confederation.

". . . it cannot secure the payment of our debts," the essay asserts of the Confederated government, "nor command the resources of our country, in case of danger. Without money, without a navy, or the means of even supporting an army of our citizens in the field, we lie at the mercy of every invader; our sea port towns may be laid under contribution, and our country ravaged."[17]

The essay is believed to be a response to the vigorous defense of the current Confederation by Rawlins Lowndes in Charleston last January. He had insisted that it was the Articles of Confederation that had guaranteed the existence of the separate States and that "the names of those gentlemen who had signed the old Confederation were eminent for patriotism, virtue, and wisdom,—as much so as any set of men that could be found in America,—and their prudence and wisdom particularly appeared in the care which they had taken sacredly to guaranty the sovereignty of each state."[18]

With such a vigorous defense for State sovereignty, it is all the more baffling that Mr. Lowndes is abdicating his leadership of the Anti-Federalists in South Carolina and has refused to serve as an elected delegate to the forthcoming ratification Convention. One observer maintains that his friends have said he feels he "knew he had failed" last January and "accepted defeat."[19]

Anti-Federalist fortunes have suffered since last January, hastened this week by Judge Lowndes' refusal to serve. His opposition to the Constitution has become the basis for personal attacks on him, said to be unlike any in his previous political experience.[20]

His parting words last January contained a recognition that his political career was at an end because "of obstinacy in standing out against" powerful members of the aristocratic ruling seacoast Charleston establishment, of which he had once been a part.[21]

Popularity was something he never "courted," he said, and when his life ceased he wished to have inscribed this epitaph on his tomb:

"Here lies the man that opposed the Constitution, because it was ruinous to the liberty of America."[22]

CHAPTER 31

★

April 18–24, 1788

On the eve of Maryland's ratification Convention this week, General George Washington for the first time openly used his prestige and political influence to ensure defeat of an Anti-Federalist effort to prevent the Annapolis conclave from becoming the seventh State to ratify the new Constitution.[1]

His personal intervention took the form of a letter that General Washington wrote on April 20 to an old friend, Thomas Johnson, the Governor of Maryland. In it, the General warned of the danger of Anti-Federalist plans to try and postpone a ratification vote.

Governor Johnson, a delegate to the Annapolis Convention that convened on April 21, circulated the letter among delegates who overwhelmingly favor approval of the document.

In the letter, a copy of which this correspondent obtained, General Washington insists that a postponement in Maryland "will be tantamount to the rejection of the Constitution" and will have a negative impact on the outcome in South Carolina and Virginia. He accuses "leading characters of the opposition" of the intent of using postponement as "*the blow*" of a dangerous weapon to wreck the new Union.

"If in suggesting this matter," the General added defensively after maintaining for months the outward appearance of neutrality, "I have exceeded the proper limit, my motive must excuse me. I have but one public wish remaining. It is, that in *peace* and *retirement*, I may see this Country rescued from the danger which is pending. . . ."[2]

One observer reports that during the first four days of the Maryland Convention this week, a majority of the Federalist delegates were determined to ratify and General Washington's letter was only an encouragement for them to proceed swiftly on a course already charted before they convened.[3]

According to another source, the Federalists on April 21 held a nighttime caucus. They agreed to a resolution that the new Constitution should be adopted swiftly because it was unlikely, after seven months of public discussion, "any new lights could be thrown on the subject" and because "each delegate was under a sacred obligation to vote comformably to the sentiments of his constituents."[4]

Earlier this month, Federalists in State-wide delegate elections to the Annapolis Convention swept fifteen counties to the Anti-Federalists' three. The campaign was punctuated by charges that the Federalists were "secretly supported" by the French government in an effort to make George Washington a king. The foes of the Constitution also alleged that the Federalist delegate landslide was secured by fraud.[5]

Anti-Federalist leaders did not put in an appearance at the Annapolis Convention until four days after it formally opened. One observer suggests this was a political tactic, hoping the Federalist majority would swiftly ratify without dissent. This would have allowed the Anti-Federalist minority to charge later that the Convention was stampeded into approval without free debate.[6]

Governor Johnson and Federalist leaders apparently anticipated the tactic and decided on a lenient and tolerant tack. They refused to challenge the fact that four of the Anti-Federalist delegates do not reside in the counties they represent—a clear violation of the delegate rules.[7]

Moreover, when dissenters like Samuel Chase on Thursday, April 24, exceeded the two-hour time limit for single speeches, the Federalists voiced no objections and let the 47-year-old lawyer and Maryland Signer of the Declaration of Independence express his rage at the new Constitution.

The Baltimore Criminal Court judge savagely assailed practically every power of the document, insisting that it was created without legitimate authority, would destroy the State governments, alter Maryland's constitution, and annul "our Bill of Rights in many of the most essential parts.

"A national or general government," Judge Chase warned, "however constructed over so extensive a country as America must end in despotism."[8]

This will come to pass, he predicted, because "The whole Constitution breathes a jealousy of the states" and the "experience of ages" teaches that men, once in power, always attempt to increase it and never part with any part of it without force.

"It is the very nature of man," he said. "The National government will possess this desire and having the means it will in time carry it into execution. I think the people themselves will assent and may be persuaded to call for the abolition of the state governments. It is at this moment the wish of many men in America and some in this state."[9]

The majority of Federalist delegates appeared angered at Judge Chase's later assertion that a national government is "calculated for a few rich and ambitious men" and that the new Congress will not represent the people at large, "but a few rich men in each state ... only the *gentry*, the *rich* and well born will be elected," he added.[10]

According to one observer, when Judge Chase sat down, "a profound silence ensued" and after an awkward stillness persisted in the Annapolis State House, Governor Johnson rose and observed that since there was no further business before the house, the delegates might adjourn for dinner.[11]

The silence that confronted Judge Chase must have been a special source of humiliation, given his past formidable influence in Maryland politics.

The humiliation may have been compounded by the fact that although Luther Martin, the State's Attorney General, listened with approval to the two-and-a-half-hour speech, he made no move to follow his friend and Anti-Federalist ally.

Attorney General Martin, famous in the State for his "leather lungs," and as a delegate to the Philadelphia Convention last year, was stricken silent, according to an observer, by a sore throat. One spectator was quoted as saying that the condition shortened the session and "saved a great deal of time & money to the state."[12]

While the Annapolis Convention delegates refused to take Judge Chase and Attorney General Martin seriously, this was not the case with William Paca. The 47-year-old lawyer, planter, and Signer of

the Declaration of Independence is respected for his role in personally using his own fortune to help finance the War of Independence
and for framing the State's Constitution after the War.

As a former three-time Governor, he is widely admired. His opposition to the Constitution is not tainted with the allegations leveled
against both Judge Chase and Attorney General Martin, that they
profited from the post–War of Independence period and oppose the
new Constitution because it might imperil their finances and
property—gained by acquiring confiscated British property with
inflated currency.

Former Governor Paca arrived at the Annapolis Convention late
on Thursday, April 24, and immediately told an evening session of the
Convention that he had "great objections to the Constitution proposed, in its current form," and intended "to propose a variety of
amendments, not to prevent, but to accompany the ratification. . . ."[13]

One observer says that the more militant Anti-Federalists supported former Governor Paca's 26 proposed amendments as a way of
diluting the final ratification vote, which is expected within a few days.[14]

Next to adjournment without voting, Federalists fear that consideration of amendments might induce other States to reconsider
their position and even force a second convention. Several State
newspapers have printed essays from the North on the subject. At
least one of the delegate elections for the Maryland ratifying Convention turned on the question of amendments.[15]

Maryland Federalists demonstrated during their four days in
Convention that they left nothing to chance. According to one source,
they have even imported from Philadelphia Dr. Thomas Lloyd to
take notes during the sessions. However, he was actually hired to
"spy on the Maryland Convention" by Philadelphia merchant Tench
Coxe.[16]

Mr. Coxe is a close political ally of Congressman James Madison of
Virginia. But Dr. Lloyd, who took notes at the contentious Penn-
sylvania ratification Convention last year, has had little to do in
Annapolis this week except record the speeches of the foes of the
Constitution, while its friends quietly wait for their opponents to
exhaust themselves.

One Anti-Federalist delegate who gave every indication this week that he could continue forever is John F. Mercer. A 28-year-old lawyer, who was a dissenting and nonsigning delegate to the Philadelphia Convention last year, he has fiercely fought ratification both at the Annapolis Convention this week and earlier in print.

Mr. Mercer is believed to be the author of a series of essays, published since last February, signed "A Farmer," that have appeared in the Baltimore-based *Maryland Gazette.*

Less inflammatory than other Anti-Federalist pieces, an essay published just this week asserts that the thirteen States "will ever be again so happy as they were under the government of Great-Britain and since the revolution" as individual sovereign States.

The consequences for the country from the late war, Mr. Mercer went on, have been an enormous private and public debt, the corrupting influence of a disordered currency, and the unleashing of "a great revolution" in the form of a new Constitution that promises the impossible—a powerful national government of perfection to cure the imperfection inherent in State governments. All government is imperfect and representative centralized government is liable to greater corruption because the power is greater.

"The elected few," Mr. Mercer adds, "are tempted to corruption by all the emoluments of government, and by that plunder which public disorder affords—they are screened from punishment by making legislation subservient to their interested purposes ... the truth is that we aimed at, and still aim at premature public splendor and private luxury, forgetting that bodies politic, like natural bodies have their duration of manly vigor and the decline of age. . . ."[17]

Maryland Federalists have dealt with Mr. Mercer, according to one source, by ascribing his opposition to "sordid human motives" rather than political idealism. They have attributed his behavior to his anger at General Washington's repeated but unsuccessful efforts to collect an old debt.[18]

General Washington this week took a more charitable view of the Anti-Federalists in Maryland and elsewhere. Writing to a close wartime friend, General John Armstrong of Pennsylvania, he deplored what he termed the misrepresentation of the opposition and their "desire to inflame the passions and to alarm the fears" and their attempts "to vilify and debase the Characters" of those who created the new Constitution.

". . . Upon the whole," he wrote to General Armstrong, "I doubt whether the opposition to the Constitution will not ultimately be productive of more good than evil; it has called forth, in its defence, abilities which would not perhaps have been otherwise exerted that have thrown new light upon the science of Government, they have given the rights of man a full and fair discussion. . . ."[19]

CHAPTER 32

★

April 25–May 1, 1788

Anti-Federalists' volleys of verbal grapeshot failed to halt the march of the "inflexibly silent" Maryland Federalists as they voted by an overwhelming 63 to 11 this week to make the State the seventh to approve the new Constitution.[1]

Results of the April 26 Annapolis vote were dispatched by express rider to General George Washington at Mount Vernon. One source reports that the General believes the decisive vote of Maryland fortifies the political position of Virginia Federalists when they convene their own ratifying Convention in Richmond the first week in June.

Maryland Federalists had circulated at Annapolis a letter from the General warning of the peril to ratification in other States if Anti-Federalists succeeded in postponing a vote.[2]

Anti-Federalists circulated their own letter, written by Thomas Jefferson to James Madison late last year. In it the U.S. Minister to France and author of the Declaration of Independence strongly urged the inclusion of a bill of rights in the Constitution.[3]

In the closing hours of the Annapolis Convention, the Anti-Federalist minority sought to use Minister Jefferson's letter as leverage to gain adoption of a bill of rights in the form of amendments.

Before the ratification vote, William Paca, former Maryland Governor, was prevented from reading to the delegates 26 amendments he had prepared. Several Federalist delegates maintained they were elected only to approve the Constitution "as speedily as possible" and "they did not consider themselves as authorized by their constituents to consider any amendments."[4]

What followed was a day and a half of Anti-Federalist verbal volleys against the Constitution and calls for a bill of rights.

Delegate John F. Mercer, for example, is reported to have said that "four fifths of the people of Maryland are now in favor of considerable Alterations and Amendments, and will insist on them. . . ."[5]

He went on to argue that powers vested in the new Congress are of a nature most liable to abuse and, therefore, "the People have a right to be secured by a sacred Declaration, defining the rights of the Individual," much in the same way that the "People were secured against the abuse of those Powers by fundamental Laws and a Bill of Rights, under the Government of Britain and under their [State] Constitutions."[6]

Judge Samuel Chase defended both the current Confederated government of States and his own State government of Maryland.

"I am a friend to our present state government," he said, "because it is wisely calculated to secure all the civil and *religious* rights of the people and fully adequate for *all internal state* purposes, and our *state* Constitution and laws afford security to property and ample protection of the poor from abuse by the officers of our state government and from any oppression of the poor by the rich and powerful."[7]

Federalists were repeatedly asked at the Annapolis Convention to answer such assertions. However, they sat "inflexibly silent" and waited until the dissenters had exhausted themselves. The 63-to-11 vote to ratify followed. Federalists drank thirteen toasts "to speedy ratification by the remaining six [states] without amendments."[8]

Prevented thus far from presenting his amendments, former Governor Paca, who voted with the Federalist majority, then rose with his 26 amendments in hand and told the Convention that he had only given his assent "to the government under the firm persuasion, and in full confidence that such amendments would be peaceably obtained so as to enable the people to live happy under the government. . . ."[9]

In a remarkable political countermarch, 66 delegates to 7 approved the formation of a Convention committee to consider Governor Paca's proposed amendments, as well as others. One observer points out that part of the sudden turnabout may trace to three factors: fear of Anti-Federalist violence; the regard in which former Governor Paca is held; and Federalists' concern that the Annapolis Convention would appear to the public as an arrogant majority opposed to amendments to protect the rights of the people.[10]

The Federalist-dominated committee approved 13 amendments, all procedural guarantees, among them rights of jury trial, safety from unlawful search and seizure, and freedom of speech, press, and religion.

However, when the Anti-Federalists sought approval of 15 other amendments—among them curbing the powers of Congress and the President—and issuing a public report, the Federalists withdrew their support, fearing Maryland Anti-Federalists were really aiming at establishing a negative public record to be used as ammunition by their allies in Virginia.

On April 26, Federalists signed the instrument of ratification and shouted down efforts to have the full Convention consider the first 13 of the 26 amendments. A move to adjourn was quickly agreed to, leaving enraged Anti-Federalists vowing to take their amendments to the press and streets with the charge of Federalist unfairness.[11]

While Federalists in Annapolis drank toasts to their victory and watched fireworks in the Maryland capital, Anti-Federalists were discussing ways to publish their version of the Convention, which consisted mainly of their speeches, since their opponents had remained silent. But the Federalists headed off this effort by seeking out Convention reporter Thomas Lloyd and taking up a collection *"to defray his expences."* He, in turn, declared his intention *"not to publish* what he had taken down."[12]

The Anti-Federalist minority then vowed that as early as next week they would publish their own version of the Annapolis Convention in the Baltimore-based *Maryland Gazette*, including the text of the amendments turned down by the full Convention.[13]

John F. Mercer, one of the dissenters, is also preparing to publish an address to the Conventions of Virginia and New York; the latter State is expected next week to hold delegate elections to its own ratifying Convention.

Mr. Mercer, who studied law under Thomas Jefferson and was a nonsigning Maryland delegate to the Philadelphia Convention, maintains that on these "two important States, the preservation of Liberty in a great measure depends." The rejection by Federalists in Maryland of amendments, he says, should serve as a warning that supporters of the Constitution cannot be trusted.[14]

A reliable source has told this correspondent that at least one Annapolis delegate, Alexander C. Hanson, is preparing for use at the forthcoming Virginia Convention a paper detailing the Federalists' view of the Maryland Convention.

Mr. Hanson, son of the first President of the Continental Congress under the current Articles of Confederation, is convinced that Anti-Federalists in his State intend an alliance with Virginia foes of the Constitution to obtain a second convention, a new document, or alterations by amendments, "calculated to produce so much incurable mischief."[15]

The 39-year-old Maryland lawyer and former assistant secretary to General Washington reveals in the defensive rebuttal he is preparing that although the Anti-Federalists in Maryland lost the ratification vote, they won a tactical political victory in their fight for amendments in the form of a bill of rights.

One observer says that the amendments advanced at Annapolis, some for the first time at any Convention, go beyond what were accepted by the Massachusetts Convention and what were proposed, but rejected, at the Pennsylvania conclave.[16]

This same observer maintains that of the amendments, both proposed by the minority and accepted by the Convention committee, the following are most likely to gain wide acceptance if any Federal bill of rights becomes part of the Constitution:

• Limiting the powers of Congress to those expressly delegated by the document,
• Providing trial by jury and against double jeopardy,
• Ensuring against oathless warrants and general warrants,
• Providing freedom of the press,
• Prohibiting the establishment of a "national religion" and guaranteeing religious liberty,
• Ensuring the right to petition for redress of grievances.[17]

Nevertheless, General Washington said in a letter this week to his wartime aide, the Marquis de Lafayette, that he concurred with the conclusion of the French nobleman and of Minister Jefferson in Paris that a bill of rights or amendments should not be considered until after nine States have approved the Constitution.

"... For, if that acceptance shall not previously take place," he added in his April 28 letter, "men's minds will be so much agitated and soured, that the danger will be greater than ever of our becoming a disunited People."[18]

It appears that General Washington and other Federalist leaders have slowly and reluctantly come to accept the need for amendments or a bill of rights. However, they fear that a faction of the Anti-Federalists is using the issue of amendments as the way to weaken or destroy the powers of the proposed national government.

One observer maintains that the Federal Convention's failure to include a bill of rights, and its outright rejection of one when proposed in Philadelphia by Virginia's Colonel George Mason, were major political mistakes.[19]

Federalist leaders for months have argued in public and in the published essays signed "Publius" that a bill of rights is unnecessary and even dangerous.

Earlier this year, Congressman James Madison rhetorically asked whether a bill of rights was essential to liberty: "The Confederation has no bill of rights," he stated.[20]

Colonel Alexander Hamilton has argued that many of the separate States do not have a bill of rights, whereas the new Constitution itself is a declaration of rights.

"I go further, and affirm," he added, "that bills of rights ... would even be dangerous. They would contain various exceptions to powers not granted; and, on this very account, would afford a colorable pretext to claim more than were granted. For why declare that things shall not be done which there is no power to do? Why, for instance, should it be said that the liberty of the press shall not be restrained, when no power is given by which restrictions may be imposed?"[21]

These arguments, according to one observer, have failed to convince a disbelieving public. Some Federalist leaders appear blind to the fact that agreeing to a bill of rights would steal the only bolt of political lightning the Anti-Federalists have left in a storm that has raged through seven State Conventions in seven months.[22]

Federalist leaders at the conclusion this week of Maryland's Convention in Annapolis first allowed a committee to consider amendments and then drew back from seeking a full Convention vote for fear they might have a negative effect on Virginia.

George Washington's undisguised support of the Federalists in Annapolis may have played a part in their leaders' efforts to suppress the amendments issue. Moreover, all know he served as President of the Federal Convention and was the first to sign the document. And since he has not made any public statements, his views cannot be attacked.

One observer believes that not only in Maryland this week but also in the six other State Conventions that have met thus far, General Washington has been a force in the deliberations, powerful but as insubstantial as a ghost.[23]

Even Luther Martin, Maryland's Anti-Federalist Attorney General, conceded in a March 19 published essay the awesome power and influence of both General Washington and Dr. Benjamin Franklin.

"The name of Washington is far above my praise," he wrote, ". . . and may that glory which encircles his head ever shine with undiminished rays. To find myself under the necessity of opposing such illustrious characters, whom I venerated and loved, filled me with regret; but viewing the system in the light I then did, and yet do view it, to have hesitated would have been criminal. . . ."[24]

CHAPTER 33

May 2–8, 1788

New York's Federalist printers may have felt as if a blacksmith's anvil had been dropped on them when returns from the New York delegate elections this week gave Anti-Federalists over two-thirds of the 65 seats at the State ratification Convention slated to meet in Poughkeepsie June 17.[1]

It came as a painful surprise to have the foes of the new Constitution capture 46 of the 65 Convention seats. For weeks the Federalist-leaning press had been forecasting that opposition in the State was waning and the leadership of the Anti-Federalist Governor, George Clinton, was being discredited and rejected.[2]

One observer points out that Governor Clinton's public image, in the wake of the delegate elections held April 29 to May 3, is now one of great political and popular strength. No Federalist brow is more furrowed over this fact than Colonel Alexander Hamilton's.[3]

"For my own part," Colonel Hamilton wrote to Congressman James Madison, who is back in Virginia preparing for his own State ratification Convention, "the more I can penetrate the views of the Anti-fœderal party in this state, the more I dread the consequences of the non adoption of the Constitution by any of the other states, the more I fear an eventual disunion and civil war. God grant that Virginia may accede. Her example will have a vast influence on our politics."[4]

Paradoxically, if Colonel Hamilton is looking to Virginia to save the Constitution, Governor Clinton is counting on Virginia and New Hampshire to limit the powers of the document, and Anti-Federalists in both States are looking to New York. New York and Virginia will convene, and New Hampshire reconvene, their Conventions next month.

For his part, Colonel Hamilton has been hammering away at the theme that the opposition of Governor Clinton and his allies amounts to a willful desire for disunion or anarchy, and for alliances with imperial foreign powers, rather than surrender some of their own power at the State level to the proposed national government.

In reply, Governor Clinton and his supporters have charged that Colonel Hamilton and the Federalists are arrogant architects of a political "tyranny of the rich" that will be created if the Constitution is adopted.

". . . our modern federalists," asserted one Anti-Federalist during the delegate election campaign, ". . . evidently aim at nothing but the elevation and aggrandisement of a few over the many. The liberty, property, and every social comfort in the life of the yeomanry in America, are to be sacrificed at the altar of tyranny. . . ."[5]

New York Federalists managed to elect delegates from four counties clustered around the commercial center on Manhattan Island. However, in the nine counties on Long Island and up the Hudson River Valley, occupied mostly by cultivators of the soil, the Anti-Federalists swept those farming hamlets. Even upstate Albany broke away from its alliance with New York merchants and cast ballots for candidates aligned with Governor Clinton.[6]

Colonel Hamilton had earlier conceded that winning Albany would be crucial. Two weeks before the delegate elections, he had ordered shipped to Albany 60 copies of *The Federalist*, bound volumes containing the series of newspaper essays appearing since last year and reported to have been written by him and Congressman Madison of Virginia under the joint *nom de plume* "Publius."[7]

The loss of Albany and a large number of seats to the Anti-Federalists must have been a double humiliation for the 33-year-old lawyer and legislator. First, because of Governor Clinton, a bitter political foe; and second, because the series of lengthy and learned essays were orginally conceived as the way of winning the election for delegates to the New York ratification Convention.[8]

This correspondent has been told by one observer that Colonel Hamilton's essay effort has suffered the same fate as his performance at the Philadelphia Convention last year: "praised by everybody and supported by none," demonstrating that wisdom and sound policy in electoral politics are never a substitute for organization.[9]

The fundamental failure of the essays, according to another observer, is the mistaken assumption that it is necessary to convince the Anti-Federalists of the need for a strong Federal Union. What is needed, this correspondent was told, is to convince them that such a creation will not endanger their personal liberties.

A bill of rights, as demanded by the Anti-Federalists, is still being dismissed by "Publius" as unnecessary, since guarantees of personal liberties, he says, are implicit in the Constitution.[10]

During the just-concluded delegate election campaign, the "Albany Antifederal Committee" issued a detailed denunciation of the powers of the proposed Constitution and its perceived threat to the existence of the States and to personal liberties. The April 10 statement, signed openly by 26 Anti-Federalists, deplores the absence of a bill of rights.

The statement also assailed Federalists for first opposing amendments and now conceding that they might be needed upon discovering they are popular with the people. This shifting of ground and of strategy is regarded as one more example of Federalist duplicity.

". . . They now acknowledge it to be defective," the statement added, "but endeavour to prevail on the people, first to adopt it, and afterwards (like Massachusetts) trust to a recommendation for future amendments. Would it be prudent or safe for the people to surrender their dearest rights and liberties, to the discretionary disposal of their future rulers? First to make a surrender and afterwards ask for terms of capitulation."[11]

Early last month the "Albany Federal Committee" expressed hope that the New York Convention might follow the example of Massachusetts last February: approve ratification while recommending nonbinding amendments.[12]

It is this formula that New York Federalists are likely to pursue when the Convention meets next month, despite the fact that Anti-Federalists will command a majority of delegates. Colonel Hamilton believes that the Anti-Federalists in Convention will be "afraid to reject the constitution at once" lest it should create a movement by Federalists to have New York City secede from the rest of the State.[13]

"We have, notwithstanding the unfavourable complexion of things," Colonel Hamilton wrote to Gouverneur Morris in Pennsylvania, "two sources of hope—one the chance of a ratification by nine states before we decide and the influence of this upon the firmness of the [Clinton] *followers*, the other the probability of a change of sentiment in the people, auspicious to the constitution. The current has been for some time running towards it. . . ."[14]

An analysis of the raw vote total of the New York delegate election offers some support for this assertion. Whereas the Anti-Federalists captured over two-thirds of the Convention seats, the popular vote was closer. Anti-Federalists received 56 percent of the 22,088 votes cast. The State currently has a population of 238,000.[15]

The narrow popular vote margin of 2,500 may, according to an observer, render the Anti-Federalist majority soft, especially since Governor Clinton is reportedly relying almost exclusively on events in Virginia and New Hampshire to aid his position in New York. The Anti-Federalists are reported also to be disorganized and have failed to maintain close and constant communications with their allies in other States.[16]

This is not the case with the Federalist minority. Colonel Hamilton, for example, is said to be arranging for a dispatch rider to travel from Concord to Poughkeepsie, New York, as soon as the New Hampshire ratifying Convention reconvenes next month and news of the vote is available. New England and New York Federalists are predicting swift approval in New Hampshire.[17]

Federalists are also confident that with Maryland's approval last week and South Carolina's expected approval sometime this month, New Hampshire, not Virginia, has the best chance of becoming the ninth State to approve the Constitution and give it legal life.

If this should happen, the New York Anti-Federalist majority might be faced with terms dictated by the Federalist minority. According to one observer, the nineteen elected Federalist delegates are superior in argument and debate; opponents of the new Constitution, with one or two exceptions, will be no match for Colonel Hamilton, Robert R. Livingston, who was on the committee that drafted the Declaration of Independence, or John Jay, the Secretary of Foreign Affairs of the current Confederated government, plus others well known in New York politics.[18]

★

Colonel Hamilton is still concerned that Anti-Federalists in New York and Virginia could keep two of the largest and most important States out of the new Federal Union. Rhode Island and North Carolina have already given indications of going their own independent way. Without New York or Virginia in the Union, it is a moot point whether the new national government could become a reality.

His anxiety may have been lessened by the confident prediction of Gouverneur Morris that he has no doubt that Virginia will ratify, principally because of the overwhelming influence of General Washington.

Last week the stylistic penman of the Constitution wrote the General, maintaining that the ratification battle has been won and the opponents of the document routed.

". . . I am led to decide that the Opposers to the new Constitution are fewer and more feeble than they were. . . . I am mistaken if some Leaders of Opposition are not more solicitous in the present Moment how to make a good Retreat than how to fight the Battle."[19]

And for the first time, General Washington this week made his own prediction: ratification by Maryland "will have a very considerable influence upon the decision in Virginia." He believes that acceptance by such a large majority will "operate very powerfully" upon those in Virginia who have been undecided. He also reaffirmed his personal belief that he has never once doubted its being adopted in his own State.[20]

Despite this optimism, Federalists in New Hampshire, New York, and Virginia must still deal with the Anti-Federalist demands for amendments before ratification rather than after.

A preview of what can be expected at the New York Convention on the amendment issue was provided by delegate Melancton Smith. The 44-year-old New York City lawyer and merchant is one of the few Anti-Federalist delegates capable of standing up in debate against Colonel Hamilton.[21]

Writing as "A Plebeian," Mr. Smith authored a pamphlet that was reviewed in the April issue of *American Magazine*, published by Noah Webster. He argues that amendments must be a condition of ratification because "it is much to be feared, that we shall hear nothing of amendments from most of the warm advocates for adopting the new government, after it gets into operation. . . .

"... Besides," Mr. Smith states, "when a government is once in operation, it acquires strength by habit, and stability by exercise.... It steals, by insensible degrees, one right from the people after another, until it rivets its powers so as to put it beyond the ability of the community to restrict or limit it.... in forming a government, care should be taken not to confer powers which it will be necessary to take back; but if you err at all, let it be on the contrary side, because it is much easier, as well as safer, to enlarge the powers of your rulers, if they should prove not sufficiently extensive, than it is to abridge them if they should be too great."[22]

CHAPTER 34

★

May 9–15, 1788

Anti-Federalist delegates from South Carolina's farming and frontier back country, accustomed to homemade hard liquor, were courted with the best Federalist sherry and Madeira as the ratification Convention began this week in the teeming port city of Charleston.[1]

The lavish entertainment of out-of-town delegates came after the Convention was gaveled to order on May 12 at the City Hall rather than the State House. The latter was gutted by a chimney fire on February 5, coincidentally following an incendiary political debate over the new Constitution in late January.[2]

Official start of the ratifying Convention had to be delayed a day until 176 of the 236 elected delegates assembled to constitute a quorum. Perhaps one reason for the delay of some delegates and the absence of others is an outbreak of contagious smallpox in Charleston and fear of contracting the disease.

Refusing to wait for the late arrivals, the Federalist majority took command of the Conventon on May 14 with a lengthy defense by Charles Pinckney III of the new Constitution.[3]

The wealthy aristocrat at 30 was one of the youngest delegates at the Philadelphia Convention last summer. As a Congressman from South Carolina, he angered Congressman James Madison of Virginia by implying in New York last year that he had a large hand in shaping the Constitution. In support of his claim, Congressman Pinckney rushed into print the plan that he had submitted to the Constitutional Convention but that had never even been formally considered.[4]

This week, the handsome, vain, but articulate South Carolina planter-lawyer had the opportunity to awe his audience of wealthy, educated Charlestonians and the unlettered, poor back-country delegates with a display of his learning. He began by maintaining that in America political power flows from the people and that rulers are servants of the people and subject to their will.

"... How different are the governments of Europe!" he exclaimed. "There the people are the servants and subjects of their rulers; there merit and talents have little or no influence; but all the honors and offices of government are swallowed up by birth, by fortune, or by rank."[5]

While Europe offers few lessons to self-governing people on this side of the Atlantic, Congressman Pinckney maintained, Europe itself has been influenced by the American Revolution. Liberty and the "rights of mankind" would not now be pervading the kingdom of France had America not led the way.

"... Let it be therefore our boast," he told the delegates in the crowded hall, "that we have already taught some of the oldest and wisest nations to explore their rights as men; and let it be our prayer that the effects of the revolution may never cease to operate until they have unshackled all the nations that have firmness to resist the fetters of despotism."[6]

Anti-Federalist delegates from the back country appeared rankled by the reference to the awakening of the "rights of mankind" in Europe. Last January, South Carolina Federalists failed to explain to the satisfaction of critics why the new Constitution contained no bill of rights for Americans. Delegate James Lincoln maintained that it was for "liberty" that the American Revolution was waged.

"... What is liberty?" he asked. "The power of governing yourselves. If you adopt this Constitution, have you this power? No: you give it into the hands of a set of men who live one thousand miles distant from you. Let the people but once trust their liberties out of their hands, and what will be the consequence? First, a haughty, imperious aristocracy; and ultimately, a tyrannical monarchy."[7]

A hard core of 75 Anti-Federalist delegates in Charleston regard Federalists like Congressman Pinckney as part of an "imperious aristocracy." Despite the fact that the back country of the State contains 80 percent of the population, a disproportionate number of seats in the South Carolina House and Senate are controlled by planters, merchants, and lawyers from the Charleston area, representing a population of only 20 percent.[8]

Ignoring this voter inequality, Mr. Pinckney told the Convention this week: ". . . we may congratulate ourselves with living under the blessings of a mild and equal government, which knows no distinctions but those of merits or talents—under a government whose honors and offices are equally open to the exertions of all her citizens, and which adopts virtue and worth for her own, wheresoever she can find them."[9]

If there is one essential element South Carolina Anti-Federalists cannot seem to find, it is strong leadership and an organizing principle upon which to focus their opposition. According to one observer, this is the same failure that befell the Anti-Federalists at the Pennsylvania and Massachusetts Conventions.[10]

Nevertheless, as the Convention in Charleston's crowded City Hall considered the Constitution paragraph by paragraph, the debate was forceful and heated on both sides. The Federalists not only endeavored to convert their opponents with words on the Convention floor, but also sought to woo them by wining and dining them in private after each daily session, when they could talk informally and off the record.[11]

Besides commanding a two-to-one delegate majority, Federalists have been charged with suppressing dissent in print. Opponents like delegate Aedanus Burke, for example, insist that printers in the State have shut their columns to Anti-Federalist essays, "afraid to offend the great men, or Merchants, who could work their ruin." As a result, according to the 45-year-old State Supreme Court Justice, "the whole weight and influence of the Press" is biased toward the Federalists.[12]

From New England to the South, opponents of the Constitution have made similar assertions ever since the ratification debate began eight months ago. An independent survey of the 95 newspapers now published throughout the thirteen States reveals that an overwhelming majority support the Constitution. One observer reports that less than a dozen newspapers in the entire nation support the Anti-Federalists.[13]

Since last fall, the alleged denial of access to newspapers by supporters of the Constitution has been turned into a freedom of press issue by the Anti-Federalists. Beginning this year, the issue has been broadened by allegations that the Continental post office has secretly conspired with the Federalists to waylay the distribution of Anti-Federalist newspapers.[14]

The Post-Master General, Ebenezer Hazard, has been the target of slashing published attacks after he ordered, as an economy measure, an end to the free mail delivery of newspapers. Since March, printers all over the country have not received their usual exchange of newspapers. (The exchange allows papers to publish news from all over the country.) Anti-Federalist printers see the post office policy as a Federalist plot.

The Philadelphia *Freeman's Journal* in its April 16 issue, for example, charged, "When the advocates of despotic power found their efforts to shackle the press unsuccessful" they used the post office to stop and destroy patriotic newspapers while letting those containing "delusion, deception and falsehood" to infect the continent. "It is remarkable that the same conduct was observed by Post Officers under the British government, when *foreign* tyrants endeavoured to enslave America."[15]

The Federalist *Massachusetts Centinel* in a May 7 editorial defended Post-Master Hazard, decrying the "torrent of abuse" that has poured forth from papers in New York and Philadelphia. The *Centinel* went on to assert that motives for the attacks were political: "Drowning men catch at *any thing* to keep their heads above water—So when argument has failed, those who experience the failure, will also catch at any thing to keep contention alive. . . ."[16]

Both Federalists and Anti-Federalists seized on the incendiary issue as a means to support, or savage, the Constitution. The Winchester *Virginia Gazette*, for instance, wrote on March 26: "If this is a *sample* of what we *may expect* from the establishment of the Federal Constitution, may we not with propriety say, from *such a government*, 'Good Lord, deliver us.'"[17]

In reply, a reader signing himself "A Federalist" penned the opinion that if the charge against the post office is true and the current Confederated Congress approves the abuse, "it affords an additional reason" for its dissolution and the establishment of a new national Congress as "more vigilant guardians of our liberties, than members of the present Congress."[18]

Late last week, the Committee on the Post Office of the Confederated Congress issued a report recommending restoration of the free exchange of newspapers via the mails—provided the newspapers are "thoroughly dry & the wrapper left open at one end" so it can clearly be seen if letters are contained therein.[19] But because the Congress has been unable to muster a quorum of seven States, the report, like so many other issues, is not likely to receive action.[20]

Post-Master General Hazard's economy measures affected both Federalist and Anti-Federalist printers, traced in large part to the current Confederated government's crisis of political confidence and also to its financial crisis. One source reports that the interest owed on the combined foreign and domestic debt now totals $10.1 million.[21]

This correspondent has learned from a source close to the President of the Congress, Cyrus Griffin, that a packet boat arriving from Europe carries news that Thomas Jefferson and John Adams, American Ministers, have just secured in Amsterdam the loan of one million Dutch guilders "upon the prospect of the New constitution being established. . . ."[22]

According to one observer, the Dutch loan, should a ninth State ratify the new Constitution, will give the new national government the means to put its financial house in order. Much of the credit for securing the loan, this correspondent has been advised, belongs to Minister Adams.[23]

Before leaving his diplomatic post in London for his return to this country, Mr. Adams reported: "It is expected in Europe that the new Constitution for the United States will be soon adopted by all, it is a general opinion that the old one, stood in great need of a Reform, and that the projected Change, will be much for our Prosperity."[24]

Many Federalists believe that the new Constitution will not only help improve the domestic economy but also provide the powers needed to deal with the swollen domestic and foreign debt. Trade with Europe is also expected to improve under the new national government.

Yet, in many of the separate States a strong prejudice still exists among Federalists and Anti-Federalists alike against Great Britain in particular and Europe in general. At the South Carolina Convention this week, for example, Congressman Charles Pinckney III bluntly told the delegates: "Foreign trade is one of the enemies" of the country and of his State, what with the flood of foreign imports.

"I consider it as the root of our present public distress," he stated, "—as the plentiful source from which our future national calamities will flow, unless great care is taken to prevent it. Divided as we are from the old world, we should have nothing to do with their politics, and as little as possible with their commerce: they can never improve, but must inevitably corrupt us."[25]

Mr. Pinckney was apparently attempting to answer those Anti-Federalists who fear that the new Constitution is nothing but a disguised European form of monarchy along the British model.

Anti-Federalist Rawlins Lowndes, in opposing ratification in South Carolina, insisted that the new Constitution was in reality modeled on the Constitution of Great Britain and pointed out the ultimate dangers that his countrymen were exposing themselves to: ". . . and this new government came so near to it, that, as to our changing from a republic to a monarchy, it was what every body must naturally expect. How easy the transition! No difficulty occurred in finding a king: the President was the man proper for this appointment. The Senate . . . will naturally say to one another, 'You see how we are situated; certainly it is for our country's benefit that we should be all lords;' and lords they are."[26]

CHAPTER 35

★

May 16–22, 1788

South Carolina's Anti-Federalists suffered total political shipwreck this week when a packet boat arrived in Charleston from Annapolis with the news that Maryland had become the seventh State to ratify the new Constitution.[1]

Dissenting delegates from the back country, already despondent about Federalist domination of the Convention, were reported to have completely "lost heart" when the news from Maryland was announced at Charleston's City Hall. Aedanus Burke privately concedes that the news is a final blow to the Anti-Federalist cause and that "further opposition was useless."[2]

Delegate Alexander Tweed broke ranks with his back-country colleagues, arguing that unlike some of his fellow farmer-frontier delegates he would not be bound to vote against the new Constitution just because his constituents opposed it.

"We, sir, as citizens," he told the packed Convention hall, "and as freemen, have an undoubted right of judging for ourselves; it therefore behoves us most seriously to consider before we determine a matter of such vast magnitude. We are not acting for ourselves alone, but, to all appearance, for generations unborn."[3]

Picking up on the posterity theme, Charles Pinckney III rose to answer attacks on the section of the Constitution that strips the States of the power to print paper money. Maintaining that the prohibition is "the soul of the Constitution," the youthful, wealthy aristocratic Congressman and delegate to the Philadelphia Convention went on to argue that "this Constitution is not framed to answer temporary purposes," but "will last for ages—that it will be the perpetual protector of our rights and properties. . . .

"But above all," he added, "how much will this section tend to restore your credit with foreigners—to rescue your national character from that contempt which must ever follow the most flagrant violations of public faith and honesty! No more shall paper money, no more shall tender-laws, drive their commerce from our shores, and darken the American name in every country where it is known."[4]

Most of the back-country delegates believe such promised economic revival will benefit only an economic elite who helped frame the document or who have supported its ratification, those willing in the process to sacrifice personal liberties and civil rights.

Delegate Patrick Dollard reminded the Convention this week that the Constitution contains no bill of rights. His constituents "are highly alarmed" at the new government's strides toward despotism. He warned of "the political mischiefs" the document will create for the South and South Carolina, which will exceed all the plagues from the fabled poisonous box of Pandora.

". . . They say," he noted of his constituents, "it is particularly calculated for the meridian of despotic aristocracy; that it evidently tends to promote the ambitious views of a few able and designing men, and enslave the rest; . . . They say they will resist against it; that they will not accept of it unless compelled to by force of arms. . . ."[5]

The Federalist majority was clearly shaken by the angry and defiant speech, particularly the suggestion that Federalists might be forced to use "the points of bayonets" to gain Anti-Federalist compliance to the new Constitution.[6]

Thomas Sumter, guerrilla leader in the swamps of South Carolina who successfully harassed the British in 1780, followed the blood and bayonet speech with a proposal aimed at influencing Virginia more than South Carolina. The 53-year-old former Indian fighter moved that the Convention postpone a vote for five months "in order to give time for the *further consideration* of the Federal Constitution."[7]

Prepared for the postponement ploy, Federalists moved swiftly and with united counterarguments, after a heated debate, easily crushed the proposal by an 89-to-46 vote. One observer notes that although the Anti-Federalists got little political guidance from General Sumter and others, the Federalists were willing to agree to recommended amendments so the back-country delegates would not return home empty-handed.[8]

It is not likely that the back-country delegates and their constituents, many of them veterans of the guerrilla war against the British, will be satisfied with anything less than a full-fledged bill of rights. The issue has been a burr under the saddle of the Federalists, particularly in South Carolina.

Dissident delegate James Lincoln wanted to know why the new Constitution is totally silent on liberty of the press.

"... Was it forgotten?" he angrily asked. He then exclaimed: "Impossible! Then it must have been purposely omitted; and with what design, good or bad, [I leave] the world to judge. The liberty of the press was the tyrant's scourge—it was the true friend and firmest supporter of civil liberty; therefore why pass it by in silence?"[9]

General Charles Cotesworth Pinckney, cousin of the younger delegate Charles Pinckney III, insisted that the issue was fully debated by the Philadelphia Convention. "The general government has no powers but what are expressly granted to it; it therefore has no power to take away the liberty of the press. . . .

"Another reason weighed particularly, with the members from this state, against the insertion of a bill of rights," General Pinckney candidly conceded. "Such bills generally begin with declaring that all men are by nature born free. Now, we should make that declaration with a very bad grace, when a large part of our property consists in men who are actually born slaves."[10]

Anti-Federalists in South Carolina are demanding a bill of rights less from concern for slaves than from the belief that the Constitution is part of an effort to reimpose a British monarchical rule on America.

One of their leaders, Rawlins Lowndes, insists that the new Constitution is based on the model of Great Britain and "On the whole, this [is] the best preparatory plan for a monarchical government" he has said. He believes it allows for an easy transition from a republic to a monarchy, and that it is "what every body must expect."[11]

Judge Lowndes named the recently returned U.S. Minister to Great Britain, John Adams, as one of the authors of this transition.

Anti-Federalists in South Carolina and elsewhere have pointed to Mr. Adams' three-volume published work, *A Defence of the Constitutions of Government of the United States of America*, insisting it advocates a monarchical government. They also maintain that the work influenced the Constitutional Convention in Philadelphia.[12]

Since the first volume was published in England before the Convention and copies reached America just as the conclave convened, it was praised by many Federalists. However, most American newspapers attacked Minister Adams for his admiration of the British Constitution, charging that he favored the rich and the well born.[13]

It was apparently from this newspaper campaign, not from having read the books themselves, that Anti-Federalists and those particularly in South Carolina have come to believe that John Adams is the actual author of the new Constitution with its alleged monarchical features patterned after the British system of government.

Last January, a poem published in the *State Gazette of South Carolina*, Charleston, embodied this belief:

On the new Constitution.

   In evil hour his pen 'squire Adams drew
Claiming dominion to his well born few:
In the gay circle of St. James's plac'd
He wrote, and, writing, has his work disgrac'd.
Smit with the splendor of a British King
The crown prevail'd, so once despis'd a thing!
Shelburne and Pitt approv'd of all he wrote,
While Rush and Wilson echo back his note.

   Tho' British armies could not here prevail
Yet British politics shall turn the scale;—
In five short years of Freedom weary grown
We quit our plain republics for a throne;
Congress and *President* full proof shall bring,
A mere disguise for Parliament and King.

   A standing army!—curse the plan so base;
A despot's safety—Liberty's disgrace.—
Who sav'd these realms from Britain's bloody hand,
Who, but the generous rustics of the land;
That free-born race, inur'd to every toil,
Who tame the ocean and subdue the soil,

Who tyrants banish'd from this injur'd shore
Domestic traitors may expel once more.

Ye, who have bled in Freedom's sacred cause,
Ah, why desert her maxims and her laws?
When *thirteen* states are moulded into *one*
Your rights are vanish'd and your honors gone;
The form of Freedom shall alone remain,
As Rome had Senators when she hugg'd the chain.

Sent to revise your systems—not to change—
Sages have done what Reason deems most strange:
Some alterations in our fabric we
Calmly propos'd, and hoped at length to see—
Ah, how deceived!—these heroes in renown
Scheme for themselves—and pull the fabric down—
Bid in its place Columbia's tomb-stone rise
Inscrib'd with these sad words—*Here Freedom lies!*[14]

Perhaps giving added currency to the belief that the British are behind the new Constitution are the American newspapers that have reported the positive reception of the Constitution in England.

The Anti-Federalist Philadelphia newspaper *Independent Gazetteer* on February 21, for example, reported that British merchants are very much pleased with the new Constitution and "they are laughing in their sleeves, at the prospect of now having it in their power to collect all *their old American debts with interest. . . .*"[15]

On March 22, the *Charleston City Gazette* reported that a British paper quoted our Minister to Great Britain, John Adams, as approving the new American Constitution "because of its approach to the English constitution; and clearly proves, that in every republican state, the power has been vested in a something like king, lords and commons, though under different names."[16]

South Carolina Federalists who were delegates in Philadelphia last year know that during that long summer of the secret conclave, Minister Adams and his published works played almost no part in their deliberations, this correspondent learned. However, because the official records of the debates remain secret and the delegates themselves sworn to secrecy, they must suffer the unfounded assertions in silence.

The belief that the British have had a hand in the creation of the new Constitution made news this week of Maryland's ratification all the more bitter for many Anti-Federalist delegates. Many are veterans of the partisan war against the British, and many also remember with hatred the foreign occupation of South Carolina and Charleston.

"The outrage & cruelty of the British," recalls delegate Aedanus Burke, "is beyond description, and the inveterate hatred & spirit of Vengeance wch. they have excited in the breasts of our Citizens is such that you can form no idea of."[17]

Memory of the war with Great Britain and the deep scars it has left were invoked this week when delegate Patrick Dollard rose to remark that the people of Prince Frederick's Parish who sent him to Charleston are brave, honest, and industrious.

". . . In the late bloody contest," he stated, "they bore a conspicuous part, when they fought, bled, and conquered, in defence of their civil rights and privileges, which they expected to transmit untainted to their posterity. They are nearly all, to a man, opposed to this new Constitution, because, they say, they have omitted to insert a bill of rights therein, ascertaining and fundamentally establishing, the unalienable rights of men, without a full, free, and secure enjoyment of which there can be no liberty, and over which it is not necessary that a good government should have the control."[18]

CHAPTER 36

★

May 23–29, 1788

Charleston's aristocratic Federalists threw reserve to the wind and "shook the air with their cheers" when South Carolina this week became the eighth State to ratify the new Constitution by a vote of 149 to 73—a more than two-to-one majority.[1]

The May 23 vote was announced at Charleston's City Hall a few minutes after five in the afternoon as a huge crowd packed the Convention hall and spilled out onto the surrounding cobblestone streets.

"When the result of the vote was announced," delegate David Ramsay related to this correspondent, "an event unexampled in the annals of Carolina took place. Strong and involuntary expressions of joy burst forth from the numerous transported spectators. The minority complained of disrespect—unpleasant consequences were expected. The majority joined with the complaining members in clearing the house, and in the most delicate manner soothed their feelings."[2]

"Soothing" took the form of Convention approval of four recommended amendments demanded by back-country Anti-Federalists.

"We had a tedious but trifling opposition," sniffed Federalist delegate Edward Rutledge of the harmless amendments that followed the formula of the February Massachusetts Convention. "We had prejudices to contend with and sacrifices to make."[3]

A copy of the resolutions passed by the Convention after the ratification vote reveals the following recommendations:

- Elections to the Federal Legislature shall be forever inseparably the province of the States.
- The States shall retain "every power not expressly relinquished by them and vested in the general government of the Union."
- The General Government of the United States "ought never to

impose direct taxes," but if duties, imposts, and excise are insufficient, Congress may requisition the States for their respective proportions to meet the needed expenses of the new national government.
• It strengthened the wording of the document that no religious oaths will be required as a qualification for office.

"Resolved that it be a standing instruction to all such delegates," the resolution concludes, "as may hereafter be elected to represent this State in the general Government to exert their utmost abilities and influence to effect an Alteration of the Constitution comformably to the foregoing Resolutions."[4]

Before the ratification vote, Anti-Federalists failed to have other amendments added. Aedanus Burke lost by a vote of 168 to 68 to have the Convention go on record as favoring one term for the President.

". . . the eligibility of the President," he told the visibly impatient majority, "after the expiration of Four Years, is dangerous to the Liberties of the peoples, calculated to perpetuate in One person during Life the high authority and influence of that Magistracy in a short time to terminate in what the good people of this State highly disapprove of, An hereditary Monarchy."[5]

Delegate David Ramsay maintained that "the minority not only acquiesced" but joined in supporting the determination of the majority.[6] But according to one observer, Federalist persuasion of dissident delegates by words, wining, and dining during the twelve-day Convention had converted only a handful to the Federalist cause.[7]

Privately, the militant minority is as bitter in its defeat as the majority is joyful in its victory. While Federalists held a "grand procession" this week through the streets of Charleston, Judge Burke reported that dissident delegates are planning their own "funeral procession" with a coffin painted black to be solemnly buried "as an emblem of the dissolution and internment of publick Liberty."[8]

When order had been restored in the City Hall, General Christopher Gadsden, 65-year-old veteran of the struggle for independence as far back as the Stamp Act Congress of 1765, spoke for the majority in closing the political conclave this week.

"I can have but little expectation," the former Governor and author of the South Carolina Constitution said, "of seeing the happy effects that will result to my country from the wise decisions of this day, but I shall say with good old Simeon: Lord, now lettest thou thy servant depart in peace, for mine eyes have seen the salvation of my country."[9]

Twenty-three years ago, General Gadsden committed South Carolina as the ninth State to oppose the British Stamp Act after Virginia's Patrick Henry led the way. Now, as the eighth State considered the new Constitution, which Patrick Henry unconditionally disapproves, he failed to use his influence to aid South Carolinian Anti-Federalists. He was with them in spirit but had, according to one observer, no inclination to fight on unfamiliar political ground.[10]

South Carolina's affirmation of the Constitution comes exactly one year to the week after the Philadelphia Convention began its secret summer of deliberations that climaxed in the creation of the document. Former Virginia Governor Henry might have influenced the Convention last summer as much as General George Washington did had he not refused to attend the Convention as an elected delegate. For Mr. Henry is the second best known, and admired, Virginian in the Union.

Next week, the Virginia Convention meets in Richmond. Apparently with an eye toward influencing its outcome, General Charles Cotesworth Pinckney was reported to have dispatched from Charleston an overland express messenger to General Washington at Mount Vernon. A second dispatch was sent by a ship going to Baltimore, with the idea that whichever one reaches him first, he will forward the South Carolina decision to Richmond.[11]

South Carolina's approval of the Constitution now raises the question whether Virginia or New Hampshire will become the necessary ninth State.

Just this week Rufus King, a Massachusetts delegate to the Philadelphia Convention, predicted in a May 25 letter to Congressman James Madison that intelligence from New Hampshire "is favorable, and I cherish a rational Expectation that they will adopt the constitution by a handsome majority. . . ."[12]

Even if New Hampshire should become the ninth State, should Virginia reject the document it would nevertheless have an impact on New York and North Carolina. Both States have elected sizable Anti-Federalist majorities to their forthcoming Conventions.

General Henry Knox, writing to General Washington from New York, concluded: "Much will depend on Virginia. Her conduct will have a powerful influence on this state and North Carolina."[13]

General Washington, in turn, knows that much depends on delegate James Madison when he confronts Patrick Henry in Richmond. One observer maintains that the 37-year-old Congressman faces two major problems.

One is that he has been attempting to win over to the Federalist cause Virginia Governor Edmund Randolph, who is still regarded by the Anti-Federalists as an influential political force against ratification. Mr. Madison is wooing Governor Randolph by agreeing with him when possible, by answering his objections while making him think the answers are his own, and by playing on his deep distrust of Patrick Henry.[14]

But then, Mr. Madison faces the tougher political problem of winning over the Kentucky delegation, reported to be hostile to ratification. Former Governor Henry has convinced the dozen elected Kentucky delegates to the Richmond Convention that the new Constitution will result in surrender of the Mississippi River to Imperial Spain, allegedly leading to impoverishing inland Virginians for the benefit of Northern commercial interests with their seaports.

What has given substance to this argument is the opposition of Eastern States to Kentucky's application to become the fourteenth State. Just this week the Continental Congress in New York is reportedly prepared to debate the issue as the Virginia Convention meets.

Mr. Madison expressed to John Brown, Kentucky Congressman, the hope that "the decision of Congress on the subject of Kentucky may be speedy & conciliatory" as one way to induce the dissident Kentucky ratification Convention delegates to vote their approval.[15]

Should the current Congress delay action on Kentucky's application, Mr. Madison indicated last week that such action would be a powerful argument *for* ratification, convinced as he is that a new Congress will be able to deal more decisively with the Mississippi River issue, Kentucky statehood, and the threat of settler security from Indian attacks.

"The new Govt. and that alone," he observed earlier to another friend, "will be able to take the requisite measures for getting into our hands the Western posts which will not cease to instigate the Savages, as long as they remain in British hands. It is said also that the Southern Indians are encouraged and armed by the Spaniards for like incursions on that side. A respectable Government would have equal effect in putting an end to that evil."[16]

Georgia approved the new Constitution on the belief that the new national government would aid in its clashes with Indian tribes. Virginia's western delegates to the Richmond Convention, also faced with Indian attacks, might be induced to vote for ratification on the same grounds.

It is clear that Mr. Madison and other Federalists fear that a failure of Kentucky's application for statehood will advance Spanish designs to make the territory a permanent colony at a time when new settlers are flooding into the frontier West.

One source reports that in 1787 alone, more than 900 flatboats on the Ohio River carried 18,000 men, women, and children along with 12,000 horses, sheep, and cattle; and 650 wagons. The westward migration has become such a flood that Rhode Island and Massachusetts are complaining they are losing their citizens to the West and with it political and economic power.[17]

Last week, Congressman Madison made it clear that he believes the future of the new Union is to be found in the West. Growing population and the formation of new States "will encourage adventurers of character and talents," he said, to settle on lands sold to them by the new national government. This in turn will strengthen the hand of the new Union to cope with Spain and Great Britain.

"As the establishment of the new Govt.," he added, "will thus promote the sale of the public lands, it must for the same reason enhance their importance as a fund for paying off the public debts, and render the navigation of the Mississippi still more an object of national concern."[18]

No doubt exists that General Washington shares Mr. Madison's belief that the future of the new American Republic is to be found in the West. The former veteran of the French and Indian War and onetime surveyor of Virginia's Shenandoah Valley has himself in recent years acquired large tracts of Western lands.[19]

However, this week General Washington's concentration and concerns are directed South toward Richmond and the opening of the crucial Virginia ratification Convention.

"... The plot thickens fast," the General wrote to his close friend and former associate, the Marquis de Lafayette, from Mount Vernon on May 28. "A few short weeks will determine the political fate of America for the present generation and probably produce no small influence on the happiness of society through a long succession of ages to come. Should every thing proceed with harmony and consent according to our actual wishes and expectations; I will confess to you sincerely, my dear Marquis; it will be so much beyond any thing we had a right to imagine or expect eighteen months ago, that it will demonstrate as visibly the finger of Providence, as any possible event in the course of human affairs can ever designate it."[20]

CHAPTER 37

★

May 30–June 5, 1788

Lean and leathery Kentucky frontiersmen sat shoulder to shoulder with smooth-faced, well-fed Tidewater merchants and plantation owners at the opening sessions of the Virginia ratifying Convention in Richmond this week. All listened in awe as the legendary Patrick Henry hurled verbal thunderbolts at the new Constitution.

"... What right had they to say, *We, the people?*" thundered the stooped 52-year-old, five-term Virginia Governor of the authors of the document. "... Who authorized them to speak the language of, *We, the people*, instead of, *We, the states?* States are the characteristics and the soul of a confederation. If the states be not the agents of this compact, it must be one great, consolidated national government...."[1]

The 170 elected delegates, meeting in Richmond's huge new Academy Hall, hardly had time to react to former Governor Henry when over the murmuring sea of voices came the clear, strong voice of the present Governor, Edmund Randolph, demanding the floor. The portly, but handsome, 34-year-old member of one of Virginia's wealthiest and most influential families had, until this week, been counted a foe of ratification.

However, his opening speech left little doubt that, despite his refusal last September to sign the Constitution in Philadelphia, he has now thrown his considerable prestige and popularity behind approval of the document. This development may prove crucial in the continual counting and courting of convention votes.[2]

"The gentleman then proceeds, and inquires why we assumed the language of 'We, the people,'" Governor Randolph told the hushed convention hall. "I ask, Why not? The government is for the people.... What harm is there in consulting the people on the construction of a government by which they are to be bound? Is it unfair? Is it unjust? . . ."[3]

One observer has told this correspondent that Governor Randolph's stunning defection to ratification may prove to be a weightier force than the spellbinding speeches of Patrick Henry or the overwhelming influence of General George Washington.[4]

The 56-year-old military hero of the American War of Independence declined election as a delegate to the Richmond ratifying Convention. Nevertheless, since last September, when the struggle for ratification began in the separate States, he has worked in the shadows to secure adoption of the Constitution. James Madison, Virginia Congressman, has worked closely with the General, providing him with a steady stream of detailed political intelligence as eight States met and ratified the document. The ninth necessary vote for adoption of the document may hinge on Virginia, the largest and most populous State.

Congressman Madison, a delegate to the ratifying Convention from Orange, is reported to have written General Washington this week that Governor Randolph has "thrown himself fully into the federal scale" and that advocates of ratification are "a good deal elated by the existing prospect."[5]

The 37-year-old chief political manager of the new Constitution is reported to have been one of the few delegates in Richmond not completely surprised by Governor Randolph's defection. According to one observer, Mr. Madison has been secretly weaning the Governor from the opposition. The Governor's speech, opposing amendments before ratification—as demanded by Patrick Henry and Colonel George Mason—is a composite echo of Mr. Madison's arguments.[6]

Colonel Mason, who also refused to sign the Constitution in Philadelphia, is reported to be infuriated at Governor Randolph's defection, denouncing him as a "young Benedict Arnold." The 62-year-old white-haired author of the Virginia Constitution and bill of rights opposes ratification, arguing that amendments are necessary to check the vast powers of the proposed national government. His militant opposition in recent months reportedly has cost him the lifelong friendship of General Washington.[7]

". . . The curse denounced by the divine vengeance," Colonel Mason warned Convention delegates this week, "will be small, compared to what will justly fall upon us, if from any sinister views we obstruct the fullest inquiry. This subject, therefore, ought to obtain the freest discussion, clause by clause. . . ."[8]

A paragraph-by-paragraph debate of the Constitution is viewed by critics of the document as a way of prolonging the Convention, allowing time for the spellbinding oratory of Patrick Henry to seduce the undecided,[9] as he has done in the courtroom and in the Virginia Legislature the last two decades.

But when Congressman Madison and other friends of ratification quickly agreed to Colonel Mason's proposal, the effect was to turn the strategy of delay into a tactical debacle for the Anti-Federalists. For example, Colonel Mason violated his own rule when he jumped ahead and denounced the clause that grants Congress the power of direct taxation before that section had come up for debate.

"The power of laying direct taxes will be more properly discussed, when we come to that part of the Constitution," Mr. Madison said, firmly but quietly reminding Colonel Mason and the Convention delegates of the clause-by-clause agreement.[10]

By insisting that the debate proceed section by section, the ratification foes have given their opposition, according to one observer, an unexpected weapon. Debate along specific principles is where Mr. Madison's talent is strongest; whereas Mr. Henry's powerful oratory would be more effective in a diffused or general discussion.[11]

In a June 4 letter to General Washington, a copy having been obtained by this correspondent, Mr. Madison appears elated that opposition leaders lack a consistent and coordinated Convention strategy.

". . . Henry & Mason made a lame figure & appeared to take different and awkward ground," he wrote. ". . . I dare not however speak with certainty as to the decision. Kentucke has been extremely tainted, is supposed to be generally adverse, and every piece of address is going on privately to work on the local interests & prejudices. . . ."[12]

Virginia's western boundary is the Mississippi River. Ever since Imperial Spain in 1784 closed the river to American navigation and trade, Patrick Henry has charged that the Northern and Middle

Atlantic shipping States have secretly conspired to keep the great river closed so they may gain commercial advantages and ruin the prosperity of Virginia.[13]

Patrick Henry's refusal to serve as a Virginia delegate to the Philadelphia Convention last year was motivated, in part, by his belief that the conclave was a furtherance of this alleged conspiracy. One observer alleges that former Governor Henry, before the election of the ratifying Convention delegates this spring, wrote "flaming letters" to people in Kentucky forecasting that the Mississippi and their prosperity would be lost to Imperial Spain forever if the new government were adopted.[14]

A majority of the Kentucky delegates to the Richmond Convention are said to oppose ratification of the Constitution. It is a tactical victory for Patrick Henry, since the Mississippi issue is believed to be the principal reason for their hostility to the document. An additional reason is the refusal of the Continental Congress in New York to act upon the petition of the frontier territory to become a separate State.[15] ". . . I shall have an opportunity in Richmd. of conversing with the members from Kentucky. . . ."[16]

The Kentucky delegates, dressed in buckskin and homespun and toting flintlock rifles used for hunting and fighting Indians, are a rude contrast to coastal delegates dressed in imported broadcloth. To reach Richmond, delegates from the frontier and interior of the State have traveled 300 to 600 miles on horseback.[17]

A recent drought has killed most of the State's young tobacco crop and turned all roads leading to Richmond into ribbons of dust, deep as a horse's fetlock. On a positive note, one observer points out that the dry weather has made many rivers and streams passable. A rainy spell in the past week would have made them impossible to cross, and would have delayed delegates from even nearby counties.[18]

Richmond was chosen the State's capital only eight years ago, in 1780, when Thomas Jefferson was Governor. The previous capital was Williamsburg. The opening Convention session this week was held in the old capitol, since the new statehouse will not be ready for occupancy until October. But the number of delegates and spectators forced a shift to the Academy building, said to be the largest structure in the still rude and rough village of Richmond.[19]

During the last two weeks, the town has become swollen with horses, delegates, and curious spectators from all over the Old Dominion. Most of the curious have come to see and hear for the first time the legendary Patrick Henry. Last week he was seen arriving at sunset from Prince Edward, driving his own topless gig. His homespun clothes were covered with the dust of the dry day. The swarms of people who have arrived this week made this Convention the largest peacetime gathering in the short history of the town.[20]

The Convention is also described by one observer as a gathering of the strongest debaters, the most powerful orators, and some of the most scholarly statesmen in America. "Seldom, in any land or age," have so many gifted and accomplished men met for argument and discussion at one time and in one place.[21]

The greatest fear of the friends of ratification is not the clamor for amendments to the Constitution, but the private plans of Patrick Henry and the use of his popularity and oratory to affect enough delegates to send the document down to a narrow defeat if a bill of rights in the form of amendments is not adopted before ratification. Most fear that Governor Henry has a secret plan up his homespun sleeve.[22]

His speeches during this first week were so lengthy that Governor Randolph complained, "Mr. Chairman, if we go on in this irregular manner, contrary to our resolution, instead of three or six weeks, it will take us six months to decide this question."[23]

Mr. Henry carried almost alone the first week of debate for the foes of an unamended Constitution. Four friends of the document took turns answering him. One delegate later testified that Patrick Henry's words of warning of the slavery to come with the new Constitution were so powerful that he involuntarily reached down to feel the chains on his wrists.[24]

"Twenty-three years ago was I supposed a traitor to my country?" Mr. Henry rhetorically asked, referring to his now-famous Stamp Act speech of May 1765. "I was then said to be the bane of sedition, because I supported the rights of my country. . . ." Then referring to the proposed Constitution, he went on, "There are many on the other side, who possibly may have been persuaded to the necessity of these [the Constitution's] measures, which I conceive to be dangerous to your liberty. Guard with jealous attention the public liberty. Suspect every one who approaches that jewel."[25]

The spellbinding nature of his delivery and the sheer energy of the no longer young orator have been a delight to his friends and a source of despair to his foes. For instance, he allowed his lengthy June 5 oration to be interrupted only briefly when he paused to receive the whispered words that one of his sons had just arrived from Southside Virginia with the news that his second wife had safely delivered a healthy baby boy. It was their sixth child and his twelfth.[26]

"I have, I fear, fatigued the committee," he concluded at the end of his three-and-a-half-hour speech, "yet I have not said the one hundred thousandth part of what I have on my mind, and wish to impart. . . ."[27]

CHAPTER 38

★

June 6–12, 1788

Patrick Henry and Governor Edmund Randolph came within a hair trigger of settling their disagreements over the new Constitution with pistol balls after an angry exchange this week on the floor of the Virginia ratifying Convention in Richmond.[1]

The explosive incident erupted when Mr. Henry taunted Governor Randolph to explain why he had opposed the Constitution in Philadelphia, later making his reasons public, and now is reversing himself to support ratification and renouncing his earlier reservations.

"That honorable member will not accuse me of want of candor," Henry mockingly told the hushed delegates in the hot Convention hall, "when I cast in my mind what [reason for opposition] he has given the public, and compare it to what has happened since.... Something extraordinary must have operated so great a change in his opinion."[2]

Sensitive to private whispers that his switch is motivated more from political ambition than from principle, Governor Randolph, his handsome face flushed and his black eyes flashing with anger, rose to answer.

"I find myself attacked in the most illiberal manner by the honorable gentleman, (Mr. Henry)," he said, his rich voice filled with self-righteous rage. "I disdain his aspersions and his insinuations.... and if our friendship must fall, *let it fall, like Lucifer, never to rise again! ...* Sir, if I do not stand on the bottom of integrity, and pure love for Virginia, as much as those who can be most clamorous, I wish to resign my existence. Consistency consists in actions, and not in empty, specious words...."[3]

Surprised at such verbal violence, Governor Henry jumped up and in fatherly tones declared he was "sorry" and did not mean to "wound the feelings of any gentleman." Indeed, he added, "every gentleman had a right to maintain his opinion."[4]

Refusing to accept the apology, Governor Randolph accused the 52-year-old veteran legislator and five-term former Governor of ignorance. Waving a copy of his public letter explaining his earlier opposition to the Constitution, the tall, portly 34-year-old Governor strode to the Convention clerk's desk and angrily threw it down, saying it should lie there *for the inspection of the curious and the malicious.*[5]

Until this explosive moment, Patrick Henry's long public life had been free of personal quarrels. However, according to one source, he felt that Governor Randolph had crossed the line between legitimate criticism and deliberate personal insult, requiring satisfaction on a field of honor with dueling pistols.[6]

This correspondent has been told that Mr. Henry dispatched to Governor Randolph's Richmond lodgings a second to work out details for a duel. Delegates on both sides were fearful of the shattering impact the spilling of blood between two so famous Virginians would have on the Convention and on the country. A great wave of relief swept over the delegates when it was disclosed that Mr. Henry decided the disagreement should be settled by ballots rather than by pistol balls.[7]

Word of the incident and stormy debate spread throughout the counties adjacent to Richmond, swelling the crowds that braved the heat and dust to gain seats in the galleries of the large new Academy Hall. The crowds this week grew so large that delegates at the opening of each day's session found it difficult to reach their seats.[8]

According to one source, both sides have used the evenings and the Sabbath to confer in secret to devise ways and means of getting votes. During this week's sessions, delegates favoring the new Constitution have complained openly on the Convention floor of alleged "out of doors" improper conduct of their opposition, which suggests that both sides are resorting to every political means available to them to secure support.[9]

The most sought-after votes are the fourteen delegates from Kentucky. One delegate reports after two weeks of debate that the Convention is evenly divided. Mr. Henry's side is confident that the use of the alleged giveaway of Mississippi River navigation rights to Spain by Northern States will keep Kentucky delegates hostile to ratification and provide political leverage for forcing acceptance of amendments to the new Constitution.[10]

Patrick Henry confirmed the worst fears of his foes this week when he played his Mississippi River card, alleging that the new Constitution will mean the loss of navigation on the valuable waterway and ruin of the commerce of Virginia and its Kentucky province.

"Common observation tells you," Mr. Henry told the hushed Convention, "that it must be the policy of Spain to get it first, and then retain it forever. If you give it up, in my poor estimation they will never voluntarily restore it. Where is the man who will believe that, after clearing the river [of Americans], strengthening themselves, and increasing the means of retaining it, the Spaniards will tamely surrender it?"[11]

All week the war of words over the waterway raged between delegates. However, it was Congressman James Madison's response that was considered the most effective. Barely heard or seen in the huge hall because of a weak voice and a slender, short stature, the 37-year-old chief political manager of the Constitution rose with notes in hat, hat in hand.[12]

Nervously rocking back and forth on the balls of his feet, Mr. Madison said Mr. Henry is factually wrong when he insists that seven States favor surrender of American navigation rights on the river to Imperial Spain. The current Confederated government has not, as charged, secretly negotiated away America's rights on the river, yet its current weakness prevents a successful settlement in the future.

"We are entitled to it; but it is not under an inefficient government that we shall be able to avail ourselves fully of that right," Mr. Madison argued. "I most conscientiously believe that it will be far better secured under the new government than the old, as we shall be more able to enforce our right. The people of Kentucky will have an additional safeguard from the change of system. . . ."[13]

Although Mr. Madison appeared striking in a suit of blue and buff, with a doubled straight collar and white ruffles on chest and at wrists, he looked pasty pale, even sickly. During last week's debates, the Virginia Congressman so exhausted himself in answering Patrick Henry, he was forced to take to his bed with a high fever and nervous stomach.[14]

"There is reason to believe that the event may depend on the Kentucky members," Mr. Madison wrote to General Washington, "who seem to lean more agst. than in favor of the Constitution. The business is in the most ticklish state that can be imagined. The majority will certainly be very small on whatever side it may finally lie; and I dare not encourage much expectation that it will be on the favorable side."[15]

Such pessimism was offset by arrival in Richmond of a dispatch rider with the news that South Carolina had ratified the Constitution on May 23. New Hampshire is expected to reconvene its own Convention next week, placing the New England State in a race with Virginia to be the necessary ninth State to approve the document for it to become legal. Supporters in Boston are preparing to speed an express rider South with the news of the New Hampshire vote.[16]

Tobias Lear, General Washington's personal secretary, is reported to have written from New Hampshire to the General saying the State ". . . to save appearances is to adopt it before the ratification can reach them from Virginia. . . ."[17]

In a letter from Mount Vernon this week, a copy having been obtained by this correspondent, the General asserts to Mr. Madison that he does not doubt or despair that Virginia will approve the new Constitution despite "the insidious arts of its opposers" to inflame the passions and fears of the multitude.

". . . I have no doubt," the General says, "but that the good sense of this Country will prevail against the local views of designing characters and the arrogant opinions of chagreened and disappointed men.

"The decision of Maryland and South Carolina by so large Majorities and the moral certainty of the adoption of the proposed constitution by New Hampshire will make *all*, except desperate men look before they leap into the dark consequences of rejection."[18]

Patrick Henry is reported to believe that no matter how many States approve the Constitution, by withholding her approval, Virginia has in her wealth and population the power to cripple a new national government even before it is formed. This week he told the Convention that Virginia must use this power to demand amendments in the form of a bill of rights.

"This state has weight and importance," Mr. Henry insisted. "Her example will have powerful influence—her rejection will procure amendments. Shall we, by our adoption, hazard the loss of amendments? Shall we forsake that importance and respectability which our station in America commands, in hopes that relief will come from an obscure part of the Union? I hope my countrymen will spurn at the idea."[19]

Mr. Henry further inflamed the amendment debate when he insisted that the "illustrious citizen" Thomas Jefferson, author of the Declaration of Independence and now U.S. Minister to France, "advises you to reject this government till it be amended. His sentiments coincide entirely with ours."[20]

In reply, James Madison, who has been corresponding with Minister Jefferson ever since the new Constitution was published last September, objected. Has it come to this, he asked the Convention, that delegates are not to follow their own reason?

"If the opinion of an important character were to weigh on this occasion, could we not adduce a character equally great on our side?" Mr. Madison asked, referring to General Washington. "Are we . . . now to submit to the opinion of a citizen beyond the Atlantic? I believe that, were that gentleman now on this floor, he would be for the adoption of this Constitution."[21]

Mr. Madison went on to insist he knows Minister Jefferson's views so well that he is certain Mr. Jefferson would favor the provision in the Constitution giving Congress the power of direct taxation.[22]

Mr. Henry has savaged this section of the document as well as the power of Congress over the militia. "Congress, by the power of taxation, by that of raising an army, and by their control over the militia, have the sword in one hand, and the purse in the other," he said at one point. "Let him candidly tell me," Mr. Henry rhetorically asked of Mr. Madison, "where and when did freedom exist, when the sword and purse were given up from the people? Unless a miracle in human affairs interposed, no nation ever retained its liberty after the loss of the sword and purse. . . ."[23]

During the last two weeks of debate, Patrick Henry's lengthy speeches have been answered by no fewer than seven Federalist delegates: James Madison, Governor Edmund Randolph, John Marshall, Edmund Pendleton, George Nicholas, Henry Lee, and Francis Corbin. According to one source, their strategy has been to hold the floor as long as possible, then, when tiring, surrender to another Federalist, in an effort to deny Mr. Henry an opportunity to bewitch the delegates with continuous oratory.[24]

Whether by accident or by design, the main burden of battling Patrick Henry has fallen on the slight shoulders of James Madison. One observer has described their confrontation as the political equivalent of the biblical confrontation between David and Goliath. Governor Henry is armed with the heavy weapon of oratorical power to persuade by emotion. Congressman Madison has the light slingshot of logic aimed to convince the mind.[25]

CHAPTER 39

★

June 13–19, 1788

Patrick Henry bewitched the Richmond ratifying Convention this week with a whirlwind of words in a "now or never" drive to defeat the new Constitution.[1]

The retired five-term Governor warned Kentucky and western Virginia delegates that acceptance of the unamended document will mean the loss of the Mississippi River forever to Imperial Spain and the ruin of their liberty and prosperity.

"It is said that we are scuffling for Kentucky votes, and attending to local circumstances," he added with a scornful scowl. "But if you consider the interests of this country, you will find that the interests of Virginia and Kentucky are most intimately and vitally connected. . . . If Congress should, for a base purpose, give away this dearest right of the people, your western brethren will be ruined. We ought to secure to them that navigation which is necessary to their very existence. If we do not, they will look upon us as betrayers of their interest."[2]

In recent years, thousands of new settlers have pushed into the Kentucky and Tennessee frontier territories. Without navigation on the Mississippi, the time-consuming and expensive shipping of Western commercial products back over the mountains to Eastern markets is becoming economically ruinous for the settlers.[3]

Imperial Spain closed the river to U.S. navigation four years ago and since then the problem of how to reopen the vital waterway, short of war, has proved to be one of the most divisive domestic political issues between Northern and Southern States.

James Madison angrily denied Patrick Henry's charges of secret diplomatic negotiations by the Continental Congress with Spain, in

247

which negotiations Congress allegedly conspired to give up American rights to the river at the insistence of Northern States. The Continental Congressman also denied charges that the new Constitution stems from the same motives and from the same men, Northerners.

The Mississippi River issue plunged the Richmond Convention into a crisis, challenging friends of the new Constitution to persuade Western frontier delegates that American rights to the river would be secured and defended under the new national government.

However, one observer reports that Patrick Henry so overwhelmed the Convention with his oratory that when he sat down a silence fell over the huge hall. Edmund Pendleton, President of the Convention and friend of ratification, was equally amazed and stunned speechless. He said later that Governor Henry's Mississippi River speech this week equaled his Stamp Act oratory in 1765 and his "Give Me Liberty or Give Me Death" address of 1775.[4]

Governor Edmund Randolph finally found his voice and accused Patrick Henry of manipulating the Mississippi River issue to scare up votes rather than to debate the merits of the Constitution. Then, according to one observer, Governor Randolph proceeded to do the same thing by responding on the Mississippi River question, appealing directly to the Kentucky and western Virginia delegates.[5]

"I contend that there is no power given to the general government to surrender that navigation," Governor Randolph said. "There is a positive prohibition . . . against it. I consider that the policy of the states, and disposition of the people, make it impossible; and I conclude that their safety is at least as great under the new as under the old government."[6]

A violent thunderstorm cut short any further rebuttal on the Mississippi issue, forcing adjournment of the June 13 session. Patrick Henry and his allies may have been dealt a setback, for the next day, when the bell in the packed assembly hall sounded start of the session, the debate shifted from the river issue.

The remaining debate this week became principally a dispassionate verbal duel between 37-year-old James Madison and 62-year-old Colonel George Mason. The section-by-section debate of the merits and the deficiencies by the two acknowledged Constitutionalists provided a striking contrast to the volcanic exchanges of Patrick Henry and Edmund Randolph.[7] The initiative was also shifted to friends of the new Constitution with the clause-by-clause debate rather than a general debate.

Unlike Patrick Henry, Colonel Mason participated in the Philadelphia Convention and has intimate, firsthand knowledge of the new Constitution. Colonel Mason refused to sign the document, insisting that without amendments in the form of a bill of rights the new national government would, in time, become an instrument of tyranny.

Colonel Mason, author of Virginia's 1776 Declaration of Rights, the first such declaration in America, is reported to have drafted a lengthy document calling for limitations on the powers of Congress to tax and to regulate commerce, and for inclusion of a Federal bill of rights to secure personal liberties.

He and Patrick Henry insist that such amendments be adopted *before* ratification of the Constitution.[8] Colonel Mason told the Convention this week that the new Constitution should contain a specific declaration that all rights not granted to the general government be reserved by the States. Otherwise, he warned, a doctrine of implied powers will be assumed by the new Congress. He predicted that "Unless there were a bill of rights, implication might swallow up all our rights."[9]

Seizing on the issue, Patrick Henry insisted that without a bill of rights, the new Constitution will follow the tyrannical path of European governments by centralizing all power. A bill of rights is a sacred concept for Virginia and for the other States, he stated.

"The officers of Congress," he warned, adjusting his wig as he warmed to his subject, "may come upon you now, fortified with all the terrors of paramount federal authority. Excisemen [tax men] may come in multitudes; for the limitation of their numbers no man knows. They may, unless the general government be restrained by a bill of rights, or some similar restriction, go into your cellars and rooms, and search, ransack, and measure, every thing you eat, drink, and wear."[10]

Delegate George Nicholas, powerful in both voice and size, struggled to his feet to reply. Five or six States do not have a bill of rights and are as free as Virginia, argued the 33-year-old delegate from

Albemarle. He then proposed, with an apparent eye toward a few wavering delegates, amendments after ratification and not before, as demanded by both Patrick Henry and Colonel Mason.

"Would you reject this government," he asked the crowded convention, "for its omission, dissolve the Union, and bring miseries on yourselves and posterity? ... [it is] said that it is not only the general wish of this State, but all the states, to have a bill of rights. If it be so, where is the difficulty of having this done by way of subsequent amendment? We shall find the other states willing to accord with their own favorite wish."[11]

It was with just such a compromise that Massachusetts last February ratified the Constitution by a narrow margin. According to one source, Congressman Madison, before the Richmond Convention, had decided to hold in reserve this very option. He apparently urged Colonel Nicholas to propose the compromise as a way to salvage at the Convention's most vulnerable point Virginia's ratification of the Constitution.[12]

After three weeks of debate, delegates are being subjected to growing pressures to adjourn. Crops not destroyed by the recent drought need tending, the Virginia Legislature is slated to reconvene next week, and for some delegates each day in Convention adds to the drain on their meager purse.[13]

Mr. Madison is said to believe that the strategy of the opposition is to drag out the debates in the hope that weary delegates will postpone voting and adjourn, in order to escape the intense heat that has baked Richmond for much of the month.

"... The parties continue to be nicely balanced," he wrote this week to Colonel Alexander Hamilton in New York. "If we have a majority at all it does not exceed three or four. If we lose it Kentucke will be the cause, they are generally if not unanimously against us."[14]

Both sides at the Convention are anxiously looking North. New York convened its own ratifying convention this week, and New Hampshire reassembled after adjourning last February without voting. Both Congressman Madison and Colonel Hamilton predict the tiny New England State will become the necessary ninth State to give the Constitution legal life.

At the Poughkeepsie, New York, convention, as Colonel Hamilton made clear this week in a letter to Mr. Madison, foes of the document greatly outnumber its friends. Even if New Hampshire approves, a rejection by New York and Virginia would mean a new national union minus two of the largest and most prestigious States.[15]

Rejection by Virginia would also have grave consequences for a new union since General George Washington would then be ineligible for election as the first President. Despite Congressman Madison's letters to the General at Mount Vernon expressing doubts whether their side has the votes to carry ratification, the General himself has no doubts.

". . . I do not believe," he wrote to General Lafayette in Paris, "that Providence has done so much for nothing. It has always been my creed that we should not be left as an awful monument to prove 'that Mankind, under the most favourable circumstances for civil liberty and happiness, are unequal to the task of Governing themselves, and therefore made for a Master.'"[16]

In recent months General Washington has written in the same optimistic terms to Thomas Jefferson, U.S. Minister to France. Just this week, Mr. Jefferson wrote from Paris to a friend that the remaining States should accept the new Constitution as Massachusetts "has done, with standing instructions to their delegates to press for amendments till they are obtained."[17]

Coincidentally, this formula is the one James Madison advanced this week at the Virginia ratifying Convention in Richmond as a way of swinging a handful of wavering delegates to the side of ratification. One observer reports that he has been working behind the scenes with key supporters to convince them to accept the compromise which will, at the same time, sugarcoat the bitter pill for Patrick Henry and George Mason.[18]

Although still staggered by his recent illness, Mr. Madison managed to answer on the Convention floor opposition objections to the powers granted the new Congress, the President, and the Judiciary. The most tense debate was between Mr. Madison and Colonel Mason over the slavery issue.

"The augumentation of slaves," Colonel Mason told the Convention with passionate conviction, "weakens the States; and such a trade is diabolical in itself, and disgraceful to mankind; yet, by this Constitution, it is continued for twenty years. As much as I value a union of all the states, I would not admit the Southern States into the Union unless they agree to the discontinuance of this disgraceful traffic."[19]

In reply, Mr. Madison pointed out that without the temporary extension of the traffic, the Southern States would not have agreed to a new union, with dreadful consequences for everyone.

"That [slavery] traffic is prohibited by our [Virginia's] laws," he quietly told the delegates, "and we may continue the prohibition [of the importation of slaves]. The Union in general is not in a worse situation. Under the Articles of Confederation, it might be continued forever; but, by this clause, an end may be put to it after twenty years. There is, therefore, an amelioration of our circumstances."[20]

CHAPTER 40

★

June 20–26, 1788

The fate of the new American Union was narrowly ensured by ten delegates this week when the Virginia ratifying Convention in Richmond approved the Constitution by a vote of 89 to 79.[1]

The razor-thin June 25 ratification victory was secured, however, only after supporters of the document agreed to recommend a bill of rights and a series of other amendments. A poll of Convention delegates reveals that without these recommendations ratification would not have been possible.[2]

James Madison admitted before the critical vote this week that the compromise he engineered was an "expedient" to sway a handful of delegates. He also acknowledges that the reconvening of the Virginia Legislature on June 23 played a part in forcing the June 25 vote. A majority of legislators is reported hostile to ratification and might have influenced undecided delegates to vote against approval of the Constitution if the Convention continued for another week.[3]

According to one observer, ratification opponents came close to serving up a staggering defeat for the Constitutionalists. Before the critical final vote, Patrick Henry offered a resolution authorizing amendments as a *condition* for ratification rather than as recommendations. It narrowly lost, 88 to 80. Conversion of a handful of delegates from the Allegheny frontier might have sent the document down to defeat.[4]

Colonel George Mason sought to win over western delegates with an attack on the judicial powers in the Constitution. Western lands, he said, might be lost by litigation if the document were ratified. Titles date back to royal land grants, and he warned that it is "utterly inconsistent with reason or good policy" to have the Federal judiciary settle disputes between citizens and their State.[5]

If State courts are not to be trusted to settle property disputes, he asked, will the State governments be trusted with the power of legislation? The States are in danger, under the new Constitution, of being destroyed by a slow, silent process, the 62-year-old, tall, white-haired statesman said, in a voice etched with alarm.

"... There are many gentlemen in the United States," Colonel Mason went on to warn, "who think it right that we should have one great, national, consolidated government, and that it was better to bring it about slowly and imperceptibly rather than all at once. ... To those who think that one national, consolidated government is best for America, this extensive judicial authority will be agreeable. ..."[6]

Sensitive to the repeated charge that the Federal Convention in Philadelphia had concealed its real aim of consolidation of the thirteen States and destruction of their autonomy, Congressman Madison demanded from Colonel Mason an unequivocal explanation of his remarks. Otherwise, he added, "these insinuations might create a belief that every member of the late federal Convention" secretly favored consolidation.[7]

Colonel Mason went out of his way to exempt Mr. Madison of harboring consolidation aims while a delegate in Philadelphia. However, one observer has told this correspondent that Mr. Madison had, early in the Federal Convention, advanced proposals to curb the power of the States, insisting that they were never sovereign and that they were merely "petty corporations."[8]

"Were I to select a power," Congressman Madison assured the Richmond Convention this week, "which might be given with confidence, it would be judicial power. This power cannot be abused, without raising the indignation of all the people of the states."[9]

One observer believes that Colonel Mason's failure to confront Mr. Madison about his inconsistencies on the consolidation issue was a crucial tactical mistake. In Virginia, popular sentiment against a strong national government is high. Had opponents of the document concentrated their fire on this particular issue and on the alleged secret plans for consolidation of the States by stages, it is more than probable that the Constitution would have been defeated.[10]

★

The spellbinding oratory of Patrick Henry throughout the Convention had an impact, but lacking a concentrated focus it was not lasting. For example, the day before the final ratification vote, Mr. Henry spoke just as a violent thunderstorm assaulted Richmond, casting the Convention Hall into darkness. Momentary flashes of lightning enhanced the drama of Governor Henry's speech.[11]

". . . When I see beyond the horizon that bounds human eyes," Mr. Henry observed as the wind violently shook the doors and shutters of the hall, ". . . and see those intelligent beings which inhabit the ethereal mansions reviewing the political decisions and revolutions which, in the progress of time, will happen in America, and the consequent happiness or misery of mankind, I am led to believe that much of the account, on one side or the other, will depend on what we now decide," his voice rising above the wind.[12]

According to observers, the storm grew so violent that Mr. Henry was forced to cut short his speech. When the Convention met the following day, on June 25, to vote on ratification, the effect of Mr. Henry's awesome oratory, with the backdrop of an angry storm, was broken. He had lost the momentum of convincing wavering Constitutionalists to join him in demanding amendments and a bill of rights as conditions of Virginia's ratification.

Congressman Madison labeled the proposal "unnecessary and dangerous," insisting that recommendation of twenty amendments and a bill of rights, the latter drawn from Colonel Mason's 1776 Declaration of Rights for Virginia, fully met the concerns of some Convention delegates.

The carefully worded compromise, similar to the one that rescued ratification in Massachusetts in February, was, according to one observer, the product of late-night strategy sessions in a now-or-never Federalist effort to outflank Patrick Henry. Rumors had been circulating in Richmond that he planned to storm out of the Convention hall. The impact of the popular five-term Virginia Governor leading nearly half of the delegates in an angry exit might have been equal to a defeat by ballots.[13]

". . . If I shall be in the minority," Governor Henry said with resignation shortly before the critical voting, "I shall have those painful sensations which arise from a conviction of *being overpowered in a good cause.* Yet I will be a peaceable citizen. . . . I wish not to go to violence, but will wait with hopes that the spirit which predominated in the revolution is not yet gone, nor the cause of those who are attached to the revolution yet lost."[14]

A sigh of relief swept through the ranks of the Federalists. Not only was Patrick Henry conceding defeat, but he was dissociating himself from suggestions that his more radical followers might resort to armed struggle. Colonel Mason earlier fed these Federalist fears when he predicted armed resistance unless amendments were adopted.[15]

In the immediate aftermath of their narrow defeat, Anti-Federalist delegates are reported to have met in the old senate chamber of the Richmond capitol to formulate a plan of resistance to the new Federal government. One observer reports that Governor Henry told the disgruntled delegates to renounce the idea of resistance and to return home to support the new Constitution and "give it fair play."[16]

However, at that same meeting Colonel Mason was unwilling to accept defeat with the same grim grace. According to one observer, Colonel Mason's address was so extreme and bitter that many of the more moderate delegates stalked out of the rump caucus in disgust.[17]

The cause for his uncharacteristic rage is believed to be what Colonel Mason termed the "treacherous" conduct of Virginia's Governor, Edmund Randolph. On the very day of the ratification vote in the Richmond Convention, the Virginia House of Delegates received a two-month-old letter written by George Clinton, Governor of New York. Addressed to Governor Randolph, the letter pledged to work with other States, especially Virginia, to tone down the powers of the Constitution by amendments.[18]

Colonel Mason flew into a fury on reading the letter, insisting that Governor Randolph had withheld it to serve the interests of those supporting ratification and did not release the document until after the Richmond Convention approved ratification.[19]

It is a debatable point among observers whether early disclosure of the correspondence would have aided the Henry–Mason forces. What is not debatable is the crucial role that General George Washington's influence played in securing the narrow margin of victory for ratification. Convention delegate James Monroe, who voted against ratification, insists that "his influence carried this government."[20]

Delegate William Grayson told the Convention the day before the vote that were it not for General Washington, not so many delegates would favor ratification.

"... We do not fear while he lives;" he said, "but we can only expect his *fame* to be immortal. We wish to know who, besides him, can concentrate the confidence and affections of all America."[21]

Had Virginia rejected the Constitution, General Washington would have been prohibited from standing for election as first President under the new Federal Constitution. Rejection would also have given the New York Convention, now in session, a powerful pretext to defeat the document, signing the death warrant for a new Union. For without Virginia and New York, the Constitution cannot survive.[22]

It is not clear at this writing, however, which State, Virginia or New Hampshire, has secured the honor of being the necessary ninth State to approve the Constitution for it to go into effect. The tiny New England State reassembled its ratifying Convention last week and express riders and packet boats may be now making their way south with news of how and when New Hampshire voted. Immediately after the June 25 vote in Richmond, express riders headed north with news of the Virginia ratification victory.[23]

According to one observer, Boston and Philadelphia exploded with a frenzy of tavern toasts, musket volleys, bonfires, and victory parades when their respective States ratified. By contrast, Richmond is sober and silent. Perhaps a recognition by friends of the ratified Constitution that the fight for amendments is far from settled.[24]

When the Virginia ratifying Convention opened on June 2, both sides realized that the fate of the document would be decided by a handful of delegates from the frontier West. Patrick Henry used the principal issue of the loss of the Mississippi River to influence the thirteen Kentucky delegates, ten of whom voted against ratification.[25]

Delegates representing frontier settlements from the Shenandoah Valley to the Ohio River were expected to vote with Kentucky. However, they voted for ratification, partly because of loyalty to their former wartime commander General Washington and partly from a belief that a strong national government would help them deal with Indian wars.[26]

Shrewd Federalist floor managers decided that one of the last delegates to make the case for ratification before it went to vote should be a Valley veteran of the War of Independence and of numerous Indian conflicts. Zachariah Johnston, spare of speech, dress, and purse, may have been more effective than the well-born and well-dressed James Madison, who has never smelled gunpowder in the heat of battle.

". . . Shall we," asked the plain-spoken Johnston, "lose our blood and treasure, which we lost in the revolution, and permit anarchy and misery to complete the ruin of this country? Under these impressions, and for these reasons, I am for adopting the Constitution without previous amendments. I will go to any length afterwards, to reconcile it to gentlemen, by proposing subsequent amendments. The great and wise state of Massachusetts has taken this step. The great and wise state of Virginia might safely do the same. I am contented to rest my happiness on that footing."[27]

CHAPTER 41

June 27–July 3, 1788

Covered with sweat and dust, an exhausted New England express rider reined in his lathered mount at City Hall in New York last week with a dispatch for the Continental Congress. New Hampshire, the dispatch disclosed, had given legal life to the new Constitution on June 21, becoming the necessary ninth State to approve the document.

The communication, delivered at noon, June 24, to Congress, was from New Hampshire President John Langdon, and announced that the tiny New England State had approved the document by a vote of 57 to 47, providing what he termed "the Key Stone in the great Arch" of the new national Union.[1]

For five hours New York City church bells noisily proclaimed the news as supporters of the Constitution toasted one another. Within half an hour after the arrival of the express rider, a fresh horse and rider were headed "for Virginia, with the *joyful tidings.*"[2]

Although details are still sketchy, a source has informed this correspondent that the ten-vote victory was secured after Federalist leaders agreed to a series of recommended amendments. The Concord conclave took care to record that it voted on Saturday, June 21, at one o'clock in the afternoon as the historic ninth State, should Virginia vote on the same day at a later hour.[3]

Approval came after nearly four months of intense Federalist campaigning. Anti-Federalists last February came within a whisker of wrecking the Convention and New Hampshire's place in history was rescued only by the Federalists' ploy to recess without voting.

When the ratifying Convention reconvened on June 18, the Anti-Federalists vainly sought another recess in the hope a delay would give the majority of Anti-Federalists at the New York Convention in Poughkeepsie time to reject the Constitution.

After four days of debate and with no breathless dispatch rider from New York on the horizon, New Hampshire Federalists tested their strength on the first day of summer, with the result that made ratification by nine necessary States an accomplished fact.[4]

According to one observer, opponents to the Constitution lacked a program on which to base their disapproval, beyond demanding a bill of rights. Then, the Federalists, in a conciliatory mood, cut the ground out from under them by agreeing to recommend amendments.[5]

Federalist leaders were intensely aware that rapid communication of the news from New Hampshire to New York and Virginia might prove decisive in those States. According to one source, Colonel Alexander Hamilton of New York had written to the President of the New Hampshire Convention on June 6 that a speedy decision and prompt communication were vital.

". . . the instant you have taken a decisive vote in favor of the Constitution," Colonel Hamilton requested of John Sullivan, the Convention President, "you send an express to me at Poughkeepsie. Let him take the *shortest route* to that place, change horses on the road, and use all possible diligence. I shall with pleasure defray all expenses, and give a liberal reward to the person."[6]

The New York Convention formally convened on June 17 at the State capital, Poughkeepsie, seventy-five miles up the Hudson River from New York City. The village of less than 3,000 had been selected as the seat of the State government after British occupation of New York City in the War of Independence.[7]

When the debate opened on June 19, two-thirds of the 65 elected delegates were reported to be hostile to an unamended new Constitution. Despite this commanding majority, the Anti-Federalists, according to one observer, looked to New Hampshire and Virginia as levers to force major concessions from the Federalist minority.[8] However, one Federalist observer thought the Anti-Federalists were embarrassed by their predicament, since he had heard rumors that a few did not want to vote against the Constitution.[9]

On June 24, an exhausted express rider from Springfield, Massachusetts, reached Colonel Hamilton in Poughkeepsie with the news that New Hampshire three days previously had become the "Ninth Pillar" in the new Federal Temple. Federalist delegate Robert R. Livington told the Convention the following day that the news from New Hampshire greatly altered the debates, the "Confederation was now *dissolved,*" thus "some might contemplate disunion without pain."[10]

Anti-Federalist John Lansing indignantly denied that any alteration had taken place, urging that their deliberations should be not influenced because nine States have ratified the Constitution. Clearly outraged at the suggestion that his side favored disunion, the former New York delegate to the Philadelphia Convention shot back that the unwarranted "insinuation" came from the other side and was "utterly false."[11]

One observer has pointed out that the New York Anti-Federalists have made it clear they intend to enter the new Union. However, their price is prior recommended amendments and they look to Virginia to come in on the same terms to reinforce their demands. For these reasons, the news from New Hampshire, brought to Poughkeepsie with great speed and expense, had little effect initially on the majority.[12]

But in Virginia, the effect of New Hampshire's news on Federalists in Northern Virginia was electrifying. General George Washington reported this week that the express rider, who had left New York at one o'clock in the afternoon of June 24 with the New Hampshire news, arrived in Alexandria, Virginia, the night of June 27. Exhausted, Colonel David Henley, in the saddle for a record sixty hours, was told upon his arrival that only a few hours earlier a dispatch had arrived from Richmond—Virginia had also narrowly approved.[13]

General Washington was reported by a source to have stood on the portico of Mount Vernon in the cool summer darkness, savoring the news that the new American Union had been midwifed to birth. Cannons of celebration echoed up and down the Potomac. Jubilant neighbors appeared on the river in small boats to invite him to victory festivities the following day in nearby Alexandria.[14]

Later, in the solitude of his study, General Washington responded to Charles Cotesworth Pinckney of South Carolina that the news from North and South allowed the citizens of Alexandria—"fœderal to a man"—to be the first in the nation to toast the prosperity of ten United States. The hero of the American Revolution also noted that this week was memorable not only because of the birth of the American Union, but also because it was the tenth anniversary of the Battle of Monmouth, New Jersey.[15]

". . . No one *can* rejoice more than I do," the General wrote to another friend, "at every step the people of this great Country take to preserve the Union. . . . Wondrously strange then, and much to be regretted indeed would it be, were we to neglect the means, and to depart from the road which Providence has pointed us to, so plainly; I cannot believe it will ever come to pass. The great Governor of the Universe has led us too long and too far on the road to happiness and glory, to forsake us in the midst of it."[16]

His soaring spirits may have been tempered by a letter from James Madison, written from Richmond. The Congressman warns the General that Patrick Henry and his allies, although having failed to defeat ratification, have secured a variety of amendments—"several of them highly objectionable. . . ."[17]

He says that former Governor Henry declared he will seize the first opportunity that is offered for "shaking off the yoke in a *Constitutional way*" by seeking to convince two-thirds of the States to convene a second Federal Convention to undo the work of the first. Or, Congressman Madison added, to elect an Anti-Federalist majority to the first Congress that "will commit suicide on their own Authority."[18]

After meeting for twenty-four days, the Virginia ratifying Convention in Richmond formally adjourned this week. However, before permanently taking their leave on June 27, Convention delegates defeated by 85 to 65 a motion to delete an amendment limiting the powers of the new national Congress to lay direct taxes or excises. Friends of the Constitution, like Mr. Madison, consider this power one of the document's cardinal virtues, while its foes consider it a cardinal vice.[19]

One observer reports that not only did strong friends of the new Constitution help ensure the 20-vote margin, but also the vote clearly indicated how much some members of the Virginia Convention fear the powers of the new national government.[20]

The celebration in Alexandria was a bright contrast to the muted calm in Richmond. At sunrise on the last day of the Convention, the State capital was alive with men and horses. By nightfall, with most delegates miles away, heading homeward on horseback, Richmond's silent, deserted dark streets gave no hint that they were the scene of a historic struggle in which members of one of the most illustrious assemblies that ever met debated the future of a nation.[21]

Congressman Madison was preparing to leave Richmond this week for the Continental Congress in New York, hand-carrying Virginia's instrument of ratification along with the twenty amendments Virginia Federalists were forced to accept as the price for narrow approval.

He is expected to pause at Mount Vernon to provide General Washington with a firsthand briefing. Already, observers are crediting James Madison with providing the intellectual and political leadership in Richmond that won out over the powerful eloquence of Patrick Henry, who has been likened to Cicero and Demosthenes.

Mr. Madison was so weakened by illness that his normally low voice sank at times during the twenty-four days of debate to a whisper. He said later that when Patrick Henry arose to reply to him, the drama of a pause or a gesture would undo an hour's work before a word was uttered. Yet he won. Extraordinary quiet logic had been pitted against thunderous and passionate eloquence.[22]

News of Mr. Madison's role in the narrow Federalist victory in Richmond reached New York this week. City residents were startled out of their sleep at 3 A.M., July 2, with the ringing of church bells, followed in a few hours by the firing of cannon. The *New York Journal* reported that Colonel David Henley had arrived back from Alexandria with the news that Virginia had become the tenth State to ratify.[23]

Immediately a fresh courier was in the saddle, heading north up the Albany post road at full stride carrying the news to the New York Convention in Poughkeepsie. Nine hours later, the courier reined in his sweating, heaving bay horse at the court house. The courier flung his reins into the hands of a waiting boy, dashed into the Convention hall, and handed his dispatch to the doorkeeper. When the news was read aloud to the delegates, Federalists cheered, a crowd gathered outside, a procession was formed, and it marched around the court house several times to fife and drum.[24]

A majority of observers concede that the decisions of New Hampshire and Virginia effectively end the ten-month struggle for ratification of the new Constitution. Nevertheless, New York Anti-Federalists refuse to abandon their drive to secure amendments as a condition for approval, for they are in the majority, whereas in Virginia the delegates were more evenly divided. Federalist delegates, anticipating that the news from Virginia would serve as a masterstroke, are depressed and dismayed that ratification in two more States has had no effect on New York's militant majority.[25]

Mr. Madison appears to be one of the few Federalists who recognize that although ratification has finally been secured, opposition to the Federal government's powers and to implementation of those powers is still very strong.

"... I am so uncharitable as to suspect that the ill will to the Constitution will produce every peaceable effort to disgrace & destroy it," he wrote to Colonel Hamilton. "Mr. Henry declared previous to the final question that although he should submit as a quiet citizen, he should wait with impatience for the favorable moment of regaining in a *Constitutional way*, the lost liberties of his country."[26]

On July 2, the Continental Congress in New York declared that, with New Hampshire's instrument of ratification in hand, the new Constitution has assumed a legal life and the Articles of Confederation have thus expired into history—exactly twelve years to the day when the Declaration of Independence had been proclaimed in Philadelphia, July 2, 1776.

CHAPTER 42

★

July 4–10, 1788

Federalists launched their campaign for the First Federal Elections by staging in Philadelphia this week a lavish July 4 "Federal Procession" to celebrate the Declaration of Independence's twelfth anniversary and the ratification of the new Constitution by ten States.

According to official eyewitnesses, the procession involved 5,000 participants, extending for a mile and a half through the city, and took three hours to complete. Thousands of spectators lined the narrow streets, and stood at open windows and on rooftops to watch float displays depicting the last dozen years of American history— from the Declaration to the ratified Constitution.[1]

The main float and the most spectacular of the procession was the "Grand Federal Edifice." Drawn by ten white horses, it stood thirty-six feet high, consisted of a domed building constructed of painted papier-mâché, and was supported by thirteen Corinthian columns. Three of the columns were incomplete to symbolize that New York, North Carolina, and Rhode Island had not yet ratified.[2]

As if to symbolize the dawn of a new era, sunrise on July 4 in Philadelphia began with the pealing of bells in Christ Church steeple, followed by the discharge of cannon from the armed frigate *Rising Sun*, anchored in the nearby Delaware River. The cool southerly breeze gently swayed ten peaceful ships whose fluttering flags displayed, in bright gold letters, the names of the ratifying States, from New Hampshire to Georgia.[3]

Military units, mounted and afoot, stepping smartly to fife and drum, were joined by marching merchants, tradesmen, mechanics, draftsmen, farmers, and over a dozen other manual trades to demonstrate to the 17,000 spectators that they believe the Constitution is

a "New Roof" for the Federal Edifice under which all will be shel-
tered in safety and prosperity. Especially if the new national government should locate in their city.[4]

The theme was put to words by Francis Hopkinson, poet, Signer of the Declaration of Independence, and one of the main planners
of this Fourth of July Federal Procession. In the service of
ratification of the Constitution, he suggested that it was a "New
Roof" to replace the rotting, leaking Articles of Confederation:

Come muster, my Lads, your mechanical Tools,
Your Saws and your Axes, your Hammers and Rules;
Bring your Mallets and Planes, your Level and Line,
And Plenty of Pins of American Pine;
For our Roof we will raise, and our Song still shall be—
A Government firm, and our Citizens free.[5]

James Wilson, another Signer of the Declaration and of the new
Constitution, gave the keynote July 4 address on the city green,
renamed *Union Green* for the occasion. He reminded the sea of
upturned faces that the benefits to flow from the new Constitution
would not become a reality unless each of them regarded his vote
as crucial in the coming First Federal Elections to be held under
the document.

". . . Let no one say that he is but a single citizen; and that his
ticket will be but one in the box. That one ticket may turn the election. In battle, every soldier should consider the public safety as
depending on his single arm. At an election, every citizen should
consider the public happiness as depending on his single vote."[6]

Federalists like Mr. Wilson anticipate that the First Federal Elections under the new Constitution are likely to be as hard fought as
the ten-month campaign for ratification. One source tells this correspondent that Federalist leaders are convinced that narrow ratification
victories in Massachusetts, New Hampshire, and Virginia, with three
States not yet deciding, have set the stage for a bitter election in the
States for control of the new national government.[7]

This week the Continental Congress in New York released a committee report that sets dates for the first election of President and

Vice President under the Electoral College. The individual States will enact legislation for the election of House members and determine the appointment of Senate members for the new First Congress.

The old Congress set the first Wednesday in December for appointing Presidential Electors in the separate States; the first Wednesday in January 1789 for the Electors to assemble and vote for President; and the first Wednesday in February for commencing proceedings under the new Constitution.[8] But it delayed further action in its July 8 report.

The *location* for the temporary seat of the new national government was left blank. This may be accounted for as rival States plot ways to lure the seat of government away from New York City. And as the State ratifying Convention is still meeting in Poughkeepsie, according to one source, its failure to ratify would most certainly mean the loss of the seat of the national government and of a valuable source of income.[9]

Samuel Osgood, a financial official of the old Congress, has advised two leading Anti-Federalist delegates to the Poughkeepsie Convention that if New York ratifies, in his opinion, the seat of the new national government is likely to remain in the city.

". . . If New York should hold out, the opposition will have all the blame laid at their door for forcing Congress to leave this city. The topic will be a feeling and a popular one. Philadelphia, I have no doubt, is desirous New York may not come in, for the purpose of getting Congress removed."[10]

At least three Federalist delegates at Poughkeepsie have used the possible loss of the seat of national government by New York as leverage against the Anti-Federalist majority. Robert R. Livingston insists that agents for Philadelphia are active in New York in a campaign to make their city the temporary capital and that New York's present position outside the Union is aiding that effort. Colonel Alexander Hamilton is making similar arguments at the ratifying Convention.[11]

Delegate John Jay, Secretary of Foreign Affairs for the old Congress, has reportedly told the Poughkeepsie Convention that the city realized annually $100,000 and that "All the Hard Money in the City of New York arise from the Sitting of Congress there."[12]

The Federalist minority's warnings of the economic loss should New York reject the document has had a sobering impact on the Anti-Federalist majority.[13]

Although the Anti-Federalists have maintained that the news last week of ratification by New Hampshire and Virginia will have no effect on their vote, evidence to the contrary is beginning to emerge. One observer reports that the fact of ratification of ten States means that New York runs the risk of economic isolation. Federalists have raised the additional threat that the southern part of the State might secede. Also, if delay causes the seat of government to be moved elsewhere, Governor George Clinton's Anti-Federalist stance would leave him very unpopular in his own State.[14]

Until this week, the Poughkeepsie Convention debates have centered on the powers and composition of Congress, particularly the power of direct taxation. Foes of the document claim they are a danger to personal liberty and the future existence of the States. The leader of the Anti-Federalists and President of the Convention, Governor Clinton, insists that though he is a friend of energetic government, the new Constitution is extreme. "Because a strong government was wanted during the late war, does it follow that we should now be obliged to accept of a dangerous one?"[15] he asked.

Privately, Governor Clinton has been accused by Colonel Hamilton of opposing the new Constitution out of fear that his own power will be diminished under the document. Colonel Hamilton has also accused his bitter political rival, in private, of demagoguery by alleging that the document is a deliberate design to consolidate and destroy the separate States.

"I insist," Colonel Hamilton told the Convention, "that it never can be the interest or desire of the national legislature to destroy the *state governments*. . . . The Union is dependent on the will of the state governments for its chief magistrate, and for its Senate. The blow aimed at the members must give a fatal wound to the head; and the destruction of the states must be at once a political suicide. Can the national government be guilty of this madness?"[16]

At the July 2 session, the Anti-Federalists turned from discussing the "dangerous" powers of the document to the absence of a bill of rights to safeguard personal liberties.

"We are told, sir," observed delegate Thomas Tredwell, "that a government is like a mad horse, which, notwithstanding all the curb you can put upon him, will sometimes run away with his rider. The idea is undoubtedly a just one. Would he not, therefore, justly be deemed a mad man, and deserve to have his neck broken, who should trust himself on this horse without any bridle at all?"[17]

The bridle the Anti-Federalists have in mind was revealed this week when delegate John Lansing offered a series of amendments to be attached to the new Constitution as a condition of its ratification. The move, coming after the news of Virginia's ratification, had the effect of changing the climate of the Convention from one of bitter opposition to opening the way for accommodation and compromise on both sides.[18]

The significant change in the climate at the New York Convention this week may also have been facilitated when contending delegates put aside their differences to participate in a convivial July 4 celebration hosted by Governor Clinton. One observer reports that both sides gave dinners and mingled with each other to drink toasts to the twelfth year of American independence.[19]

However, upstate in Albany a July 4 celebration was reported to have turned bloody. Anti-Federalists paraded into the city, setting a copy of the Constitution on fire. Federalists retrieved the charred document and began parading up the streets of Albany only to encounter an angry Anti-Federalist mob. As many as eighteen were reported injured in the melee. An Anti-Federalist leader later had misgivings, and explained that it would not have happened if both sides had "not been heated with Liquor."[20]

In sharp contrast, the July 4 Federal Procession in Philadelphia, for all the artillery discharges and trumpets, ended quietly and the 17,000 celebrants "*soberly* retired to their respective homes," although ten toasts of American porter, beer, and cider had been drunk to the newly ratified American Union.[21] Federalists and Anti-Federalists alike may have taken to heart Francis Hopkinson's ringing close in his "Ode": "United thus, and thus united, free."[22]

According to one observer, the lavish and expensive day-long celebration was both an end . . . and a beginning. It was an end to the ten-month war of ideas that had begun in Philadelphia with the Federal Convention and fought out in the often bitter ratification battles in the State Conventions. It was a beginning of a collective faith in the future of a united group of States.[23]

Although the Federal Procession was staged as the kickoff of a Federal campaign to sweep the First Federal Elections so as to control the new national government, it was also, according to one observer, the first extensive use of the arts in a national political effort. Federalist election themes were clearly manifest in this week's July 4 Procession. The floats, marchers, costumes, and slogans were deliberately arranged to present the new Constitution as the last link in a historical chain first forged in July 1776.

"The connection of the great event of independence," explains one Signer of the Declaration, Dr. Benjamin Rush, who was one of the planners of the event, "the French alliance, the Peace, and name of General Washington with the adoption of the Constitution was happily calculated to unite the most remarkable transports of the mind which were felt during the war with the great event of the day, and to produce such a tide of joy as has seldom been felt in any age or country. Political joy is one of the strongest emotions of the human mind."[24]

CHAPTER 43

★

July 11–17, 1788

New York City has been alive with dire predictions of violence and bloodshed this week if the State ratifying Convention in Pough-keepsie rejects the new Constitution.

A bloody clash between inebriated Federalists and Anti-Feder-alists in Albany at a July 4 celebration may have fanned talk in New York City of recourse to the sword if the Anti-Federalists prevail.

Federalist leader General Samuel Webb, an aide to General Wash-ington during the War of Independence, was reported to have said that the negative reports reaching New York City from Pough-keepsie have produced "rage" in the city's inhabitants, who are open-ly talking of seceding from the State if the Federalists are defeated.

". . . Should they not adopt it in a few days," General Webb informed a friend, "a resolution will pass for the new Congress to meet at Philadelphia, which will be a fatal stroke to our commerce, and where it will end God only knows. . . . I do not believe the life of the Governor [George Clinton] and his party would be safe in this place."[1]

One observer points out that it is difficult to separate bluster from real intentions. Federalists in New Hampshire had also threatened to take up the sword if ratification in their State failed. Whereas in Pennsylvania Anti-Federalists are reported to be organizing armed resistance to the new Constitution since their State has ratified.

In an apparent show of defiance of Anti-Federalist Governor Clin-ton, his opponents in New York City are planning an elaborate pub-lic procession for July 23 to celebrate the ratification of the Constitution by ten States, although New York State's Convention is still in session and deadlocked.[2]

Samuel A. Otis, a Massachusetts Congressman sitting in the Continental Congress, has raised the issue of possible violence, even though New York City Federalists are adamant in pressing ahead with the planned celebration before a Convention decision. He said: "... I dont know but we are in danger of running into excess in regard to processions. Perhaps my gravity and aversion to parade may have induced this opinion. It is an implied triumph over minority which always irritates."[3]

It is uncertain whether talk of possible violence induced Congressman Otis to vote with his colleagues in the Continental Congress this week to delay consideration of an ordinance establishing procedures for the First Federal Elections under the newly ratified Constitution until the New York ratifying Convention votes to accept or reject. One source maintains that a bitter behind-the-scenes struggle is unfolding in the old Congress over what city will be selected as the seat for the new national government.[4]

This may explain, however, why for the first time in many years all thirteen States are represented in the Continental Congress, even though the members number exactly one-third of those who signed the Declaration of Independence. Chronic absenteeism has been a major reason for its alleged ineffectiveness. This year, for example, the old Congress assembled in January, but it was not until May that it commanded the necessary seven-State quorum to conduct business.[5]

Congressman James Madison, recently arrived in New York City from Richmond, reported that Colonel Alexander Hamilton has written from Poughkeepsie that if New York City were to be selected as the seat of the national government, that action might influence the Convention to approve the new Constitution, with recommended rather than conditional amendments.[6]

According to one observer, the Poughkeepsie Convention has been bitterly deadlocked, not over whether ratification itself will be effected, but over what form in order that it may command a majority vote.[7]

On July 11, delegate John Jay proposed that the Constitution be ratified, with recommended amendments—the form that was approved by New Hampshire, Virginia, and Massachusetts. However, Governor Clinton and the Anti-Federalist majority insist that such amendments be made a condition of ratification. Mr. Jay countered that Congress had no power to accept New York on such special terms while other States had approved unconditionally. The 43-year-old Secretary of Foreign Affairs warned that if New York withheld ratification until such amendments were considered, she might be out of the Union for at least two years and would have no part in organizing the new government.

"These are not threats," he told the delegates who understood the economic implications of his words. "This is prudence. Let us join with our Neighbors to obtain the same Ends in the same Way. Let us agree and be unanimous. . . . We will have our Constitution you will have your A[men]dments."[8]

Governor Clinton rose to oppose Mr. Jay, arguing that the form of the new government must not be mistaken for substance. In Ancient Rome, he pointed out, the Senate existed but the real substantive power rested with the reigning tyrant. The new national government, with its extensive powers, will, Governor Clinton grimly predicted, terminate the existence of the States, and the liberties of the people will be crushed unless amendments are added to curb such powers.

". . . The evils pointed out in the system are now within our power to remedy—" the 48-year-old Governor told the Convention delegates, "but if we suffer ourselves to be influenced by specious reasoning unsupported by example to an unconditional adoption of an imperfect government, the opportunity will be forever lost, for history does not furnish a single instance of a government once established, voluntarily yielding up its powers to secure the rights and liberties of the people."[9]

Colonel Hamilton, in what sources say was an argumentative and impassioned rebuttal, insisted the only power the current Convention had was to adopt or reject absolutely: ". . . that it had indeed a power to recommend, because this was a natural right of every freeman; but it had none to dictate to or embarrass the union by any restrictions or conditions whatever. . . ."[10]

Instead of reconciling opponents, Colonel Hamilton's speech angered many of the Anti-Federalists. One went so far as heatedly to imply that his words amounted to a declaration of war.

"I see the advocates of the Constitution," the delegate stated, "are determined to force us to a rejection. We have gone great lengths and have conceded enough—but nothing will satisfy them:— if convulsions and a civil war are the consequence, I will go with my party."[11]

One observer reports that during the last three weeks of floor debate, the speeches of Colonel Hamilton and Robert R. Livingston have been filled with sneering sarcasm. The effect has been to make themselves obnoxious to the Anti-Federalist majority when divisiveness calls for conciliation. Delegate John Jay saved the situation by the use of a flattering courtesy toward his opponents, persuading them not to use their numbers to crush the minority by demanding an immediate vote.[12]

A source has told this correspondent that the majority of 46 Anti-Federalist delegates, made up mostly of village lawyers, farmers, and small-town politicians, has been unable to unite on a positive plan to rebut the arguments of the 19 Federalist delegates. Like most of the majority, Governor George Clinton has assumed the role of a negative leader rather than a positive proponent. He is willing to vote for ratification with conditional amendments, and he will not change his position.[13]

Another observer says that this week may have witnessed the crumbling of majority opposition in the face of the persistent minority drive to ratify, and the acceptance by ten other States. The basic weakness of the majority has been a lack of alternatives to outright rejection and a reliance almost exclusively on an illusionary alliance with Anti-Federalist forces in New Hampshire and Virginia.[14]

The narrow victories for ratification in both States late last month have, according to this observer, thrown Governor Clinton's forces into confusion, demonstrating that even before the New York Convention opened in Poughkeepsie a majority of Anti-Federalists were more disorganized than they cared to admit.

John Jay, in a letter to General Washington on May 29, a copy of which this correspondent obtained, may have accurately perceived the weakness of Governor Clinton's majority when he observed that many in the opposition were "Friends to Union and mean well." He also noted that the "Southern part of the State will at all Events adhere to the Union, and if necessary . . . seek a Separation from the northern." And about the leaders, he added, "I cannot find that they have as yet so looked forward to contingent Events, or even to those the most probable, as to have united in or formed any System adapted to them—"[15]

The close communication and cooperation among Federalists during the last eleven months of the ratification struggle are believed, by most observers, to have contributed to their victories, even though by narrow margins. Had the Anti-Federalists in New York and Virginia established effective cooperation and early communications, and presented a unified leadership, they could have forced acceptance of any form of ratification they chose to adopt.

For most of this year, the poor mail service among the States has led to the Anti-Federalist charge that their opponents have deliberately delayed delivery of their newspapers, pamphlets, and correspondence.

For example, Richard Henry Lee, Virginia Congressman, replied to General John Lamb, the organizer of a belated New York–based intra-State opposition organization, that he had only just received a letter on June 27 that General Lamb had posted from New York on May 18.

General Lee, the intellectual leader of the Anti-Federalists, immediately replied to the overdue letter—received two days after Virginia had narrowly ratified—and insisted that had General Lamb's plans for cooperation between New York and Virginia arrived sooner, they would have had "salutary consequences" on the Richmond ratifying Convention.

"It will be considered, I believe, as a most extraordinary epoch in the history of mankind," Congressman Lee wrote, "that in a few years there should be so essential a change in the minds of men. 'Tis really astonishing that the same people, who have just emerged from a long and cruel war in defence of liberty, should now agree to fix an elective despotism upon themselves and their posterity!"[16]

Two other failed efforts of the Virginia Anti-Federalists to form a working alliance with other States have only deepened the bitter belief that Federalists had deliberately delayed their mail communications for political advantage.

Last November, for instance, the Virginia Legislature passed a resolution inviting other States to confer on amendments to the new Constitution. Edmund Randolph, Virginia's Governor, who did not sign the Constitution but who was being wooed by James Madison, did not dispatch copies of the resolution to Governors of other States until December 27. Then, Governor Clinton of New York did not receive his copy until March 7, a delay of over two months, and too late for the New York Legislature to consider the invitation, as it had already adjourned.[17]

Governor Clinton wrote an unofficial reply, dated May 8, accepting the invitation for the two States to cooperate on amendments to the new Constitution. The letter was not made public until nearly two months later, and one day after Virginia's narrow ten-vote margin to ratify. When learning of the delay, Colonel George Mason bitterly assailed the Governor, alleging he withheld the Clinton letter in order to favor supporters of the new Constitution.[18]

Despite the belief of some New York and Virginia Anti-Federalists that the Federalists achieved their narrow ratification victory by unfair means, James Monroe is one of the few opponents of ratification who may have accurately assessed the single overriding influence that made possible narrow approval of the Constitution.

The 30-year-old Monroe acutely observed this week that the almost certain prospect that General George Washington would be chosen first President of the new national government defeated chances of the Anti-Federalists. "Be assured, his influence carried this government," he wrote in code to Thomas Jefferson in Paris.[19]

CHAPTER 44

★

July 18–24, 1788

In rare overt political use of his enormous prestige and influence, General George Washington demanded this week that the Continental Post-Master General be sacked.

In an angry letter dated July 18 to John Jay, Secretary of Foreign Affairs, a copy having been obtained by this correspondent, the General denounced a recent decision by the Post-Master General, Ebenezer Hazard, to stop the free postal delivery of newspapers between printers in the nation's cities. The decision was part of an economy measure and went into effect as the country is preparing for the First Federal Elections under the new Constitution.

"... The interruption in that mode of conveyance," the General wrote from Mount Vernon to Secretary Jay in New York City, "has not only given great concern to the friends of the Constitution...but it has afforded its enemies very plausible pretexts for dealing out their scandals, and exciting jealousies by inducing a belief that the suppression of intelligence, at that critical juncture, was a wicked trick of policy, contrived by an Aristocratic Junto."[1]

During the ratification campaign, Anti-Federalists alleged that Federalists bribed postal officials to delay or destroy their letters, pamphlets, and newspapers. However, one observer points out that General Washington is well aware that a majority of the nation's newspapers are pro-Federalist and that a halt to the free exchange of newspapers will hamper political influence of public opinion in the coming national elections. General Washington's demand that Post-Master General Hazard repeal his ban or be replaced marks the climax of furor on both sides using the mails for political advantage. The Post-Master General is reported to believe he has become a victim of his own desire to save public funds.[2]

★

Funds, private and public, were not spared this week when New York City staged, through its freshly swept streets, a "Grand Procession" down Broadway to Bowling Green where New Yorkers had toppled a statue of George III only thirteen years before. Although the July 23 parade was staged to celebrate ratification of the new Constitution, one observer reports that the banners, floats, and tableaus had the clear intent of influencing New York State's Convention, being held in Poughkeepsie, to end its bitter deliberations and become the eleventh State to approve the document.[3]

In a drizzling rain that delighted the Anti-Federalists but failed to dampen the spirits of Federalists, a crowd of over 6,000 watched as the procession was led by two horsemen with trumphets and one piece of artillery.

The most enthusiastic reception was reserved for the Federal ship *Hamilton*, a float drawn by ten horses, firing a thirteen-gun salute and manned by a crew of thirty seamen and marines. The bow of the ship displayed a bust of Colonel Alexander Hamilton holding a copy of the new Constitution to honor his signing the document for New York and his efforts during the ratification struggle.[4]

The Continental Congress adjourned its deliberations and most members watched the estimated three-and-a-half-hour procession and later joined some 6,000 New Yorkers who sat down to an outdoor dinner of roasted bullock, mutton, and ham. Protected from the rain by a huge canopy of canvas, the massive meal concluded with toasts to "The Convention of the State of New York; may they soon add an eleventh pillar to the Federal Edifice."[5]

The North Carolina Congressional delegation deliberately stayed away from both the procession and the victory dinner. Hugh Williamson says that his State's delegates had "stayed at home" out of "the respect we owed" North Carolina since it had not ratified the new Constitution.[6]

Congressman Williamson, a North Carolina delegate to the Federal Convention, may have remained aloof from the New York celebration because when his State's ratifying Convention met this week in Hillsboro, Anti-Federalist delegates were more than double the number of Federalists.[7]

According to one source, unlike the Anti-Federalist majority at the Poughkeepsie, New York, Convention, the leader of the opposition in North Carolina is intent not on debate but on using his majority to defeat ratification with dispatch. Willie Jones, a 47-year-old English-educated planter, refused to serve as a delegate to the Federal Convention, and although he is wealthy and from the upper classes, he commands the loyalty of the masses as a patriot and an ultra-democrat in theory.[8]

In the opening hours of the Convention this week, Mr. Jones formally moved for a ratification vote, saying it would save time and money since "the Constitution had so long been the subject of the deliberation of every man in this country, and that the members of the Convention had had such ample opportunity to consider it. . . ."[9]

Federalist James Iredell, immediately on his feet to object, pointed out that none of the ten previous Conventions had acted in such haste. Such a subject of great consideration, the 37-year-old English-educated lawyer contended, had been formed after much debate and deliberation. What would the constituents of each delegate think if the Convention voted without a conscientious discharge of his duty through mature debate and discussion? he asked.

"This Constitution," he counseled the Convention, "ought to be discussed in such a manner that every possible light may be thrown upon it. If those gentlemen who are so sanguine in their opinion that it is a bad government will freely unfold to us the reasons on which their opinion is founded, perhaps we may all concur in it."[10]

William Goudy, an ally of Mr. Jones, clearly indicated that the Anti-Federalist majority is not awed by the great names and men of learning and of the law who created the new Constitution. The fundamental issue, he told the Hillsboro Convention on July 23, is the concession of the powers, on the part of the people, to their rulers and thereby risking the danger of consolidation of the separate States.

". . . If we give away more power than we ought," he said, "we put ourselves in the situation of a man who puts on an iron glove, which he can never take off till he breaks his arm. Let us beware of the iron glove of tyranny."[11]

The following day, William Davie, a North Carolina delegate to the Federal Convention, sought to refute the Anti-Federalist charge that the new Constitution meant the consolidation and destruction of the power of the separate States:

"... the state governments are the pillars upon which this government is extended over such an immense territory, and are essential to its existence. The House of Representatives are immediately elected by the people. The senators represent the sovereignty of the states; they are directly chosen by the state legislatures, and no legislative act can be done without their concurrence. The election of the executive is in some measure under the control of the legislatures of the states, the electors being appointed under their direction."[12]

Nevertheless, the Federalist minority in North Carolina privately concedes its cause is hopeless and that argument is not likely to change many opposition minds under the intelligent, militant direction of Willie Jones.

One observer believes that the planter-politician is the only Anti-Federalist leader in the entire country who, in commanding a majority, has a consistent program and is pursuing it with dispatch. Had the Anti-Federalists in other States, this observer adds, been as well organized as the North Carolinians, they would not now be in full retreat on nearly all political fronts.[13]

The Anti-Federalist majority at the New York Convention in Poughkeepsie was reported this week to be in full political retreat. On July 23, for example, the retreat was led by a handful of nervous delegates when they moved to change the formula of ratification from "on condition" to "in full confidence" that New York's proposed 32 amendments would be accepted by the other States. This was nothing less than unconditional ratification, as demanded by the Federalist minority. It was expediency, not conviction, that won ratification by three votes.[14]

The next day, Anti-Federalist diehards, led by the Governor, George Clinton, sought to reverse their retreat by proposing the right of New York to withdraw from the new Union if its amendments were not submitted to a second convention within a certain number of years. Twelve delegates deserted Governor Clinton and voted with the Federalists to defeat the proposal by three votes.[15]

According to one observer, it was not the arguments of Federalists John Jay and Colonel Alexander Hamilton that won over some of their opponents, but the influence of Virginia's James Madison. Colonel Hamilton wisely read to the Poughkeepsie Convention a letter written by the Virginia Congressman.[16]

"... My opinion is," Mr. Madison wrote to Colonel Hamilton on July 20, "that a reservation of a right to withdraw if amendments be not decided on under the form of the Constitution within a certain time, is a *conditional* ratification, that it does not make N. York a member of the New Union, and consequently that she could not be received on that plan." He then unequivocally stated in his letter: "The Constitution requires an adoption *in toto,* and *for ever.*"[17]

Mr. Madison's words carried weight with a dozen Anti-Federalists already fearful of the economic consequences of New York out of the new Union. According to another observer, the Anti-Federalists also fear that the alternatives to ratification might be the risk of civil conflict, of secession by New York's southern counties, and an end to their own political as well as professional careers (as the chief defectors are merchants or lawyers).[18]

Another motive has been suggested this week by Congressman Madison. Many New York delegates are considering the economic factor of New York City's "fair chance" at retaining the seat of the national government.[19]

However, he stated in a July 21 letter from New York to General Washington at Mount Vernon, that the Continental Congress has delayed action on "putting the new Machine into operation" because of heated competition among various Congressmen to have their respective States selected as the seat of the Federal government. The consequence of a prolonged delay, the politically astute 37-year-old lawmaker says, is to give enemies of the Constitution the opportunity to organize and eventually elect House and Senate members to the First Congress who will be hostile to the new national government.[20]

General Washington's worry that the post office's policy of ending the free exchange of newspapers might also adversely affect Federalists' election fortunes, clearly indicates that neither the military hero of the War of Independence nor the chief political manager of the Constitution is taking anything for granted, even with the battle for ratification won.

Expressing his concern in his letter to Foreign Secretary Jay, for example, General Washington suggests that he "weigh the expediency" of "dropping such hints" to those in power to have the post office restore the free delivery of newspapers. He went on to suggest that we emulate England: "Mail Coaches as a great modern improvement" might be adopted in America and replace mail carried on horseback.

"I trust we are not too old, or too proud to profit by the experience of others," he added with dry wit.[21]

Ever since the Constitution was first published in the nation's newspapers, General Washington has been sensitive to the critical part they would play in winning ratification of the document. His alarm and anxiety because of Post-Master General Hazard's halt to free postal delivery of newspapers stem from the same perception of the vital role the press must play in the forthcoming First Federal Elections.

"It is a matter in my judgment of primary importance that the public mind should be relieved from inquietude on this subject," wrote the person whom everyone in America expects to be unanimously elected the first President under the new Constitution.[22]

CHAPTER 45

★

July 25–31, 1788

New York narrowly navigated its way into the new national Union this week only to have the helmsman of the new Constitution express angry alarm that New York Federalists may have unwittingly given the enemies of the document the means to steer the ship toward the reefs of shipwreck.

The July 26 ratification vote of 30 to 27 at the conclusion of the five-week Poughkeepsie Convention was the closest of any of the eleven State ratification conclaves. Although the thin three-vote approval was unconditional, the ratification document contains a circular letter to be signed by George Clinton, New York Governor, and sent to other States calling for a second convention to adopt amendments for a bill of rights.[1]

According to one observer, the letter had first been proposed on the Convention floor by Colonel Alexander Hamilton as a Federalist concession in exchange for the Anti-Federalist majority accepting unconditional ratification. The honest compromise has left both sides in New York State faintly dissatisfied.[2]

Whereas John Jay, Secretary of Foreign Affairs and a Federalist delegate, views the letter as a harmless expedient to ratification, James Madison, in New York at the Continental Congress, is reported by one source to be furious at and unforgiving of Mr. Jay for drafting an instrument for a second convention, an idea which the latter himself had earlier denounced. Mr. Madison is fearful that a second conclave would give Anti-Federalists an opportunity to undo the work of the Philadelphia Convention by amending the document to death.[3]

" . . . It has a most pestilent tendency," Congressman Madison angrily wrote to General Washington of the New York Circular

Letter. "If an Early General Convention cannot be parried, it is seriously to be feared that the system which has resisted so many direct attacks may be at last successfully undermined by its enemies."[4]

Most Federalists were in a self-congratulatory mood that the last of the large States has come into the Union. When an express rider from Poughkeepsie reached New York City the day of the ratification vote with the news, it set off general rejoicing. Cannon were fired from ships in the city harbor and Federalist supporters formed a procession and went cheering and shouting through the streets.[5]

Toasting and drinking, punctuated by an occasional skyward salute of muskets, prompted an ale-sodden mob to storm the offices of the *New York Journal*, vowing to teach the lone dissenting "Anti" publisher in the city a "public lesson in humility." The Federalist mob is reported to have upset type cases, smashed furniture, shattered windows, and scattered ink and paper throughout the publication's shop as punishment for its printing critical comments of the Federalist parade held on July 23.[6]

The Federalist press ignored the mob's destruction, preferring to praise New York's narrow approval and to heap scorn on the Circular Letter attached to the ratification document. The letter is expected to be widely printed in newspapers outside New York State. The *Pennsylvania Gazette* in Philadelphia, sharing Mr. Madison's concern about the political consequences of the Circular Letter, fired a fierce editorial broadside.

"The *alterations* (not amendments) of the Federal Constitution proposed by the Convention of New York. . .are so numerous, that if it were possible to admit them, they would annihilate the Constitution, and throw the United States not only back again into anarchy, but introduce poverty, misery, bloodshed and slavery into every state in the Union."[7]

While Federalists are united in their approval of New York's ratification, they are at odds with each other over what city should be chosen as the seat of the new national government. The Continental Congress on July 28, after weeks of delay, has set dates early next year for the selection and balloting of Presidential Electors and for convening the First Congress under the new Constitution.[8]

This correspondent has been unable to obtain details of the spirited debate in the old Congress over what city will be chosen as the seat of the new government, but the French envoy to the Continental government in New York has provided fragmentary details from his private journal.

According to Comte de Moustier, Southern delegates favor Philadelphia over New York City because of greater commercial ties with the Quaker city. A more central location, Southerners believe, would minimize Northern political influence with the new government. However, neither the advocates of New York nor those of Philadelphia have, at this writing, the votes to prevail.

"Other delegates had less patriotic motives," the French envoy wrote in his journal for July 28. "One voted for New York because his wife's family is settled there, another because he courts several young ladies, a third because the air of that city agrees with his health, etc. It is believed that Mr. [James] Madison has been so strongly in favor of Philadelphia only because he is to marry a woman who holds an annuity there."[9]

The French diplomat also notes that the Virginia delegation is split; Richard Henry Lee favors his own State along the shores of the Potomac. If the new Congress sits in Philadelphia, Congressman Lee is quoted as saying, it will again be subject to Robert Morris's attending to all the "financial operations" and that will "cause the revival of the pernicious stockjobbing which had ruined the states" during the War of Independence.

The French envoy adds that "Mr. [Alexander] Hamilton alleged that the delegates from New York were going to lose their popularity if the new Congress did not remain in that state because they had solemnly promised it at the [New York] Convention if the new Constitution were ratified there. . . . It is astonishing that the personal interest of each delegate is so active in attracting Congress to his own state."[10]

Politics aside, the French diplomat himself has astonished residents of Boston, New York, and Philadelphia. Ever since he took up his diplomatic post earlier this year, he has shocked those societies by bringing along his sister-in-law who, it is rumored, is also his mistress. Mr. Madison is reported to be leading an effort to have the American Minister to Paris, Thomas Jefferson, request his recall.

"Moustier proves a most unlucky appointment," Mr. Madison wrote in code to Mr. Jefferson. "He is *unsocial proud* and *niggardly and betrays a sort of fastidiousness toward this country. He suffers also from his illicit connection with Madame de Brehan* which is *universally known* and *offensive to American manners—she* is *perfectly soured toward this country.* . . . On *their journeys* it is *said they often neglect the* most obvious *precautions for veiling their intimacy—.* . . ."[11]

The desire for the French envoy's recall comes at a time when Mr. Jefferson is involved in delicate negotiations with the French government over trade and debt matters. Moreover, the French monarchy is currently caught up in a severe economic crisis with revolutionary implications, and is unable or unwilling to enact similar political and economic reforms that are embodied in the newly ratified American Constitution.

One observer reports that Minister Jefferson may seek to solve the delicate problem by asking the Marquis de Lafayette in Paris to make the case personally for Comte de Moustier's recall before the French Minister for Foreign Affairs Montmorin.[12]

Increasing foreign trade, solving America's swollen foreign debt, and securing new hard currency loans from Europe are three issues that have been used by Federalists to justify ratification of the new Constitution.

This week at the North Carolina Convention, for example, Samuel Johnston, the Governor, sought to use the real, and imagined, economic ills of the State and of the nation to answer delegates' objections to granting powers of direct taxation to the new Congress.

". . . The United States are bankrupts," he told the July 26 session at Hillsboro. "They are considered such in every part of the world. They borrow money, and promise to pay: they have it not in their power, and they are obliged to ask of the people, whom they owe, to lend them money to pay the very interest. This is disgraceful and humiliating. By these means we are paying compound interest. . . . Shall we continue the same practice? Shall we not rather struggle to get over our misfortunes?"[13]

Although the Federalist minority has commanded the Convention floor with persuasive arguments all this week, the two-to-one Anti-Federalist majority is reported to have remained unmoved in its conviction that the new Constitution should be rejected, even if it means that North Carolina would remain outside the new Union.

Anti-Federalist leader Willie Jones took that uncompromising position this week and even invoked the name of Thomas Jefferson to support his position. Minister Jefferson had earlier suggested to Mr. Madison that nine States should ratify the document while the remaining four withheld their approval until amendments were guaranteed. Apparently obtaining a copy of the letter or learning of its contents, Anti-Federalists have effectively used the letter to the dismay of Mr. Madison.[14] For Mr. Jefferson subsequently changed his mind.

But Mr. Jones told the North Carolina delegates this week that he does not trust any new Congress to keep its word and he has greater confidence in a second Federal convention or in the individual State Legislatures adopting a bill of rights in the form of amendments.

"... In either case," he said in a speech on July 31, "it may take up about eighteen months. For my part, I would rather be eighteen years out of the Union than adopt it in its present defective form."[15]

Delegate James Iredell, who has carried the bulk of the debate for the Federalists, was clearly appalled and alarmed. Only three States ratified unanimously, he argued, while the others vigorously advanced a demand for amendments to protect the liberties of the people. This fact, he added, clearly places great pressure on the new Congress to act.

"... There is a very great probability," he told the delegates, "if not an absolute certainty, that amendments will be obtained. ... We are not, at any event, in a condition to stand alone. God forbid we should be a moment separated from our sister states! If we are, we shall be in great danger of a separation forever. I trust every gentleman will pause before he contributes to so awful an event."[16]

According to one observer, such arguments have had almost no effect on the Anti-Federalist majority. Since the conclave first met in Hillsboro on July 21, Federalists have been unable to draw out the opposition in debate. Rather than answer arguments, the Anti-

Federalist majority has been content to respond with word quibbling and sarcasm. Their leader, Willie Jones, has spoken hardly at all, but it is his individual strength of will that is in control of the majority.[17]

An underlying, unspoken factor that has not been publicly debated is the Anti-Federalists' concern that the Northern-dominated Congress could outvote the South. Personal freedoms should be protected, but there is the subtle implication that Southern interests should also be protected.[18]

Before the North Carolina Convention, Federalists confidently predicted that the State would follow Virginia's lead and ratify with a recommendation for amendments. However, the tone and tenor of the debates in North Carolina and the Circular Letter from the New York Convention this week clearly indicate that Congressman Madison's fears for the future of the new Constitution may be well founded.

"... The great danger in the present crisis," he wrote to Thomas Jefferson, "is that if another Convention should be soon assembled, it would terminate in discord, or in alterations of the federal system which would throw back *essential* powers into the State Legislatures."[19]

CHAPTER 46

★

August 1–7, 1788

North Carolina rang down the curtain on the eleven-month ratification drama this week when, by a lopsided margin of 183 to 84, its Convention voted neither to reject nor to accept the new Constitution.[1]

The Hillsboro Convention's action on August 2 may have resulted from the influence of Patrick Henry's Anti-Federalist forces in neighboring Virginia. Willie Jones, leader of the Anti-Federalist majority at the North Carolina Convention, offered, without alteration, a resolution that had originally been submitted to the Virginia ratifying Convention. It proposed amendments, for a bill of rights, as a *condition* for the State joining the new Union.

"... We run no risk," he told the delegates, "of being excluded from the Union when we think proper to come in. Virginia, our next neighbor, will not oppose our admission. We have a common cause with her. She wishes the same alterations."[2]

During the nearly two weeks that the North Carolina Convention met, the Federalist minority argued in vain that rejection of the Constitution would have dangerous economic and political consequences for the State and for the new Union. Federalist delegate James Iredell maintained that North Carolina should follow Virginia's example and approve the document with *recommended* amendments rather than remain out of the Union until alterations were approved by the other States.

"... Had she held out," he said of Virginia, "it would have been a subject of most serious alarm. But she thought the risk of losing the union altogether too dangerous to be incurred. She did not then know of the ratification of New Hampshire. If she thought it necessary to adopt, when only eight states had ratified, is it not much more necessary for us after the ratification by ten?"[3]

Dismissing the dangers of remaining out of the Union as "fanciful," Mr. Jones believes that by withholding ratification, North Carolina will accumulate sufficient leverage to force a second convention of the States. He hopes that North Carolina's failure to ratify will, in the words of Thomas Jefferson, fly "like an electrical shock through America and Europe."[4]

The huge Anti-Federalist majority's vote at Hillsboro was dictated as much by population and geography as by conviction. North Carolina, which includes counties in Tennessee, is a large State with its population widely dispersed; many are in isolated interior communities comprising self-sufficient farmers and frontiersmen. Most believe the State government is unresponsive to their views because it is for the most part in the hands of commercial men who live near the Atlantic seacoast. The new national government would be considered even more remote and unresponsive to the people's interests.[5]

Many of the delegates are Presbyterians from the north of Ireland, by way of Virginia, and fiercely Protestant. The Baptists in the northern section of the State are also generally opposed to the Constitution. This may help explain why, in the concluding days of the Convention, the issue of the absence of a religious test in the new Constitution produced an intense debate.

Delegate Henry Abbot said he had in some measure been satisfied that the people could worship God according to their own consciences. But he nevertheless shared the concern of others that Presidential treaty-making powers might be used to impose the Roman Catholic religion on the country.[6] Many wished to know what *religion* will be founded in the Union, he said. Since every Federal and State officeholder will be required to swear an oath, he asked, if there is no religious test, to whom will they swear support—the ancient pagan gods of Jupiter, Juno, Minerva, or Pluto?

"... The exclusion of religious tests," he said, "is by many thought dangerous and impolitic. They suppose that if there be no religious test required, pagans, deists, and Mahometans might obtain offices among us, and that the senators and representatives might all be pagans."[7]

Federalist delegate Iredell responded by holding up for all delegates to see a printed pamphlet describing the "very serious danger" that the Pope of Rome might be elected President. Such fears, he said, are as unfounded as fear of electing one of the Kings of Europe the American President. Every person conversant with the history of mankind knows how religious tests have been used for persecution and waging bloody wars.

". . . America has set an example to mankind," the 37-year-old lawyer added, "to think more modestly and reasonably—that a man may be of different religious sentiments from our own, without being a bad member of society. The principles of toleration, to the honor of this age, are doing away those errors and prejudices which have so long prevailed, even in the most intolerant countries."[8]

The spirit of toleration by the Anti-Federalist majority came to an abrupt, inconclusive end on August 1. Refusing to entertain a Federalist motion to vote on its plan for unconditional ratification with recommended amendments for a bill of rights, the majority followed Willie Jones and on August 2 voted for withholding ratification until amendments are secured.[9]

One observer reports that when news of what North Carolina has done this week reaches New York and Congressman James Madison, it is likely to increase his growing alarm over the possibility that Anti-Federalists in Virginia, Pennsylvania, and New York will join with North Carolina and successfully convene a second Federal convention, which will then amend the new Constitution to death.[10]

Mr. Madison is also disturbed over petty sectional politics that have surfaced in the Continental Congress over a temporary seat for the new national government. The dispute is taking on the semblance of a power struggle between North and South. This week, for example, to prevent Philadelphia and New York from being selected, Congress surprised everyone by temporarily approving Baltimore.[11]

Then, two days later, on August 6, the Continental Congress reversed its earlier decision and designated New York City. The French envoy to the New York City–based Congress alleges that South Carolina broke ranks with the Southern States, which favor

Philadelphia as a more central location, for reasons of the heart and not regional preference.

"The delegates from South Carolina," observes Comte de Moustier, "incapable of making a firm decision and attached to some New York women, by means of being importuned by the New Yorkers, were not able to resist their entreaties and it was proposed to replace the word Baltimore with the word New York, which passed with a majority of seven states, 5 states being opposed to it and Georgia divided."[12]

The determination of the place for commencing proceedings under the new government was one part of the entire ordinance under consideration. The ordinance also provides for the organization of the new government—including the dates for the Electors to be chosen and the Presidential election. The first two votes were for *place*. The following day the ordinance as a whole was put to a vote.

Rhode Island, which had not called a ratifying Convention but which retains its seat in the old Continental Congress, became an important pawn in the sectional struggle. The tiny New England State was instrumental, along with South Carolina, in defeating Philadelphia in favor of New York City. But then it lived up to its reputation for consistently opposing the new Constitution by refusing to join in the vote for the whole ordinance. A vote could have been construed as an implicit acceptance of the new government.[13]

The delegation departed for home, leaving Congress deadlocked. Without Rhode Island, the quorum of seven States cannot be obtained to pass the whole ordinance.[14]

The delays, indecisions, and deadlock of the past six weeks are likely to require the intervention of George Washington. His own view of what city should be chosen as the temporary seat of the new national government is likely to be crucial—just as his behind-the-scenes influence at the Philadelphia Convention and during the long ratification debates ensured the document's final creation and adoption.

Regarding the choice for a temporary capital, the General has written to Congressman Madison, a copy having been obtained by this correspondent, suggesting that some kind of compromise will be necessary: "the several parts should submit to the inconveniences for the benefits which they derive from the conveniences of the compact."[15]

Mr. Madison is reportedly concerned about Anti-Federalist efforts to convene a second convention. Whereas General Washington is reportedly more concerned over the delay of the Continental Congress in implementing the first requirements to begin the new national government. He is also worried, this correspondent has learned, about his own personal finances.

This week, for example, the General wrote Dr. James Craik, his family physician, apologizing for his delinquency in discharging his account. He candidly confessed: "I never felt the want of money so sensibly since I was a boy of 15 years old as I have done for the last 12 months and probably shall do for 12 months more to come."[16]

Like so many planters in the last few years, the General is land rich and cash poor. A drought last year forced him to borrow heavily. According to one observer, his cash shortage reached a humiliating crisis when he had to put off the Fairfax County sheriff three separate times for collection of back taxes on Mount Vernon. Also, he was warned that his undeveloped lands in Greenbrier County, in western Virginia, will be sold unless back taxes are paid.[17]

General Washington and other supporters of the new Constitution see the document as an instrument as much for financial reform as for political reform. The chronic shortage of gold and silver as a circulating medium and each State's issuing of inflated paper money under the old Articles of Confederation have been cited as major causes for the economic hard times.

The recently ratified document prohibits the States from coining money, or from printing paper money or bills of credit. And it specifies that only gold and silver will be used by the States as legal tender in payment of debt.[18]

At the close of the North Carolina Convention this week, when the Anti-Federalist majority proposed its series of amendments, along the lines of Virginia's recommended ones, it included a bombshell: an amendment to curb the power of the new Congress to levy direct taxes and to deny federal control over paper money issued by the States.[19]

Next to the power to levy direct taxes, the most heated economic debate at the Hillsboro Convention centered on the paper-money issue. Many delegates fear that with the chronic shortage of gold and silver, and with paper money swept away, they would be left without the means to pay their taxes and to meet other financial obligations.[20]

". . . As to paper money, it was the result of necessity," insisted delegate Joseph M'Dowell. "We were involved in a great war. What money had been in the country was sent to other parts of the world. What would have been the consequence if paper money had not been made? We must have been undone. Our political existence must have been destroyed."[21]

Samuel Johnston, North Carolina Governor, replied that although paper money assisted in financing the War of Independence and the payment of officers and enlisted men, its effect since the formal peace of 1783 has been destructive to all economic classes in the country. Only the new Constitution can rid the country of the evil, the Governor said, and instill confidence in those at home and abroad who are currently hoarding hard currency.

". . . Before the emission of the paper money, there was a great deal of hard money among us," he pointed out to the Convention delegates. ". . . There is more specie in the country than is generally imagined; but the proprietors keep it locked up. No man will part with his specie. It lies in his chest. It is asked, Why not lend it out? The answer is obvious—that, should he once let it get out of his power, he never can recover the whole of it. If he bring suit, he will obtain a verdict for one half of it. This is the reason of our poverty."[22]

General George Washington, in spite of his personal financial woes, is optimistic that an economic revival is under way in both agriculture and manufactured goods. He writes Thomas Jefferson in Paris that "we may perhaps rejoice that the People have been ripened by misfortune for the reception of good government."

He went on to admit that he "had indulged the expectation, that the New Government would enable those entrusted with its Administration to do justice to the public creditors and retrieve the National character. . . . If the system can be put in operation without touching much the Pockets of the People, perhaps, it may be done; but, in my judgment, infinite circumspection and prudence are yet necessary in the experiment."[23]

Looking back on the last eleven months, General Washington has confided to friends that the greatest danger and consequences from the passionate opposition to ratification would have been general chaos before any new government could even be established; that would have meant "political shipwreck, without the aid of one friendly star to guide us into Port."[24]

The General is reportedly gratified that some of the most militant opponents have pledged support for the new national government now that the issue has been decided. Nevertheless, he is warning Federalists that sharp political reefs remain.

Anti-Federalists will seek, he predicts, to secure election to the First Congress "in order to embarrass the wheels of government and produce premature alterations in its Constitution." He is urging Federalists "to be on their guard so far as not to suffer any secret machinations to prevail, without taking measures to frustrate them."

As he wrote to a wartime aide, "I wish I may be mistaken in imagining, that there are persons, who, upon finding they could not carry their point by an open attack against the Constitution, have some sinister designs to be silently effected, if possible. But I trust in that Providence, which has saved us in six troubles yea in seven, to rescue us again from any imminent, though unseen, dangers. Nothing, however, on our part ought to be left undone."[25]

Although the new Constitution has been given legal life with the approval of the nine necessary States, and the expectation is that the hero of the American Revolution will be the Union's first President, he continues to deny that he has any desire other than to live out his last years in retirement at his beloved Mount Vernon. Nevertheless, this does not prevent him from formulating and articulating his own vision about the future.

In writing to a member of the Irish Parliament, Sir Edward Newenham, the General expresses hope that the United States may steer clear of European politics and its wars. Perhaps these nations will in time adopt good national governments "and become respectable in the eyes of the world," he predicted. He also believes that as long as America remains united and faithful to itself, none of the maritime powers, particularly those with possessions in the New World or the West Indies, shall be able to prevent her from becoming a great respectable commercial nation.

"... It is true," he went on, "that, for the want of a proper Confœderation, we have not yet been in a situation fully to enjoy those blessings which God and Nature seemed to have intended for us. But I begin to look forward, with a kind of political faith, to scenes of National happiness, which have not heretofore been offered for the fruition of the most favoured Nations.... We have an almost unbounded territory whose natural advantages for agriculture and Commerce equal those of any on the globe. In a civil point of view we have unequalled privilege of choosing our own political Institutions and of improving upon the experience of Mankind in the formation of a confœderated government, where due energy will not be incompatible with unalienable rights of freemen....

"... You will permit me to say," General Washington adds, "that a greater Drama is now acting on this Theatre than has heretofore been brought on the American Stage, or any other in the World. We exhibit at present the Novel and astonishing Spectacle of a whole People deliberating calmly on what form of government will be most conducive to their happiness...."[26]

POSTSCRIPT

A Reporter's Reflections

The Philadelphia Convention was Act One, the just-concluded ratification ordeal was Act Two, and the forthcoming First Federal Elections are Act Three. Many of the principals in the first two acts are certain to be major players in the third.

Perhaps this is the only public drama wherein the star was seen on-stage during the first act, but not heard. He was seen on-stage during the second act but heard only off-stage. Yet his very existence has been critical in the first two acts and very likely will be indispensable in the third act.

General George Washington these last eleven months has seemed a godlike ghost, an American Moses at his Mount Vernon Sinai, who, in time, is expected to descend and lead the American people into the promised land armed with the new Constitution as a covenant for freedom, prosperity, and happiness. Without the General's support, never publicly stated, and behind-the-scenes strategy plotted with James Madison, little doubt exists that the document would have gone down to defeat.

Even with his support, the new Constitution would have suffered defeat had the Federalists not promised amendments or a bill of rights. Despite this expedient promise, in four key States the margin of victory was narrow: New York by 3 votes, Virginia and New Hampshire by 10, and in Massachusetts by 19 out of 355 delegates.

An analysis, moreover, of the nine States and 1,648 delegates who actually voted, shows that 545, or 33 percent, voted to reject despite the promise of future amendments, or a bill of rights. In six of the nine Conventions, only the promise of future amendments made passage possible.

297

It is now clear to this correspondent that despite their superior leadership, organization, and near dominance of the newspapers, the Federalists came perilously close to defeat by misjudging their Anti-Federalist opponents. For the first six months during the ratification debate, Federalists refused to recognize the political importance of the bill of rights issue.

The Federalists' failure to convince critics that sections of the new Constitution were themselves a bill of rights, or that rights not specified were retained by the States, appears to have arisen initially from the secrecy that had surrounded the Philadelphia Convention. Their refusal to release records of the debates only deepened critics' distrust of the advocates of the document. Nevertheless, those delegates who opposed the document in Philadelphia honored their oath of secrecy, perhaps, in part, because of the presence of General Washington.

Efforts to rush the ratification process, first in the Continental Congress when it forwarded the document to the States, and later in Pennsylvania, convinced the more militant Anti-Federalists that a conspiracy had been hatched to rob the people of their liberties and the States of their sovereignty by a power-hungry aristocratic elite. Such repeated assertions, given wider circulation in a handful of Anti-Federalist newspapers, clearly cast a shadow over the document and its supporters.

The use or sanction of violence, irregularities in the election of ratifying Convention delegates, and the arrogant conduct of the Federalists at the Pennsylvania and Connecticut ratifying Conventions made even more credible the critics' charge that a conspiracy was afoot. As this negative news spread to other parts of the country, it clearly alienated many moderate supporters.

The rapid ratification by Delaware, Pennsylvania, New Jersey, Georgia, and Connecticut, in a period of six weeks, established a critical momentum for the Federalists. At the same time, it produced a nearly fatal overconfidence. So much so that supporters of the new Constitution were blinded to the importance of a bill of rights and to the historical and human elements that produced a broad base of support for the inclusion of such a bill in the new Constitution in the form of amendments.

★

The most vocal advocates for a bill of rights, whether in the ratifying Conventions or elsewhere, are older men who have lived through what they perceive as the tyrannical rule of the British. Many had actively participated in the political and military struggle for independence. A bill of rights is in most of the State constitutions and is seen as a safeguard of personal liberties and a check on abuse of power by State governments.

When the new Constitution emerged from the secrecy of Philadelphia with a novel, new form of government with sweeping powers, but without a bill of rights, it was perceived as an instrument for the destruction and consolidation of the separate States. Charges that the document is the product of power-hungry aristocrats, secretly seeking to reimpose a king and with him a British-style rule, fed fears that the hard-won independence, at great cost, is to be swept away.

In three New England States, the clause in the Constitution that extends slavery for twenty years served to reinforce the belief in the minds of some that the document is a potential design for future despotism and a death warrant for personal liberties. In the ratifying Conventions of Connecticut, Massachusetts, and New Hampshire, a number of delegates specifically voted against approval out of a moral conviction that a new Constitution willing to continue the enslavement of black Africans could just as easily impose slavery on white Americans.

The Massachusetts Convention was a watershed for Federalists. Clearly in the minority, the Federalists disguised their arrogance with a mask of patient, polite persuasion to secure a nineteen-vote majority. However, in private they employed spying and threats, packed the spectator galleries with supporters, and concluded a political deal with the popular Governor of the State, who successfully presented himself as a reluctant physician prepared to bind up the wounds of the ratifying Convention.

Neutralizing influential Samuel Adams, the only Anti-Federalist leader capable of commanding a majority to vote for rejection, was crucial to Federalist success. Just as crucial was the political bargain concluded with vain John Hancock. Seduced with the prospect of his name being put forth as President, he was coached off-stage to introduce the idea of recommended amendments.

Just as the Anti-Federalists lacked a leader to materialize at the Boston Convention, with Sam Adams successfully silenced, the Anti-Federalists in New Hampshire and New York also lacked decisiveness and a strong leader.

Only in North Carolina did such a leader emerge—Willie Jones—with the political skills to convince the majority to risk staying out of the Union by rejecting ratification. New Hampshire's Joshua Atherton was articulate as a leader, but not as effective as Mr. Jones in mobilizing the majority under the relentless pressure of the Federalist minority.

Vocal, but politically feeble, Anti-Federalists in Pennsylvania, Maryland, and South Carolina looked to Virginia to save their cause after Massachusetts ratified. Remarkably, the Anti-Federalists in New York, led by its Governor, George Clinton, counted more on Patrick Henry in Virginia than on their own numerical strength as a majority.

On the other hand, the Federalist minority in New York had both articulate leaders and a program. They successfully manipulated the Convention to accept ratification less on the merits of the new Constitution than out of fear that New York would suffer retribution should the State's voters blame the Convention delegates for negative economic consequences that might flow from disunion.

There is little evidence to support the repeated Federalist assertion that critics of the Constitution favored disunion, or even the formation of separate confederations. Nevertheless, the charge appears to have had some effect on wavering delegates, primarily because of the British, Spanish, and Indian threats along the frontiers.

The promise that the new Constitution would return economic prosperity to the country consolidated support in the regions nearest the coast and the main centers of commerce—Boston, New York, Philadelphia, and Charleston. Added to this hard-core support were former officers who had served under General Washington, although a handful did side with opponents of the document.

The Anti-Federalists drew their principal strength from farmers and frontiersmen in the interior, although in several State Conventions some delegates from the interior voted for ratification. Like those to the Virginia and Georgia Conventions, delegates were concerned about security from Indian attacks and future economic prosperity.

Although there is some evidence that a majority of Americans favored the Anti-Federalists in varying degrees, limited access to newspapers proved critical in the Anti-Federalist failure to communicate and to mobilize such support. Even more crucial was the failure of Anti-Federalist leaders in various States to coordinate their efforts and to communicate with one another to the same degree as their Federalist opposition.

With perhaps some justice, Anti-Federalists maintain that their opponents controlled the postal service and deliberately delayed or lost letters, newspapers, and pamphlets. It is a matter of record that even though the Federalists controlled most newspapers, they sanctioned a campaign to drive out of business the few Anti-Federalist newspapers that were publishing.

Even if the Anti-Federalists had not been dealt a serious setback by delays of the mail, and not lacked equal access to the press, the failure of a national leader to emerge would by itself probably have crippled their cause. In eight of the nine State Conventions where opposition was offered—whether as a vocal minority or a clear majority—leadership, a program, and a sound strategy were clearly lacking.

Patrick Henry in Virginia was the only leader with the stature and national respect capable of leading the Anti-Federalist opposition. But he did not emerge on the scene until Virginia's Convention met, and his focal points were the Mississippi River issue, and general distrust of the document and of its advocates.

Governor Henry and Anti-Federalist penman Richard Henry Lee appear to have committed their first tactical error by declining to serve as elected delegates to the Philadelphia Convention. The record, moreover, does not reveal that Governor Henry sought actively to use his fame, prestige (second nationally only to General Washington's), and pen to influence men and events in the States beyond Virginia's borders to the degree that General Washington did.

Governor Henry's oratorical brilliance at the Virginia Convention equaled, or excelled, his past performances. Nevertheless, he failed against the careful plotting and preparation of James Madison. One even gains the impression that Governor Henry entered the Virginia Convention relying solely on his powers of oratorical persuasion, while neglecting to prepare a long-range strategy and formula for victory. Yet, he and his allies, like Colonel George Mason, had had almost seven months to plan a strategy.

What is remarkable about the just-concluded eleven-month ratification struggle is that, despite all their strengths and advantages, the Federalists came so close to defeat.

And despite all their weaknesses and disadvantages, the Anti-Federalists forced their opponents to promise amendments as the price for what still remains an embryonic, imperfect new Union that could easily become stillborn.

Patrick Henry and other Anti-Federalists regard the promises of amendments with deep distrust and are skeptical that the Federalists will honor such pledges. Part of their distrust is rooted in the conviction that the advocates of the new Constitution prevailed by unfair means and, in some cases, by force and fraud.

As a consequence, a sizable influential segment in the thirteen States is hostile toward the creation of the new national government. If General Washington is elected President in the forthcoming First Federal Elections, as is widely expected, he cannot hope to succeed faced with hostile foreign powers at the States' borders and an angry militant minority within the Union. Such a combination has the potential for igniting a civil war.

Almost certainly the Anti-Federalists will continue to use the issue of amendments, or a bill of rights, during the elections and in the new Congress as a way of achieving some of their goals. The more militant will surely use the threat of calling a second convention if the Federalists and the new Congress show any signs of delay or dishonor in implementing their promises for amendments.

★

The creation of the new Constitution and the often profound and profane public debate over its acceptance are unprecedented experiences. Nothing like the document or the debates these last fifteen months has ever happened before, making it difficult for this correspondent to draw any definite conclusion about the future.

One thing is certain. The last fifteen months have been historic in the sense that for the first time in the known world, the matter of how political power should be used both to serve a nation and to preserve the liberty of its individual citizens has been set down in a document and openly debated in public.

Federalists argue that a centralized power—contained, checked, balanced, and held accountable—can serve the ends of prosperity, peace, and personal liberty if administered by enlightened leaders.

Anti-Federalists argue, in effect, that when man is entrusted with power, experience has proved that he is so corrupted by it that only a severe decentralization and fragmentation of power can, in the long range, save personal liberty from being sacrificed.

So fundamental and clashing are these propositions that they will not cease with the conclusion of the ratification struggle. Indeed, they will very likely agitate and animate future American politics forever.

APPENDIX 1

American Newspapers Publishing in 1787–88*

Connecticut

AMERICAN MERCURY, HARTFORD
CONNECTICUT COURANT, HARTFORD
CONNECTICUT GAZETTE, NEW LONDON
CONNECTICUT JOURNAL, NEW HAVEN
FAIRFIELD GAZETTE
MIDDLESEX GAZETTE, MIDDLETOWN
NEW HAVEN CHRONICLE
NEW HAVEN GAZETTE
NORWICH PACKET
WEEKLY MONITOR, LITCHFIELD

Delaware

DELAWARE COURANT, WILMINGTON
DELAWARE GAZETTE, WILMINGTON

Georgia

GAZETTE OF THE STATE OF GEORGIA, SAVANNAH
GEORGIA STATE GAZETTE, AUGUSTA

Maryland

MARYLAND CHRONICLE, FREDERICKTOWN
MARYLAND GAZETTE, ANNAPOLIS
MARYLAND GAZETTE, BALTIMORE

* *Documentary History of the Ratification of the Constitution.* Short titles of selected newspapers and magazines.

MARYLAND JOURNAL, Baltimore
PALLADIUM OF FREEDOM, Baltimore

Massachusetts

AMERICAN HERALD, Boston
AMERICAN RECORDER, Charlestown
BERKSHIRE CHRONICLE, Pittsfield
BOSTON GAZETTE
CONTINENTAL JOURNAL, Boston
CUMBERLAND GAZETTE, Portland, Maine
ESSEX JOURNAL, Newburyport
HAMPSHIRE CHRONICLE, Springfield
HAMPSHIRE GAZETTE, Northampton
HERALD OF FREEDOM, Boston
INDEPENDENT CHRONICLE, Boston
MASSACHUSETTS CENTINEL, Boston
MASSACHUSETTS GAZETTE, Boston
SALEM MERCURY
WORCESTER MAGAZINE/MASSACHUSETTS SPY

New Hampshire

FREEMAN'S ORACLE, Exeter
NEW HAMPSHIRE GAZETTE, Portsmouth
NEW HAMPSHIRE MERCURY, Portsmouth
NEW HAMPSHIRE RECORDER, Keene
NEW HAMPSHIRE SPY, Portsmouth

New Jersey

BRUNSWICK GAZETTE, New Brunswick
NEW JERSEY JOURNAL, Elizabeth Town
TRENTON MERCURY

New York

ALBANY GAZETTE
ALBANY JOURNAL
AMERICAN MAGAZINE, New York
COUNTRY JOURNAL, Poughkeepsie
DAILY ADVERTISER, New York
HUDSON WEEKLY GAZETTE

IMPARTIAL GAZETTEER, NEW YORK
INDEPENDENT JOURNAL, NEW YORK
NEW YORK GAZETTEER
NEW YORK JOURNAL
NEW YORK MORNING POST
NEW YORK MUSEUM
NEW YORK PACKET
NORTHERN CENTINEL, LANSINGBURGH

North Carolina

NORTH CAROLINA GAZETTE, EDENTON
NORTH CAROLINA GAZETTE, NEW BERN
STATE GAZETTE OF NORTH CAROLINA, NEW BERN
WILMINGTON CENTINEL

Pennsylvania

AMERICAN MUSEUM, PHILADELPHIA
CARLISLE GAZETTE
COLUMBIAN MAGAZINE, PHILADELPHIA
EVENING CHRONICLE, PHILADELPHIA
FEDERAL GAZETTE, PHILADELPHIA
FREEMAN'S JOURNAL, PHILADELPHIA
GERMANTAUNER ZEITUNG
INDEPENDENT GAZETTEER, PHILADELPHIA
LANCASTER ZEITUNG
PENNSYLVANIA CHRONICLE, YORK
PENNSYLVANIA GAZETTE, PHILADELPHIA
PENNSYLVANIA HERALD, PHILADELPHIA
PENNSYLVANIA JOURNAL, PHILADELPHIA
PENNSYLVANIA MERCURY, PHILADELPHIA
PENNSYLVANIA PACKET, PHILADELPHIA
PHILADELPHISCHE CORRESPONDENZ
PITTSBURGH GAZETTE

Rhode Island

NEWPORT HERALD
NEWPORT MERCURY
PROVIDENCE GAZETTE
UNITED STATES CHRONICLE, PROVIDENCE

South Carolina

CHARLESTON MORNING POST/CITY GAZETTE
COLUMBIAN HERALD, CHARLESTON
SOUTH CAROLINA WEEKLY CHRONICLE, CHARLESTON
STATE GAZETTE OF SOUTH CAROLINA, CHARLESTON

Vermont

VERMONT GAZETTE, BENNINGTON
VERMONT JOURNAL, WINDSOR

Virginia

KENTUCKE GAZETTE, LEXINGTON
NORFOLK AND PORTSMOUTH JOURNAL, NORFOLK
VIRGINIA CENTINEL, WINCHESTER
VIRGINIA GAZETTE, PETERSBURG
VIRGINIA GAZETTE, WINCHESTER
VIRGINIA GAZETTE AND INDEPENDENT CHRONICLE, RICHMOND
VIRGINIA GAZETTE AND WEEKLY ADVERTISER, RICHMOND
VIRGINIA HERALD, FREDERICKSBURG
VIRGINIA INDEPENDENT CHRONICLE, RICHMOND
VIRGINIA JOURNAL, ALEXANDRIA

APPENDIX 2

Chronology of State Ratification Conventions, 1787–90, and Final Votes

1787

February 21	Continental Congress Calls Constitutional Convention
May 14	Convention Meets in Philadelphia; Quorum Not Present
May 25	Convention Begins with Quorum of Seven States
September 17	Constitution Signed and Convention Adjourns
September 20–27	Continental Congress Reads, Debates, and Transmits Constitution to the States
December 7	Delaware Ratifies, 30 to 0
December 12	Pennsylvania Ratifies, 46 to 23
December 18	New Jersey Ratifies, 38 to 0
December 31	Georgia Ratifies, 26 to 0

1788

January 9	Connecticut Ratifies, 128 to 40
February 6	Massachusetts Ratifies, 187 to 168
March 24	Rhode Island Rejects Constitution in Referendum, 2,711 to 239
April 26	Maryland Ratifies, 63 to 11
May 23	South Carolina Ratifies, 149 to 73
June 21	New Hampshire Ratifies, 57 to 47
June 25	Virginia Ratifies, 89 to 79

July 2　　　　　　　　New Hampshire Ratification Read to Congress as the Necessary Ninth State to Give the Constitution Legal Life

July 26　　　　　　　New York Ratifies, 30 to 27

August 2　　　　　　North Carolina Refuses to Ratify

1789

September 26　　　　Congress Adopts Bill of Rights and Submits It to the States for Ratification

November 21　　　　North Carolina in Second Convention Ratifies, 194 to 77

1790

May 29　　　　　　　Rhode Island Ratifies, 34 to 32

APPENDIX 3

The Constitution
of the United States, 1787

WE THE PEOPLE of the United States, in Order to form a more perfect Union, establish Justice, insure domestic Tranquility, provide for the common defence, promote the general Welfare, and secure the Blessings of Liberty to ourselves and our Posterity, do ordain and establish this Constitution for the United States of America.

ART. I

Sec. 1. All legislative Powers herein granted shall be vested in a Congress of the United States, which shall consist of a Senate and House of Representatives.

Sec. 2. The House of Representatives shall be composed of Members chosen every second Year by the People of the several States, and the Electors in each State shall have [the] Qualifications requisite for Electors of the most numerous Branch of the State Legislature.

No Person shall be a Representative who shall not have attained to the Age of twenty five Years, and been seven Years a Citizen of the United States, and who shall not, when elected, be an Inhabitant of that State in which he shall be chosen.

Representatives and direct Taxes shall be apportioned among the several States which may be included within this Union, according to their respective Numbers, which shall be determined by adding to the whole Number of free Persons, including those bound to Service for a Term of Years, and excluding Indians not taxed, three fifths of all other Persons. The actual Enumeration shall be made within three Years after the first Meeting of the Congress of the United States, and within every subsequent Term of ten Years, in such Manner as they shall by Law direct. The Number of Representatives shall not exceed one for every thirty Thousand, but each State shall have at Least one Representative; and until such enumeration shall be made, the State of New Hampshire shall be entitled to chuse three, Massachusetts eight, Rhode-Island and Providence Plantations one, Connecticut five, New-York six, New Jersey four, Pennsylvania eight, Delaware one, Maryland six, Virginia ten, North Carolina five, South Carolina five, and Georgia three.

When vacancies happen in the Representation from any State, the Executive Authority thereof shall issue Writs of Election to fill such Vacancies.

The House of Representatives shall chuse their Speaker and other Officers; and shall have the sole Power of Impeachment.

Sec. 3. The Senate of the United States shall be composed of two Senators from each State, chosen by the Legislature thereof, for six Years; and each Senator shall have one Vote.

Immediately after they shall be assembled in Consequence of the first Election, they shall be divided as equally as may be into three Classes. The Seats of the Senators of the first Class shall be vacated at the Expiration of the second Year, of the second Class at the Expiration of the fourth Year, and of the third Class at the Expiration of the sixth Year, so that one third may be chosen every second Year; and if Vacancies happen by Resignation, or otherwise, during the Recess of the Legislature of any State, the Executive thereof may make temporary Appointments until the next Meeting of the Legislature, which shall then fill such Vacancies.

No Person shall be a Senator who shall not have attained to the Age of thirty Years, and been nine Years a Citizen of the United States, and who shall not, when elected, be an Inhabitant of that State for which he shall be chosen.

The Vice President of the United States shall be President of the Senate, but shall have no Vote, unless they be equally divided.

The Senate shall chuse their other Officers, and also a President pro tempore, in the Absence of the Vice President, or when he shall exercise the Office of President of the United States.

The Senate shall have the sole Power to try all Impeachments. When sitting for that Purpose, they shall be on Oath or Affirmation.

When the President of the United States is tried, the Chief Justice shall preside: And no person shall be convicted without the Concurrence of two thirds of the Members present.

Judgment in Cases of Impeachment shall not extend further than to removal from Office, and disqualification to hold and enjoy any office of honor, Trust or Profit under the United States: but the Party convicted shall nevertheless be liable and subject to Indictment, Trial, Judgment and Punishment, according to Law.

Sec. 4. The Times, Places and Manner of holding Elections for Senators and Representatives, shall be prescribed in each State by the Legislature thereof; but the Congress may at any time by Law make or alter such Regulations, except as to the Places of chusing Senators.

The Congress shall assemble at least once in every Year, and such Meeting shall be on the first Monday in December, unless they shall by Law appoint a different Day.

Sec. 5. Each House shall be the Judge of the Elections, Returns and Qualifications of its own Members, and a Majority of each shall constitute a Quorum to do Business; but a smaller Number may adjourn from day to day, and may be authorized to compel the Attendance of absent Members, in such Manner, and under such Penalties as each House may provide.

Each House may determine the Rules of its Proceedings, punish its Members for disorderly Behaviour, and, with the Concurrence of two thirds, expel a Member.

Each House shall keep a Journal of its Proceedings, and from time to time publish the same, excepting such parts as may in their Judgment require Secrecy; and the Yeas and Nays of the Members of either House on any question shall, at the Desire of one fifth of those Present, be entered on the Journal.

Neither House, during the Session of Congress, shall, without the

Consent of the other, adjourn for more than three days, nor to any other Place than that in which the two Houses shall be sitting.

Sec. 6. The Senators and Representatives shall receive a Compensation for their Services, to be ascertained by Law, and paid out of the Treasury of the United States. They shall in all Cases, except Treason, Felony and Breach of the Peace, be privileged from Arrest during their Attendance at the Session of their respective Houses, and in going to and returning from the same; and for any Speech or Debate in either House, they shall not be questioned in any other Place.

No Senator or Representative shall, during the Time for which he was elected, be appointed to any civil Office under the Authority of the United States which shall have been created, or the Emoluments whereof shall have been encreased during such time; and no Person holding any Office under the United States, shall be a Member of either House during his Continuance in Office.

Sec. 7. All Bills for raising Revenue shall originate in the House of Representatives; but the Senate may propose or concur with Amendments as on other Bills.

Every Bill which shall have passed the House of Representatives and the Senate, shall, before it become a Law, be presented to the President of the United States; If he approve he shall sign it, but if not he shall return it, with his Objections to that House in which it shall have originated, who shall enter the Objections at large on their Journal, and proceed to reconsider it. If after such Reconsideration two thirds of that House shall agree to pass the Bill, it shall be sent, together with the Objections, to the other House, by which it shall likewise be reconsidered, and if approved by two thirds of that House, it shall become a Law. But in all such Cases the Votes of both Houses shall be determined by Yeas and Nays, and the Names of the Persons voting for and against the Bill shall be entered on the Journal of each House respectively. If any Bill shall not be returned by the President within ten Days (Sundays excepted) after it shall have been presented to him, the Same shall be a Law, in like Manner as if he had signed it, unless the Congress by their Adjournment prevent its Return, in which Case it shall not be a Law.

Every Order, Resolution, or Vote to which the Concurrence of the Senate and House of Representatives may be necessary (except on a question of Adjournment) shall be presented to the President of the United States; and before the Same shall take Effect, shall be approved by him, or being disapproved by him, shall be repassed by two thirds of the Senate and House of Representatives, according to the Rules and Limitations prescribed in the Case of a Bill.

Sec. 8. The Congress shall have Power To lay and collect Taxes, Duties, Imposts and Excises, to pay the Debts and provide for the common Defence and general Welfare of the United States; but all Duties, Imposts and Excises shall be uniform throughout the United States;

To Borrow Money on the credit of the United States;

To regulate Commerce with foreign Nations, and among the several States, and with the Indian Tribes;

To establish an uniform Rule of Naturalization, and uniform Laws on the subject of Bankruptcies throughout the United States;

To coin Money, regulate the Value thereof, and of foreign Coin, and fix the Standard of Weights and Measures;

To provide for the Punishment of counterfeiting the Securities and current Coin of the United States;

To establish Post Offices and post Roads;

To promote the Progress of Science and useful Arts, by securing for limited Times to Authors and Inventors the exclusive Right to their respective Writings and Discoveries;

To constitute Tribunals inferior to the supreme Court;

To define and punish Piracies and Felonies committed on the high Seas, and Offences against the Law of Nations;

To declare War, grant Letters of Marque and Reprisal, and make Rules concerning Captures on Land and Water;

To raise and support Armies, but no Appropriation of Money to that Use shall be for a longer Term than two Years;

To provide and maintain a Navy;

To make Rules for the Government and Regulation of the land and naval Forces;

To provide for calling forth the Militia to execute the Laws of the Union, suppress Insurrections and repel Invasions;

To provide for organizing, arming, and disciplining the Militia, and for governing such Part of them as may be employed in the Service of the United States, reserving to the States respectively, the Appointment of the Officers, and the Authority of training the Militia according to the discipline prescribed by Congress;

To exercise exclusive Legislation in all Cases whatsoever, over such District (not exceeding ten Miles square) as may, by Cession of particular States, and the Acceptance of Congress, become the Seat of the Government of the United States, and to exercise like Authority over all Places purchased by the Consent of the Legislature of the State in which the Same shall be, for the Erection of Forts, Magazines, Arsenals, dock-Yards, and other needful Buildings;—
And

To make all Laws which shall be necessary and proper for carrying into Execution the foregoing Powers, and all other Powers vested by this Constitution in the Government of the United States, or in any Department or Officer thereof.

Sec. 9. The Migration or Importation of such Persons as any of the States now existing shall think proper to admit, shall not be prohibited by the Congress prior to the Year one thousand eight hundred and eight, but a Tax or duty may be imposed on such Importation, not exceeding ten dollars for each Person.

The Privilege of the Writ of Habeas Corpus shall not be suspended, unless when in Cases of Rebellion or Invasion the public Safety may require it.

No Bill of Attainder or ex post facto Law shall be passed.

No Capitation, or other direct, Tax shall be laid, unless in Proportion to the Census or Enumeration herein before directed to be taken.

No Tax or Duty shall be laid on Articles exported from any State.

No Preference shall be given by any Regulation of Commerce or Revenue to the Ports of one State over those of another: nor shall Vessels bound to, or from, one State, be obliged to enter, clear, or pay Duties in another.

No Money shall be drawn from the Treasury, but in Consequence of Appropriations made by Law; and a regular Statement and

Account of the Receipts and Expenditures of all public Money shall be published from time to time.

No Title of Nobility shall be granted by the United States: And no Person holding any Office of Profit or Trust under them, shall, without the Consent of the Congress, accept of any present, Emolument, Office, or Title, of any kind whatever, from any King, Prince or foreign State.

Sec. 10. No State shall enter into any Treaty, Alliance, or Confederation; grant Letters of Marque and Reprisal; coin Money; emit Bills of Credit; make any Thing but gold and silver Coin a Tender in Payment of Debts; pass any Bill of Attainder, ex post facto Law, or Law impairing the Obligation of Contracts, or grant any Title of Nobility.

No State shall, without the Consent of the Congress, lay any Imposts or Duties on Imports or Exports, except what may be absolutely necessary for executing its inspection Laws: and the net Produce of all Duties and Imposts, laid by any State on Imports or Exports, shall be for the Use of the Treasury of the United States; and all such Laws shall be subject to the Revision and Controul of the Congress.

No State shall, without the Consent of Congress, lay any Duty of Tonnage, keep Troops, or Ships of War in time of Peace, enter into any Agreement or Compact with another State, or with a foreign Power, or engage in War, unless actually invaded, or in such imminent Danger as will not admit of delay.

ART. II

Sec. 1. The executive Power shall be vested in a President of the United States of America. He shall hold his Office during the Term of four Years, and, together with the Vice President, chosen for the same Term, be elected, as follows:

Each State shall appoint, in such Manner as the Legislature thereof may direct, a Number of Electors, equal to the whole Number of Senators and Representatives to which the State may be entitled in the Congress: but no Senator or Representative, or Person Holding an Office of Trust or Profit under the United States, shall be appointed an Elector.

The Electors shall meet in their respective States, and vote by Ballot for two Persons, of whom one at least shall not be an Inhabitant of the same State with themselves. And they shall make a List of all the Persons voted for, and of the Number of Votes for each; which List they shall sign and certify, and transmit sealed to the Seat of the Government of the United States, directed to the President of the Senate. The President of the Senate shall, in the Presence of the Senate and House of Representatives, open all the Certificates, and the Votes shall then be counted. The Person having the greatest Number of Votes shall be the President, if such Number be a Majority of the whole Number of Electors appointed; and if there be more than one who have such Majority, and have an equal Number of Votes, then the House of Representatives shall immediately chuse by Ballot one of them for President; and if no person have a Majority, then from the five highest on the List the said House shall in like Manner chuse the President. But in chusing the President, the Votes shall be taken by States, the Representative from each State having one Vote; A quorum for this Purpose shall consist of a Member or Members from two thirds of the States and a Majority of all the States shall be necessary to a Choice. In every Case, after the Choice of the President, the Person having the greatest Number of Votes of the Electors shall be the Vice President. But if there should remain two or more who have equal Votes, the Senate shall chuse from them by Ballot the Vice President.

The Congress may determine the Time of chusing the Electors, and the Day on which they shall give their Votes; which Day shall be the same throughout the United States.

No Person except a natural born Citizen, or a Citizen of the United States, at the time of the Adoption of this Constitution, shall be eligible to the Office of President; neither shall any Person be eligible to the Office who shall not have attained to the Age of thirty five Years, and been fourteen Years a Resident within the United States.

In Case of the Removal of the President from Office, or of his Death, Resignation, or Inability to discharge the Powers and Duties of the said Office, the Same shall devolve on the Vice President, and the Congress may by Law provide for the Case of Removal, Death, Resignation or Inability, both of the President and Vice President, declaring what Officer shall then act as President, and such Officer shall act accordingly, until the Disability be removed, or a President shall be elected.

The President shall, at stated Times, receive for his Services, a Compensation, which shall neither be encreased nor diminished during the Period for which he shall have been elected, and he shall not receive within that Period any other Emolument from the United States, or any of them.

Before he enter on the Execution of his Office, he shall take the following Oath or Affirmation:—"I do solemnly swear (or affirm) that I will faithfully execute the Office of President of the United States, and will to the best of my Ability, preserve, protect and defend the Constitution of the United States."

Sec. 2. The President shall be Commander in Chief of the Army and Navy of the United States, and of the Militia of the several States, when called into the actual Service of the United States; he may require the Opinion, in writing, of the principal Officer in each of the executive Departments, upon any Subject relating to the Duties of their respective Offices, and he shall have Power to grant Reprieves and Pardons for Offences against the United States, except in Cases of Impeachment.

He shall have Power, by and with the Advice and Consent of the Senate, to make Treaties, provided two thirds of the Senators present concur; and he shall nominate, and by and with the Advice and Consent of the Senate, shall appoint Ambassadors, other public Ministers and Consuls, Judges of the supreme Court, and all other Officers of the United States, whose Appointments are not herein otherwise provided for, and which shall be established by Law: but the Congress may by Law vest the Appointment of such inferior Officers, as they think proper, in the President alone, in the Courts of Law, or in the Heads of Departments.

The President shall have Power to fill up all Vacancies that may happen during the Recess of the Senate, by granting Commissions which shall expire at the End of their next Session.

★

Sec. 3. He shall from time to time give to the Congress Information of the State of the Union, and recommend to their Consideration such Measures as he shall judge necessary and expedient; he may, on extraordinary Occasions, convene both Houses, or either of them, and in Case of Disagreement between them, with Respect to the Time of Adjournment, he may adjourn them to such Time as he shall think proper; he shall receive Ambassadors and other public Ministers; he shall take Care that the Laws be faithfully executed, and shall Commission all the Officers of the United States.

Sec. 4. The President, Vice President and all civil Officers of the United States, shall be removed from Office on Impeachment for, and Conviction of, Treason, Bribery, or other high Crimes and Misdemeanors.

ART. III

Sec. 1. The judicial Power of the United States, shall be vested in one supreme Court, and in such inferior Courts as the Congress may from time to time ordain and establish. The Judges, both of the supreme and inferior Courts, shall hold their Offices during good Behaviour, and shall, at stated Times, receive for their Services, a Compensation, which shall not be diminished during their Continuance in Office.

Sec. 2. The judicial Power shall extend to all Cases, in Law and Equity, arising under this Constitution, the Laws of the United States, and Treaties made, or which shall be made, under their Authority;—to all Cases affecting Ambassadors, other public Ministers and Consuls;—to all Cases of admiralty and maritime Jurisdiction;—to Controversies to which the United States shall be a Party;—to Controversies between two or more States;—between a State and Citizens of another State;—between Citizens of different States;—between Citizens of the same State claiming Lands under Grants of different States, and between a State, or the Citizens thereof, and foreign States, Citizens or Subjects.

In all Cases affecting Ambassadors, other public Ministers and Consuls, and those in which a State shall be Party, the supreme Court shall have original Jurisdiction. In all the other cases before mentioned, the supreme Court shall have appellate Jurisdiction, both as to Law and Fact, with such Exceptions, and under such Regulations as the Congress shall make.

The Trial of all Crimes, except in Cases of Impeachment, shall be by Jury; and such Trial shall be held in the State where the said Crimes shall have been committed; but when not committed within any State, the Trial shall be at such Place or Places as the Congress may by Law have directed.

Sec. 3. Treason against the United States, shall consist only in levying War against them, or in adhering to their Enemies, giving them Aid and Comfort. No Person shall be convicted of Treason unless on the Testimony of two Witnesses to the same overt Act, or on Confession in open Court.

The Congress shall have Power to declare the Punishment of Treason, but no Attainder of Treason shall work Corruption of Blood, or Forfeiture except during the Life of the Person attainted.

ART. IV

Sec. 1. Full Faith and Credit shall be given in each State to the Public Acts, Records, and judicial Proceedings of every other State. And the Congress may by general Laws prescribe the Manner in which such Acts, Records and Proceedings shall be proved, and the Effect thereof.

Sec. 2. The Citizens of each State shall be entitled to all Privileges and Immunities of Citizens in the Several States.

A Person charged in any State with Treason, Felony, or other Crime, who shall flee from Justice, and be found in another State, shall on Demand of the executive Authority of the State from which he fled, be delivered up, to be removed to the State having Jurisdiction of the Crime.

No Person held to Service or Labour in one State, under the Laws thereof, escaping into another, shall, in Consequence of any Law or Regulation therein, be discharged from such Service or Labour, but shall be delivered up on Claim of the Party to whom such Service or Labour may be due.

Sec. 3. New States may be admitted by the Congress into this Union; but no new States shall be formed or erected within the Jurisdiction of any other State; nor any State be formed by the Junction of two or more States, or Parts of States, without the Consent of the Legislatures of the States concerned as well as of the Congress.

The Congress shall have Power to dispose of and make all needful Rules and Regulations respecting the Territory or other Property belonging to the United States; and nothing in this Constitution shall be so construed as to Prejudice any Claims of the United States, or of any particular State.

Sec. 4. The United States shall guarantee to every State in this Union a Republican Form of Government, and shall protect each of them against Invasion; and on Application of the Legislature, or of the Executive (when the Legislature cannot be convened) against domestic Violence.

ART. V

The Congress, whenever two thirds of both Houses shall deem it necessary, shall propose Amendments to this Constitution, or, on the Application of the Legislatures of two thirds of the several States, shall call a Convention for proposing Amendments, which, in either Case, shall be valid to all Intents and Purposes, as Part of this Constitution, when ratified by the Legislatures of three fourths of the several States, or by Conventions in three fourths thereof, as the one or the other Mode of Ratification may be proposed by the Congress; Provided that no Amendment which may be made prior to the Year One thousand eight hundred and eight shall in any Manner affect the first and fourth Clauses in the Ninth Section of the first Article; and that no State, without its Consent, shall be deprived of its equal Suffrage in the Senate.

ART. VI

All Debts contracted and Engagements entered into, before the Adoption of this Constitution, shall be as valid against the United States under this Constitution, as under the Confederation.

This Constitution, and the Laws of the United States which shall be made in Pursuance thereof; and all Treaties made, or which shall be made, under the Authority of the United States, shall be the supreme Law of the Land; and the Judges in every State shall be bound thereby, any Thing in the Constitution or Laws of any State to the Contrary notwithstanding.

The Senators and Representatives before mentioned, and the Members of the several State Legislatures, and all executive and judicial Officers, both of the United States and of the several States, shall be bound by Oath or Affirmation, to support this Constitution; but no religious Test shall ever be required as a Qualification to any Office or public Trust under the United States.

ART. VII

The Ratification of the Conventions of nine States, shall be sufficient for the Establishment of this Constitution between the States so ratifying the Same.

Done in Convention by the Unanimous Consent of the States present the Seventeenth Day of September in the Year of our Lord one thousand seven hundred and Eighty seven and of the Independence of the United States of America the Twelfth. In witness whereof We have hereunto subscribed our Names.

G° WASHINGTON—Presid[t]
and deputy from Virginia

New Hampshire NICHOLAS GILMAN
JOHN LANGDON

Massachusetts NATHANIEL GORHAM
RUFUS KING

Connecticut	W^m SAM^L JOHNSON ROGER SHERMAN
New York	ALEXANDER HAMILTON
New Jersey	DAVID BREARLEY JONA: DAYTON WIL: LIVINGSTON W^M PATERSON
Pennsylvania	GEO. CLYMER THO^s FITZSIMONS B FRANKLIN JARED INGERSOLL THOMAS MIFFLIN GOUV MORRIS ROB^T MORRIS JAMES WILSON
Delaware	RICHARD BASSET GUNNING BEDFORD JUN JACO: BROOM JOHN DICKINSON GEO: READ
Maryland	DAN^l CARROLL DAN of S^t THO^s JENIFER JAMES M^cHENRY
Virginia	JOHN BLAIR JAMES MADISON JR
North Carolina	Wm BLOUNT RICH^d DOBBS SPAIGHT HU WILLIAMSON

South Carolina	PIERCE BUTLER
	CHARLES COTESWORTH PINCKNEY
	CHARLES PINCKNEY
	J. RUTLEDGE
Georgia	ABR BALDWIN
	WILLIAM FEW

NOTES

Chapter 1

1. Flexner, *Washington*, 138.
2. Harwell, *Washington*, 549–50.
3. Hamilton, *Papers*, 275.
4. Beeman, *Patrick Henry*, 144.
5. Washington, *Writings*, 29:278. "To Patrick Henry. Mount Vernon, September 24, 1787."
6. Van Doren, *Great Rehearsal*, 178.
7. Ibid.
8. Farrand, *Records*, 3:98. "Philada. Sept. 20, 1787."
9. Ibid.
10. Brant, *Madison*, 162–63.
11. Madison, *Papers*, 10:172. "From Edward Carrington. New York Sept. 23. 1787."
12. Van Doren, *Great Rehearsal*, 177.
13. Elliot, *Debates*, 1:305.
14. Ibid.
15. Burnett, *Letters of Continental Congress*, 8:648.
16. Ibid.
17. Ibid.
18. Ibid., Preface, xivii.
19. Lee, *Letters*, 439. "To George Mason. New York, October 1st, 1787."
20. Farrand, *Records*, 2:648.
21. Ford, *Pamphlets*, 139.
22. Storing, *Complete Anti-Federalist*, 2:104–5. See also 104, *fn*10.
23. Hamilton, *Papers*, 4:276–77.
24. *Commentaries*, 1:243. "*Pennsylvania Gazette*, 10 October."

Chapter 2

1. McMaster, *Pennsylvania*, 4.
2. Ibid., 4–5.
3. Bowen, *Miracle*, 274.
4. Storing, *Complete Anti-Federalist*, 3:8–9.
5. Van Doren, *Great Rehearsal*, 180.
6. Storing, *Complete Anti-Federalist*, 3:13.
7. Ibid., 3:14–15.
8. Lee, *Letters*, 2:440. "To [George Mason]. New York, October 1st, 1787."
9. Ibid., 439.
10. Ibid., 438.
11. Madison, *Papers*, 10:180–81. "To George Washington. N York Sepr. 30. 1787."
12. Flexner, *Washington*, 141.
13. Washington, *Writings*, 29:277. "To Clement Biddle, Head of Elk, September 19, 1787."
14. Spaulding, *George Clinton*, 175.
15. Ibid.
16. Brant, *Madison*, 170.
17. Allen, *Essential Antifederalist*, 11.
18. Ibid., 11–12.
19. Ibid.
20. Ibid., 13.

Chapter 3

1. Storing, *Complete Anti-Federalist*, 2:142.
2. Ibid., 2:130.
3. Ibid., 2:137.
4. Ibid., 2:141.
5. Ibid., 2:142.
6. Rossiter, *Grand Convention*, 286.
7. Ford, *Pamphlets*, 155. "Wilson's Speech, Oct. 6, 1787."
8. Ibid., 156–57.
9. Ibid., 157.
10. Ibid., 161.
11. Van Doren, *Great Rehearsal*, 182.
12. Mason, *Papers*, 1001–2. "To George Washington. Gunston Hall Octor. 7th, 1787."

13. Washington, *Writings*, 24:285. See also Mason, *Papers*, 1002, *fn.*
14. Flexner, *Washington*, 135, *fn.*
15. Farrand, *Records*, 3:103–4. "To George Humphreys. Mount Vernon October 10th. 1787."
16. Storing, *Complete Anti-Federalist*, 2:214–16.
17. Brant, *Madison*, 166.
18. Storing, *Complete Anti-Federalist*, 2:225–27. "Letters from The Federal Farmer, October 7, 1787."
19. Ibid., 2:228.
20. Brant, *Madison*, 166.
21. Storing, *Complete Anti-Federalist*, 2:240. "Letters from The Federal Farmer, October 10, 1787."
22. Van Doren, *Great Rehearsal*, 179.
23. Jensen, *Making of American Constitution*, 122.
24. Reardon, *Edmund Randolph*, 123.
25. Elliot, *Debates*, 1:482. "A Letter of His Excellency, Edmund Randolph, Esq., on the Federal Constitution; addressed to The Honorable the Speaker of the House of Delegates, Virginia. Richmond, Oct. 10, 1787."
26. Ibid., 1:490.
27. Ibid.
28. Conway, *Edmund Randolph*, 93.

Chapter 4

1. *Commentaries*, 1:507. "George Lee Turberville to Arthur Lee. Richmond, 28 October."
2. Beveridge, *John Marshall*, 1:325.
3. Madison, *Writings*, 5:41. "To Thomas Jefferson. New York, Oct. 24, 1787."
4. *Commentaries*, 1:150.
5. Farrand, *Records*, 3:306–7. "Hugh Williamson to James Madison. New York, June 2nd, 1788."
6. Madison, *Papers*, 10:195, *fn*2. "To George Washington. New York Octr. 14, 1787."
7. Ibid., 10:194.
8. Beeman, *Patrick Henry*, 141.
9. Madison, *Writings*, 5:43. "To George Washington. New York, October 28, 1787."
10. Washington, *Writings*, 29:293. "To James Madison. Mount Vernon, Oct 22, 1787."

11. Williams, *Pinckneys*, 270–71.
12. *Documentary History of the Constitution*, 4:327. "[James Monroe] to the honble James Madison New York. Richmond Oct 13, 1787."
13. Madison, *Papers*, 10:197. "To George Washington. New York Octr 18, 1787."
14. Washington, *Writings*, 29:289. "To Henry Knox. Mount Vernon October 15, 1787."
15. Ibid., 29:290. "To David Stuart. Mount Vernon, October 17, 1787."
16. Storing, *Complete Anti-Federalist*, 3:59. "*Pennsylvania Herald* 17 October, 1787."
17. Ibid., 3:61.
18. Ibid., 3:58.
19. McDonald, *E Pluribus Unum*, 213.
20. Lee, *Letters*, 2:455. "To [the] Governor [of Virginia] [Edmund] Randolph. New-York, Oct. 16th, 1787."
21. Groce, *William Samuel Johnson*, 152.
22. Ibid.
23. *Commentaries*, 1:403. "The Attack on the Non-signers of the Constitution, Philadelphia, 17 October."
24. Farrand, *Records*, 3:128. "Elbridge Gerry to President of Senate and Speaker of House of Representatives of Massachusetts. New York Oct 18, 1787."
25. *Commentaries*, 1:407. "Elbridge Gerry to James Warren. New York, 18 October."
26. Ibid., 1:382–83. "*Boston Gazette*, 15 October 1787."
27. McDonald, *E Pluribus Unum*, 213.
28. Bancroft, *Formation of the Constitution*, 2:230.
29. Brant, *Madison*, 170.
30. Rossiter, *Federalist Papers*, 47.
31. *Commentaries*, 1:407. "Don Diego de Gardoqui to Conde de Floridablanca. New York, 18 October."
32. Ibid., 1:386. "Philadelphia *Freeman's Journal*, 17 October."

Chapter 5

1. William Henry, *Patrick Henry*, 2:320.
2. Meade, *Patrick Henry*, 334.
3. Reardon, *Edmund Randolph*, 125.
4. Ibid., 126–27.
5. Beeman, *Patrick Henry*, 142.

6. Ibid., 143.
7. Meade, Patrick Henry, 335.
8. William Henry, *Patrick Henry*, 323.
9. Mason, *Papers*, 3:1002.
10. *Commentaries*, 1:404. "The Attack on the Non-signers of the Constitution. Philadelphia, 17 October."
11. Miller, *George Mason*, 219.
12. Bancroft, *Formation of the Constitution*, 2:232.
13. Brant, *Madison*, 171–72.
14. *Commentaries*, 1:457–59. "Centinel II. Philadelphia *Freeman's Journal*, 24 October." "Centinel" was later identified as George Byran, a Pennsylvania legislator.
15. Warren, *Making of the Constitution*, 762.
16. Farrand, *Records*, 3:76. "Thomas Jefferson to John Adams. Paris, Aug 30, 1787."
17. Madison, *Papers*, 10:205. "Editorial Note."
18. Storing, *Complete Anti-Federalist*, 2:110.
19. Ibid., 2:111.
20. Madison, *Writings*, 5:17. "To Edmund Randolph. New York, October 21, 1787."
21. O'Connor, *William Paterson*, 164.
22. Conway, *Edmund Randolph*, 96.
23. Ibid.
24. Brant, *Madison*, 168.

Chapter 6

1. *Documentary History of the Constitution*, 4:358–60. "Gouv Morris to His Excellency Gen Washington, Mount Vernon. Philadelphia 30 October 1787."
2. Flexner, *Washington*, 141.
3. McDonald, *Hamilton*, 107.
4. Chadwick, *The Federalist*, No. 1:2–3. "The Fate of an Empire," by Alexander Hamilton.
5. McDonald, *Hamilton*, 107.
6. Spaulding, *George Clinton*, 175.
7. Ibid.
8. McDonald, *Hamilton*, 106.
9. Chadwick, *The Federalist*, No. 1:13. "The Fate of an Empire," by Alexander Hamilton.
10. Ibid., No. 1:5.

11. Mitchell, *Biography of the Constitution*, 126.
12. Ibid.
13. *Commentaries*, 1:411. "Brutus I, *New York Journal*, 18 October."
14. Ibid., 1:529. "Brutus II, *New York Journal*, 1 November."
15. Ibid., 1:486–87. "Publius, The Federalist I, New York *Independent Journal*, 27 October."
16. Chadwick, *The Federalist*, No. 2:6,7, "The Most Important Question Facing America in 1789," by John Jay.
17. Storing, *Complete Anti-Federalist*, 5:126–28. "A Proposal for Reviving Christian Conviction, *Virginia Independent Chronicle*, 31 October 1787."
18. *Commentaries*, 1:515. "Nicholas Gilman to President John Sullivan of New Hampshire, New York, 31 October (excerpt)."
19. Beveridge, *John Marshall*, 1:331, *fn2*.
20. *Commentaries*, 1:542–43. "An Old Whig V, Philadelphia *Independent Gazetteer*, 1 November."
21. Ibid., 1:521. "*Pennsylvania Gazette*, 31 October."
22. Madison, *Writings*, 5:41. "To Thomas Jefferson. New York, Oct 24, 1787."
23. Burnett, *Letters of Continental Congress*, 8:667. "The Secretary of Congress to the Governors of North Carolina, South Carolina, and Georgia. Office of Secretary of Congress. October 27th, 1787."
24. Hamilton, *Papers*, 4:306. "To George Washington. [New York, October 30, 1787.]"
25. Flexner, *Washington*, 144.
26. *Commentaries*, 1:486–87. "Purpose and Authorship."
27. *Documentary History of the Constitution*, 4:359. "Gouv Morris to His Excellency Gen Washington, Mount Vernon. Philadelphia 30 October 1787."

Chapter 7

1. Van Doren, *Great Rehearsal*, 182.
2. McMaster, *Pennsylvania*, 1:12.
3. Van Doren, *Great Rehearsal*, 182.
4. McDonald, *E Pluribus Unum*, 211.
5. Beveridge, *John Marshall*, 1:327.
6. *Commentaries*, 1:343. "James Wilson: Speech at a Public Meeting in Philadelphia, 6 October."

7. Ibid., 1:549. "Elbridge Gerry to the Massachusetts General Court. *Massachusetts Centinel,* 3 November."
8. Ibid., 1:547. "Elbridge Gerry and the Constitution."
9. Bancroft, *Formation of the Constitution,* 2:258–59.
10. *Commentaries,* 1:561."A Landholder I. *Connecticut Courant,* 5 November."
11. Ibid. "To the Holders and Tillers of Land," by Oliver Ellsworth.
12. Wright, *Economic History,* 235.
13. *Commentaries,* 1:563. "A Landholder I. *Connecticut Courant,* 5 November. To the Holders and Tillers of Land."
14. Chadwick, *The Federalist,* No. 3:14. "Unity Under One Federal Government," by John Jay.
15. Ibid., No. 4:18. "National Security Depends upon a Strong and United Union," by John Jay.
16. *Commentaries,* 2:460, Appendix II. "Americans Abroad Comment on the Constitution."
17. Ibid., 2:462. "Abigail Adams to Cotton Tufts. London, 6 November (excerpt)."
18. Ibid., 2:462. "Thomas Lee Shippen to William Shippen, Jr. London, 6 November (excerpt)."
19. Ibid., 2:460. "John Brown Cutting to John Rutledge, Jr. London, 1 November (excerpt)."
20. Storing, *Complete Anti-Federalist,* 2:116. Letters of "Cato": "To the Citizens of the State of New-York."
21. Ibid., 2:160. Letters of "Centinel": "To the People of Pennsylvania."
22. *Commentaries,* 2:504, Appendix III. "Quaker Opposition to the Protection of Slavery in the Constitution."
23. Storing, *Complete Anti-Federalist,* 6:30. Essays by "Cincinnatus": "To James Wilson, Esq. 6 December 1787."

Chapter 8

1. Munroe, *Federalist Delaware,* 108.
2. Ibid., 108–9.
3. Flower, *John Dickinson,* 250.
4. *Documentary History of the Constitution,* 4:378. "Samuel Powell to His Excellency George Washington. Philadelphia, 13 November 1787."

5. Storing, *Complete Anti-Federalist*, 6:17. "Cincinnatus III, 15 November 1787."
6. Chadwick, *The Federalist*, No. 5:19–20. New York *Independent Journal*, "The Dangers from Foreign Aggression," by John Jay.
7. Ibid., No. 5:22.
8. Ibid., No. 6:24. New York *Independent Journal*, 14 November 1787, "History Confirms the Dangers From War Between the States and From Domestic Conflict," by Alexander Hamilton.
9. Ibid., No. 6:23–25.
10. Adams, *Dictionary of American History*, 2:329.
11. Burnett, *Letters of Continental Congress*, 7:667. "The Secretary of Congress to the Governors of North Carolina, South Carolina, and Georgia. Office of Secretary of Congress, October 27th, 1787."
12. Madison, *Writings*, 5:41.
13. Adams, *Dictionary of American History*, 2:329.
14. Storing, *Complete Anti-Federalist*, 5:135. "Essays by A Georgian. *Gazette of the State of Georgia*, 15 November 1787."
15. *Commentaries*, 2:84. "David Ramsay to Benjamin Rush. Charleston, 10 November."
16. Flexner, *Washington*, 144–45.
17. Washington, *Writings*, 29:310. "To Bushrod Washington. Mount Vernon, November 10, 1787."
18. Lodge, *Washington*, 2:39–40.
19. *Commentaries*, 1:566. "George Washington in the Constitutional Convention."
20. Ibid., 2:253. "*Boston Gazette*, 12 November."
21. Ibid., 2:117. "The News-Mongers' Song for the Winter of 1788. *Albany Gazette*, 15 November."

Chapter 9

1. Bancroft, *Formation of the Constitution*, 2:242.
2. McMaster, *Pennsylvania*, 214.
3. *Ratification*, 2:280.
4. Ibid., 2:290–91. "A Plain Citizen, To the Honorable the Convention of the State of Pennsylvania. *Independent Gazetteer*, 22 November."
5. Mason, *Papers*, 3:991. "Mason's Objections Written on the Committee of Style Report [*ca* 16 September 1787]," *Massachusetts Centinel*, November 21.

6. *Commentaries*, 2:128. "Elbridge Gerry to John Wendell, Cambridge, 16 November."
7. Bancroft, *Formation of the Constitution*, 2:261–62.
8. Bowen, *Miracle*, 189.
9. Beveridge, *John Marshall*, 1:339.
10. Storing, *Complete Anti-Federalist*, 6:50. "A Countryman from Dutchess County, 21 November 1787."
11. De Pauw, *Eleventh Pillar*, 114–16.
12. Chadwick, *The Federalist*, No. 7:33. "Possible Causes of Internal War," by Alexander Hamilton.
13. Ibid., No. 8:37. "Preservation of the Union Is Essential to Insure Independence from Europe," by Alexander Hamilton.
14. Ibid., No. 9:40. "A Firm Union Will Provide a Barrier Against Domestic Faction and Insurrection," by Alexander Hamilton.
15. Ibid., No. 9:41.
16. *Commentaries*, 2:175. "Publius: The Federalist 10. New York *Daily Advertiser*, 22 November."
17. Madison, *Writings*, 5:55. "To George Washington. New York, November 18, 1787."
18. Madison, *Papers*, 10:259–60. "Madison's Authorship of *The Federalist*, 22 November 1787–1 March 1788."
19. Chadwick, *The Federalist*, No. 10:49. "Securing the Public Good and Private Rights Against the Dangers of Faction," by James Madison.
20. Ibid., No. 10:52.

Chapter 10

1. Bancroft, *Formation of the Constitution*, 2:247.
2. McMaster, *Pennsylvania*, 2:752–53. "Sketches of Members of the Convention."
3. Ibid., 1:249. "The Debate in Convention."
4. Ibid.
5. Schwartz, *Bill of Rights*, 2:642.
6. *Ratification*, 2:322–23.
7. Ibid., 3:92.
8. Ibid., 3:125.
9. Storing, *Complete Anti-Federalist*, 4:71. "Letters of Agrippa I."
10. Ibid.
11. Chadwick, *The Federalist*, No. 11:58. "A Strong Union Would Develop More Favorable Trade Relations," by Alexander Hamilton.

12. Ibid., No. 11:55.
13. Ibid., No. 11:58.
14. Ibid., No. 12:60. "The Benefits of Indirect Taxation for the Union," by Alexander Hamilton.
15. Ibid., 12:63.
16. *Commentaries*, 2:229. "Louis Guillaume Otto to Comte de Montmorin. New York, 26 November."
17. Van Doren, *Great Rehearsal*, 297.
18. *Commentaries*, 2:278. "Maryland's Constitutional Convention Delegates Address the State House of Delegates, 29 November."
19. Ibid., 2:293. "Daniel Carroll to Benjamin Franklin. Annapolis, 2 December."
20. Farrand, *Records*, 3:159. Appendix A, CXLVI*b:* "Luther Martin Before the Maryland House of Representatives. Maryland Novr. 29th, 1787."

Chapter 11

1. *Ratification*, 2:447–48.
2. Ibid., 2:474–75.
3. McMaster, *Pennsylvania*, 1:283.
4. Ibid., 1:284.
5. Ibid., 1:299–300.
6. Ibid., 1:301.
7. *Commentaries*, 2:333. "Samuel Adams to Richard Henry Lee. Boston, 3 December."
8. Storing, *Complete Anti-Federalist*, 4:129–30.
9. Jensen, *Making of American Constitution*, 134.
10. Washington, *Writings*, 29:328. "To John Langdon. Mount Vernon, December 3, 1787."
11. Ibid., 29:323. "To David Stuart. Mount Vernon, November 30, 1787."
12. Ibid., 29:324.
13. Chadwick, *The Federalist*, No. 14:68–69. "The Founders Pursued A New and More Noble Course at the Constitutional Convention for America and the World," by James Madison.
14. Ibid., No. 14:72–73.
15. Ibid., No. 15:76. "Defects of the Articles of Confederation," by Alexander Hamilton.
16. Ibid., No. 16:82. "Inefficient Government Is Leading America Toward a Slow Death," by Alexander Hamilton.

17. Ibid., No.17:88. "State Government Should Possess More Power and Authority Than the Federal Government," by Alexander Hamilton.
18. Ibid., No.17:87.

Chapter 12

1. *Ratification,* 3:105, 106, 110.
2. Beveridge, *John Marshall,* 1:330.
3. McMaster, *Pennsylvania,* 1:364.
4. *Ratification,* 3:112.
5. Ibid., 3:113.
6. Ibid., 3:110.
7. Ibid., 3:109.
8. Bowen, *Miracle,* 209–10.
9. *Ratification,* 3:105–7.
10. Ford, *Pamphlets,* 167. "Fabius," Letter I, by John Dickinson.
11. McMaster, *Pennsylvania,* 1:420.
12. *Ratification,* 2:595–96.
13. McMaster, *Pennsylvania,* 1:420.
14. *Ratification,* 2:552.
15. Ibid., 2:584.
16. McMaster, *Pennsylvania,* 1:365.
17. *Ratification,* 2:549.
18. McMaster, *Pennsylvania,* 2:365.
19. *Ratification,* 2:599.
20. Ibid., 2:603.
21. Jensen, *Making of American Constitution,* 133.
22. Van Doren, *Great Rehearsal,* 183.
23. Storing, *Complete Anti-Federalist,* 3:145.
24. Van Doren, *Great Rehearsal,* 187.
25. Schwartz, *Bill of Rights,* 2:628.
26. *Ratification,* 2:606.
27. Ibid., 2:607–8.

Chapter 13

1. *Ratification,* 3:177.
2. Munroe, *Federalist Delaware,* 108.
3. *Ratification,* 3:186.
4. Ibid., 3:190.
5. Ibid., 3:192–93.

6. Storing, *Complete Anti-Federalist*, 3:165.
7. Schwartz, *Bill of Rights*, 1:592. "Thomas Jefferson—James Madison Correspondence, 1787–1789."
8. Ibid.
9. Madison, *Papers*, 10:332. "To Thomas Jefferson. New York Decr. 20, 1787."
10. Chadwick, *The Federalist*, No. 22:113. "The Outdated and Ineffective Articles of Confederation," by Alexander Hamilton.
11. Ibid., No. 23:121. "The Necessity of a Strong National Government," by Alexander Hamilton.
12. Ibid., No. 24:127–28. "The Power of Raising Armies Should Remain With the Legislative Branch of the Federal Government," by Alexander Hamilton.
13. Storing, *Complete Anti-Federalist*, 4:135. "Essays by Candidus, II, 20 December 1787."
14. Madison, *Writings*, 5:73. "To George Washington. New York, December 20, 1787."
15. Washington, *Writings*, 29:340. "To Charles Carter. Mount Vernon, December 14, 1787."

Chapter 14

1. *Ratification*, 2:670. "The Carlisle Riot and Its Aftermath. 26 December 1787–20 March 1788."
2. Van Doren, *Great Rehearsal*, 180, 182.
3. Beveridge, *John Marshall*, 1:330.
4. McMaster, *Pennsylvania*, 1:23.
5. Ibid., 2:487.
6. *Commentaries*, 3:87. "Charles Nisbet to the Earl of Buchan. Carlisle, 25 December (excerpt)."
7. Storing, *Complete Anti-Federalist*, 4:259. "Essay by Poplicola. *Boston Gazette and the Country Journal*, 24 December 1787."
8. *Commentaries*, 3:77. "The Landholder VIII. *Connecticut Courant*, 24 December."
9. Ibid., 3:78.
10. Farrand, *Records*, 2:370.
11. *Commentaries*, 3:82. "New England. *Connecticut Courant*, 24 December."
12. Barry, *Rutledge of South Carolina*, 332.
13. Storing, *Complete Anti-Federalist*, 2:259. "Letters from The Federal Farmer."

14. *Commentaries*, 3:82. "New England. *Connecticut Courant*, 24 December."
15. Schwartz, *Bill of Rights*, 1:464. "Attacks by Richard Henry Lee, Elbridge Gerry, and Luther Martin, 1787–1788."
16. Storing, *Complete Anti-Federalist*, 4:154. "Essays by Helvidius Priscus. (Boston) *Independent Chronicle* and *Massachusetts Gazette*, December 1787–February 1788."
17. Chadwick, *The Federalist*, No. 25:133. "The Common Defense of America Should Be Handled by the Legislative Discretion of the Federal Government," by Alexander Hamilton.
18. Ibid., No. 25:130.
19. *Ratification*, 3:232. "Joseph Clay to John Pierce. Savannah, 17 October (excerpt)."
20. Burnett, *Letters of Continental Congress*, 8:691. "The Secretary of Congress to the Governor of Connecticut (Samuel Huntington). Office of Secretary of Congress, Decr. 27th, 1787."
21. Ibid.

Chapter 15

1. Bancroft, *Formation of the Constitution*, 2:254.
2. *Ratification*, 3:294. "Governor George Handley to Governor John Sevier. Augusta, 19 February."
3. Burnett, *Letters of Continental Congress*, 8:667. "The Secretary of the Congress to the Governors of North Carolina, South Carolina and Georgia. October 27, 1787."
4. *Ratification*, 3:285. "The Aftermath of Ratification."
5. Ibid., 3:395. "Chief Justice Henry Osborn's Charge to the Chatham County Grand Jury. 4 March (excerpt)." A reference to silver coins being cut, literally, in two, thus being mutilated and their value diminished according to the fluctuating values of paper money or bills of credit.
6. Farrand, *Records*, 2:309–10.
7. *Ratification*, 3:535.
8. Ibid., 3:400–401. "A Landholder" II.
9. Ibid., 3:392–93. "A Farmer: To the Farmers of Connecticut, *New Haven Gazette*, 18 October."
10. Chadwick, *The Federalist*, No. 30:157–58. "The Necessity of a General Power of Taxation in the Federal Government," by Alexander Hamilton.

11. Ibid., No. 31:162. "Justification for a General Power of Taxation," by Alexander Hamilton.
12. Ibid., No. 32:164. "The Necessity of Concurrent Jurisdiction Between the States and the Federal Government in Relation to Taxation," by Alexander Hamilton.
13. Storing, *Complete Anti-Federalist*, 2:395. "Brutus" VI, 27 December 1787.
14. Ibid., 3:397.
15. Washington, *Writings*, 29:351. "To Thomas Jefferson. Mount Vernon, January 1, 1788."
16. *Documentary History of the Constitution*, 4:424. "Th: Jefferson to Col Forest. Paris Dec. 31. 1787."
17. *Commentaries*, 2:495. Appendix II, "Marquis de Lafayette to George Washington. Paris, 1 January 1788 (excerpt)."

Chapter 16

1. *Ratification*, 3:562.
2. Ibid., 3:563.
3. Van Doren, *Great Rehearsal*, 194–95.
4. Bowen, *Miracle*, 277.
5. Van Doren, *Great Rehearsal*, 195.
6. *Ratification*, 3:546.
7. Ibid., 3:330–32.
8. Ibid., 3:425. "Speech by Benjamin Gale, 12 November."
9. Ibid.
10. *Commentaries*, 2:401. "Landholder VI. *Connecticut Courant*, 10 December."
11. *Ratification*, 3:557.
12. Ibid., 3:564.
13. *Documentary History of the Constitution*, 4:434. "Jon Trumbull to [George Washington]. Hartford 9th Jan 1788."
14. Rutland, *Ordeal*, 95.
15. Brown, "The Aftermath of Shays's Rebellion....in Massachusetts."
16. Bancroft, *Formation of the Constitution*, 2:263–64.
17. Van Doren, *Great Rehearsal*, 291.
18. Bowen, *Miracle*, 283.
19. *Commentaries*, 3:563. "Appendix 1. *Worcester Magazine*, First Week in January."
20. Ibid., 3:293. "*Massachusetts Gazette*, 8 January. Resolutions of

the TRADESMEN of the Town of BOSTON. Boston, January 7, 1787 [1788]."

21. Ibid., 3:291. "Reports of the Boston Tradesmen Meetings, 8–9 January"; and "Christopher Gore to Rufus King. Boston, 6 January (excerpt)."

Chapter 17

1. Van Doren, *Great Rehearsal*, 197.
2. Elliot, *Debates*, 2:32–33.
3. Ibid., 2:33–34.
4. Harding, *Contest over Ratification*, 74–75.
5. Elliot, *Debates*, 2:10.
6. Rutland, *Ordeal*, 87.
7. Madison, *Papers*, 10:399. "To George Washington. N.York, Jany. 20, 1788."
8. McDonald, *Hamilton*, 107.
9. Spaulding, *George Clinton*, 175.
10. *Documentary History of the Constitution*, 4:643. "John Jay to [George Washington], New York 29 May 1788."
11. *Commentaries*, 3:342. "Governor George Clinton: Speech to the New York Legislature, Poughkeepsie, 11 January."
12. Ibid., 3:368. "The Report of New York's Delegates to the Constitutional Convention, New York *Daily Advertiser*, 14 January."
13. Spaulding, *George Clinton*, 172.
14. Chadwick, *The Federalist*, No. 37:193. "The Genius of the Republican Form of Government," by James Madison.
15. Ibid., No. 38:197. "History Demonstrates the Wisdom of Improvements Made by Members of the Constitutional Convention," by James Madison.
16. Ibid., 199.
17. Harding, *Contest over Ratification*, 78.
18. *Documentary History of the Constitution*, 4:449–50. "R. King to J. Madison, Esq. Boston 20 Jan 1788."

Chapter 18

1. Harding, *Contest over Ratification*, 84.
2. *Documentary History of the Constitution*, 4:457. "R King [to James Madison]. Boston 23. Jan. 1788."

3. Bancroft, *Formation of the Constitution*, 2:266.
4. Elliot, *Debates*, 2:80.
5. Ibid., 2:88.
6. Ibid., 2:51.
7. Rutland, *Ordeal*, 104. A "penitent local citizen" later admitted authorship of the article. He had overheard a statement that efforts were being made to silence one delegate. There was also another report that "*a bag of money* had been sent down to Boston to quiet the Antifederalists." Rutland noted, "As with most accusations, the story had spread faster than the retraction."
8. Madison, *Papers*, 10:400–401. "From Rufus King. Boston, 20 Jan 1788."
9. Rutland, *Ordeal*, 101.
10. Elliot, *Debates*, 2:80–81.
11. Ibid., 2:95.
12. Forbes, *Paul Revere*, 370.
13. McDonald, *E Pluribus Unum*, 216.
14. Harding, *Contest over Ratification*, 85.
15. McDonald, *E Pluribus Unum*, 216–17.
16. Madison, *Papers*, 10:445. "From Rufus King. Boston 30. Jan 1788 Wednesday."
17. *Commentaries*, 4:60. "Massachusetts Convention: Amendments to the Constitution. Boston, 6 February."
18. Madison, *Papers*, 10:436. "From Nathaniel Gorham. Charles Town Jany. 27h. 1788."
19. Rutland, *Ordeal*, 90–91.
20. Chadwick, *The Federalist*, No. 42:226. "Powers of the Federal Government in Relation to Foreign Affairs and Intercourse Among the States," by James Madison.

Chapter 19

1. *Commentaries*, 3:562. "John Hancock and the Constitution, 3 January–4 January."
2. Bowen, *Miracle*, 289.
3. Rutland, *Ordeal*, 107.
4. Ibid., 97.
5. Elliot, *Debates*, 2:102.
6. Ibid.

7. Ibid.
8. Ibid., 2:104.
9. Van Doren, *Great Rehearsal*, 200.
10. Elliot, *Debates*, 2:107.
11. Bancroft, *Formation of the Constitution*, 2:268.
12. Ibid.
13. Elliot, *Debates*, 2:115.
14. Harding, *Contest over Ratification*, 87–88.
15. Elliot, *Debates*, 2:122.
16. Ibid., 2:122–23.
17. Harding, *Contest over Ratification*, 88.
18. Bancroft, *Formation of the Constitution*, 2:269.
19. Rutland, *Ordeal*, 107.
20. Mitchell, *Biography of the Constitution*, 141.
21. Elliot, *Debates*, 2:124–25.
22. *Documentary History of the Constitution*, 4:472. "R King to James Madison Jun Esquire New-York. Boston Sunday 3d Feb. 1788."
23. Rutland, *Ordeal*, 107.
24. *Commentaries*, 3:563. "John Hancock and the Constitution, 3 January–4 February."

Chapter 20

1. Bancroft, *Formation of the Constitution*, 2:273.
2. Libby, *Geographical Distribution of the Vote*, 12–14.
3. *Documentary History of the Constitution*, 4:492. "C. Gibbs to His Excellency General Washington. Boston Feby 9th 1788."
4. Harding, *Contest over Ratification*, 89–90.
5. Elliot, *Debates*, 2:131.
6. Ibid., 2:134.
7. Ibid., 2:143.
8. Ibid., 2:148.
9. Ibid.
10. Rutland, *Ordeal*, 108.
11. Harding, *Contest over Ratification*, 98.
12. Ibid.
13. Schwartz, *Bill of Rights*, 2:675.
14. Ibid.
15. Rutland, *Ordeal*, 110.

16. Elliot, *Debates*, 2:176.
17. Ibid., 2:183.
18. Harding, *Contest over Ratification*, 103.
19. Rutland, *Ordeal*, 109.
20. Ibid., 113.
21. Madison, *Papers*, 10:533. "To Edmund Pendleton. New York Feby. 21. 88."
22. *Commentaries*, 4:67.
23. Bancroft, *Formation of the Constitution*, 2:273.
24. Bowen, *Miracle*, 291.
25. *Commentaries*, 4:242.
26. Harding, *Contest over Ratification*, 106.
27. *Commentaries*, 4:176–77.

Chapter 21

1. Rossier, *Grand Convention*, 289.
2. Rutland, *Ordeal*, 117.
3. Ibid.
4. Elliot, *Debates*, 2:214.
5. Schwartz, *Bill of Rights*, 2:758.
6. *Documentary History of the Constitution*, 4:491. "C. Gibbs to His Excellency General Washington. Boston Feby. 9th 1788."
7. Rossiter, *Grand Convention*, 289.
8. Madison, *Papers*, 10:510. "To George Washington. N. York Feby. 15 [1788]."
9. Van Doren, *Great Rehearsal*, 204–5.
10. Storing, *Complete Anti-Federalist*, 4:238. "A Friend to the Rights of the People and A Friend of the Republic."
11. Ibid., 4:242.
12. Ibid.
13. McDonald, *Novus Ordo Seclorum*, 42.
14. Chadwick, *The Federalist*, No. 52:286. "The U.S. House of Representatives," by James Madison.
15. Ibid., No. 53:293–94. "The Role of Annual Elections in the Preservation of Liberty," by James Madison.
16. Beveridge, *John Marshall*, 1:266.
17. Ibid., *fn*7.
18. Washington, *Writings*, 29:409. "To Marquis de Lafayette. Mount Vernon, February 7, 1788."

19. *Commentaries*, 4:540. "The Controversy over the Post Office and the Circulation of Newspapers."
20. *Ratification*, 2:643.
21. *Commentaries*, 4:540. "The Controversy over the Post Office and the Circulation of Newspapers."
22. Rutland, *Ordeal*, 129–30.
23. *Commentaries*, 4:552. "Centinel XV, Philadelphia *Independent Gazetteer*, 22 February (excerpt)."
24. Rutland, *Ordeal*, 135.
25. *Commentaries*, 4:458. "Philadelphiensis VIII, Philadelphia *Freeman's Journal*, 23 January."

Chapter 22

1. *Commentaries*, 4:83, *fn*5.
2. Ibid.
3. Durant, *Rousseau and Revolution*, 872.
4. Ibid., 944.
5. Madison, *Papers*, 10:533. "To Edmund Pendleton. New York Feby. 21. 88."
6. Malone, *Jefferson*, 187–89.
7. *Commentaries*, 4:82. "Comte de Moustier to Comte de Montmorin. New York, 8 February (excerpt)."
8. *Documentary History of the Constitution*, 4:502–3. "John Adams to His Excellency John Jay Secretary of State. Grosvenor Square Feb. 14, 1788."
9. *Commentaries*, 4:195. "John Adams on the Constitution. *New York Journal*, 23 February."
10. Malone, *Jefferson*, 170–71. Dumas Malone makes the point that Jefferson's attitude was of importance, and he would have had far greater influence except that communications lagged so far behind events. Letters often took two or three months for delivery. He nevertheless was kept abreast of events as much as possible by visitors, regular correspondence, and newspapers that were sent him.
11. Madison, *Papers*, 10:338. "From Thomas Jefferson. Paris Dec. 20, 1787."
12. Libby, *Geographical Distribution of the Vote*, 49.
13. *Documentary History of the Constitution*, 4:516. "[Benjamin Lincoln] to His Excellency General Washington. Boston Feby 20 1788."

14. Rutland, *Ordeal*, 118.
15. Ibid.
16. Storing, *Complete Anti-Federalist*, 4:243. "A Friend of the Republic, *AntiFœderalist No. II.*, (New Hampshire) *Freeman's Oracle.* 8 February 1788."
17. Rossiter, *Grand Convention*, 284.
18. Warren, *Making of the Constitution*, 759.
19. *Documentary History of the Constitution*, 4:506. [Benjamin Franklin] to M. Le Veillard at Passy. Philada Feb 17th 1788."
20. Madison, *Papers*, 10:343. "From William Short. Paris Dec. 21, 1787."
21. Palmer, *French Revolution*, 50–51.
22. Durant, *Rousseau and Revolution*, 946–47.
23. Ibid., 946.

Chapter 23

1. Rossiter, *Grand Convention*, 289.
2. Rutland, *Ordeal*, 119–20.
3. Van Doren, *Great Rehearsal*, 205.
4. *Documentary History of the Constitution*, 4:523–24. "John Langdon to His Excellency General Washington. Portsmouth Feb 28, 1788."
5. Rutland, *Ordeal*, 121.
6. *Commentaries*, 4:180. "The Adjournment of the New Hampshire Convention. Exeter, 22 February."
7. Flexner, *Washington*, 146–47.
8. Rutland, *Ordeal*, 122.
9. Madison, *Papers*, 10:554. "To Edmund Pendleton. N. York Mar. 3. 88."
10. Ibid., 10:554. "To Edmund Randolph. N. York Mar. 3. 88."
11. Ibid., 10:526. "To George Washington. New York Feby 20, 1788."
12. Bancroft, *Formation of the Constitution*, 300.
13. Beveridge, *John Marshall*, 1:365.
14. Libby, *Geographical Distribution of the Vote*, 89.
15. *Commentaries*, 4:152–53. "Harry Innes to John Brown. Danville, Ky., 20 February."
16. Ibid., 4:262. "Samuel McDowell et al. to the Court of Fayette County, Ky., 28 February."
17. Burnett, *Letters of Continental Congress*, 8:784. "James Madison to Thomas Jefferson. New York Augst. 23d. 1788."

18. Madison, *Papers*, 10:355. "To Edmund Randolph. N. York Jany. 10, 1788."
19. Rakove, *Beginnings of National Politics*, 350.
20. Adams, *Dictionary of American History*, 5:362–63.
21. Rutland, *Ordeal*, 177.
22. Bancroft, *Formation of the Constitution*, 301.

Chapter 24

1. Rutland, *Ordeal*, 126.
2. Rossiter, *Grand Convention*, 87–88.
3. Bowen, *Miracle*, 13.
4. Farrand, *Records*, 2:42.
5. *Commentaries*, 1:35. "Charles Vaughan to Benjamin Franklin. Boston, 27 February."
6. Ibid., 4:526.
7. Ibid., 4:517.
8. Ibid., 1:35.
9. Rutland, *Ordeal*, 195.
10. *Commentaries*, 2:165. "Philadelphia *Freeman's Journal*, 21 November [1787]." The newspaper editors neglected to mention that Rhode Island had 948 slaves; those born after 1784 were free, but complete emancipation had not yet been achieved. Rossitor, *Grand Convention*, 84.
11. *Commentaries*, 4:408. "Rufus King to Tench Coxe. New York, 18 March (excerpt)."
12. Ibid., 4:305. "The Landholder X. *Connecticut Courant*, 3 March."
13. Rutland, *Ordeal*, 195.
14. Madison, *Papers*, 10:493–94. "From Edward Carrington. Manchester Feby. 10th: 1788."
15. Brant, *Madison*, 188.
16. Rutland, *Ordeal*, 189.
17. Beveridge, *John Marshall*, 1:359.
18. Grigsby, *History of the Virginia Federal Convention*, 36, *fn*41.
19. Washington, *Writings*, 29:431. "To James Madison. Mount Vernon, March 2, 1788."
20. Lodge, *Washington*, 2:39–40.
21. Flexner, *Washington*, 156.
22. Harwell, *Washington*, 555.
23. Ibid.

Chapter 25

1. *Commentaries*, 4:348. "Luther Martin: Reply to Maryland Landholder No. X. *Maryland Journal*, 7 March."
2. Ibid., 4:343.
3. Farrand, *Records*, 3:278. "Luther Martin's Reply to the Landholder. Baltimore, March 3, 1788."
4. Rutland, *Ordeal*, 75.
5. Farrand, *Records*, 3:171. "The Landholder [Oliver Ellsworth], VIII," first printed in the *Connecticut Courant*, December 24, 1787.
6. Ibid., 3:272–73. "The Landholder [Oliver Ellsworth]. To the Honourable Luther Martin, Esq.," first printed in the *Maryland Journal*, February 29, 1788.
7. Ibid., 3:291. "Luther Martin's Reply to the Landholder. Baltimore, March 19, 1788," first printed in the *Maryland Journal*, March 21, 1788.
8. Rutland, *Ordeal*, 151.
9. Ibid., 153.
10. Washington, *Writings*, 29:471–72. "To James McHenry. Mount Vernon, April 27, 1788."
11. Ibid.
12. Harwell, *Washington*, 552.
13. Farrand, *Records*, 3:294–95. "Luther Martin's Reply to the Landholder. Baltimore, March 19, 1788," first printed in the *Maryland Journal*, March 21, 1788.
14. Ibid., 3:283. "Luther Martin's Reply to the Landholder. Baltimore, March 14, 1788," first printed in the *Maryland Journal*, March 18, 1788.
15. Ibid., 2:648.
16. *Commentaries*, 4:32. "Centinel XIV. Philadelphia *Independent Gazetteer*, 5 February. To the People of Pennsylvania."
17. Rossiter, *Grand Convention*, 115–16.
18. Risjord, *Chesapeake Politics*, 74–75.
19. Rutland, *Ordeal*, 152–53.
20. Washington, *Writings*, 29:411. "To Marquis de Lafayette. Mount Vernon, February 7, 1788."

Chapter 26

1. *Commentaries*, 4:365–66. "Philadelphiensis XI. Philadelphia *Independent Gazetteer*, 8 March."

2. Chadwick, *The Federalist*, No. 69:378. "The Powers and Limitations of the Office of President," by Alexander Hamilton."
3. Ibid., No. 69:374–75.
4. Farrand, *Framing*, 204.
5. Farrand, *Records*, 3:74.
6. Farrand, *Framing*, 174.
7. Farrand, *Records*, 1:299.
8. Warren, *Making of the Constitution*, 770.
9. Farrand, *Records*, 1:66. "June 1, 1787."
10. *Commentaries*, 4:445. "*Gazette of the State of Georgia*, 20 March. Extract of a letter from the Hon. William Pierce, Esq. to St. George Tucker, Esq. dated New York, Sept. 28, 1787."
11. Chadwick, *The Federalist*, No. 70:380. "The Necessity for a Vigorous Executive," by Alexander Hamilton.
12. *Commentaries*, 4:468. "Publication and Sale of the Book Edition of *The Federalist*, 22 March." A volume was forwarded to General Washington, and among other distributions, forty were sent to Virginia's Governor Edmund Randolph, a delegate to the upcoming ratifying Convention, for distribution to other delegates.
13. Brant, *Madison*, 187.
14. *Commentaries*, 4:465. "George Washington on the Ratification of the Constitution by Massachusetts."
15. Ibid., 1:513–14. "Gouverneur Morris to George Washington. Philadelphia, 30 October."
16. Ibid., 2:501. "Marquis de Lafayette to George Washington. Paris, 4 February (excerpts)."
17. Ibid., 1:253–54. The editors note that "the weekly *Pennsylvania Gazette*, a Federalist newspaper, was the most widely reprinted newspaper in the United States....paragraphs dealing with the Constitution (in the September 26 issue) were each reprinted between eighteen and fifty times."
18. Washington, *Writings*, 29:190. "To James Madison. Mount Vernon, March 31, 1787." See also *Commentaries*, 1:169.
19. *Commentaries*, 1:168. "Monarchical Tendencies in America."
20. Farrand, *Framing*, 175.
21. Farrand, *Records*, 3:302. "Pierce Butler to Weedon Butler. Mary Villa, May ye 5th. 1788."

Chapter 27

1. Morris, *Encyclopedia of American History*, 120.

2. Rutland, *Ordeal*, 126.
3. *Documentary History of the Constitution*, 4:554–55. "John Collins to His Exy the President of Congress. State of Rhode-Island and Providence-Plantations. In General Assembly. April 5th 1788."
4. *Commentaries*, 4:406. "The Landholder XII. *Connecticut Courant*, 17 March."
5. McDonald, *Novus Ordo Seclorum*, 175–76.
6. Rossiter, *Grand Convention*, 88.
7. *Commentaries*, 4:403–4, *fn3*.
8. Ibid., 2:504. Appendix III, "Quaker Opposition to the Protection of Slavery in the Constitution."
9. Ibid., 2:510. Appendix III, "Samuel Hopkins to Moses Brown. Newport, 22 October."
10. *Commentaries*, 4:250–51. "Benjamin Rush to Jeremy Belknap. Philadelphia, 28 February."
11. Madison, *Papers*, 11:14. "To George Nicholas. Orange 8 April 1788."
12. Ibid., 11:4. "From Cyrus Griffin. N: york 24 March 1788."
13. Ibid., 11:5. "To Eliza House Trist. Orange, March 25, 1788."
14. Brant, *Madison*, 188–89.
15. *Commentaries*, 4:208. "Hugh Williamson: Speech at Edenton, N.C. New York *Daily Advertiser*, 25–27 February." This was an address to the freemen of Edenton and the County of Chowan, North Carolina.
16. Storing, *Complete Anti-Federalist*, 2:225. "Letters from the Federal Farmer. October 8th, 1787."
17. *Commentaries*, 2:224. "John Quincy Adams to William Cranch. Newburyport, 14 October."
18. Ibid., 1:84. "John Adams: A Defence of the Constitutions."
19. *Documentary History of the Constitution*, 4:183–84. "James Madison to Thomas Jefferson. Philad. June 6th 1787."
20. *Commentaries*, 2:501–2. "Abigail Adams Smith to John Quincy Adams. London, 10 February (excerpt)."
21. Ibid., 1:86. "John Adams: A Defence of the Constitutions."
22. Madison, *Papers*, 11:296. "To Thomas Jefferson. New York Ocr. 17, 1788." Italics indicate words written in code.

Chapter 28

1. Rutland, *Ordeal*, 272.

2. Trenholme, *North Carolina*, 108.
3. Ibid., 162.
4. Washington, *Writings*, 29:452. "To Benjamin Lincoln. Mount Vernon, April 2, 1788."
5. Ibid., 29:451.
6. Rutland, *Ordeal*, 121–23.
7. Madison, *Papers*, 11:8. "From George Nicholas. Charlottesville April 5th, 88."
8. Reardon, *Edmund Randolph*, 134.
9. Trenholme, *North Carolina*, 113.
10. Ibid.
11. Rutland, *Ordeal*, 272.
12. Trenholme, *North Carolina*, 107–8.
13. Risjord, *Chesapeake Politics*, 318.
14. Ibid., 317.
15. Trenholme, *North Carolina*, 140–41.
16. Rutland, *Ordeal*, 198.
17. Madison, *Papers*, 11:20. "To George Washington. Orange April 10, 1788."
18. Brant, *Madison*, 188.
19. Risjord, *Chesapeake*, 302.
20. Madison, *Papers*, 11:11. "From Cyrus Griffin. N:Y: April 7th [1788]."
21. Reardon, *Edmund Randolph*, 134–35.
22. Ibid., 135.
23. Madison, *Papers*, 11:28.
24. Beveridge, *John Marshall*, 1:362.
25. Washington, *Writings*, 29:357–58. "To Governor Edmund Randolph. Mount Vernon, January 8, 1788."

Chapter 29

1. Rutland, *Ordeal*, 156.
2. Risjord, *Chesapeake Politics*, 285.
3. Rutland, *Ordeal*, 156.
4. Bancroft, *Formation of the Constitution*, 2:280.
5. Risjord, *Chesapeake Politics*, 287–88.
6. *Commentaries*, 4:502. "Luther Martin: Address No. III. *Maryland Journal*, 28 March. To the Citizens of Maryland."
7. Rutland, *Ordeal*, 155.

8. Risjord, *Chesapeake Politics*, 289.
9. Rutland, *Ordeal*, 151.
10. *Commentaries*, 4:475. "Centinel XVII. Philadelphia *Independent Gazetteer*, 24 March."
11. Ibid., 4:217, 476.
12. *Ratification*, 2:709.
13. Ibid., 2:644.
14. Ibid., 2:645.
15. Fleming, *Man Who Dared Lightning*, 487.
16. Van Doren, *Franklin*, 759.
17. *Documentary History of the Constitution*, 4:570–71. "[Benjamin Franklin] To the Editor of the *Federal Gazette*."
18. *Commentaries*, 4:532, *fn*1.
19. Rutland, *Ordeal*, 144.
20. Ibid.
21. Madison, *Papers*, 11:19. "To Edmund Randolph. Orange April 10th. 1788."
22. Ibid., 11:20. "To George Washington. Orange April 10. 1788."
23. Freeman, *Washington*, 6:134.
24. Risjord, *Chesapeake Politics*, 283–84.
25. Rutland, *Ordeal*, 150–51.
26. McDonald, *Novus Ordo Seclorum*, 220.

Chapter 30

1. Rutland, *Ordeal*, 166.
2. Storing, *Complete Anti-Federalist*, 5:148.
3. Elliot, *Debates*, 4:265–66.
4. Ibid., 4:266.
5. Ibid., 4:272.
6. *Commentaries*, 4:537. "*Pennsylvania Gazette*, 19 March."
7. Ibid., 4:510.
8. Elliot, *Debates*, 4:283–85.
9. Williams, *Pinckneys*, 272.
10. *First Federal Elections*, 1:147. Introduction.
11. Ibid.
12. Ibid., 1:148.
13. Williams, *Pinckneys*, 272–73.
14. Rutland, *Ordeal*, 165.
15. Madison, *Papers*, 11:20. "To George Washington. Orange April 10, 1788."

16. Ibid., 11:13. "To George Nicholas. Orange 8 April 1788."
17. *Commentaries*, 4:26. "Civis: To the Citizens of South Carolina. Charleston *Columbian Herald*, 4 February."
18. Elliot, *Debates*, 4:287.
19. Storing, *Complete Anti-Federalist*, 5:148.
20. Rutland, *Ordeal*, 165.
21. Elliot, *Debates*, 4:308.
22. Ibid., 4:311.

Chapter 31

1. Freeman, *Washington*, 6:134.
2. Washington, *Writings*, 29:463–64. "To Thomas Johnson. Mount Vernon, April 20, 1788."
3. Bancroft, *Formation of the Constitution*, 2:181.
4. Risjord, *Chesapeake Politics*, 289.
5. Rutland, *Ordeal*, 155–56.
6. Ibid., 156–57.
7. Risjord, *Chesapeake Politics*, 290.
8. Storing, *Complete Anti-Federalist*, 5:80–81. "Samuel Chase. Notes of Speeches Delivered to the Maryland Ratifying Convention. April 1788."
9. Ibid., 85.
10. Ibid., 88–89.
11. Risjord, *Chesapeake Politics*, 290.
12. Rutland, *Ordeal*, 157.
13. Elliot, *Debates*, 2:548.
14. Rutland, *Ordeal*, 157.
15. Risjord, *Chesapeake Politics*, 289.
16. Ibid.
17. Storing, *Complete Anti-Federalist*, 5:66–69. "Essays by A Farmer. (Baltimore) *Maryland Gazette*, February–April 1788."
18. Rutland, *Ordeal*, 154.
19. Washington, *Writings*, 29:466. "To John Armstrong. Mount Vernon, April 25, 1788."

Chapter 32

1. Bancroft, *Formation of the Constitution*, 2:283.
2. Freeman, *Washington*, 6:135.
3. Madison, *Papers*, 11:64–65. "From Daniel Carroll. May 28th. 1788."
4. Elliot, *Debates*, 2:548.

5. Storing, *Complete Anti-Federalist*, 5:103.
6. Ibid., 5:105.
7. Ibid., 5:81.
8. Rutland, *Ordeal*, 158.
9. Elliot, *Debates*, 2:549.
10. Risjord, *Chesapeake Politics*, 291–93.
11. Ibid., 292–93.
12. Rutland, *Ordeal*, 159.
13. Storing, *Complete Anti-Federalist*, 5:92.
14. Ibid., 5:106.
15. Madison, *Papers*, 11:70. "From Alexander Contee Hanson. Annapolis June 2, 1788."
16. Schwartz, *Bill of Rights*, 2:729.
17. Ibid., 2:729–30.
18. Washington, *Writings*, 29:478. "To Marquis de Lafayette. Mount Vernon, April 28, 1788."
19. Rutland, *Ordeal*, 32–33.
20. Chadwick, *The Federalist*, No. 38:200. "History Demonstrates the Wisdom of Improvements Made by Members of the Constitutional Convention," by James Madison.
21. Ibid., No. 84:465. "The Constitution as a Bill of Rights," by Alexander Hamilton.
22. Rutland, *Ordeal*, 33–34.
23. Flexner, *Washington*, 150.
24. Farrand, *Records*, 3:294. "Luther Martin's Reply to the Landholder. Baltimore, March 19, 1788." *Maryland Journal*, March 21, 1788.

Chapter 33

1. Bancroft, *Formation of the Constitution*, 2:340.
2. Spaulding, *George Clinton*, 176.
3. Rutland, *Ordeal*, 238.
4. Hamilton, *Papers*, 5:3. "To James Madison. [New York, June 8, 1788]."
5. Spaulding, *George Clinton*, 176–77.
6. Ibid., 176.
7. *Commentaries*, 4:468. "Publication and Sale of the Book Edition of *The Federalist*, 22 March."
8. McDonald, *Hamilton*, 107.
9. Ibid., 114.

10. De Pauw, *Eleventh Pillar*, 116.
11. Storing, *Complete Anti-Federalist*, 6:126.
12. *Commentaries*, 4:65.
13. Hamilton, *Papers*, 5:3. "To James Madison. [New York, June 8, 1788.]"
14. Ibid., 4:651. "To Gouverneur Morris. [New York, May 19, 1788.]"
15. De Pauw, *Eleventh Pillar*, 185.
16. Rutland, *Ordeal*, 237.
17. Hamilton, *Papers*, 5:2. "To John Sullivan [president of the New Hampshire Ratifying Convention]. New York, June 6, 1788."
18. Spaulding, *George Clinton*, 178.
19. *Documentary History of the Constitution*, 4:603. "Gouv Morris to His Excellency Gen Washington Mount Vernon. Richmond 29 April 1788."
20. Washington, *Writings*, 29:488. "To Benjamin Lincoln. Mount Vernon, May 2, 1788."
21. Spaulding, *George Clinton*, 179.
22. Storing, *Complete Anti-Federalist*, 6:130. "Address by A Plebeian. New York, 1788." A reprint appeared in the Philadelphia *Independent Gazetteer* in May.

Chapter 34

1. Rutland, *Ordeal*, 167.
2. Williams, *Pinckneys*, 282.
3. Ibid., 284–85.
4. Bradford, *Worthy Company*, 212.
5. Elliot, *Debates*, 4:319.
6. Ibid., 4:320.
7. Schwartz, *Bill of Rights*, 2:743–44.
8. *First Federal Elections*, 1:147.
9. Elliot, *Debates*, 4:323.
10. Rutland, *Ordeal*, 166.
11. Williams, *Pinckneys*, 285.
12. Rutland, *Ordeal*, 165.
13. Ibid., 135.
14. *Commentaries*, 4:540. "The Controversy over the Post Office and the Circulation of Newspapers."
15. Ibid., 4:586. "A Friend to the People. Philadelphia *Freeman's Journal*, 16 April."
16. Ibid., 4:589–90. "*Massachusetts Centinel*, 7 May."

17. Ibid., 4:574. "Winchester *Virginia Gazette,* 26 March–9 April."
18. Ibid., 4:575. "A Federalist: To the Editors, 2 April."
19. Ibid., 4:589. "Confederation Congress: Report of Committee on the Post Office, 7 May."
20. Burnett, *Letters of Continental Congress,* 8:733. "John Brown to James Madison. New York, May 12, 1788."
21. Wright, *Economic History of the United States,* 237.
22. Burnett, *Letters of Continental Congress,* 737. "Cyrus Griffin to James Madison."
23. Malone, *Jefferson,* 2:191.
24. *Commentaries,* 4:481. "John Adams to Governor George Clinton. London, 26 March (excerpt)."
25. Elliot, *Debates,* 4:321–22.
26. Ibid., 4:311.

Chapter 35

1. Williams, *Pinckneys,* 285.
2. Rutland, *Ordeal,* 167.
3. Elliot, *Debates,* 4:333.
4. Ibid., 4:333–36.
5. Ibid., 4:337–38.
6. Ibid., 4:338.
7. Ibid.
8. Rutland, *Ordeal,* 168.
9. Schwartz, *Bill of Rights,* 2:744.
10. Ibid., 2:745–46.
11. Elliot, *Debates,* 4:311.
12. *Commentaries,* 1:85. "John Adams: A Defence of the Constitutions."
13. Ibid., 1:84.
14. Ibid., 3:486. "*State Gazette of South Carolina,* 28 January." The poem was reprinted in newspapers in other cities, from Boston to Philadelphia.
15. Ibid., 4:519. "Accounts from England, 18 February–22 March."
16. Ibid., 4:520.
17. Williams, *Pinckneys,* 184.
18. Elliot, *Debates,* 337.

Chapter 36

1. Bancroft, *Formation of the Constitution,* 2:293.

2. Van Doren, *Rehearsal*, 214.
3. Rutland, *Ordeal*, 168.
4. Schwartz, *Bill of Rights*, 2:756–57. See also *Documentary History of the Constitution*, 2:138–40.
5. Williams, *Pinckneys*, 286.
6. Van Doren, *Great Rehearsal*, 214.
7. Williams, *Pinckneys*, 286–87.
8. Rutland, *Ordeal*, 168–69.
9. Bancroft, *Formation of the Constitution*, 2:293–94.
10. Rutland, *Ordeal*, 169.
11. Williams, *Pinckneys*, 287.
12. *Documentary History of the Constitution*, 4:626. "Rufus King to James Madison Esq. New York 25. May 1788."
13. Ibid., 4:627. "H. Knox to His Excellency Gen Washington. New York 25 May 1788."
14. Brant, *Madison*, 191.
15. Madison, *Papers*, 11:60. "To John Brown. Orange May 27, 1788."
16. Ibid., 11:49–50. "To George Nicholas. Orange May 17th. 1788."
17. Bowen, *Miracle*, 171, 175.
18. Madison, *Papers*, 11:45–46. "To George Nicholas. Orange, May 17th. 1788."
19. Bowen, *Miracle*, 172.
20. Washington, *Writings*, 29:507–8. "To Marquis de Lafayette. Mount Vernon, May 28, 1788."

Chapter 37

1. Elliot, *Debates*, 3:22.
2. Meade, *Patrick Henry*, 352.
3. Elliot, *Debates*, 3:28–29.
4. Beveridge, *John Marshall*, 1:378.
5. Madison, *Papers*, 11:77. "To George Washington. Richmond June 4, 1788."
6. Brant, *Madison*, 196.
7. Rutland, *Ordeal*, 103.
8. Elliot, *Debates*, 3:3.
9. Rutland, *Ordeal*, 226.
10. Elliot, *Debates*, 3:34.
11. Brant, *Madison*, 195.
12. Madison, *Papers*, 11:77. "To George Washington. Richmond June 4, 1788."

13. Grigsby, *Virginia Federal Convention*, 1:41.
14. Meade, *Patrick Henry*, 338.
15. Rutland, *Ordeal*, 197–98.
16. Madison, *Papers*, 11:60. "To John Brown. Orange May 27, 1788."
17. Grigsby, *Virginia Federal Convention*, 1:58.
18. Ibid., 1:25.
19. Dabney, *Richmond*, 33–42.
20. Meade, *Patrick Henry*, 342.
21. Beveridge, *John Marshall*, 1:356.
22. Rutland, *Ordeal*, 220.
23. Elliot, *Debates*, 3:61.
24. Grigsby, *Virginia Federal Convention*, 1:119.
25. Elliot, *Debates*, 3:45.
26. Meade, *Patrick Henry*, 357–58.
27. Elliot, *Debates*, 3:64.

Chapter 38

1. Reardon, *Edmund Randolph*, 143.
2. Elliot, *Debates*, 3:138.
3. Ibid., 187–88.
4. Ibid.
5. Grigsby, *Virginia Federal Convention*, 1:164–65.
6. Ibid.
7. Meade, *Patrick Henry*, 363.
8. Grigsby, *Virginia Federal Convention*, 1:151.
9. Beveridge, *John Marshall*, 1:401–3.
10. Rutland, *Ordeal*, 231–32.
11. Elliot, *Debates*, 3:326.
12. Beveridge, *John Marshall*, 1:394.
13. Elliot, *Debates*, 3:331.
14. Brant, *Madison*, 202.
15. Madison, *Papers*, 11:134. "To George Washington. Richmond June 13th. 1788."
16. *Documentary History of the Constitution*, 4:701. "Rufus King to Col. A. Hamilton. Boston 12 June 1788."
17. Ibid., 4:677. "Tobias Lear to His Excellency General Washington. Portsmouth N.H. 2d June 1788."
18. Washington, *Writings*, 29:520–22. "To James Madison. Mount Vernon, June 8, 1788."

19. Elliot, *Debates*, 3:315.
20. Ibid., 3:152.
21. Ibid., 3:329.
22. Ibid., 3:328–29.
23. Ibid., 3:169.
24. Reardon, *Edmund Randolph*, 141.
25. Brant, *Madison*, 194.

Chapter 39

1. Brant, *Madison*, 210.
2. Elliot, *Debates*, 3:251–52.
3. Meade, *Patrick Henry*, 365.
4. Grigsby, *Virginia Federal Convention*, 1:245–46.
5. Reardon, *Edmund Randolph*, 145.
6. Elliot, *Debates*, 3:364.
7. Reardon, *Edmund Randolph*, 145.
8. Rutland, *George Mason*, 99.
9. Elliot, *Debates*, 3:445.
10. Ibid., 3:448–49.
11. Ibid., 3:451.
12. Brant, *Madison*, 216.
13. Rutland, *Ordeal*, 234.
14. Madison, *Papers*, 11:144. "To Alexander Hamilton. Richmond June 16, 1788."
15. McDonald, *Hamilton*, 114.
16. Washington, *Writings*, 29:525. "To Marquis de Lafayette. Mount Vernon, June 19, 1788."
17. *Documentary History of the Constitution*, 4:714. "Th: Jefferson to T. Lee Shippen, esq. Paris June 19, 1788."
18. Rutland, *Ordeal*, 245.
19. Elliot, *Debates*, 3:452.
20. Ibid., 3:453.

Chapter 40

1. Meade, *Patrick Henry*, 372.
2. Beveridge, *John Marshall*, 1:468.
3. Madison, *Papers*, 11:166. "To Alexander Hamilton. Richmond June 22, 1788."

4. Rutland, *Ordeal*, 250.
5. Elliot, *Debates*, 3:523.
6. Ibid., 3:522.
7. Ibid.
8. Grigsby, *Virginia Federal Convention*, 1:285 *fn.*
9. Elliot, *Debates*, 3:535.
10. Beveridge, *John Marshall*, 1:446.
11. Grigsby, *Virginia Federal Convention*, 316.
12. Elliot, *Debates*, 3:625.
13. Beveridge, *John Marshall*, 1:472.
14. Elliot, *Debates*, 3:652.
15. Rutland, *Ordeal*, 247.
16. William Henry, *Patrick Henry*, 2:412.
17. Rutland, *Ordeal*, 251.
18. Ibid., 252.
19. Ibid.
20. Flexner, *Washington*, 139.
21. Elliot, *Debates*, 3:616.
22. McDonald, *Hamilton*, 114.
23. Reardon, *Edmund Randolph*, 149.
24. Rutland, *Ordeal*, 250.
25. Reardon, *Edmund Randolph*, 148.
26. Beveridge, *John Marshall*, 1:476.
27. Elliot, *Debates*, 3:649.

Chapter 41

1. *First Federal Elections*, 1:769.
2. Ibid., 1:24. "*New York Journal*, 26 June."
3. Bancroft, *Formation of the Constitution*, 2:318.
4. Rutland, *Ordeal*, 212.
5. Ibid.
6. *First Federal Elections*, 1:23. "News of New Hampshire Ratification Reaches Congress. Wednesday, 25 June 1788."
7. De Pauw, *Eleventh Pillar*, 187.
8. Rutland, *Ordeal*, 239.
9. Ibid.
10. Elliot, *Debates*, 2:322.
11. Ibid., 2:324–25.
12. De Pauw, *Eleventh Pillar*, 209–10.

13. *First Federal Elections*, 1:25, *fn2*.
14. Flexner, *Washington*, 148–49.
15. Washington, *Writings*, 30:9–10. "To Charles Cotesworth Pinckney. Mount Vernon, June 28, 1788."
16. Ibid., 30:11. "To Benjamin Lincoln. Mount Vernon, June 29, 1788."
17. Madison, *Papers*, 11:182. "To George Washington. Richmd. June 27, 1788."
18. Ibid., 2:183.
19. Grigsby, *Virginia Federal Convention*, 1:351.
20. Meade, *Patrick Henry*, 372.
21. Grigsby, *Virginia Federal Convention*, 1:355.
22. Brant, *Madison*, 227.
23. *First Federal Elections*, 1:28.
24. De Pauw, *Eleventh Pillar*, 214–15.
25. Ibid., 215.
26. Madison, *Papers*, 11:182. "To Alexander Hamilton. Richd. June 27 [1788]."

Chapter 42

1. Silverman, *Cultural History*, 582.
2. Ibid.
3. Van Doren, *Great Rehearsal*, 242–43.
4. Ibid., 250.
5. *Commentaries*, 4:97. "*Pennsylvania Gazette*, 6 February." The poem was reprinted throughout the States fifteen times by March 26, 1788.
6. *First Federal Elections*, 1:242. "James Wilson's Fourth of July Oration, 1788 (excerpt)." Wilson's speech was printed in the *Pennsylvania Gazette*, July 9, and reprinted in several other States.
7. Ibid., 1:17. "Introduction."
8. Burnett, *The Continental Congress*, 712.
9. De Pauw, *Eleventh Pillar*, 229–30.
10. *First Federal Elections*, 1:35. "Samuel Osgood to Melancton Smith and Samuel Jones, New York, 11 July (excerpt)."
11. Ibid., *fn3*.
12. De Pauw, *Eleventh Pillar*, 230.
13. Ibid.
14. Spaulding, *George Clinton*, 181–82.
15. Elliot, *Debates*, 2:359.

16. Ibid., 2:353.

17. Ibid., 2:405.

18. De Pauw, *Eleventh Pillar*, 219–20.

19. Ibid., 217.

20. Rutland, *Ordeal*, 256.

21. Bowen, *Miracle*, 309.

22. Ibid.

23. Van Doren, *Great Rehearsal*, 250–51.

24. Silverman, *Cultural History*, 579.

Chapter 43

1. *First Federal Elections*, 1:36. "Samuel B. Webb to Catherine Hogeboom, New York, 17 July (excerpt)."

2. Silverman, *Cultural History*, 585.

3. Burnett, *Letters of Continental Congress*, 8:763. "Samuel Alleyne Otis to George Thatcher. New York 17 July 1788."

4. *First Federal Elections*, 1:13. "Introduction."

5. Burnett, *The Continental Congress*, 703–5.

6. Madison, *Papers*, 11:187. "To Edmund Randolph. N. York July 16. 88."

7. De Pauw, *Eleventh Pillar*, 218.

8. Ibid., 221–22.

9. Storing, *Complete Anti-Federalist*, 6:185.

10. Hamilton, *Papers*, 5:157.

11. Ibid., 5:158, *fn*4. A statement quoted in the New York *Daily Advertiser*, July 16, 1788, in an article commenting on Hamilton's remarks. The newspaper reported that Anti-Federalists "retired with malice still more embittered, and an obstinacy more confirmed than before."

12. De Pauw, *Eleventh Pillar*, 220–23.

13. Spaulding, *George Clinton*, 179.

14. Rutland, *Ordeal*, 237–38.

15. *Documentary History of the Constitution*, 4:643. "John Jay to George Washington. New York 29 May 1788—"

16. Lee, *Letters*, 2:475. "To General John Lamb. Chantilly in Virginia, June 27, 1788." General Lamb was an officer in the Revolutionary War and later a prominent member of the Clinton party in New York. The Anti-Federalist society of which he was chairman was opposed to adoption without amendment.

17. De Pauw, *Eleventh Pillar*, 211–12.

18. Reardon, *Edmund Randolph*, 163.
19. *Documentary History of the Constitution*, 4:789. "Ja. Monroe to [Thomas Jefferson]. Fredrick'sburg July 12. 1788."

Chapter 44

1. Washington, *Writings*, 30:16. "To the Secretary for Foreign Affairs. Mount Vernon, July 18, 1788."
2. Rutland, *Ordeal*, 134. See also *Commentaries*, 4:540–42, Appendix II: "The Controversy over the Post Office and the Circulation of Newspapers."
3. Silverman, *Cultural History*, 585.
4. Burnett, *Letters of Continental Congress*, 8:765, *fn*4. See also Van Doren, *Great Rehearsal*, 240–41.
5. De Pauw, *Eleventh Pillar*, 239–40. Reported in *Independent Journal*, New York, August 6, 1788.
6. Burnett, *Letters of Continental Congress*, 8:768. "Hugh Williamson to James Iredell. New York, July 26th, '88."
7. Trenholme, *North Carolina*, 151.
8. Ibid., 129, 148. See also 129, *fn*133.
9. Elliot, *Debates*, 4:4.
10. Ibid., 4:6.
11. Ibid., 4:10.
12. Ibid., 4:21.
13. Rutland, *Ordeal*, 273.
14. Spaulding, *George Clinton*, 181.
15. Ibid.
16. De Pauw, *Eleventh Pillar*, 244.
17. Madison, *Papers*, 11:189. "To Alexander Hamilton. N.York Sunday Evening [20 July 1788]."
18. Rutland, *Ordeal*, 263.
19. Madison, *Papers*, 11:190. "To George Washington. N.York July 21, 1788."
20. Ibid., 11:190–91.
21. Washington, *Writings*, 30:17. "To the Secretary for Foreign Affairs. Mount Vernon, July 18, 1788."
22. Ibid.

Chapter 45

1. Spaulding, *George Clinton*, 181.

2. De Pauw, *Eleventh Pillar*, 261.
3. Morris, *Witness*, 251.
4. Madison, *Papers*, 11:230. "To George Washington. New York Augst. 11. 1788."
5. McMaster, *A History*, 1:499.
6. Rutland, *Ordeal*, 265.
7. *First Federal Elections*, 1:46. "*Pennsylvania Gazette*, 6 August."
8. Ibid., 1:50. "Journals of Congress, Monday, 28 July."
9. Ibid., 1:52. "Journal of Comte de Moustier, 28 July."
10. Ibid., 1:55. "Journal of Comte de Moustier, 30 July."
11. Madison, *Papers*, 11:383. "To Thomas Jefferson. Philadelphia Decr. 8, 1788." Italics indicate coded words.
12. Malone, *Jefferson*, 2:198. *Fn*37: Moustier, spared the embarrassment of a recall, was given leave to return to France, arriving in Paris late November 1789. Jefferson was spared the embarrassment of having to encounter Moustier as he had already departed for the United States.
13. Elliot, *Debates*, 4:89.
14. Rutland, *Ordeal*, 216–17.
15. Elliot, *Debates*, 4:226.
16. Ibid., 4:233.
17. Rutland, *Ordeal*, 274.
18. Ibid., 275.
19. Madison, *Papers*, 11:226. "To Thomas Jefferson. New York Augst. 10. 1788."

Chapter 46

1. Rutland, *Ordeal*, 275.
2. Elliot, *Debates*, 4:226.
3. Ibid., 4:232. Virginia's narrow ratification, by ten votes, had to do more with having a ninth State to approve, and with being able to put forth George Washington's name as President. Without approval, Virginia could not take part in the elections. Virginians, and the Union, had a great deal more to lose than did North Carolina if their State had adopted a wait-and-see attitude.
4. Rutland, *Ordeal*, 278.
5. Van Doren, *Great Rehearsal*, 236–37.

6. Editor: Except for Great Britain, from which many settlers had fled precisely because of religious persecution, the great world powers were headed by Roman Catholic monarchs.

7. Elliot, *Debates*, 4:192.

8. Ibid., 4:193.

9. Trenholme, *North Carolina*, 188.

10. Rutland, *Ordeal*, 282.

11. *First Federal Elections*, 1:63, *fn2*.

12. Ibid., 1:75. "Journal of Comte de Moustier, 6 August."

13. Burnett, *The Continental Congress*, 715.

14. *First Federal Elections*, 1:76. "Journals of Congress, Thursday, 7 August." The Continental Congress required a majority vote of the thirteen states, not a majority of those that were sitting, nor, at this turning point in history, of those that had ratified. North Carolina and Rhode Island were still members of the Continental Congress. As one member states: ". . .all is undone again for the present." Ibid., 1:77–80.

15. Washington, *Writings*, 30:33. "To James Madison. Mount Vernon, August 3, 1788."

16. Ibid., 30:36. "To Doctor James Craik. Mount Vernon, August 4, 1788."

17. Harwell, *Washington*, 555.

18. Wright, *Economic History*, 242.

19. Rutland, *Ordeal*, 276.

20. Trenholme, *North Carolina*, 142.

21. Elliot, *Debates*, 4:88.

22. Ibid., 4:90.

23. Washington, *Writings*, 30:83. "To Thomas Jefferson. Mount Vernon, August 31, 1788."

24. Ibid., 30:41. "To Charles Pettit. Mount Vernon, August 16, 1788."

25. Ibid., 30:62–63. "To Benjamin Lincoln. Mount Vernon, August 28, 1788."

26. Ibid., 30:72–73. "To Sir Edward Newenham. Mount Vernon, August 29, 1788."

BIBLIOGRAPHY

The following is an alphabetical list of the sources cited and abbreviated in the Notes. It is not intended as an inclusive list of reference sources on the ratification debates in the thirteen States, or of the personalities on-stage (and in the wings—for example, Thomas Jefferson). Boldface indicates that the Notes refer to that brief title, rather than to the editor.

Adams, James Truslow, ed. *Dictionary of American History.* Vol. 5. New York: Charles Scribner's Sons, 1940.

Allen, W. B., and Lloyd, Gordon, eds. *The Essential Antifederalist.* Lanham, Md.: University Press of America, 1985.

Bancroft, George. *History of the Formation of the Constitution of the United States of America.* 2 vols. 2d ed. New York: D. Appleton and Company, 1882.

Barry, Richard. *Mr. Rutledge of South Carolina.* 1942. New York: Arno Press, Books for Libraries Press, 1971.

Beeman, Richard R. *Patrick Henry: A Biography.* New York: McGraw-Hill, 1974.

Beveridge, Albert J. *The Life of John Marshall.* Vol. 1, *Frontiersman, Soldier, Lawmaker: 1755–1788.* Boston: Houghton Mifflin Company, 1916.

Bowen, Catherine Drinker. *Miracle at Philadelphia.* London: Hamish Hamilton, 1966.

Bradford, M. E. *A Worthy Company—Brief Lives of the Framers of the United States Constitution.* Marlborough, N.H.: Plymouth Rock Foundation, 1982.

Brant, Irving. *James Madison: Father of the Constitution—1787–1800.* Indianapolis and New York: Bobbs-Merrill Company, 1950.

Brown, Richard D. "The Aftermath of Shays's Rebellion and the Ratification of the Federal Constitution in Massachusetts." Bridgeport: University of Connecticut, 1985.

Burnett, Edmund Cody. *The Continental Congress.* New York: Macmillan Company, 1941. Reprint. Westport, Conn: Greenwood Press, a division of Williamhouse-Regency, 1975.

———, ed. *Letters of Members of the Continental Congress.* Vol. 8, *January 1, 1785, to July 25, 1789, with Supplement 1783–1784.* Washington, D.C.: Carnegie Institution of Washington, 1936. Reprint. Gloucester, Mass.: Peter Smith, 1963.

Chadwick, Michael Loyd, ed. *The Federalist: A Collection of Essays, Written in Favor of the Constitution of the United States. . .by Alexander Hamilton, John Jay, and James Madison, Jr.* Washington, D.C.: Global Affairs Publishing Company, 1987.

Conway, Moncure Daniel. *Omitted Chapters of History Disclosed in the Life and Papers of Edmund Randolph.* New York: Da Capo Press, 1971.

Dabney, Virginius. *Richmond: The Story of a City.* New York: Doubleday & Company, 1976.

De Pauw, Linda Grant. *The Eleventh Pillar, New York State and the Federal Constitution.* Published for the American Historical Association. Ithaca, N.Y.: Cornell University Press, 1966.

Documentary History of the Constitution of the United States of America. Vol. 4, *1786–1870.* Washington, D.C.: U.S. Department of State, 1905. Reprint. New York: Johnson Reprint Corp., 1965.

Documentary History of the First Federal Elections: 1788–1790. Vol 1. Edited by Merrill Jensen and Robert A. Becker. Madison: University of Wisconsin Press, 1976.

Documentary History of the Ratification of the Constitution, The. Madison: State Historical Society of Wisconsin, 1976–86. A multivolume source organized into four sections. References in Notes are to two specific sections and to volumes within those sections.

    Commentaries on the Constitution: Public and Private. 4 vols. Edited by John P. Kaminski and Gaspare J. Saladino.

    Ratification of the Constitution by the States. 11 vols. Edited by Merrill Jensen.

Durant, Will and Ariel. *Rousseau and Revolution.* New York: Simon & Schuster, 1967.

Elliot, Jonathan, ed. *The Debates in the Several State Conventions on the Adoption, of the Federal Constitution. . . .* 5 vols. 2d ed. Philadelphia: J.B. Lippincott & Co., 1861.

Farrand, Max. *The Framing of the Constitution of the United States.* New Haven: Yale University Press, 1913, 1976.

————, ed. *The Records of the Federal Convention of 1787.* Rev. ed. in 4 vols. New Haven and London: Yale University Press, 1966.

Fleming, Thomas. *The Man Who Dared the Lightning: A New Look at Benjamin Franklin.* New York: William Morrow and Company, 1971.

Flexner, James Thomas. *George Washington and the New Nation (1783–1793).* Boston: Little, Brown and Company, 1969–70.

Flower, Milton E. *John Dickinson: Conservative Revolutionary.* Charlottesville: University Press of Virginia, for the Friends of the John Dickinson Mansion, 1983.

Forbes, Esther. *Paul Revere and the World He Lived In.* 1942. Reprint, with a new Foreword by Daniel J. Boorstin. New York: Book-of-the-Month Club, American Past, 1983.

Ford, Paul Leicester, ed., with Notes and Bibliography. *Pamphlets on the Constitution of the United States Published During Its Discussion by the People, 1787–1788.* Brooklyn: 1888. Reprint. New York: Da Capo Press, 1968.

Freeman, Douglas Southall. *George Washington—A Biography: Patriot and President.* Vol. 6. New York: Charles Scribner's Sons, 1954.

Grigsby, Hugh Blair. *The History of the Virginia Federal Convention of 1788.* Vol. 1. Richmond: Virginia Historical Society, 1890.

Groce, George C., Jr. *William Samuel Johnson: A Maker of the Constitution.* New York: AMS Press, 1967.

Hamilton, Alexander. *The Papers of Alexander Hamilton.* Edited by Harold C. Syrett. Vol. 4, *January 1787–May 1788.* New York and London: Columbia University Press, 1962.

Harding, Samuel Bannister. *The Contest over the Ratification of the Federal Constitution in the State of Massachusetts.* Longmans, Green, and Co., 1896. Reprint. New York: Da Capo Press, 1970.

Harwell, Richard. *Washington: An Abridgment in One Volume of the Seven-Volume George Washington by Douglas Southall Freeman.* New York: Charles Scribner's Sons, 1968.

Henry, William Wirt. *Patrick Henry: Life, Correspondence and Speeches.* Vol. 2. New York: Charles Scribner's Sons, 1891.

Jensen, Merrill. *The Making of the American Constitution.* Princeton, N.J.: D. Van Nostrand Company, 1964.

Lee, Richard Henry. *The Letters of Richard Henry Lee.* Edited by James Curtis Ballagh. Vol. 2, *1779–1794.* New York: Macmillan Company, 1914.

Libby, Orin Grant. *The Geographical Distribution of the Vote of the Thirteen States on the Federal Constitution, 1787–8.* New York: Burt Franklin, 1894. Reprint. 1969.

Lodge, Henry Cabot. *George Washington*. American Statesmen Series. Boston: Houghton Mifflin Company, 1889.

Madison, James. *The Papers of James Madison*. Editor-in-Chief, Robert A. Rutland. Vol. 10, *27 May 1787–3 March 1788*. Vol. 11, *7 March 1788–1 March 1789*. Chicago: University of Chicago Press, 1977.

———. *The Writings of James Madison*. Edited by Gaillard Hunt. Vol. 5, *1787–1790*. New York: G.P. Putnam's Sons, 1904.

Malone, Dumas. *Jefferson and the Rights of Man*. Boston: Little, Brown and Company, 1951.

Mason, George. *The Papers of George Mason 1725–1792*. Edited by Robert A. Rutland. Vol. 3, *1787–1792*. Chapel Hill: University of North Carolina Press, 1970.

McDonald, Forrest. *Alexander Hamilton: A Biography*. New York: W.W. Norton & Company, 1982.

———. *E Pluribus Unum: The Formation of the American Republic 1776–1790*. Boston: Houghton Mifflin Company, 1965.

———. *Novus Ordo Seclorum: The Intellectual Origins of the Constitution*. Lawrence: University Press of Kansas, 1985.

McMaster, John Bach. *A History of the People of the United States: From the Revolution to the Civil War*. Vol. 1. New York: D. Appleton and Company, 1893.

McMaster, John Bach, and Stone, Frederick D., eds. *Pennsylvania and the Federal Constitution 1787–1788*. 2 vols. Published by the Historical Society of Pennsylvania, 1888. Reprint. New York: Da Capo Press, 1970.

Meade, Robert Douthat. *Patrick Henry: Practical Revolutionary*. Philadelphia: J.B. Lippincott Company, 1969.

Miller, Helen Hill. *George Mason: Constitutionalist*. Gloucester, Mass.: Peter Smith, 1966.

Mitchell, Broadnus, and Mitchell, Louise Pearson. *A Biography of the Constitution of the United States: Its Origins, Formation, Adoption, Interpretation*. New York: Oxford University Press, 1964.

Morris, Richard B. *Witness at the Creation: Hamilton, Madison, Jay, and the Constitution*. A Lou Reda Book. New York: Holt, Rinehart, and Winston, 1983.

———, ed. *Encyclopedia of American History*. New York: Harper & Row, 1970.

Munroe, John A. *Federalist Delaware, 1775–1815*. New Brunswick, N.J.: Rutgers University Press, 1954.

O'Connor, John E. *William Paterson, Lawyer and Statesman: 1745–1806.* New Brunswick, N.J.: Rutgers University Press, 1974.

Palmer, R. R. *The World of the French Revolution.* New York: Harper & Row, 1967.

Rakove, Jack N. *The Beginnings of National Politics: An Interpretive History of the Continental Congress.* New York: Alfred A. Knopf, 1979.

Reardon, John J. *Edmund Randolph: A Biography.* New York: Macmillan Company, 1974.

Risjord, Norman K. *Chesapeake Politics 1781–1800.* New York: Columbia University Press, 1978.

Rossiter, Clinton. *The Federalist Papers: Alexander Hamilton, James Madison, John Jay.* New York: New American Library, 1961.

———. *1787: The Grand Convention.* New York: Macmillan Company, 1966.

Rutland, Robert Allen. *George Mason: Reluctant Statesman.* Baton Rouge: Louisiana State University Press, 1961.

———. *The Ordeal of the Constitution: The Antifederalists and the Ratification Struggle of 1787–1788.* Norman: University of Oklahoma Press, 1966.

Schwartz, Bernard. *The Bill of Rights: A Documentary History.* Vol. 2. New York: Chelsea House Publisher with McGraw-Hill Book Company, 1971.

Silverman, Kenneth. *A Cultural History of the American Revolution: Painting, Music, Literature, and the Theatre in the Colonies and the United States from the Treaty of Paris to the Inauguration of George Washington: 1763–1789.* New York: Thomas Y. Crowell Company, 1976.

Spaulding, E. Wilder. *His Excellency George Clinton.* New York: Macmillan Company, 1938.

Storing, Herbert J., ed., with Commentary and Notes. *The Complete Anti-Federalist.* 7 vols. Chicago: University of Chicago Press, 1981.

Trenholme, Louise Irby. *The Ratification of the Federal Constitution in North Carolina.* New York: AMS Press, 1967.

Van Doren, Carl. *Benjamin Franklin.* New York: Viking Press, 1938.

———. *The Great Rehearsal.* New York: Viking Press, 1948.

Warren, Charles. *The Making of the Constitution.* New York: Barnes & Noble, 1967.

Washington, George. *The Writings of George Washington from the Orig-*

inal *Manuscript Sources: 1745–1799*. Vol. 29, *Sept 1, 1786–June 19, 1788*. Vol. 30, *June 20, 1788–January 21, 1790*. Edited by John C. Fitzpatrick. Washington, D.C.: United States Government Printing Office, 1939.

Williams, Frances Leigh. *A Founding Family: The Pinckneys of South Carolina*. New York: Harcourt Brace Jovanovich, 1978.

Wright, Chester W. *Economic History of the United States*. New York: McGraw-Hill Book Company, 1941.

INDEX

★

ABOUT THE AUTHOR

★

Jeffrey St. John is the winner of the Benjamin Franklin Award "for excellence in writing on the Constitution's import and the nation and people." The award is presented jointly by the National Press Foundation, Washington, D.C., and the Commission on the Bicentennial of the U.S. Constitution.

He has also received two Emmys, one for his work in translating historical subjects to television, and is the recipient of the George Washington Medal, Freedoms Foundation, Valley Forge, Pennsylvania, for his newspaper writings.

Child of Fortune is the second of three works on the creation of the U.S. Constitution. The first, *Constitutional Journal*, was published in 1987, having appeared in part initially as a newspaper series in the *Christian Science Monitor*. Completing the trilogy will be reports on the First Federal Elections and the creation of the Bill of Rights, to be published to mark the bicentennial of the adoption of the Bill of Rights by the States.

The author of five other works, he has also written articles on history for the *Christian Science Monitor, New York Times, Wall Street Journal, Philadelphia Inquirer, Chicago Tribune, Los Angeles Times*, and other newspapers through the Los Angeles Times Syndicate.

He conceived and wrote a weekly syndicated column, "Headlines & History," and narrated a radio version that was heard on Mutual Broadcasting and overseas on Voice of America.

His career in broadcasting includes the NBC-TV "Today" show; news commentator on CBS-TV "Morning News," CBS Radio Network, and Mutual Radio Network; and moderator and producer of public affairs programs for television stations in New York and Washington.

He is the scriptwriter for and associate producer of the feature film *A Republic If You Can Keep It,* produced for the American Studies Center in Washington, D.C., by Main Street Productions, Richmond, Virginia.

He keeps his reportorial skills sharpened as a state correspondent for the *Richmond News Leader* covering county government affairs in historic Southside Virginia, where he and his wife, Kathryn, reside.